John Goodsir, William Turner, Henry Lonsdale, T. S. A Orr

The anatomical Memoirs of John Goodsir

John Goodsir, William Turner, Henry Lonsdale, T. S. A Orr

The anatomical Memoirs of John Goodsir

ISBN/EAN: 9783743333420

Manufactured in Europe, USA, Canada, Australia, Japa

Cover: Foto ©ninafisch / pixelio.de

Manufactured and distributed by brebook publishing software (www.brebook.com)

John Goodsir, William Turner, Henry Lonsdale, T. S. A Orr

The anatomical Memoirs of John Goodsir

CONTENTS OF VOL. II.

DIVISION I.

		PAGE
I.	On the Origin and Development of the Pulps and Sacs of the Human Teeth (Edinburgh Medical and Surgical Journal, Jan. 1839.)	1
II.	On the Follicular Stage of Dentition in the Ruminants, with some Remarks on that Process in the other Orders of Mammalia (Transactions of British Association for Advancement of Science, August 1839.)	53
III.	On the Mode in which Musket-Bullets and other Foreign Bodies become inclosed in the Ivory of the Tusks of the Elephant (Transactions of Royal Society of Edinburgh, January 18, 1841.)	56
IV.	On the Supra-Renal, Thymus, and Thyroid Bodies (Philosophical Transactions, January 22, 1846.)	66
V.	On the Morphological Relations of the Nervous System in the Annulose and Vertebrate Types of Organisation (Edinburgh Philosophical Journal, January 1857.)	78
VI.	On the Morphological Constitution of the Skeleton of the Vertebrate Head (Edinburgh Philosophical Journal, January 1857.)	88
VII.	On the Morphological Constitution of Limbs (Edinburgh Philosophical Journal, January 1857.)	198

DIVISION II.

		PAGE
VIII.	On the Employment of Mathematical Modes of Investigation in the Determination of Organic Forms . . . . . (Daily Mail, July and August 1849.)	205
IX.	On the Horizontal Curvature of the Internal Femoral Condyle; on the Movements and Relations of the Patella, Semilunar Cartilages, and Synovial Pads of the Human Knee-Joint . . . . . . (Edinburgh Medical Journal, July 1855.)	220
X.	On the Mechanism of the Knee-Joint . . (Abstract in Proceedings of Royal Society, Edinburgh, January 18, 1858.)	231
XI.	On the Curvatures and Movements of the Acting Facets of Articular Surfaces .	246
XII.	Lecture on the Retina . . . . (Edinburgh Medical Journal, October 1855.)	265
XIII.	On the Mode in which Light acts on the Ultimate Nervous Structures of the Eye, and on the Relations between Simple and Compound Eyes . . . . . (Proceedings of Royal Society, Edinburgh, April 6, 1857.)	273
XIV.	Lecture on the Lamina Spiralis of the Cochlea (Edinburgh Medical Journal, December 1855.)	282
XV.	On the Electrical Apparatus in Torpedo, Gymnotus, Malapterurus, and Raia . . (Edinburgh Medical Journal, August and September 1855.)	289
XVI.	A Brief Review of the Present State of Organic Electricity . . . . . (Edinburgh Philosophical Journal, October 1855.)	306

CONTENTS.

	PAGE
XVII. On the Conferva which vegetates on the Skin of the Gold-Fish	345
(Annals and Magazine of Natural History, IX., 1842.)	
XVIII. History of a Case in which a Fluid periodically ejected from the Stomach contained Vegetable Organisms of an undescribed form (Sarcina Ventriculi)	351
(Edinburgh Medical and Surgical Journal, LVII., 1842.)	
XIX. On a Diseased Condition of the Intestinal Glands	372
(Edinburgh Monthly Journal of Medical Science, April 1842.)	
XX. Structure and Pathology of Kidney and Liver	379
(London and Edinburgh Monthly Medical Journal, May 1842.)	

Anatomical and Pathological Observations.—Edin. 1845.

XXI. Centres of Nutrition . . .	389
XXII. The Structure and Functions of the Intestinal Villi	393
XXIII. Absorption, Ulceration, and the Structures engaged in these Processes . . .	403
XXIV. The Process of Ulceration in Articular Cartilages . . .	408
XXV. Secreting Structures . . .	412
XXVI. The Testis and its Secretion in the Decapodous Crustaceans . .	429
XXVII. The Structure of the Serous Membranes .	436

		PAGE
XXVIII.	STRUCTURE OF THE LYMPHATIC GLANDS	439
XXIX.	THE STRUCTURE OF THE HUMAN PLACENTA	445
XXX.	THE STRUCTURE AND ECONOMY OF BONE	461
XXXI.	THE MODE OF REPRODUCTION AFTER DEATH OF THE SHAFT OF A LONG BONE	465
XXXII.	THE MODE OF REPRODUCTION OF LOST PARTS IN THE CRUSTACEA	471
XXXIII.	OF THE ANATOMY AND DEVELOPMENT OF THE CYSTIC ENTOZOA	476
XXXIV.	DESCRIPTION OF AN ERECTILE TUMOUR	504

(Monthly Medical Journal, 1845.)

| XXXV. | DESCRIPTION OF A CONGENITAL TUMOUR OF THE TESTIS | 506 |

(Northern Journal of Medicine, 1845.)

| XXXVI. | THE CURVATURES OF THE ARTICULAR SURFACES AND THE GENERAL MECHANISM OF THE HIP-JOINT | 508 |

EXPLANATION OF THE PLATES.

DEVELOPMENT OF THE TEETH.—Plate I. page 1.

a. Fig. 1. A tooth-germ—a bulging on a mucous membrane.
b. Diagrams illustrating the three stages of dentition.
   Fig. 1. Follicular. 2. Saccular. 3. Eruptive stage.
c. Diagrams illustrative of the formation of a temporary and its corresponding permanent tooth from a mucous membrane.
   Fig. 1. Mucous membrane. Fig. 2. Mucous membrane, with a granular mass deposited in it. Fig. 3. A furrow or groove on the granular mass. (Primitive dental groove.)
Fig. 4. A papilla (a tooth germ) on the floor of the groove.
Fig. 5. The papilla enclosed in a follicle in the bottom of the groove (the latter in the condition of a secondary dental groove).
Fig. 6. The papilla acquiring the configuration of a pulp, and its sac acquiring opercula. The depression for the cavity of reserve behind the inner operculum.
Fig. 7. The papilla become a pulp, and the follicle a sac, in consequence of the adhesion of the opercular lips. The secondary dental groove in the act of closing.
Fig. 8. The secondary groove adherent, except behind the inner operculum, where it has left a shut cavity of reserve for the formation of the pulp and sac of the permanent tooth.
Fig. 9. The last change rendered more complete by the deposition of the granular body (the enamel organ of Hunter, Purkinje, and Raschkow). Deposition of tooth substance commencing.
Fig. 10. The cavity of reserve receding from the surface of the gum, and dilating it at its distal extremity, in which a pulp is forming. Rudimentary opercula developing near its proximal extremity and dividing it into a follicular and an extra-follicular compartment. Temporary tooth pulp nearly covered with tooth substance, and granular body almost absorbed.
Fig. 11. The cavity of reserve become a sac with a pulp, and further removed from the surface of the gum. Temporary tooth pulp covered with tooth substance, and granular body absorbed. (See Hunter, *Nat. Hist. of Human Teeth*, p. 95.)
Fig. 12. The temporary tooth acquiring its fang by the triple

action described in the paper, and its sac approaching the surface of the gum.

Fig. 13. The fang of the temporary tooth longer, and its sac touching the mucous membrane of the mouth.

Fig. 14. The temporary tooth sac again a follicle; free portion of the latter becoming shorter, and fang of the tooth receding from the bottom of its socket. Permanent tooth sac removing further from the surface of the gum.

Fig. 15. The temporary tooth completed. Free portion of the sac become the vascular border of the gum; adherent portion become what is commonly denominated the periosteum of the fang, but which in fact is a triplex membrane—viz. mucous membrane, submucous tissue, and periosteum of alveolus or jaw bone. The permanent tooth sac much removed from the gum, but connected with it by a cord which passes through the foramen behind the temporary alveolus.

Fig. 16. The fang of the permanent tooth lengthening, and the crown approaching the gum. Fang of temporary tooth undergoing absorption.

Fig. 17. The same change more advanced.

Fig. 18. The permanent tooth appearing through the gum. Shedding of the temporary tooth.

Fig. 19. The perfected permanent tooth.

Fig. 20. The shed temporary tooth.

d. Diagrams illustrative of the formation of the three molar teeth from the non-adherent portion of the primitive dental groove.

Fig. 1. The non-adherent portion of the primitive dental groove.

Fig. 2. The papilla and follicle of the first molar on the floor of the non-adherent portion, which is now a portion of the secondary groove.

Fig. 3. The papilla and follicle of the first molar become a pulp and sac. The lips of the secondary groove adhering, so that the latter has become the posterior or great cavity of reserve.

Fig. 4. The sac of the first molar increased in size, and advanced along a curved path into the substance of the coronoid process or maxillary tuberosity. The cavity of reserve lengthened out or advanced along with it.

Fig. 5. The sac of the first molar returned by the same path to its former position. The cavity of reserve again shortened.

Fig. 6. The cavity of reserve sending backwards the sac of the second molar.

Fig. 7. The sac of the second molar advanced along a curved path into the coronoid process or maxillary tuberosity. The cavity of reserve lengthened for the second time.

Fig. 8. The sac of the second molar returned to the level of the dental range. The cavity of reserve shortened for the second time.

Fig. 9. The cavity of reserve sending off the pulp and sac of the wisdom tooth.

Fig. 10. The sac of the wisdom tooth advanced along a curved line into the maxillary tuberosity or coronoid process.

Fig. 11. The sac of the wisdom tooth returned to the extremity of the dental range.

MUSKET-BULLETS IN TUSKS OF ELEPHANTS.
Plate II. page 56.

Fig. 1. A portion of a section of a wounded tusk; a cement; b regular ivory deposited previous to the wound; c irregular ivory deposited after the wound.

Fig. 2. A diagram illustrative of the mode of connection between the Retzian tubes of the primary and secondary regular ivory, and the cells and Retzian tubes of the different inosculating systems of the irregular ivory, after inclosure of a ball; a cement with its osseous corpuscles; b primary regular ivory with its Retzian tubes; c the ball; d the irregular ivory with its systems of tubes and cells; e secondary regular ivory

Fig. 3. A copper ball inclosed in a sphere of irregular ivory, on the surface of which are the orifices of Haversian canals. Some of the orifices have closed, and present the appearance of irregular projections. The mass has begun to be attached to the regular ivory of the tusk, and would in time have been inclosed in it. The ball must either have passed across from the opposite side of the tusk, or must have sunk below the level of the hole by which it entered.

Fig. 4. Section of a tusk across the cavity of which a ball has passed, and become inclosed in the ivory of the wall opposite the hole by which it entered. The hole is filled with irregular ivory, coated externally with cement. The cement over the ball has been disarranged by the shock. This section proves that the track of a ball across the pulp is not necessarily ossified.

Fig. 5. Section of a tusk across the base of which a spear-head has penetrated and remained in the wound. The weapon has therefore been separated from the pulp by deposition of irregular ivory in the form of a tube; a cement; $b\,b$ irregular ivory deposited previous to the wound; $c\,c$ regular ivory deposited after the wound; d irregular ivory inclosing a vacant space e, the seat of an abscess or sinus, and continuous with the cavity of f, a mass of irregular ivory (coated with regular ivory) in the form of a tube surrounding the foreign body. As irregular ivory always contracts in drying, more than any other kind of dental substance, that portion of the section marked $g\,g$ has been bent outwards.

Fig. 6. The same section viewed in profile; a the broken shaft of the spear; *b* an irregular mass of cement formed round the orifice of the wound by the membrane of the tusk follicle, and which would have closed the wound had the weapon been removed. The wound inflicted has in this instance, as in many others, stunted the growth of the tusk at *c c*, so as to render the part formed after the injury narrower and weaker.

Fig. 7. A longitudinal section of a tusk in which a gun-shot wound had terminated in abscess of the pulp; *a a* cement; *b b* regular ivory deposited before the injury; *c c* regular ivory deposited after the injury; *d d* irregular ivory bounding the abscess; *e e* masses of cement and irregular ivory at the margin of the shot-hole.

Fig. 8. The external aspect of a portion of a tusk, which had been transversely fractured; *a a* the line of fracture united externally by irregular masses of cement.

Fig. 9. The internal aspect of the same portion of tusk; *a a* the line of fracture united by irregular ivory, a portion of which is arranged in a reticular form. This reticular ivory is interesting, as affording a natural analysis of the peculiar arrangement of parts in the irregular ivory described in the paper. Each bar of the reticular ivory is traversed longitudinally by a medullary canal, from which radiate secondary canals and Retzian tubes, the whole being coated with regular ivory. This reticular ivory differs from the ordinary form of ossified pulp, only in the greater distance between the Haversian or medullary canals, so that portions of the pulp have remained unossified between them.

DEVELOPMENT OF THE SUPRA-RENAL, THYMUS, AND THYROID BODIES.—Plate III. page 66.

Fig. 1. A portion of an early embryo of the sheep.
- *a*. Heart.
- *b*. Lungs still in front of the intestinal tube.
- *c*. Wolffian body.
- *d*. Lateral mass of blastema, out of which is formed the supra-renal capsule, thymus, and thyroid.
- *e*. Cardinal vein.
- *f*. Jugular vein.
- *g*. Ductus Cuvieri.

Fig. 2. A portion of the early embryo of the sheep.
- *a*. Intestinal tube and ductus vitelli.
- *b*. Liver.
- *c*. Omphalo-mesenteric vein.
- *d*. Omphalo-mesenteric artery.
- *e*, *f*. Mass of blastema on the inner side of the Wolffian body, and

EXPLANATION OF THE PLATES.   xiii

around the **trunks of** the omphalo-mesenteric vessels; this is the posterior part of the lateral mass of blastema marked *d* in Fig. 1, and becomes in the course of development the supra-renal capsule.

Fig. 3. An early embryo of the sheep.
  a. Head, branchial arches, and rudiment of the eye.
  b. Heart.
  c. Ductus Cuvieri entering the auricle, and receiving
  d. The jugular, and
  e. The cardinal vein.
  f. The lateral blastema.
  g. Wolffian body.
  h. Umbilical cord, to which is passing
  i. The allantois.
  j. The omphalo-mesenteric artery, and
  k. Omphalo-mesenteric vein; traces of the umbilical vessels are also seen in the parietes of the abdomen.
  l. The liver and intestinal tube.
  m. Lungs.

Fig. 4. Jugular veins and lateral masses of blastema in the sheep, soon after the latter have joined across the middle line.
  a. The triangular absorption of the cervical portion, which is the first indication of the separation of the thyroid.

Fig. 5. The next stage, in which the thyroid is more distinct.

Fig. 6. The thyroid is now quite distinct, and differs from the thymus in being opaque; the latter exhibits opaque spots in a semi-transparent matrix.

Fig. 7. The thyroid and thymus have assumed their perfect form.

Fig. 8. A portion of the supra-renal capsule of the adult green monkey, slightly compressed. It exhibits the minute nucleated particles of which it consists. Among these, at pretty regular distances, are seen the germinal spots.

Fig. 9. A portion of the thymus of the brown bear, slightly compressed. It exhibits the nucleated particles of which it consists. These are grouped in spherical masses around centres from which they appear to have derived their origin.

Fig. 10. A portion of the thymus from a human fœtus. It has been taken from the surface of the gland, so as to exhibit the areolar fibres which form its delicate capsule. The pressure of the glass plates has almost obliterated the spherical grouping in the cells.

Fig. 11. A portion of the membrane which covered the contiguous surfaces of the lobes of the thymus of a human fœtus (the membrane lining the reservoirs of Sir A. Cooper). It has the same structure as in Fig. 10. It exhibits no germinal membrane, but consists of an areolar or fibrous texture intermixed with the cells of the organ, the fibres being more fasciculated, and running a straighter course than in the substance of the organ.

Fig. 12. A portion of the thyroid from a human fœtus, slightly compressed. It exhibits the same structure as the thymus, but its fibrous texture is more developed.

Fig. 13. A portion of the same thyroid to show its vascular network, in the meshes of which, as in Fig. 12, the cells are seen arranged in groups.

CENTRES OF NUTRITION.—Plate IV. page 389.

Fig. 1. A portion of the middle and internal membranes of a large encysted tumour situated under the tongue, and removed by Professor Syme.
  a. The middle or second membrane, which is a germinal membrane, consisting of flattened cells, the lines of junction of which are faintly visible, the **nuclei** remaining as the germinal spots of the membrane.
  b. The internal membrane, a layer of small cells, somewhat spherical, with slightly granular contents.
      The external membrane of the cyst, consisting of areolar and elastic fibres, contained the blood-vessels of the morbid growth.
      The cyst contained a soft mass resembling thick honey in consistence. The outer layer of this mass was white, and consisted of large, flat, transparent cells or scales, with few or no traces of nuclei. The larger internal part of the mass was reddish-grey, and consisted of ovoidal cells, resembling those of the external layer, except that they were turgid with a transparent oily-like fluid, and contained nuclei in various stages of development.

Fig. 2, *a.* Fig. 3, *a.* Cells of the meliceritous mass—those without nuclei being those of the white external layer, the others belonging to the reddish-grey part of the mass, presenting nuclei in various stages of development.
  b b. Some of the latter cells, in which the nuclei have become so much developed as to distend their cells beyond the average size. In these enlarged cells, it will be remarked that the nuclei, instead of remaining as single germinal spots for each cell, have broken up into numerous spots or centres of nutrition.
      In a tumour of this kind, the cyst and its contents are two distinct parts, and perform two distinct actions. The cyst is the active agent in withdrawing materials of nutrition for itself and its contents from the vessels which ramify in its outer tunic. The organs which accomplish this are the germinal spots in its middle tunic, which, in virtue of forces

of attraction in each, select and remove from the capillary vessels the matter necessary for the formation of the cells of the internal layer. These after solution pass in succession into the cavity of the cyst, to serve as nutriment for the contained cellular mass.

This mass is evidently the principal element of the morbid growth. The cyst is a subsidiary or accessory part, arranged for the protection and due supply of nourishment for its principal. The cells of which this mass consists have each its own nucleus or germinal centre. These cells would appear to be of two classes—those whose nuclei produce young cells in their interior for their own nutrition, but not for the reproduction of new mother-cells, and those which act as reproductive individuals for the whole morbid growth. These latter cells are marked $b\ b$ in Figs. 2 and 3, and contain numerous nutritive centres or germinal spots in their interior. The flat cells of the white external layer appear to be those individuals of the first class, which are about to close their existence, their nuclei having disappeared; their food, therefore, no longer supplied to them, and their position in the mass removed to the exterior by the eccentric development of the younger and more active neighbouring cells. In a morbid mass of this kind, as in the textures and organs of an animal generally, certain parts are set aside as reproducers, the remaining parts performing the functions of the whole mass, texture, or organ; just as in certain communities of animals certain individuals are set aside to reproduce the swarm, the others are devoted to the duties of the hive.

Fig. 4. Two portions of the primary or germinal membrane from the tubes of the tubular portion of the human kidney. The germinal spots of the gland are seen imbedded in the substance of the membrane. The external layer of this membrane, which may occasionally be seen with the nuclei detached from it, is the basement or homogeneous membrane of Mr. Bowman. In other instances, as when the epithelia are but slightly developed, it becomes difficult to decide whether we have merely the germinal membrane, or both the membrane and its epithelia before us.

INTESTINAL VILLI.—PLATE IV. page 389.

Fig. 5. Extremity of a villus immediately before absorption of chyle has commenced. It has cast off its protective epithelium, and displays, when compressed, a network of peripheral lacteals. The granular germs of the absorbing vesicles, as yet undeveloped, are seen under its primary membrane.

Fig. 6. Extremity of a villus, with its absorbent vesicles distended with chyle, and the trunks of its lacteals seen through its coats.
Fig. 7. Protective epithelium-cells from a villus in the dog.*
Fig. 8. Protective epithelium-cells cast off preparatory to absorption of chyle; instead of nuclei, they present, in their interior, groups of globules.
Fig. 9. A group of the same cells adhering by their distal extremities.
Fig. 10. Secreting cells thrown out of the follicles of Lieberkühn during digestion.
Fig. 11. Diagram of mucous membrane of jejunum when absorption is not going on. a. Protective epithelium of a villus. b. Secreting epithelium of a follicle. c c c. Primary membrane, with its germinal spots or nuclei, d d. e. Germs of absorbent vesicles. f. Vessels and lacteals of villus.
Fig. 12. Diagram of mucous membrane during digestion and absorption of chyle. a. A villus, turgid, erect; its protective epithelia cast off from its free extremity;† its absorbent vesicles, its lacteals and blood-vessels turgid. b. A follicle discharging its secreting epithelia.

PROCESS OF ULCERATION IN ARTICULAR CARTILAGE.
Plate IV. page 389.

Fig. 13. a. A section of articular cartilage and absorbent membrane. In the lower part of the section the cartilage-corpuscles retain their natural size and appearance; as they approach the rugged ulcerated edge, they increase in size, and contain numerous young cells, apparently the progeny of their nuclei; beyond this edge, rounded masses of cells, originally contained within the cartilage-corpuscles, are seen embedded in the cellular absorbent mass.
b. Absorbent cells of the false membrane, with two globular masses derived from the cartilage-corpuscles.

SECRETING STRUCTURES.—Plates IV. V.
Plate IV. page 389.

Fig. 14. Four secreting cells from the ink-bag of *Loligo sagittata*.
Fig. 15. Five cells from the liver of *Patella vulgata*. In this instance the bile is contained in the cavities of the secondary cells, which constitute the nucleus of the primary cell.

* It may be noted that both in figures 7 and 9 the clear space at the broad free ends of the columnar intestinal epithelial cells, to which several German anatomists have recently directed attention, is figured by the author.—Eds.

† The author subsequently abandoned the idea that the epithelial cells were cast off during absorption.—Eds.

Fig. 16. Three cells from the kidney of *Helix aspersa*. The contained secretion is dead white, and presents a chalky appearance.

Fig. 17. Two cells from the vesicles of the testicle of *Squalus cornubicus*. The contained bundles of spermatozoa are developed from the nucleus—each spermatozoon being a spiral cell.

Plate V. page 412.

Fig. 1. Five cells from the mamma of the bitch. In addition to their nuclei, these cells contain milk-globules.

Fig. 2. A portion of duct from the testicle of *Squalus cornubicus*. A few nucleated cells, the primary or germinal cells of the future acini, are attached to its walls.

Fig. 3. The primary cell of an acinus in a more advanced stage. The nucleus has produced a mass of young cells. The pedicle appears to have been formed by the germinal cell carrying forward the wall of the duct. A diaphragm accordingly presents itself across the neck of the pedicle.

Fig. 4. A primary cell in a more advanced stage.

Fig. 5. A primary cell still more advanced.

Fig. 6. Some of the secondary cells, products of the nucleus of the primary cell, are cylindrical, and are arranged in a spiral.

Fig. 7. The change into cylinders, and the spiral arrangement completed.

Fig. 8. *a*. One of the secondary cells; its nucleus a mass of young cells. *b*. A secondary cell elongated into a cylinder, each cell of its composite nucleus elongated into a spiral. *c*. The spiral cells or spermatozoa, free.

Fig. 9. A bunch of acini, in various states of development, maturity, and atrophy.

The four following figures are diagrams, arranged so as to illustrate the intimate nature of the changes which occur in vesicular glands when in a state of functional activity.

Fig. 10. A portion of gland-duct with two acini. One of the acini is a simple primary cell; the other is in a state of development, its nucleus producing young cells.

Fig. 11. Both acini are advancing; the second has almost reached maturity.

Fig. 12 The second acinus is ready to pour out its contents, the first to take its place.

Fig. 13. The second acinus is in a state of atrophy, the first is ripe.

Fig. 14. Two follicles from the liver of *Carcinus mænas*. The colourless germinal spot is at the blind extremity of the follicle. The secreting cells become distended with bile and oil as they recede from the germinal spot.

THE STRUCTURE OF THE LYMPHATIC GLANDS.
Plate V. page 412.

Fig. 15. A portion of the germinal membrane of the human intra-glandular lymphatics, with its germinal spots or nutritive centres diffused over it.

Fig. 16. A portion of the same membrane, in which the component flattened cells, with the centres, have been rendered transparent, and are beginning to separate, by the action of acetic acid. Five of the glandular epithelia adhere to the membrane.

Fig. 17. A diagram of a lymphatic gland, showing the intra-glandular network, and the transition from the scale-like epithelia of the extra-glandular to the nucleated cells of the intra-glandular lymphatics.

Fig. 18. A portion of an intra-glandular lymphatic, showing along one edge the thickness of the germinal membrane, and upon it the thick layer of glandular epithelia.

THE STRUCTURE OF THE PLACENTA.—Plates V. VI.
Plate V. page 412.

Fig. 19. The extremity of a placental villus.
- *a.* The external membrane of the villus, the lining membrane of the vascular system of the mother.
- *b.* The external cells of the villus, cells of the central portion of the placental decidua.
- *c c.* Germinal centres of the external cells.
- *d.* The space between the maternal and fœtal portions of the villus.
- *e.* The internal membrane of the villus, the external membrane of the chorion.
- *f.* The internal cells of the villus, the cells of the chorion.
- *g.* The loop of umbilical vessels.

Fig. 20. This drawing illustrates the same structures as the last, and has been introduced to show the large space which occasionally intervenes between the internal membrane and the external cells. It would appear that into this space the matter separated from the maternal blood by the external cells of the villus, is cast before being absorbed through the internal membrane, by the internal cells. This space, therefore, is the cavity of a secreting follicle, the external cells being the secreting epithelia, and the maternal blood-vessel system the capillaries of supply. This maternal portion of the villus, and its cavity, correspond to the glandular cotyledons of the ruminants, and the matter thrown into the cavity to the milky secretion of these organs.

Fig. 21. A portion of the external membrane, with external cells of the villus.
    a. Cells seen through the **membrane**.
    b. Cells seen from within the villus.
    c. Cells seen in profile along the edge of the villus.
Fig. 22. The extremity of a villus treated with acetic acid. All the parts are distinctly visible, and the germinal centres of the internal cells are seen surrounding the umbilical vessel.
Fig. 23. A villus with a terminal decidual bar, along the cavity of which the external cells are seen to be continued, so as to pass forwards in the direction of the parietal decidua.

Plate VI. page 445.

Fig. 1. A portion of the external membrane of a villus, with a lateral decidual bar. This portion of membrane is seen from its fœtal aspect, and in this three or four germinal centres of the external cells are perceptible.
Fig. 2. A drawing of the extremity of a villus treated with acetic acid. In this villus all the parts described are distinctly seen, and indicated by the same letters as in Fig. 19, Plate V.
Fig. 3. The extremity of a villus, with a terminal decidual bar, treated with acetic acid, to show the nuclei of the decidual cells in the cavity of the bar, and on the external membrane of the villus.
Fig. 4. Two tufts connected by a terminal decidual bar.
Fig. 5. A tuft with a lateral bar passing off from its stem.
Fig. 6. A diagram illustrating the arrangement of the placental decidua.
    a. Parietal decidua.
    b. A venous sinus passing obliquely through it by a valvular opening.
    c. A curling artery passing in the same direction.
    d. The lining membrane of the maternal vascular system, passing in from the artery and vein lining the bag of the placenta, and covering *e e* the fœtal tufts, passing on to the latter by two routes, first by their stems from the fœtal side of the cavity, and secondly by the terminal decidual bars *f f* from the uterine side, and from one tuft to the other by the lateral bar *g*. Throughout its whole course this membrane is in contact with decidual cells, except along the stems of the tufts, and the fœtal side of the placenta, where the decidual cells have degenerated into fibrous or areolar fibres. All that portion of the decidua which is in connection with the bars, villi, and tufts, is the central or functional portion of the decidua, and along with the lining membrane of the maternal vascular system, or external membrane of the tufts, constitutes the true maternal portion of the placenta.

h. Two diagrams illustrating the fœtal cellular elements of the placental tufts. These are the internal membrane, and the internal cells of the tufts, and along with the loops of umbilical blood-vessels constitute the true fœtal portion of the placenta.

THE TESTIS AND ITS SECRETION IN THE DECAPODOUS CRUSTACEANS.—Plates VII. VIII.

Plate VII. page 429.

Fig. 1. Figures of Entozoa from the tubuli seminiferi of *Orchestia littoralis*, probably allied to filaria, and supposed by M. Kölliker to be the spermatozoa. This opinion, however, is incorrect, as may be seen in the accompanying drawings, where figures are given representing all the details of the development of the true spermatozoa. These are all produced from cells, whereas the entozoa under consideration are never seen within cells, but are in all cases generally seen floating free in the seminal vessels. These filaria have only been seen, so far as I am aware, in Amphipoda and Isopoda. If they are spermatozoa, they must be produced from cells; and from what has been stated in the text, it will be seen that in all the crustacea, these cells, before producing the spermatozoa, undergo several metamorphoses; and that the final changes take place in the spermatheca of the female, where the seminal animalcules are produced. In Amphipoda and Isopoda, where these supposed filaria exist, we always find them high up in the testicle, and not occasionally, but in great numbers. In the tertiary seminal cells also, which are floating about among them, not the slightest vestige of the worm can be observed. I am inclined to suppose, therefore, that these thread-like worms, supposed by Kölliker to be spermatozoa, are only parasites.

Fig. 2. Representation of a primary germinal cell projecting from the wall of the seminal tube. It has just burst, and the young secondary cells are escaping and descending the tube; during the descent they increase in size, from their nucleus throwing off nucleoli, the latter forming the tertiary generation. In this figure it will be observed that the cell-walls of the parent are quite smooth and unbroken, so that in all probability the young arise from that portion of the cell attached to the seminal tube.

Fig. 3 Is a small quantity of the fluid from the spermatheca of the female crab, showing the tertiary or spermatozoal cells after they have burst from the secondary. As described in the text, the spermatheca appears to be the organ in which the seminal fluid undergoes the final and essential change which fits it for impregnation.

Fig. 4. This figure shows the adult seminal secondary cells from the dilated parts of the seminal tube. They are full of tertiary cells. The fluid amongst which they are floating is thick and albuminous, much more so than it is higher up or lower down the tube, and the large, clear, transparent-looking masses, are the pabulum for the nourishment of the cells It is much more abundant in this part of the organ than anywhere else, and accordingly great numbers of the secondary cells, in all stages of development, are constantly found here. If a small quantity of the seminal fluid from that portion of the testicle immediately preceding the dilated part be placed under the microscope, it will be seen that the nuclei of the secondary cells are just throwing off small nucleoli, and that the parent cell is not very much larger than when it burst from the primary. In the same part also, little or no pabulum is observed. As we proceed downwards, however, we find them increasing rapidly in size ; and, at the same time, an immense quantity of pabulum floating about in large masses. The lower part of the tube and the vas deferens are almost destitute of pabulum, the cells being satiated.

Fig. 5. The secondary cells of *Hyas araneus* from the vas deferens. The walls of the parent cells are remarkably thin. The parent secondary cells are of enormous size in this species.

Fig. 6 Represents the testicles of *Carcinus mænas*, of the natural size, and shortly before they have reached the maximum state of development. The portion included between *a a* is the tubular or hepatic, that between *b b* is the dilated or gastric. The vasa deferentia are not seen in this species so well as in *Hyas araneus*, Fig. 8, *c c*. It is in the gastric division that the pabulum lies in such quantities.

Fig. 7 Is the internal or sheathed portion of the external organs of *Cancer pagurus*; proximal extremity.

Fig. 8. Testes of *Hyas araneus*. *a a*. Tubular portion. *b b*. Follicular portion. *c c*. Vasa deferentia.

Fig. 9. External organs of *Cancer Pagurus*. *a*. Is the internal or sheathed portion *in situ*. *b*. Is the sheath or external portion.

Fig. 10. External organs of *Hyas araneus*. *A*. Sheath. *B*. Sheathed portion.

PLATE VIII. page 431.

Fig. 1. First stage of development of secondary seminal cell of *Galathea strigosa*.

Figs. 2, 3, 4. Second, third, and fourth stages of development of the secondary cell.

Figs. 5, 6, 7, 8, 9, 10, 11, 12, 13. Various stages of development of the secondary cell of lobster.

Figs. 14, 15, 16, 17. The same treated with acetic acid.

Fig. 18. Tertiary or spermatozoal cells.

Fig. 19. Secondary cell of lobster seen from armed extremity, to show the three setæ.

Fig. 20. Primary cell, or cæcum of testicle of *Pagurus bernhardus* full of secondary cells. *c*. Attachment. *b*. Free extremity. *a*. Nucleus.

Fig. 21. Primary seminal cell of *Pagurus bernhardus* filling with secondary cells. As already described, these cells grow in pairs from discs on the walls of the seminal tubes, and hang free in the cavity of the tube. It has also been described how the secondary cells are produced from the parent nucleus, namely, by means of successive growths, each of which carries off a fold of nucleus before it.

   a. Disc from which the primary seminal cells grow.
  b b. The discs on each side of it.
  c c. The origins of the primary seminal cells.
   d. One of the primary cells cut off.
   e. Nucleus of the primary cell in a state of activity; it has just thrown off a series of young, marked
   f. In the diagram.
   g. Are several old walls of former growths.
   h. Full extremity of primary cell.

Fig. 22. A small portion of the testicle of *Pagurus bernhardus* magnified, showing the manner in which the cæca hang from the walls of the seminal tube.

Fig. 23. Small drop of seminal fluid of lobster, showing the secondary cells before the armature had expanded.

Fig. 24. Small drop of seminal fluid of lobster from vas deferens. That part of the figure above *a a*, as seen under the microscope, presents one dense mass of secondary cells floating down towards *b*, where a few are seen separate.

Fig. 25. A cæcum from the testicle of *Carcinus mœnas*, showing a germinal spot at its apex just being filled with secondary cells.

Fig. 26. The germinal spot enlarged.

REPRODUCTION OF LOST PARTS IN THE CRUSTACEA.
Plates IX. XII.
Plate IX. page 471.

Fig. 1 Represents the raw surface of the proximal or adherent portion of the leg of *Cancer pagurus*, after the animal has thrown off the distal portion. The figure represents the parts of the natural size, and only a few hours after the separation had taken place.

Fig. 2 Is a representation of the same part, after the young leg had grown to some size. It will be observed that the cicatrix, which was formed upon the raw surface a few hours after

EXPLANATION OF THE PLATES. xxiii

separation, has now become very strong, covers the young germ, thus acting as a means of defence from external injury.

Figs. 3, 4, 5, Are the same parts in progressive states of development. Fig. 5 presents a bifurcated character; probably from some accidental cause it thus appears smaller than it is in the normal state.

Fig. 6 Represents the raw surface of the leg, already alluded to in *Carcinus mænas*, some time after separation. A nucleated cell is seen in the centre. This drawing was made from a very small specimen, and was only procured in the stage represented after great difficulty.

Fig. 7 Represents a longitudinal section of a very young germ, for the purpose of showing its mode of development. The fibrous-looking band which surrounds it externally, is a circular canal which belongs to a system of vessels described in the text. The four striated bodies which lie next to this canal are the rudiments of the four joints of the future limb. The striated appearance arises from the muscles already so far developed, and the albuminous matter within, and which they enclose, appears to be pabulum for their farther nourishment. The more defined globules, which may be observed floating amongst the albumen, are oil-globules. In the development of this leg, it will be observed that the external segments, or those which are analogous to the thigh and first tibial joints, are largest and most fully formed,—a fact we would be led to expect, from the circumstance of their formative cells being the first thrown off from the original parent nucleus, and consequently the first that would take on a central or more independent action. From a similar mode of development, we see that the second tibial and tarsal joints are the smallest, as they are the last formed of the centres. The last or distal phalanx is the smallest of the internal segments; those nearest the circular vessel are the largest, as was to be expected from the centres which formed them, being the oldest and the first formed from the earlier generations of cells; and those again within them are smaller, being formed from the later generations thrown off by the original parent.

Fig. 8. Cells from the external series represented by *c* in Fig. 9.

Fig. 9. Transverse section of raw surface of proximal or attached extremity of the reproductive organ in leg of *Cancer pagurus*. This is the surface and appearance which is seen immediately upon the leg falling off; if it is seen half-an-hour, or a little more, after the separation, it is covered with a thickish film, which shortly becomes a strong opaque cicatrix hiding everything beneath it. The vessels seen in Fig. 15 are also omitted, for the purpose of showing the structure of the reproductive body more clearly.

a. Is the circular vessel, of the system of vessels mentioned in the text, and it surrounds
   b. A fluid or semi-fluid mass, containing small nucleated cells, from which the germ is probably derived.
   c. Is a large mass of very large cells surrounding the circular vessel, which appear to act as a magazine of nutritive matter for the young germ during its growth.
   d. Is the shell membrane, which is surrounded externally by the shell.

Fig. 10. A young limb of *Carcinus mænas* still enclosed within its original cyst, which is formed probably from the cicatrix mentioned above. Magnified two diameters.

Fig. 11. Is a very young leg of the common lobster. The reproduced leg of this species is not enclosed in a cyst, and it is not folded upon itself, but projects straight forward. Nat. size.

Fig. 12. Is a figure of the natural size of one of the large claws of *Pagurus bernhardus*, shortly after it has burst from its containing cyst.

Fig. 13. Enlarged view of Fig. 11.

Fig. 14. One of the large claws of *Carcinus mænas* still enclosed within the cyst. From observations made, it appears that these young legs remain within the cyst until their own covering or shell is of sufficient strength to act as a means of defence. They do not obtain a true shell for some time after the cyst has burst.

Fig. 15. Raw surface of proximal extremity of leg in *Cancer pagurus*, shortly after the animal has thrown off the distal portion. This figure is made for the purpose of showing the distribution of the peculiar vessels, and their mode of running from the circumference towards the circular vessel in the centre.

Fig. 16. Longitudinal section of young leg still within the cyst.
   a. Part of old leg containing the reproductive organ.
   b. External cells.
   c. Smaller nucleated cells.
   d d. Cyst of young leg.
   e. Femur of young leg.
   f. First tibial joint of young leg.
   g. Second tibial joint.
   h. Tarsal joint.

Fig. 17. Natural size of young leg.

Fig. 18. Portion of blind extremity of one of the peculiar vessels which are attached to the blood-vessel running to the leg, Plate XII. Fig. 14. The contents are oil-globules, but in the figure have somewhat the appearance of nucleated cells.

Fig. 19. An enlarged view, for the purpose of showing the connection of these vessels.

Fig. 20. Two of the blind extremities from raw surface of leg, where they present a clavate appearance.

Fig. 21. View of the extremity, showing the dark spot supposed to be a germinal spot.

Plate XII.

Fig. 9. Small longitudinal portion of shell from the large claw of *Cancer pagurus*, showing the thickness of the annulus or ring in it at the point of separation.

Fig. 12. Longitudinal section of one of the legs of *Cancer pagurus*, showing the natural position and relations of the reproductive organ.
- *a a.* Femur.
- *b b.* Reproductive organ.
- *c.* Natural appearance of line of separation
- *d.* Coxa.

Fig. 13. Enlarged foramen as it is seen on raw surface after the separation. This has been hardened in boiling water, which gives it a much more defined appearance, and also enlarges it more than it naturally should be.

Fig. 14 Is a small portion of the femoral artery, about half-an-inch in extent beyond the line of separation, which is covered as represented by the peculiar vessels.
- *a.* Distal extremity of blood-vessel.

ON THE ANATOMY AND DEVELOPMENT OF THE CYSTIC ENTOZOA.—Plates VI. X. XI. XII.

Plate X. page 476.

Fig. 1. Magnified view of one of the young of *Acephalocystis armatus* still attached to the germinal membrane of a secondary parent. It is taken from the group shown in Fig. 2, and is still in an early stage of development, the circlet of teeth still being minute and not fully developed. The absorbing series of cells may be seen internally.

Fig. 2. Small portion of the germinal membrane of a secondary parent of *Acephalocystis armatus* highly magnified.

Fig. 3. Small portion of germinal membrane of *Acephalocystis armatus* in a state of degeneration; nothing is seen in the membrane, which is quite homogeneous, except the small cells figured *a*.
- *b.* Is the commencement of one of the cretaceous fatty masses described in the text.

Fig. 4. Several of the stages of development of Cysticercus.
- *a.* First stage represents spines; hardly if at all seen.
- *b.* Their first decided appearance.
- *c.* Third stage.

        d. Fourth stage.

Fig. 5. Small portion of the germinal membrane of *Acephalocystis armatus.*

Fig. 6. Small portion, highly magnified, of the granular matter from the cyst of Cysticercus.

Fig. 7. Small portion of the inner surface of the external membrane of *Acephalocystis armatus* while in a state of degeneration.

Fig. 8. Ovum from the pedicle of Cysticercus.

Fig. 9. Small portion of the germinal membrane of *Acephalocystis monroii*, highly magnified.

    a. Fibrous basis.
    b. Germinal vesicles.
    c. Secondary acephalocysts within the germinal vesicles; this portion was taken from the large parent cyst, which is the primary animal, buried in the liver; and each of the smaller vesicles marked *c* belong therefore to the secondary generation, their progeny again being the tertiary generation.

Fig. 10 Is a specimen of *Cysticercus neglectus* ruptured at the fundus of the sac, apparently for the escape of the young germs into the cavity of the cyst, where they become attached.

Fig. 11. Small portion of the cyst of *Cysticercus neglectus* magnified, showing its vascularity, and the mode of attachment of the young Cysticerci to its internal surface.

Fig. 12. View from above the pedicle of Cysticercus, showing the disposition of the teeth. In all works hitherto published on Helminthology, there has been a great want of proper figures or descriptions of the true generic and specific characters of these animals, a point of the utmost importance for obtaining a proper knowledge of them: with this view the author has paid scrupulous attention to the leading characters, and these he has placed in the form of a synopsis at the end of the chapter. All the drawings have been made with the view of illustrating these characters more fully. The disposition of the teeth, and their forms, are perhaps the most certain external characters.

Plate XI. page 482.

Fig. 4. Magnified view of a small portion of the external or tubular membrane of *Diskostoma acephalocystis.*

    a. Larger disc.
    b. Smaller one on its surface.
    c. Tubuli.
    d. Extremities of tubes.
    e e. Gemmules, which at this stage of development may act as absorbents.

Fig. 5. Natural size of *Diskostoma acephalocystis.*

Fig. 6. *Diskostoma acephalocystis* in various stages of development.

a a a. Small cells arising from the attached surface of the tubular membrane. This is the manner in which the original group increases in size.

  b. More advanced.

  c. First stage of second mode of development, or that for the extending of the parasite to as yet uninfested parts of the body, for the purpose of forming new groups.

  d. Second stage.

  e. Third stage.

  f. Root where the original germ became fixed.

  g. External or tubular membrane.

Fig. 10. Section of *Astoma acephalocystis*, showing its internal structure

Plate XII. page 487.

Fig. 1. Portion of sac of Cysticercus, much magnified.

  a. Absorbing cells of absorbing membrane.

  b b. Separate ova, after their escape from the pedicle.

Fig. 2. *Cysticercus neglectus* very much magnified.

Fig. 3. Small portion of omentum containing *Cysticercus neglectus*, showing the bodies considered to be young Cysticerci attached; the omentum has been folded over, and the young (*a*) are seen attached to the fold.

Fig. 4. The natural size of the animal supposed to be a new Cœnurus—*Cœnurus hepaticus*.

Fig. 5. Magnified view of the head of *Acephalocystis armatus* in a more advanced stage than the former figure.

Fig. 6. The germinal membrane from which it was taken.

Fig. 7. The absorbing membrane of cyst of *Cysticercus rattus* highly magnified.

Fig. 8. Teeth of *Cysticercus rattus* highly magnified.

Fig. 10. Ovum of *Cysticercus rattus* highly magnified.

Fig. 11. Ova from pedicle of *Cysticercus rattus* highly magnified.

Plate VI. page 445.

Fig. 8. *Gymnorhynchus horridus* within its cyst.

Fig. 9. ——————————— exposed.

Fig. 10. First stage of *Cœnurus cerebralis*.

Figs. 11, 12, 13, 14. Second, third, fourth, and fifth stages of the discoidal period of development of *Cœnurus cerebralis*.

Fig. 15. One of the first stages in the vertical period of development.

Fig. 16. *Sphairidion acephalocystis* highly magnified.

Fig. 7. *Neuronaia monroii*. (J. Goodsir.)

  a. Suctorial mouth.

  b. Acetabulum.

  c. Orifice of organs, supposed to be reproductive.

  d. Posterior orifice, by which the sigmoidal " cisterna chyli "

  e. Opens, and apparently also,

    f. The thick-walled peculiar sac.
    g. Pyriform sac, a receptacle for the ova.
    i. Male organs.
        The figure also presents the arrangement of the dermal spines, and the general form of the animal.

PLATE XI. page 482.

Fig. 2. The anterior extremity and suctorial mouth of *Neuronaia monroii* more highly magnified.

Fig. 7. The cyst of *Neuronaia monroii* in a bundle of nervous filaments. The fissured appearance of the cyst, with its epithelia, is represented in this drawing.

    I am inclined to believe that the function of the cyst in this and the other Cystic Entozoa is to supply nourishment to the enclosed animal, drawing it from the surrounding parts, and throwing it into the cavity, the structure and action being identical with that in the encysted tumours as already described.

    The bulbous extremities of the cysts of *Trichina spiralis* contain masses of germinating cells, to which I am inclined to attribute the same function.

Figs. 8, 9, 11. The clavate extremities of the cysts of *Trichina spiralis*, with their germinating absorbent cells.

    The epithelium and absorbent cells of the cysts of the entozoa may be considered as permanent yelk-cells in the economy of these persistent embryos.

Figs. 1 and 3. Magnified drawings of *Sarcina ventriculi* described, but badly figured by me in the *Edinburgh Medical and Surgical Journal*, No. 151. I am still of opinion, notwithstanding the arguments of Mr. Busk, in the *Microscopical Journal*, that this body is a vegetable parasite, its sudden occurrence and sudden disappearance being not more extraordinary than the rapid development of many cellular structures; the glandular epithelium, for instance, during secretion. That it is a Gonium, as has been suspected by Professor Link, appears to me improbable, as would be admitted, I believe, by that great botanist, if he had had an opportunity of observing its peculiar vegetable aspect, so different from that of an infusorial animal.

DIVISION I.

DEVELOPMENT AND MORPHOLOGY.

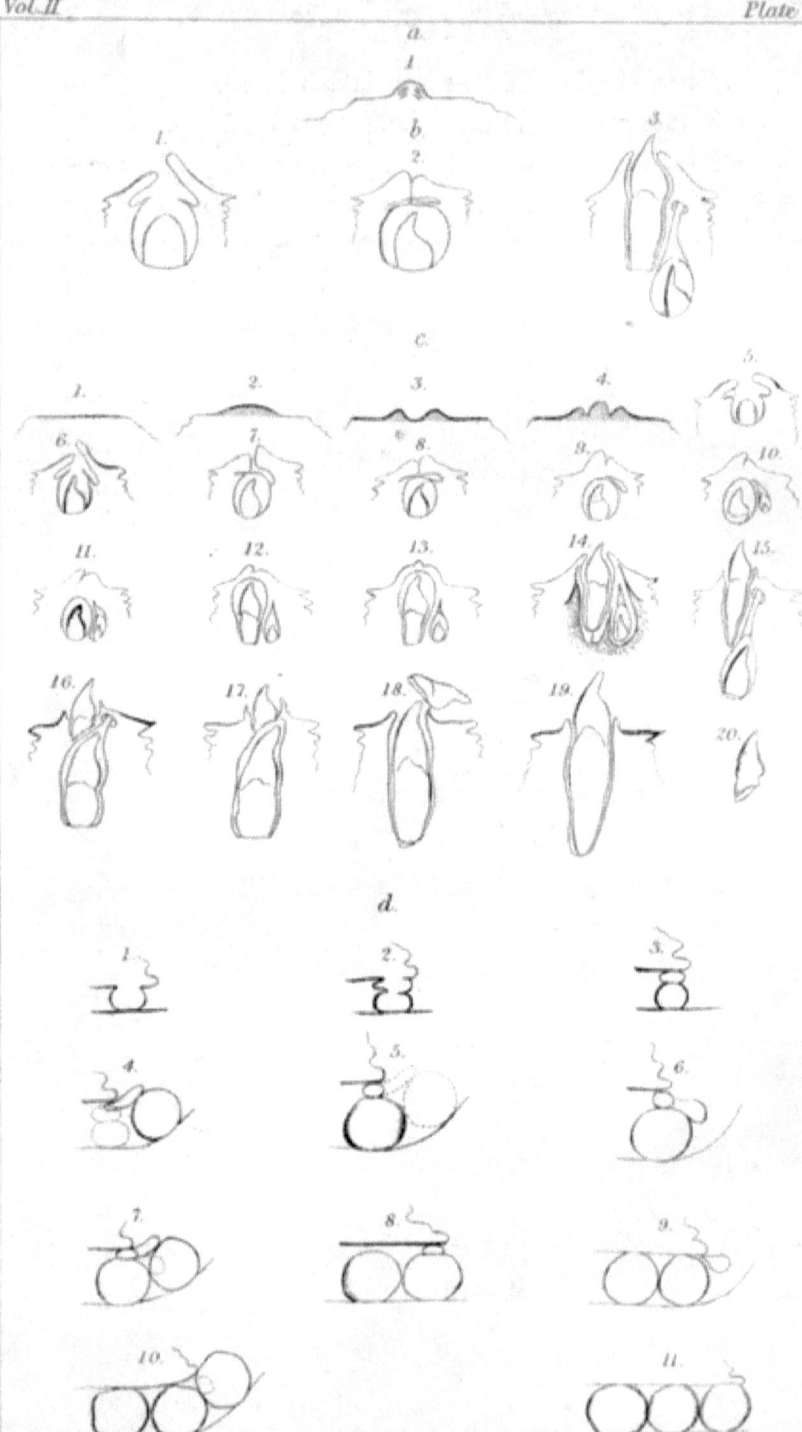

DIVISION I.

I.—ON THE ORIGIN AND DEVELOPMENT OF THE PULPS AND SACS OF THE HUMAN TEETH.— PLATE I.

"Il est peu de sujets en medecine sur lesquels on ait tant écrit que sur les dents ; deux cent volumes contiendraient à peine tout ce qu'on en a imprimé ! Mais est-ce à dire que tout soit connu à cet egard ? Est-ce à dire que la matière ait été epuisée et qu'il ne reste plus rien à faire ? Nullement. L'Anatomie n'a pas encore le dernier mot de la nature sur cet intéressant sujet et il reste encore, quoiqu'on en dise, quelques doutes à eclaircir et plus d'une difficulté à résoudre."—BLANDIN, *Anat. du Systeme Dentaire*, 1836.

SECTION I.—EXAMINATIONS OF THE DENTAL ARCHES AT DIFFERENT AGES.

1. An embryo (Fig. 1), which measured $7\frac{1}{2}$ lines from the vertex to the point of the coccyx, weighed 15 grains, and appeared to be about the sixth week,* was selected and prepared for the purpose of examining the state

Fig. 1.

* It is difficult to determine the exact age of an embryo. The ages given in the text, therefore, must be considered as approximations, being probably rather under-rated. I have given a full-sized sketch of the youngest subject in which I have observed any of the phenomena of dentition, with the weight and measurements of a few of the others. In researches of this kind, the sequences of phenomena are of more importance than their periods of appearance.

Velpeau, *Embryologie ou Ovologie Humaine;* Breschet, *Etudes Anatomiques, etc., de l'œuf dans l'espèce Humaine:* Sœmmering, *Icones Embryonum Humanorum.*

of the palate and dental arches. The cheeks were divided transversely from the commissures of the lips with fine scissors; the jaws were separated, removed, and fixed to the bottom of a small capsule full of water. The point of the tongue was removed. The configuration of the mouth was then determined by means of a half-inch lens and two needles, bent at the points, and fixed in slender handles.

Upper Jaw.—The roof of the mouth was bounded anteriorly and laterally by the free edge of the lip (*a*, Fig. 2), which is at this age thin and of great transverse extent. Within the lip (*a*), but separated from it by a groove (*b*), to be more particularly described afterwards, there was observed a lobe of a horse-shoe shape (*c*), narrow anteriorly at the median line, broader, flatter, and of a rounded form on each side posteriorly. Coming out from above the internal

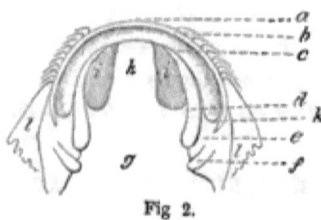

Fig 2.

posterior edges of this lobe (*c*), and firmly adhering to it, two other lobes (*d d*) were seen; flat, rounded, and curving backwards and inwards posteriorly, gradually disappearing by pointed extremities anteriorly. From the posterior extremities of each of the lobes now described (*d d*), and of the horse-shoe lobe (*c*), a thin semitransparent membranous fold (*e e*) passed backward on each side, attached externally to the sides of the capacious bucco-pharyngeal cavity, bounded internally by a free edge opposed to its fellow of the opposite side, and terminating posteriorly on the lateral walls of the pharynx. Adhering to the inferior surface of each of these folds was seen a smaller lobe (*f f*) somewhat similar to the two last, and situated a little behind them. The needle placed under the folds showed that they were free and floating, except at their exterior or adherent edges, and that they constituted a partial division of the large common nasal, buccal, and pharyngeal cavity into a superior and an inferior compartment. The upper wall of this common cavity was smooth and flat posteriorly (*g*); but anteriorly it was contracted and terminated in a longitudinal bar (*h*), which ran forwards to be attached to the superior surface of the horse-shoe lobe at the median line, and to the other parts in that neighbourhood. Under the bar (*h*) a deep cavity (*i i*) was seen, which communicated with the exterior of the face by two small *foramina*, which constituted at this period the whole external nasal organ. As before-mentioned, a groove (*b*) was observed between the lip (*a*) and the external edge of the horse-shoe lobe (*c*). This groove (*b*) was deep, and its walls and lips were in close apposition. It terminated posteriorly on each side (*k k*) by becoming more shallow, and curving backwards and inwards on the inferior surface of the membranous folds (*e e*). There was a median frenum between the lip and the horse-shoe lobe.

Lower Jaw.—The under lip (*a*, Fig. 3), resembled the upper, and was separated along its whole extent by a groove (*b*) similar to the one above, from a semicircular lobe (*c*). Anteriorly this lobe (*c*) was divided into two median large (*d d*), and two lateral smaller lobules (*e e*), the whole being firmly adherent to the floor of the mouth in front of the tongue and its *frenum*, which were both well developed. The lateral parts of the lobe (*c*) were rather indistinct, but at the point where the free edge of the lip terminated, it extended transversely and posteriorly, became thick and bulbous (*f f*), and exhibited on its surface a narrow shallow groove of a sigmoidal form (*g g*), which was continuous with the groove behind the lip. There was a median labial frenum.

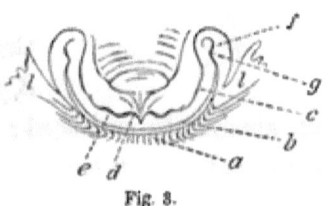

Fig. 3.

On the external sides of the membranous folds in the

upper, and of the posterior parts of the lobe in the lower jaw, the cut surfaces of the cheeks made by the scissors were seen (*l l, l l*).

The mucous membrane over its whole extent was thin, and of a greyish-yellow colour, the lobes granular, very friable, and of a dead white. The breadth of the upper alveolar arch was $1\frac{1}{3}$ line, and the length of the same was 1 line.

2. The jaws of an embryo which measured 1 inch, weighed 20 grains, and appeared to be about the seventh week, were prepared and examined as in the former case.

Upper Jaw.—The free edge of the lip (*a*, Fig. 4) was not so extended as at the sixth week. The horse-shoe lobe (*c*) had become broader and more developed posteriorly, and anteriorly exhibited three lobules, one median (*m*), and two lateral and anterior (*n n*). The two lobes observed on each side of the palate in the former embryo (*d d, f f*, Fig. 2), had disappeared, having apparently coalesced; the posterior one (*f*) being curved forwards to join the anterior (*d*), in the point (*s*, Fig. 4), while the combined mass had contracted itself towards the front of the mouth within the limits of the horse-shoe lobe (*c*).

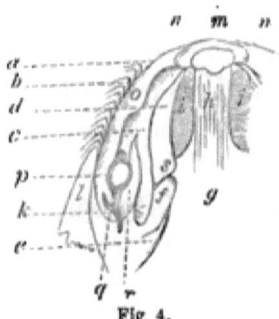

Fig. 4.

The cleft had slightly diminished, but was still of sufficient width to display the whole of the undivided nasal cavity.

The lip (*a*) was so lax as to admit of being moved by the middle. The horse-shoe lobe (*c*) could also be pressed by the same means inwards and backwards. When these two parts were separated, the mucous membrane was seen to form a duplicature (*b*), between the lips and a ridge (*o*), which extended from the posterior part of the dental arch to the outer extremity of the lateral lobule (*n*).

The median portion of the dental arch was formed by the two lateral lobules (*n n*), which separated the lips from the median lobule (*m*), and extended also a little on each side of it.

The lateral portions of the arch presented externally the ridge (*o*), formerly mentioned, smooth and convex on its external surface, internally moulded into three curves, the anterior long and shallow, the second deeper, the third or posterior almost semicircular. Behind the last curve, the internal edge of the ridge formed a deep notch, which swept outward and forward, so as to mould the former into an almost isolated lobule (*q*). The ridge now disappeared, but its edge continued backwards and inwards, winding around the posterior extremity of the horse-shoe lobe (*c*), so as to form a groove (*k k*, Figs. 2 and 4), on the surface of the soft mucous membrane. The internal division of the lateral parts of the dental arch was formed by three bulgings, apparently productions from the horse-shoe lobe (*c*), and which were separated from the curves of the ridge (*o*), by a groove which was deeper at their sides than in their intervals. The anterior one was lengthened and indistinct, the middle one was more developed, the posterior circular, convex, and altogether isolated. The isolation of this bulging was produced by a longitudinal lobule (*r*), apparently cut off from the external edge of the horse-shoe lobe (*c*), and forming a partial inner ridge corresponding with the outer one. This new lobule (*r*) reached back as far as the posterior extremity of the horse-shoe lobe (*c*), and terminated anteriorly near the middle of the centre bulging.

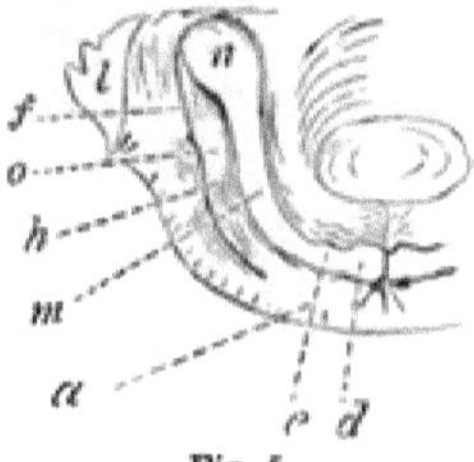

Lower Jaw.—In the situation of the dental arch, there existed a groove (*h*, Fig. 5), very distinct posteriorly, but having no outer lip anteriorly. The inner lip (*m*), presented posteriorly a large lobe

Fig. 5.

(n), under which the needle was easily inserted for a short distance. In the middle, this lip (m) was thin, elevated, and curved over the groove (h). Anteriorly it became broader, and curved still more over the groove, and was divided into two median larger lobules (d), and two lateral smaller (e). Between the two median (d) there was a notch at the attachment of the lingual frenum. The outer lip (f) was deficient anteriorly, so that the groove was bounded in that situation by the under lip (a), which was loose, free, and turned outwards. Posteriorly the outer lip (f) was well developed, and came out from under the posterior lobe (n) of the inner lip, so as to render the grove (h) pointed, and curved backwards and inwards. This lip (f) extended only about half-way towards the median line, and appeared flat, or in the same continuous plane with the floor of the groove. It was also curved outwards, so as to overhang the labial mucous membrane.

The groove presented an elevation (o) of its floor near its posterior extremity. There was a labial frenum. The mucous membrane possessed the same physical properties as at the sixth week. The lobes were not so granular, but tougher and more consistent. Breadth of superior arch 1½ line, length 1.

3. The jaws of an embryo at the second month, having been prepared in the usual manner, presented the following appearances :—

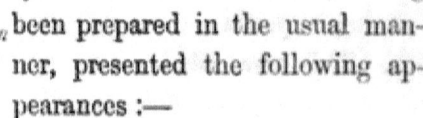

Fig. 6.

Upper Jaw.—The lip (a, Fig. 6) was more movable, and its free edge less extended. The cleft in the palate had diminished, existing only as a small angular deficiency (x) in the pendulous portion. The horse-shoe lobe was still perceptible under the form of a bulging (c), represented as turned aside to exhibit the objects under it. The lobule (r) had increased in size, so as to extend further backwards, and to appear on the posterior lateral parts of the palate. The median lobule (m) had become triangular, the anterior edge being formed by the curve of the palate somewhat pointed in front, the lateral edges being straight and meeting in an angle behind, from which the median line of suture or raphe of the palate proceeded. The median lobule (m) had increased relatively, the lateral lobules (n n) only absolutely. The posterior portion of the dental groove (k) was longer, wider, and not so much curved.

The bulging or papilla (1) was more distinctly isolated; and at the anterior extremity of the second curve in the ridge (o), another papilla (2) had appeared as a production from the latter. This papilla (2) was bounded externally by a lamina (p), which was also a production from the edge of the ridge (o), and was notched at its inner margin, where it was applied to the side of the papilla.

The dental groove then terminated in a point, at the outer extremity of the lateral lobule (n). There was a labial frenum.

Lower Jaw.—The posterior portion of the dental groove had undergone no material change, but had become deeper, and contained in the situation of the elevation marked (o, Fig. 5), a distinct rounded papilla (1, Fig. 7). Further on, another papilla (2) bounded externally by a notched lamina (a)

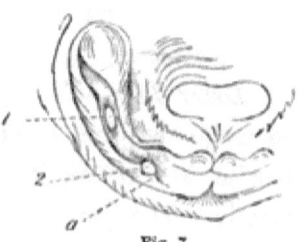

Fig. 7.

had appeared. This combined papilla and lamina was exactly similar in its configuration and relations to that marked (2, Fig. 6). The anterior part of the groove had become more distinct, not because it had acquired an outer lip, but because its floor had risen above the level of the labial mucous membrane. There was a labial frenum. The breadth of the superior arch was 1⅔ line; length 1⅓.

4. The jaws of an embryo nine weeks old were examined under water.

Upper Jaw.—No material change had taken place in the configuration of the palate, except that the median lobule (*m*, Fig. 8), had diminished relatively, and in the transverse direction, while the lateral lobules (*n*) had increased relatively, and also in the transverse direction. A longitudinal lobule (*y*), had also appeared on the surface of the median lobule (*m*). The cleft (*x*) in the soft palate was smaller.

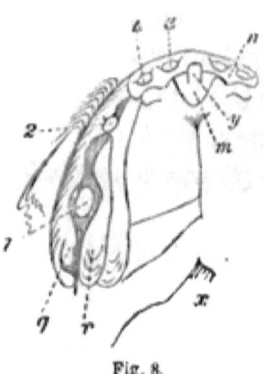

Fig. 8.

The posterior part of the dental groove was wider. The papilla (1), had become more prominent, and the lips of the groove had almost met before and behind it. The papilla (2) is larger. A little further on, corresponding with the lateral lobule (*n*), on each side, two papillæ (3 and 4), with notched laminæ in front of them, had appeared. The centrals (3), or those on each side of the median line, were the most distinct.

Lower Jaw.—The lips of the dental groove had approached so as to require separation by the needle to exhibit its contents distinctly. The papilla (1 or 2, Fig. 9) had undergone little change, but two very indistinct bulgings (3 and 4) had appeared on each side of the labial frenum, the centrals (3) being the

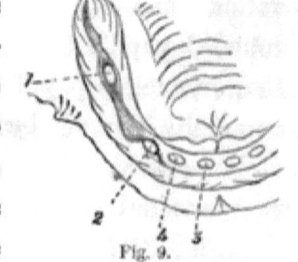

Fig. 9.

largest. The breadth of the superior arch was 1⅔ line; the length 1⅓ line.

5. In an embryo of the tenth week the following appearances presented themselves:—

Upper Jaw.—Very little change had taken place in the lateral lobules (*n*, Fig. 10), or the median (*m*) and its additional lobule (*y*). They had all increased absolutely, and if any relative change had taken place, it was in the transverse diminution of the median (*m*) and the movement forward of its additional lobule (*y*). The palate had advanced anteriorly, so as not only to have encroached in some degree upon the median and lateral lobule, but also to have thrown itself into folds immediately behind them. The outline of the horse-shoe lobe (which is represented in the sketch as turned aside to exhibit the dental groove), was still observed. There was an indistinct uvula. The papillæ (1 and 2) had sunk completely into follicles, and could only be seen by looking into the open mouths of the latter. The mouth of (1) was bordered by four laminæ or lids, that of (2), by three, as represented in the sketch. The papillæ (3 and 4) had not increased much, but their notched laminæ had become more distinct. At the posterior extremity of the floor of the dental groove, on the inner side of the lobule (*q*, Figs. 4, 6, 8, 10), a slight bulging (5, Fig. 10) was seen.

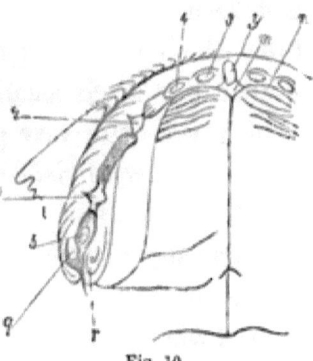

Fig. 10.

The upper lip had receded in the neighbourhood of the median line, so as to have disappeared almost entirely at that spot, the centre of the upper dental arch being exposed.

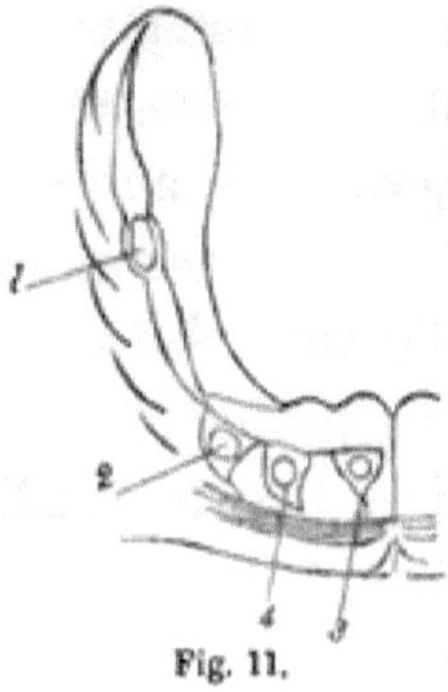

Fig. 11.

Lower Jaw.—The bulgings on each side of the median line (3, 4, Fig. 11), which were so indistinct in the last subject, had become well developed and inclosed in follicles, through the mouths of which they were seen. A similar change was observed in reference to the papilla (2). The follicles had been produced by the stretching across of productions from the outer lip (which was very indistinct) towards similar but much smaller productions from the inner lip (which was still very prominent). The lines of junction of the septa were visible, and the mouths of the follicles presented an unfinished appearance. The papilla (1) had become surrounded by an incomplete follicle, in consequence of the production of a notched lamina from the outer lip of the groove, which lamina was almost met by a smaller slip of membrane from the inner lip. The breadth of the superior arch was 2 lines, length 1⅜ line.

6. *11th or 12th week.*—*Upper Jaw.*—The median lobule (*m*, Fig. 12) had diminished so much transversely, as to have become antero-posterior; while its supplementary lobule had become attached to the frenum of the lip. The lateral lobules (*n*) had increased much transversely, and appeared each to be divided into an anterior and a posterior portion. They were compressed by the true palate, which was folded at this part, as at the tenth week, into wrinkles, the longest and anterior of which stretched across the median line from the right to the left side. The papillæ (3 and 4), with their follicles, were fully developed. The other two papillæ (1 and 2, Fig. 10) had not undergone much change, but the small bulging (5, Fig. 10) had now become a distinct papilla, and its follicle had begun to show itself. The uvula was well marked.

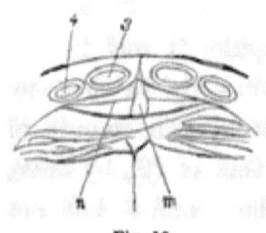
Fig. 12.

Lower Jaw.—The lines of junction of the interfollicular

septa had almost disappeared, and the mouths of the follicles had become more distinct. The mouths of the three anterior follicles had an anterior lip, the free edge of which was directed somewhat inwards. It was necessary to lift up this lip with the needle to obtain a view of the contained papilla. At the posterior part of the dental groove, another papilla with a notched lamina, both productions from the external lip, had appeared (5, Fig. 13). Breadth of superior arch 12½ lines; length, 2.

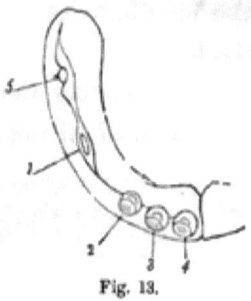

Fig. 13.

7. *13th week.—Upper Jaw.*—There was little change in the configuration of the palate since the former week. The lobe running across the median line was still visible. The frenum of the upper lip had become closely attached to, and continuous with, the median lobule. The outlines of the horse-shoe lobe were still perceptible, and on its external side the lobule, all along marked (*r*), was visible. The outer lip of the dental groove, or the external alveolar process, was equally developed all around. The upper lip was still much retracted. There were ten papillæ inclosed in open-mouthed follicles, and ranged at nearly equal distances all around the dental groove.*
The four anterior papillæ were flattened from before backwards with a straight edge, and were somewhat similar to the future incisive teeth. The next one on each side was a simple cone. The two posterior on each side were also conical, but flattened transversely, so as considerably to resemble carnivorous molars. Each of these papillæ adhered by its base to the fundus, while its apex, as during the eleventh and twelfth weeks, presented itself at, or, as in the present instance, protruded from, the mouth of its

---

* Arnold, *Salzburg Med.-Chirurg. Zeitung*, 1831, Erster Band, p. 236. Valentin, *Handbuch der Entwickelungs-geschichte des Menschen*, p. 482.

follicle. The point of the needle could be introduced through the mouth, so as to move the papilla about in the interior of the follicle.

By removing the outer lip of the dental groove, and the outer wall of all the follicles by the scissors, a good view was obtained of the configuration of these parts (Fig. 14). The follicles were observed to be mere duplications of the membrane of the groove, and consequently of the *general gastro-intestinal mucous membrane*. The inner surface of the follicles was of a greyish-yellow colour. The papillæ had increased relatively so as to protrude from the mouths of their follicles. They were granular, friable, and of a dead-white colour.

Fig. 14.

Lower Jaw.—No remarkable change had taken place in the lower jaw, except in the relative enlargement of the papillæ, and in the distinct development of the follicle of the posterior papilla (5, Fig. 13). The outer lip of the dental groove was not very distinctly marked, but the inner was well developed. The breadth of the superior arch was 3 lines, and the length was also 3 lines.

8. *14th week.*—*Upper Jaw.*—The median lobule had undergone little change, the lateral lobules had become broader from before backwards, apparently in consequence of the retraction of the palate, which, instead of exhibiting on its anterior part the confused transverse wrinkles formerly mentioned, presented on its lateral divisions (corresponding to the horse-shoe lobe) four or five parallel rugæ, which were apparently remains of the wrinkles. The upper lip had again become full, so that its free edge was on a level with the surface of the palate. The soft outer edges of the palate and the anterior edges of the lateral lobules were now closely applied to the outer lip of the dental groove, so as to close the

latter in a valvular manner. When these edges—viz. the continuous semicircular outline of the whole palate—were raised by the needle, the dental groove and its contents—viz. ten papillæ in their follicles—were seen. It was observed that the follicles had increased relatively, the papillæ only absolutely, in consequence of which the latter, instead of projecting from, had receded within, the mouths of the former. The mouths of the follicles had apparently become smaller. This had arisen in consequence of the greater development of the laminæ which were seen in the earlier stages. There were two, an anterior and a posterior, for the four anterior follicles; three, an internal and two external for the third on each side; and four for the two posterior on each side (Fig. 15). Close upon the inner side of the mouth of each of the follicles there was observed a little depression in the form of a crescent, its concave edge being towards the former. These depressions were most distinctly marked at the four or six anterior follicles, where they were situated immediately behind their inner lips (*a a a a a*).

Fig. 15.

Lower Jaw.—The papilla had receded. The laminæ of the follicles were more developed (Fig. 16). Little depressions or lunulæ had appeared similar to those in the upper jaw. When the membrane of the dental groove with its adherent follicles and their pulps,

Fig. 16.

was stripped off, the dental nerves and vessels were found running along under the follicles, and distributing vascular branches and a nervous twig to each of them (Fig. 14). Each of the individual follicles, with its papilla, vascular branches, and nervous twig, exactly resembled a large hair-bulb with its nerve and vessels exposed after the hair has been extracted. Breadth of the superior arch, 3½ lines; length, 3 lines.

9. *15th week.—Upper Jaw.*—The outer edges of the palate, which in the last embryo lay unattached on the outer lip of the dental groove, in the present subject adhered firmly to it, except along a small portion posteriorly (*a*, Fig. 17).

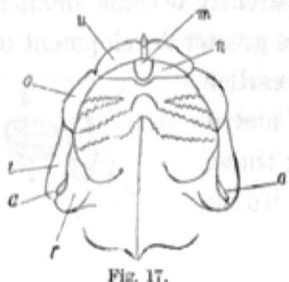

Fig. 17.

This adhesion was firm anteriorly on both sides of the median line, then became weaker, and posteriorly at the non-adherent portion (*a*), between the lobules (*r* and *t*), the lips of the groove retained their original smooth edges. When the lips of this non-adherent portion were separated by the needles, its floor and walls exhibited nothing but the greyish-yellow mucous membrane of the original groove. The outer lip of the dental groove was visible all around the external margin of the palate, and was divided on both sides into three parts, an anterior (*u*), a lateral (*o*), and a posterior (*t*). On the inner side of the latter was seen the longitudinal lobule, which has hitherto been marked (*r*). The median lobule (*m*) was rounded anteriorly, and had a process (*y*, Figs. 8 and 10), which stretched forwards between the lobules (*u u*). This was the additional lobule formerly mentioned. The sides of the median lobule were straight and converged to its posterior extremity, which was circular, and was received into a curve in the middle of a transverse band, constituting the anterior boundary of the palate, which appeared to have receded still more than in the last subject, and to have exposed still more completely the lateral lobules (*n n*). The four rugæ seen in the last subject had become ridges beautifully crenated, and converging, as represented in the sketch, towards a curve, reversed and opposite to the one formerly mentioned in the middle of the transverse band of the palate. This last curve was the result of the anterior junction of the lobes ($d\,d$, Fig. 2), and was traced through all its phases to its present state. The median suture of the palate proceeded from it posteriorly. The dental groove being torn open by means of the needles, its lips were found to have adhered pretty firmly, as before mentioned, but a feeble adhesion only had taken place between its walls so as to allow its contents to be restored to their original condition by means of a blunt instrument. This was carefully done under water, and the mouths of all the follicles with their laminæ were displayed. The latter were more developed than in the last subject, and completely concealed the papilla. The former required to be lifted up in order to display the latter. Careful observation during the separation of the contents of the groove disclosed the important fact that the general adhesion had not obliterated the little crescent-shaped depressions behind the mouths of the follicles. These retained the smooth greyish-yellow colour of the walls of the original groove, and from this circumstance could be distinguished from the general flocculent appearance of the other parts.

Lower Jaw.—The outer lip of the dental groove had increased in size, and was as prominent as the inner, except posteriorly, where the latter still retained its posterior lobe; but the most remarkable change which had taken place since last week was the complete adhesion of both lips, as in the upper jaw, with the exception of a small portion posteriorly, which still retained the peculiar appearance of the dental groove, and in which nothing could

Fig. 18.

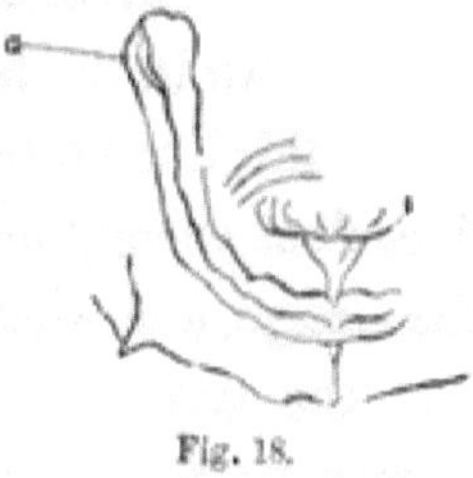

be seen but the smooth mucous membrane (a, Fig. 18). When the dental groove was torn open, as was done in the upper jaw, the laminæ (which were highly developed) of the follicles, and the walls of the groove, were found to be rough and flocculent from adhesions, with the exception of the little depressions formerly mentioned, which still retained their original appearance.

Breadth of the superior arch, 5 lines; length, 4 lines.

10. 16*th week.*— *Upper Jaw.*—The palate retained the appearance it had in the last subject, with the exception of the median lobule, which had become narrow in front, and broad posteriorly. The raphe of the dental groove had become firmer, so as to give a much more defined and permanent appearance to the non-adherent portion posteriorly, which was now seen to great advantage, its fine greyish mucous membrane gradually running at its edges into the white tough substance of the palate and gums.

Having separated the lips of the non-adherent portion (*a*, Fig. 19), a papilla, sunk in an open follicle, with three or four laminæ, was visible (6). The membrane of the palate and maxillary arch being stripped from the bone, and its surface of adhesion examined, lines corresponding with the sutures of the bones were observed; one the median, another the intermaxillary, and a third with the palato-maxillary. Five tooth-sacs were also observed on both sides of the maxillary arch. These were divided into three groups, two in the first or anterior, one in the second, and two in the third or posterior. These groups were covered with a flocculent spongy membrane, which was easily stripped off by the forceps, and when this was carefully done, it became evident that the sacs which were formerly grouped together by this membrane were individually isolated, and formed of a thin grey diaphanous membrane, similar to the one formerly mentioned as covering the bottom of the dental groove, and constituting the membrane of the follicles. The careful detachment of the external spongy membrane from the posterior group showed, what was not at first observed, that there was at the posterior part of the posterior sac another very small one, which by careful examination was seen to be the fundus of the open follicle in the non-adherent portion of the dental groove.

The adhesion of the lip and walls of the groove had now become so strong, that it was impossible to separate them. The only way, therefore, in which its contents could be examined was by transverse sections. When these sections were made between the different sacs, they displayed scarcely any traces of the dental groove; but when they passed through any place perpendicular to the surface of the gum, and near to the middle of any of the sacs, they exhibited the appearances represented in the marginal sketch (Fig. 20). The deciduous tooth pulp (a), which was lately a free papilla; (b), the section of its sac, which was a follicle when the pulp was a papilla; (d), the line of adhesion of part of the walls of the dental groove leading from the shut sac to (c), the raphe of the groove; (e), the section of the non-adherent portion of the groove in the situation of the lunula, which existed behind (f), the inner laminæ of the sac (b), in its former follicular condition. From the consideration of this section (Fig. 20), the mode in which the original follicle, the non-adherent depression behind the inner laminæ, and the walls of the dental groove, were connected after full adhesion of all the neighbouring parts, will be easily understood. The little cavity (e) adhered by its anterior and inferior extremity to the line of adhesion (d), so that it and the sac of the milk-tooth were both connected to the raphe of the edges of the dental grooves by lines of attachment, which resembled two petioles proceeding from a common footstalk. These lines of attachment were not tubular, but resisted all efforts to push a fine probe or bristle through them; they were merely opaque remains of the surfaces of junction contrasting with the semitransparent substance of the gums. Parallel sections through all the sacs exhibited similar appearances. When the contents of the sacs were examined, the pulps were found to have acquired the configuration of the bodies of the future teeth. The bases by which the molar pulps formerly adhered to the bottoms of their sacs, and which may be denominated their primary bases, had become almost divided into three secondary bases, which corresponded with the internal and two external fangs of the future teeth. This division was so far accomplished by the advancement of the internal grey membrane of the sac, under the form of small compressed canals between the base of the pulp and the external spongy membrane. These canals, which were three in number, one external and two internal, did not meet in the middle under the pulp. Deposition of *tooth-substance* (Zahn-substanz) had commenced on the edges and tubercles.

The sacs were twice as large as their contained pulps, and in the space (*g*, Fig. 20), which existed between them, there was observed a very soft flocculent gelatinous substance, which had no attachment to the pulp, and did not appear to adhere to any part of the sacs, except the laminæ and the parts adjoining them.

Lower Jaw.—The adhesion of the dental groove was not so strong as in the upper jaw. The open portion (*a*, Fig. 18), was fully defined, and exhibited on its floor the orifice of a follicle, containing a papilla. In other respects the lower was similar to the upper jaw.

Breadth of superior arch 7 lines; length 5 lines.

11. *5th month.*—Fœtus minutely injected with size and vermilion.

Upper Jaw.—The lobes (*t, o, u,* Fig. 21) had become highly developed. The anterior one (*u*) was convex anteriorly, with a sharp edge directed backwards, and corresponded with the incisive teeth. The central lobe (*o*) had become shorter, but more prominent, like a canine tooth. The posterior (*t*) had united firmly with the longitudinal lobe all along marked (*r*), so as to close the open portion of the groove (*a,* Fig. 17), which was described in the two last subjects. The raphe of the groove between these two lobes was serrated, and a vessel was seen traversing each denticulation. The raphe then ran close along the inner edges of the bases of the lobes (*o* and *u*). The median lobule was triangular, the base posterior; the apex in front continuous with the labial frenum, and situated between the anterior pointed extremities of the lobules, (*u, u*). The lateral lobules were very distinct. The other less important changes which had taken place in the palate may be understood by comparing Figs. 21 and 17.

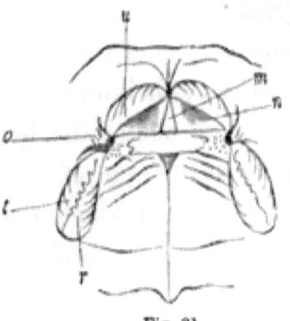

Fig. 21.

The membrane of the palate, with the sacs of the teeth, was removed from the bone. The fundus of the follicle (6, Fig. 19), had now assumed the appearance of a sac, and the other ten, instead of being grouped, had become isolated. The branch of the dental artery, which supplied each of the sacs and their pulps, was seen, when it reached the fundus of the former, to give off a number of twigs, which, radiating from their common centre, proceeded perpendicularly towards the gum, near which they inosculated with others proceeding from it. The combined vessels then formed a pretty minute network in the spongy membrane formerly described.

Transverse sections were now made by the scissors through all the sacs. The general appearance of these sections was similar to that of those at the fourth month; but the gelatinous granular substance between the pulp and the sac was of the consistence of very firm jelly, closely and intimately adherent to the whole interior of the sac, with the exception of a narrow strip all round the base of the pulp, along which strip the grey membrane of the sac retained its original appearance, and through which the radiating saccular twigs were visible, being strongly and beautifully contrasted with the cream-coloured surface of the granular substance. The mass of the granular substance had a peculiar greyish-white colour; its surface was cream-coloured, and had a dry chalky appearance. It had a tendency to tear in a direction perpendicular to the internal surface of the sac. Although closely applied, it did not adhere to the pulp, but, as stated above, surrounded it on all sides till within a short distance of its base—"whatever eminences or cavities the one *had*, the other *had* the same, but reversed, so that they *were* moulded exactly to each other." In the incisives its principal mass lay "against the hollowed inside of the tooth, and in the molars it *was* placed directly against their base like a tooth of the opposite jaw." In the pulps of the molars, which had three canals which *now* passed completely across their bases, the granular substance sent a process into each of them. These processes did not meet in the centre, but disappeared near to it, and left, as in the case of the general mass, a minute portion of the grey membrane of the sac between themselves and the secondary bases of the pulp.* In the case of the molars also the dental arterial

---

* The only authors, as far as I know, who have observed and described this gelatinous body, are Mr. Hunter in his *Natural History of the Teeth*, p. 94, and Purkinje and Raschkow, in the work of the latter, entitled, *Meletemata circa Mammalium dentium evolutionem*. Not having been able, hitherto, to procure Raschkow's work, I can only state from Burdach (*Physiologie*, French ed. tom. iii. p. 498), that Purkinje's opinion appears to coincide with Mr. Hunter's as to its being the organ which secretes that enamel. Mr. Hunter has not described the processes which this body sends under the pulp, or the

branch divided into three twigs, one for each secondary base of the pulp, and from all of these, radiating perpendicular ramuscules proceeded, as in the case of a pulp with a primary base.

The arterial network, which was formed in the external spongy membrane by the inosculation of these vessels with those proceeding from the gums, transmitted small branches, which ramified with such minuteness in the substance and on the surface of that portion of the grey membrane to which the granular matter adhered, that, when the latter was removed, the former appeared to the naked eye a mass of vermilion, but under a one-fourth of an inch lens exhibited a network of the most minute injection. No injected vessel could be seen in the granular substance.* The main dental twig, after giving off all these branches, arrived at the base or secondary bases of the pulp, and immediately divided into many branches, which ramified in a contorted flattened position, between the base or bases of the pulp and the membrane of the sac. From these, smaller ramifications were transmitted into the substance of the pulp, which ramified in considerable numbers in the centre of its mass, but scarcely at all near its surface or on its membrane, except in the neighbourhood of, and at the point where, deposition of *tooth-*

space left between it and the base of the latter; but his description is in other respects so correct and characteristic, that it is difficult to account for the manner in which the first part of his chapter on the formation of the enamel has been so much misunderstood. Dr. Blake (p. 34) (although he described the granular body as the inner membrane of the tooth-sacs, and as possessing "no vessels capable of conveying red blood") supposed that Mr. Hunter meant by "another pulpy substance," the sacs of the permanent teeth. Mr. Bell also in a note, vol. ii. Palmer's ed. *Hunter's Works*, p. 43, states that after most accurate observations, he had come to the conclusion that the "pulpy substance" mentioned by Hunter is nothing more than the inner membrane of the sac turgid with blood and earthy matter preparatory to the secretion of the enamel.

* Blake, *Essay on the Structure and Formation of the Teeth*, p. 4.

substance had commenced, immediately beneath which the vascularity was intense, both in the substance under, and on the surface a little beyond, the edge of the scale.* This surrounding vascularity had the appearance of a zone, and was situated in the substance and on the surface of an elevated portion of the pulp, which surrounded the scale of tooth-substance.

The granular substance in contact with the tooth-substance and its border had begun to be absorbed, and had consequently become thinner in that situation than elsewhere, allowing the subjacent vascularity to appear through it. No vessel could be detected in the granular substance to account for the absorption of its inner surface.

The ten little cavities had undergone no change, except that the two or four anterior had become rather longer, and were situated further from the surface of the groove, so as to be placed rather behind than below the sacs. The anterior cavity, in particular, although its walls were still in contact, and required to be separated by the needles under water to see its interior, had become pear-shaped. The fundus or portion furthest from the gum exhibited on its floor a fold, which lay in the direction of the edge of the future permanent tooth, and near its apex there were two other minute folds, one on the anterior wall, the other on the posterior. Beyond this the cavity terminated in an opaque IMPERVIOUS line, which soon disappeared. The substance of the gums had become infiltrated with a quantity of gelatinous matter very similar to the granular substance of the sacs. In consequence of this infiltration the line of junction of the walls of the dental groove had become obliterated, the substances of the gums had become thicker, and the sacs more removed from the surface.

The open portion of the groove (*a*, Fig. 19) had disappeared,

* Serres, *Essai sur l'Anatomie et la Physiologie des Dents*, p. 20.

but a longitudinal section showed that the *lips* only had adhered, the *walls* had not. The follicle (6, Fig. 22) had become a sac, in consequence of which a cavity (*b*) remained between it and the surface of the gum. Gelatinous substance had been deposited in the sac (6), and in the neighbourhood of the cavity below it (*b*), as in the other sacs.

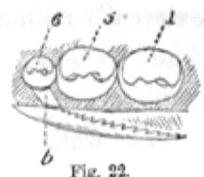

Fig. 22.

The lower jaw exhibited changes analogous to those in the upper.

12. *Child at Birth.*—A longitudinal section was made through the posterior part of the under jaw, when the sacs and pulps of the posterior milk-molar, and of the first permanent molar, and the arrangements represented in Fig. 23, were observed. (5) The sac and pulp of the posterior milk-molar; (6) the sac and pulp of the first permanent molar; (*b*) the cavity marked (*b*, Fig. 22).

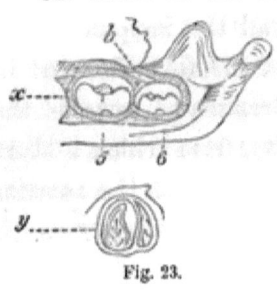

Fig. 23.

The sac of the permanent tooth (6) was now almost wholly imbedded in the base of the coronoid process of the jaw. The cavity (*b*) which was attached to the upper part of the sac of the permanent tooth by its posterior extremity, adhered by its anterior extremity to that point of the gum which was attached to the anterior edge of the base of the coronoid process, so as to drag its surface at that point into a dimple. The cavity (*b*) was consequently longer than it was at its first formation.

The granular substance had wholly disappeared. The interior of the sacs had a villous highly-vascular appearance, like a portion of injected intestinal mucous membrane. The original opening of the sac (6) into the cavity (*b*) was indicated on its inner surface by an indistinct circular lip. The sacs of one of the central incisives of the same fœtus exhibited externally nothing peculiar. After a transverse section, it was found to be composed of two, the temporary and permanent combined.

The walls of the temporary sac (*b*, Fig. 23) were composed of an external membrane, which was rather thick and condensed; the inner could be separated from it, and had the appearance, as in the molar sacs, of an injected villous membrane. The little permanent sac was situated in the substance of the outer membrane of the temporary sac, as if the latter had been split to receive it. It was lined by a membrane similar to that of the temporary, and exhibited near the lower end of its posterior wall the incipient pulp, which was evidently a development of the fold observed in that situation at the fifth month. It terminated towards the gum by an indistinct pointed extremity, from which a short opaque impervious line proceeded, near to which the anterior and posterior folds, observed at the fifth month, were seen.

13. The lower jaw of an infant about eight or nine months old, in which the central incisives had cut the gum, was prepared by removing a section from its external posterior lateral aspect, so as to expose the sacs of the posterior milk-molar, and of the anterior permanent molar (*x*, Fig. 24). The latter (6), instead of being buried in the base of the coronoid process, was situated further forward, and the cavity (*b*) having been displayed by a longitudinal section of the former, was found, comparatively speaking, to have recovered its original small extent, being attached inferiorly to the top of the sac (6), and superiorly to the anterior edge of the base of the coronoid process.

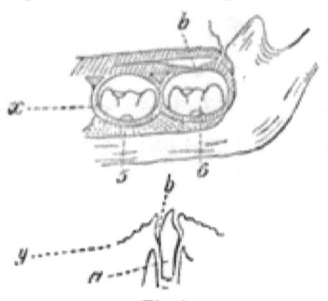

Fig. 24.

Upon examining the two incisive teeth which had cut the gum, it was found that a bristle could be inserted between their surfaces and the gum for one-third of an inch. Through the soft parts a transverse section was made, which was afterwards continued through the jaw and one of the teeth by means of a very fine saw.

It was now observed that the tooth (*a*, Fig. 24, *y*) had acquired nearly two-thirds of its fang, and that the *sac* had again become an open follicle (*b*). This follicle was shorter than the whole length of the tooth by the length of the protruding portion of the latter. At the mouth of the follicle, its lining membrane was continuous with the surface of the gums, and continued free till it arrived at the termination of the enamel, where it united to the surface of the fang of the tooth, but could be separated from it as a continuous membrane, and at the lower end of the root it became continuous with the surface of the pulp, whose base was yet considerable. Upon removing the bone in front of the neighbouring lateral tooth, which had not yet passed through the gum, it was observed that the extremity of its fang, or rather the fundus of its sac, was deeper in the jaw than that of the central by a length equal to the protruding portion of the latter. This change of level had not, however, taken place in the case of the alveoli, that of the central being rather deeper than the lateral. The space intervening between the bottom of the alveolus of the central tooth and the fundus of its sac was occupied by a spongy filamentous tissue, through which the dental vessels and nerves proceeded.

14. The lower jaw of an infant, which had cut all its milk-teeth, and which was probably between four and five years old, was prepared in the same manner as the last.

The sac of the anterior permanent molar (6, Fig. 25) was situated under the gum in front of the coronoid process, and a new sac and pulp of a smaller size (7) had appeared buried in

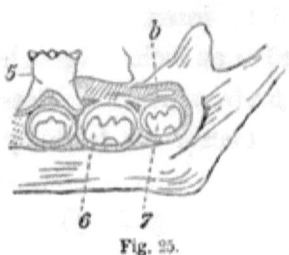

Fig. 25.

the base of that process. The cavity (*b*) was again lengthened out, being attached anteriorly, at the anterior edge of the base of the process, to the gum, and posteriorly to the top of the new sac (7). That portion of the cavity formerly attached to the sac (6) was now almost obliterated.

13. The posterior part of the lower jaw of a child about six years old was prepared by removing a section from its internal posterior aspect, and making at the same time a longitudinal section of the gum. The sac (7, Fig. 26) had advanced from under the coronoid process; and another very small sac and pulp had appeared enclosed in a bony crypt under the process, and communicat-

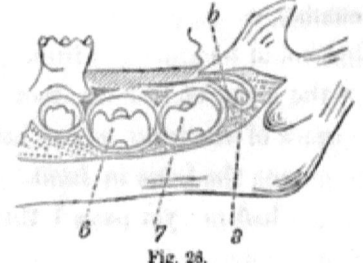

Fig. 26.

ing through the upper part of the bony cell of the sac (7) with the gum, where it terminated in an opaque line or tail, the last remains of the surface of adhesion of the dental groove.

SECTION II.—A DESCRIPTION OF THE PULPS AND SACS FROM THEIR FIRST APPEARANCE IN THE EMBRYO TILL THE ERUPTION OF THE WISDOM-TEETH.

When we examine the upper jaw of a human embryo at the sixth week, there is perceived between the lip and a semi-circular lobe of a horse-shoe form (which is the primitive condition of the palate) a deep narrow groove which terminates on each side, behind the former, by curving inwards on the soft mucous membrane. As this groove becomes gradually wider, and the lip more lax in a direction from behind forwards, there appears on its floor posteriorly, and proceeding in the same direction, a ridge (the external alveolar process) which speedily divides the original groove into two others; the outer one forming the duplicature of mucous membrane from the inside of the lip to the outside of the alveolar process, the inner one constituting what may be very properly denominated the *primitive dental groove*, as the germs of the teeth appear in it.

The inner side of the ridge already mentioned, after being cut into three grooves whose concavities look inwards, and of which the posterior is the deepest, terminates in a rounded lobule, which is continuous with it anteriorly, while externally, internally, and posteriorly, it is bounded by that portion of the original groove which was situated behind the semicircular lobe. The curves of the ridge are occupied by bulgings of the semicircular lobe, so that the ridge and lobe, with their curves and bulgings, are exactly similar to the arrangement of the mucous membrane of the second compartment of the stomach of the porpoise.

At some period between the sixth and seventh week a longitudinal portion is cut off from the internal posterior edge of the semicircular lobe, extending as far forwards as the middle bulging, and about the same time the posterior bulging becomes isolated and defined, under the appearance of an ovoidal papilla, the long diameter of which is antero-posterior. This papilla is the germ of the anterior superior milk-molar tooth, the first tooth-germ which appears in the development of the human body. It is at this period a simple free granular papilla, like many others on the surface of the mucous membrane and skin.

About the eighth week or second month a second papilla appears at the point of projection of the ridge, between the middle and anterior curve. This papilla, which is the germ of the superior milk canine tooth, is rounded and granular, and is bounded externally by a triangular lamina, which spreads out into, and is continuous with, the inner edge of the ridge, having its apex notched so as to fit the external aspect of the papilla.

During the ninth week the ridge advances in an indistinct manner to the median line, and there appears on each side of that line an oblong papilla with a notched lamina in front of it, and immediately afterwards another smaller papilla and lamina external to the former. These last papillæ are the germs of the incisive teeth, and are placed in connection with the lateral elements of the intermaxillary system.

The primitive dental groove, which before the appearance of the incisive germs terminated anteriorly at the outer extremity of the lateral intermaxillary lobules, now extends forwards to the median line. The longitudinal lobule, and the lobule opposite to it also, have lengthened out posteriorly, and the intervening portion of the primitive groove has become wider and not so curved. The sides of the groove before and behind the anterior molar papilla have been gradually approaching one another.

During the tenth week the incisive papillæ make very little advance, their anterior laminæ only increasing somewhat in size. Processes from the sides of the primitive dental groove, particularly the external one, approach and finally meet before and behind the papilla of the anterior molar, so as to inclose it in a follicle, through the mouth of which it may be seen. A similar follicle is gradually formed round the canine by the advancement inwards of its external notched lamina, which at first appeared as a production of the ridge or external lip of the groove. The germ of the posterior milk-molar also appears as a small papilla towards the end of this week behind the anterior molar, at the side and apparently as a production from the rounded lobule, which terminates posteriorly the outer ridge.

During the eleventh and twelfth week the incisives advance steadily. Septa pass between them from the outer to the inner side of the groove, so that their papillæ become completely sunk in well-developed follicles. No material change takes place in the anterior molar or canine ; but the posterior molar papilla enlarges, and the terminal lobule of the outer ridge folds gradually round it, so as to constitute its follicle, behind which there still remains a portion of the primitive groove.

The changes which ensue during the thirteenth week consist in the completion of the follicle of the posterior molar, and in the gradual change which takes place in the shape of the different papillæ. Instead of remaining, as hitherto, simple, rounded, blunt masses of granular matter, each of them assumes a particular shape. The incisives acquire in some degree the appearance of the future teeth ; the canines become simple cones ; and the molars become cones flattened transversely, somewhat similar to carnivorous molars. During this period, too, the papillæ grow faster than the follicles, so that the former protrude from the mouth of the latter, while the depth of the latter varies directly as the length of the fangs of their future corresponding teeth, the canine follicle being deepest, etc. etc. While the papillæ are changing their shape, the mouths of the follicles are undergoing a change which consists in the development of their edges, so as to form opercula, which correspond in some measure with the shape of the crowns of the future teeth. There are two of these opercula in the incisive follicles, one larger, anterior, and rather external, the second smaller, posterior, and internal. There are three for the canines, an external and two internal, and four or five for the molars, each corresponding with a tubercle ; while their edges correspond with the grooves on the grinding surfaces of these teeth.*

* It would be interesting to ascertain whether the opercula of the human

The inner lip of the dental groove (or the outer edge of the palate), which has been increasing for some time past, is now, at the fourteenth week, so large as to meet and to apply itself in a valvular manner to the outer lip or ridge, which has also been increasing. The follicles at this time grow faster than the papillæ, so that the latter recede into the former. The molar papillæ gradually acquire two or three additional small compressed tubercles on their sides, and their apices become less conical, so that they still more resemble the molar teeth of the carnivorous mammals.* The opercula of the follicles continue to increase, so as almost to hide their contained papillæ.

The *primitive dental groove*, which at this period contains ten papillæ in as many follicles, and is situated on a higher level than at first, may be now more properly denominated the *secondary dental groove*. It is when in its secondary condition that the groove affords a provision for the production of all the permanent teeth, with the exception of the first or anterior

tooth-follicles may not be rudimentary organs, which are to attain their utmost development in the sacs of the elephantoid, ruminant, and other compound teeth, under the form of depending folds for the secretion of the intersecting enamel and cement plates.

One may easily conceive the mode of formation of a composite tooth-sac, by supposing the opercula, after their edges have met, to dip down back to back between the divisions of the pulp, till they almost meet the common body of the latter.

* This is another instance of the law of progressive development, by virtue of which an organ, in the course of its formation, passes through phases which correspond to permanent conditions of the same organ in other animals. A human molar tooth-pulp is at first rounded, as in certain fishes; then conical, as in other fishes and reptiles; then conical, but flattened transversely, gradually acquiring two or more additional conical tubercles, as in the carnivorous mammals; and finally, by the equalisation of the primary and secondary tubercles, assuming the shape of the molars in the quadrumanous animals and man. In the elephantoid, ruminant, and rodent animals, it probably undergoes a further and ultimate change in the deepening of the rudimentary grooves on the grinding surface.

molars. It is about the fourteenth or fifteenth week that we begin to observe preparations made for this provision, by the gradual appearance of a little depression in the form of a crescent, immediately behind the inner operculum of each of the milk-tooth follicles. The concave edges of these depressions are in contact with the attached margins of these opercula. Those of the centre incisives appear first, then the laterals, canines, anterior bicuspids, posterior bicuspids. About this time the opercula close the mouths of the follicles, but without adhering, the anterior closing first, then the laterals, and so on in succession. The lips and walls of the secondary groove now begin to cohere in a direction from behind forwards, the opercula and every part of the groove, with the exception of the ten depressions for the permanent teeth, becoming rough, flocculent, and adherent. The follicles have now become the *sacs;* the papillæ the *pulps* of the milk-teeth; and the crescent-formed depressions vacant *cavities of reserve,* to furnish delicate mucous membrane for the future formation of the *pulps* and *sacs* of the *ten* anterior permanent teeth.

The general adhesion does not invade that portion of the primitive dental groove which is situated behind the posterior milk-molar follicle. This small portion retains its original appearance, greyish-yellow colour, and smooth edges, for a fortnight or three weeks longer, and affords a nidus for the development of the papilla and follicle of the anterior permanent molar-tooth, the fundus of its follicle being situated immediately behind the sac of the posterior milk-molar. The *cavities of reserve* for the ten anterior permanent teeth are at this period minute compressed sacs, with their sides in contact, and situated between the surface of the gum and the milk-sacs.

The papillæ of the milk-teeth, from the time that their follicles close,* become gradually moulded into their peculiarly

---

* Herissant in the *Mem. de l'Academie Royale*, 1754, p. 664, described two gums—the "gencive permanent," and the "gencive passagere." His ideas

human shape. The molar pulps begin to be perforated also by three canals, which, proceeding from the surface to their centres, gradually divide their primary base into three secondary bases, which become developed into the fangs of the future teeth. While this is going on, the sacs grow more rapidly than the pulps, so that there speedily exists an intervening space in which is deposited a gelatinous granular substance, at first in small quantity, and adherent only to the proximal surfaces of the sacs; but ultimately, about the fifth month, closely and intimately attached to the whole interior of these organs, except for a small space of equal breadth, all round the base of the pulp, which space retains the original grey colour of the inner membrane of the follicle; and as the primary base of the pulp becomes perforated by the canals formerly mentioned, the granular matter sends processes into them, which, adhering to the sac, reserve the narrow space described above between themselves and the secondary bases. These processes of granular matter do not meet across the canals, but disappear near their point of junction. The granular matter is closely applied, but does not adhere to the surface of the pulp. "Whatever eminences or cavities the one has, the other has the same, but reversed, so that they are moulded exactly to each other."

Each branch of the dental artery, as it arrives at the fundus of its destined sac, sends off a number of radiating twigs, which run in the substance of the cellular submucous tissue (which constitutes the outer membrane of the sac) towards the gum, from which others proceed to inosculate with them. The

on the subject appear to have been derived from the examination of jaws in which the lips and walls of the secondary dental groove "gencive passagere," had not become completely adherent or obliterated. In this way the indistinct mouths of the milk-tooth sacs on the floor of the groove "gencive permanent," did not escape the notice of this most accurate observer. The cartilages of the gum described by Serres (*Essai*, p. 10) are to be considered as the walls of the groove in the semicartilaginous condition which they assume after closure.

combined twigs then **ramify minutely in the true membrane of the sac without sending the smallest twig into the granular substance.*** The dental branch, after giving off these saccular twigs, divides into a number of **contorted ramifications between the base of the pulp and the sac, which from smaller ramusculi are transmitted into the pulp itself.** In the case of the molars, the main branches divide into three secondary branches, one for each of the secondary bases. From these, three sets of saccular twigs, and three packets of contorted pulp-vessels, take their origin.

While these changes have been taking place in the sacs of the milk-teeth, the follicle of the first permanent molar closes, and granular matter is deposited in its sac. The walls of that portion of the secondary groove below it do not adhere; the edges alone do so. There is, therefore, a cavity of considerable size below the sac of this tooth, or between it and the surface

---

* Mr. Fox (*Natural History of the Human Teeth*, p. 20) and Mr. Bell (*Anatomy of the Teeth*, p. 54, and in a note, p. 39, vol. ii. Palmer's edition of Hunter's Works) have both misunderstood the statements of Mr. Hunter and Dr. Blake on the relative vascularity of the membranes of the tooth-sacs. (Hunter's *Natural History*, p. 84, and Blake, p. 4.) What Blake denominates the internal lamella is the enamel pulp of Hunter, Purkinje, and Raschkow, the gelatinous granular substance described in the text. He, with great accuracy states that it is "more tender and delicate, and seems to contain no vessels capable of conveying red blood." Under the denomination "external lamella" he includes the proper vascular mucous membrane of the sac, and the external spongy submucous tissue. In his search after the germs of the permanent teeth, Blake's attention appears to have been directed to the tooth-sacs when in the condition he describes. Mr. Hunter, again, who had a most correct conception of the constitution of the sacs, has, with his usual sagacity, not confounded the granular body, or, as he denominates it, "another pulpy substance," with the proper membranes of the sacs. Accordingly, in his account of the relative vascularity of the membranes of the sacs, he, when describing the manner in which a tooth is formed, has taken no notice of the pulpy substance. Dr. Blake describes the membranes of the sacs at an early period; Mr. Hunter, again, in a child at birth, at which time the external membrane is not very vascular, and has assumed somewhat of the appearance of a fibro-cartilage.

of the gum. This cavity is a reserve of delicate mucous membrane to afford materials for the formation of the second permanent molar, and of the third permanent molar or wisdom-tooth.

A little before this period *tooth-substance* begins to be deposited on the tubercles and apices of the pulps, which have acquired round the point of deposition a raised border and a zone-like vascularity; and, synchronous with this deposition, absorption takes place on the inner surface of the granular matter immediately in contact with it. No vessel can be detected running to the point of absorption, but ultimately the granular matter becomes so thin as to allow the subjacent vascularity to appear. The absorption goes on increasing as the tooth-substance is deposited, and when the latter reaches the base of the pulp the former disappears, and the interior of the dental sac assumes the villous vascular appearance of a mucous membrane. This change is nearly completed about the seventh or eighth month.

Up to this period little change has taken place in the ten anterior, or in the two posterior or great cavities of reserve. The ten anterior have been gradually receding from the surface of the gum, so as to be posterior, instead of inferior, to the milk-sacs. The two or four anterior began about the fifth month to dilate at their distal extremities, across which a fold appears (which is the germ of the future pulp) lying in the direction of the cutting edge of the future tooth; and at the proximal or acute extremities of the cavities two other folds, an anterior and a posterior, appear.* These round off the un-

* These two folds are strictly analogous to the opercula of the milk-tooth sacs. They never attain, however, the same high development as those of the latter, remaining in a rudimentary state, apparently in consequence of the almost saccular condition of the cavities of reserve. The existence of these laminæ in a rudimentary state proves that in the formation of the permanent teeth there is a strict adherence to the law of follicular development even when, in man at least, there is no apparent necessity for it.

defined apices of the cavities, and are strictly analogous to the opercula of the milk-follicles.

The distal fold gradually acquires the appearance of a tooth-pulp, while the proximal disappear by the obliteration of the little undefined space beyond them.

The cavities of reserve have now become tooth-sacs, and under this form they continue to recede from the surface of the gum, imbedding themselves in the submucous cellular tissue, which has all along constituted the external layer of the milk-sacs, and in which the larger saccular vessels ramify before arriving at the true mucous membranes of the sacs. This implantation of the permanent in the walls of the temporary tooth-sacs gives the former the appearance of being produced by a GEMMIPAROUS process from the latter.*

The dental groove was originally imbedded in an alveolar groove. As the dental interfollicular septa are developed in the former, osseous septa also begin to be formed in the latter. These osseous septa are at first in the form of bridges, but ultimately, at the sixth month, become complete partitions.

* It was this imbedding of the permanent in the walls of the temporary tooth-sacs which deceived Dr. Blake, and led him to suppose that the former derived their origin from the latter. Mr. Fox supported the same view of the subject; and Mr. Bell, in his own work (*Anatomy*, etc. etc. *of the Teeth*, p. 61), and more lately in his notes in Palmer's edition of Mr. Hunter's Works, vol. ii. p. 37, has strongly urged the same doctrine. Mr. Bell has stated that Mr. Hunter's "account of the manner in which the permanent teeth are formed is exceedingly imperfect," but it is evident that if the account of the origin of these teeth given in the text be correct, Mr. Hunter was not in error when he supposed both sets to be of independent origin. Mr. Hunter was so correct a thinker, that he did not account the circumstance of contiguity to be a proof of dependence. He was apparently ignorant of the origin of both sets, and in his usual cautious manner, when *describing structure* makes no observation on the subject. The author of the *Edinburgh Dissector* holds the same opinion as Mr. Hunter on this subject; and in his excellent chapter on the teeth, although he does not disprove the opinions of Dr. Blake and others, cautions the student against supposing Mr. Hunter to be incorrect on this subject.

As the sacs increase in size, the alveoli increase also, and when the permanent form slight projections behind the temporary tooth-sacs, niches* are formed for them in the posterior walls of the alveoli. Whilst this increase in the bulk of the sacs and alveoli is going on, there is no proportionate increase in the length of the jaw, in consequence of which, the sac of the anterior permanent molar has been insinuating itself into, and at the eighth month, or the full time, is almost wholly imbedded in, the maxillary tuberosity,† and has become situated on a higher level than the milk-sacs, during which it has not only drawn the surface of the gum upwards and backwards, but has also lengthened out the great or posterior cavity of reserve.

About this time the fangs of the milk-incisives begin to be formed, in the accomplishment of which three contemporaneous actions are employed—viz. the lengthening of the pulp, the deposition of tooth-substance upon it, and the adhesion to the latter of that portion of the inner surface of the sac which is opposite to it.

While the fangs of the milk-teeth, particularly those in the front of the jaw, are lengthening in the manner now described, the pulps and sacs of the permanent teeth continue to increase, and the bony crypts which contain them to enlarge in proportion, the lower edges of the latter insinuating themselves between the two former. As this process continues, the jaw lengthens more rapidly, and when the infant is eight or nine months old, there is so much room in the alveolar arch, that the anterior permanent molar tooth begins to resume its former position in the posterior part of the dental arch, and the great cavity of reserve again to return to its original size and situation.

About this time the central incisives begin to pass through

---

* Bell, *Anatomy*, etc. *of the Teeth*, p. 62.
† Hunter, *Nat. Hist. Human Teeth*, pp. 101, 102, 103.

the gum—a process which is accomplished in the following manner :—The body of the tooth having been fully formed, and coated with enamel, has also been acquiring a portion of its fang by the triplex action formerly described; in consequence of which, a reaction takes place between the bottom of the socket and the unfinished extremity of the fang. This reaction causes the body of the tooth and the non-adherent portion of the sac gradually to approach, and the former finally to pass through the surface of the gum. Till the time that the edge of the tooth passes through the gum, the fundus of the sac, and consequently the base of the pulp with the extremity of the fang, never change their common relative position in the jaw. At the moment, however, that the tooth passes through the gum (when the non-adherent portion of the sac resumes its primitive follicular condition, its inner membrane becoming continuous with the mucous membrane of the mouth) the non-adherent portion of the sac shortens more rapidly than the fang lengthens, in consequence of which the adherent portion with the fang itself separates from the fundus of the alveolus and the body of the tooth advances through the gum.* A space is thus left between the top of the alveolus and the fundus of the sac, occupied by cellular tissue, and traversed by the vessels and nerves. The alveolar cavity at the same time rapidly adapts itself to the new condition of its contents, advancing its edges so as to clasp the root, which has during these rapid changes been steadily lengthening—a process which now goes on with greater rapidity, as it is conducted in a comparatively empty

* The movement of the unfinished extremity of an incisive tooth from the fundus of its alveolus will explain what I have commonly remarked, and what must have been observed by medical practitioners, that from the time that the edge of the tooth appears through the gum, it advances more rapidly than can well be accounted for by the usual rate of lengthening of its fang. This advance is not invariably rapid, but may be observed in all the incisive teeth, if careful daily examination be made during a normal dentition.

space. The pulp continues to lengthen till its base is no larger than the fasciculus of vessels and nerve which enters it. The orifice of the cavity of the tooth also diminishes to the same size, and through it the surface of the pulp becomes continuous with the adherent portion of the sac and consequently with the mucous membrane of the mouth. The adherent portion of the sac has now attained its maximum, and the free or open portion its minimum size, having been reduced to that narrow portion of the gum which forms a vascular border and groove round the neck of the perfected tooth.*

During the period that the milk-teeth have been advancing along with their sockets to their perfect state and ultimate position in the jaw, the permanent sacs have been receding in an opposite direction, and have, as well as their bony crypts, been enlarging, the edges of the latter, insinuating themselves so far between the former and the milk-sacs, that at last they are only connected by their proximal extremities, and ultimately, when the lower edges of the crypts sink so far as to have become the posterior lips of the alveoli of the milk-teeth, the notches of communication between the latter and the permanent alveoli are forced, under the form of foramina, into a position on the anterior surface of the palate, one behind each milk-alveolus. The sacs of the bicuspids having assumed a position directly above the milk-molars, the hole

* This vascular border may be seen in healthy gums which have not been disturbed by the deposition of tartar, and is beautifully displayed in two wet injected preparations in the Bell collection, Museum of the Royal College of Surgeons, Edinburgh (Bell, C. iii. Nos. 25 and 56).

It is interesting to observe that one of the first physiological effects of mercury—viz. excitation of the gastro-intestinal compound glands and simple mucous follicles—is also displayed in a similar manner in the borders which surround the necks of the teeth, which are the remains of the free portions of the tooth-sacs, while it at the same time acts upon the adherent portions and their submucous tissue, raising the teeth from their sockets, and affecting the jaw from contiguity.

of communication is never removed from the sockets of the latter.

The cords of communication which pass through these foramina are not tubular, although in some instances a portion of the unobliterated extrafollicular compartment of the original little cavity of reserve may be detected in them. They are merely those portions of the gum which originally contained the lines of adhesion of the depressions for the permanent teeth in the *secondary dental groove,* and which have been subsequently lengthened out, in consequence of the necessarily retired position in which the permanent teeth have been developed during the active service of the temporary set. The cords and foramina are not obliterated in the child, either because the former are to become useful as "gubernacula," and the latter as "itinera dentium," or much more probably, in virtue of a law, which appears to be a general one in the development of animal bodies—viz. *that parts or organs which have once acted an important part, however atrophied they may afterwards become, yet never altogether disappear so long as they do not interfere with other parts or functions.*

The sacs of the permanent teeth derive their first vessels from the gums; ultimately they receive their proper dental vessels from the milk-sacs, and as they separate from the latter into their own cells, the newly-acquired vessels conjoining into common trunks, retire also into permanent dental canals.

It was stated above that, in the child at the seventh or eighth month, when the central incisives were passing through the gums, the jaw had lengthened so much as to allow the first permanent molar to retire from the maxillary tuberosity, and to resume in some measure its position downwards and forwards in the same line with the other teeth, and also to reduce the great cavity of reserve to its primitive size. This cavity of reserve now begins to lengthen, to bulge out, and to curve backwards and upwards at its posterior extremity, under the form of a sac, into the mass of the maxillary tuberosity; a papilla or pulp appears in its fundus, and a process of contraction separates it from the remainder of the cavity of reserve, which still adheres to its proximal wall by one extremity, while by the other it is continued into the substance of the gum under the anterior molar. This new sac, which is that of the second permanent molar, now occupies the position in the maxillary tuberosity which the first permanent did before it. It afterwards leaves this retired position, in consequence of the lengthening of the jaw allowing it to fall downwards and forwards into the line, and on a level with the other teeth.* Before it leaves the tuberosity altogether, the posterior extremity of the remainder of the cavity of reserve sends backwards and upwards its last offset—the sac and pulp of the wisdom-tooth, which speedily occupies the tuberosity after the second molar has left it, and ultimately, when the jaw again lengthens for the last time, at the age of nineteen or twenty, takes its place at the posterior extremity of the range of the adult teeth.

The wisdom-teeth are the second products of the posterior

* The curved lines which the posterior cavities of reserve, and the sacs of the molar teeth, describe in their progress to and from the maxillary tuberosity, and the coronoid process, and the peculiar position in which the pulps are consequently developed, explain satisfactorily certain normal and abnormal conditions of these teeth :—1. The curves which the combined grinding surfaces of the molar teeth present, convex downwards and backwards in the upper jaw, concave upwards and forwards in the lower. 2. The peculiar manner in which the fangs of the molars, particularly the inferior, are bent backwards. 3. The occasional horizontal position of the wisdom-teeth, the crowns of the inferior being directed forwards, those of the superior backwards. This abnormal position is the cause of much annoyance and danger to the patient, and of difficulty to the surgeon.

or great cavities of reserve, and the final effects of development in the *secondary dental groove.**

In the lower jaw, as in the upper, dentition commences in a deep narrow groove, situated between the lip and a semicircular lobe. This groove, instead of terminating in a simple curve posteriorly, as in the upper jaw, becomes shallow, and assumes a sigmoidal form upon the surface of the posterior bulbous ovoidal portion of the lobe.

About the seventh week the lip becomes very loose, and separates widely from the lobe, between which and the former a ridge appears, growing from behind forwards, and dividing the original groove into two, an outer one—the labial duplicature of mucous membrane, and an inner—the *primitive dental groove.* This ridge, which, as in the upper, does not yet extend to the incisive portion of the jaw, is flat, or in the same continuous plane with the bottom of the dental groove, and its lip is turned out, or overhangs the labial mucous membrane. The inner lip of the groove is formed by the semicircular lobe, which has become thin, and arched over the groove, particularly anteriorly, where it is cut into four festoons, two on each side of the median line; and posteriorly, where it still retains the appearance of an oval lobe, from under which the outer lip or ridge appears to proceed. The groove curves inwards between the two lips posteriorly, under a form which is evidently a development of the original sigmoidal groove.

Near the posterior extremity of the groove there is an elevation of a small portion of its floor, which speedily becomes the germ or papilla of the inferior anterior milk-molar tooth—the second tooth which appears in the primitive

---

* It is probable that the successive dentitions of the elephant are conducted in a cavity of reserve, which must consequently exist even in the adult animal, till a late period of its life. If such be the case, the molar dentition of the elephant, and the formation of the human adult molars, are analogous processes.

development of the human body. During the eighth week the elevation already mentioned becomes a papilla, lengthened from behind forwards, and flattened transversely. About the same time another papilla, bounded by a notched lamina, similar to those on the upper jaw, makes its appearance further forward in the groove. This papilla is the germ of the inferior milk-canine. The dental groove is about the same time continued forward to the median line, not by the advancement of its outer ridge, but by the elevation of its floor. Its posterior portion also has become wider and not so curved.

During the succeeding week the incisives make their appearance, the centrals first.

From this time all the eight papillæ continue to increase. The notched laminæ shoot inwards to the inner lip of the groove, near which they meet and join slight projections from it. About the eleventh or twelfth week the germ of the posterior milk-molar appears in the curved portion of the groove, and is developed in the usual manner.

Crescent-like depressions appear in the secondary groove, on the inner side of the mouths of the milk-follicles, as in the upper jaw.

The secondary groove adheres, leaving a posterior open portion, in which are developed the papilla and follicle of the first permanent molar. This follicle closes, as well as the lips of the portion of groove above it. There are now in the jaw ten milk-tooth sacs, two permanent-tooth sacs, ten anterior cavities of reserve, and two great or posterior cavities of reserve;* the ten anterior for the development of the incisives,

* The mucous membrane constituting the cavities of reserve exists in a condition which has hitherto been considered by anatomists as peculiar to the serous membranes. A dental cavity of reserve is a shut sac, lined by a true mucous membrane, which is isolated from the general mucous system, and performs no special function, till it is called upon to supply what it alone can afford, materials for the development of a tooth.

canines, and bicuspids; the two posterior for that of the second and third **molar**,* the coronoid process acting the part which the maxillary tuberosity did in the upper jaw.

SECTION III.

1. *On the Division of Dentition into Stages.*—As dentition is a process, not only very complicated in its details, but of very lengthened duration, extending over nearly eight months of intra-uterine, and above twenty years of extra-uterine existence, the understanding and further investigation of it may be facilitated by dividing it into stages. The most natural division, one which is not artificial, but clearly indicated by the phenomena themselves, is into three stages, according to the position of the pulp in relation to its containing cavity—1*st*, follicular stage; 2*d*, saccular; 3*d*, eruptive. We ought probably to consider, as anterior to the follicular, the papillary stage† during which the follicle or sac does not exist, and the future pulp is a simple papilla on the free surface of the gastro-intestinal mucous membrane. As this stage,

---

* The cavities of reserve are occasionally somewhat undefined, two or three being conjoined, particularly posteriorly. Sooner or later, however, they become distinct. The great cavity frequently stretches forwards over the sacs of the milk-molars.

† Most anatomists have supposed the germs of the teeth to appear as shut sacs, full of a fluid, the pulps being formed by inspissation of the latter, or by development from the walls of the former. Neither Mr. Hunter nor Mr. Bell has stated anything very definite on this subject. The pulp must be considered as the principal part of the organ, and as the element which appears first. The sac is a mere subsidiary part, supplied for purposes of development and nourishment. *Handbuch der Anatomie des Menschen*, von. H. Hildebrandt, besorgt. von E. H. Weber, Erster Band, p. 212; *Handbuch der Entwickelungs-geschichte des Menschen*, von Valentin, p. 482; Arnold, *Salzburg Medicinisch-Chirurgisch Zeitung*, 1831, Erster Band, p. 236; Cruveilhier, *Anatomie Descriptive*, vol. i. p. 518; Serres, *Essai sur l'Anatomie*, etc., *des Dents*, p. 59; Ph. Fr. Blandin, *Anatomie du Systeme Dentaire*, etc., p. 87; Blake, *Essay on the Human Teeth*, p. 2.

however, is short in its duration, and simple in its details, it may be included in the first stage.

The first or follicular stage comprehends all the phenomena which present themselves from the first appearance of the dental groove and papillæ till the latter become completely hid by the closure of the mouths of their follicles, and of the groove itself. It is upon this hitherto unknown stage of dentition that I have insisted so much in the former sections of this paper.

The second or saccular stage is the one with which anatomists have been so long familiar, during which the papillæ are pulps, and the open follicles which contain them are shut sacs, when the tooth-substance and the enamel, constituting the teeth themselves, are deposited. It is during this stage, also, that some of the most interesting phenomena in the formation of the alveolar processes present themselves.

The third or eruptive stage includes the completion of the teeth, the eruption and shedding of the temporary set, the eruption of the permanent, and the necessary changes in the alveolar processes.

When viewed in reference to an individual tooth, these three stages are distinct; but when viewed in reference to both sets, and to the whole process of dentition, they become somewhat intermingled.

When considered in the latter point of view, we may state that the follicular stage commences at the sixth or seventh week, and terminates at the fourth or fifth month of intrauterine existence; that the saccular commences at the termination of the first, and lasts for certain of the teeth till the sixth or eighth month, and for others till the twentieth or twenty-fifth year of extra-uterine existence; and that the third or eruptive commences at the sixth or eighth month, and lasts till the twentieth or twenty-fifth year.

On the Anterior Permanent Molar Teeth.—The anterior permanent molar is the most remarkable tooth in man, as it forms a transition between the milk and permanent set. If considered anatomically, it is decidedly a milk-tooth; if physiologically, a permanent one. In a former part of this paper, it was stated that the papilla and follicle of this tooth were developed in a small portion of the primitive dental groove, which remained open for that purpose till the fourth or fifth month, while all the other permanent teeth were productions, not from the primitive groove, but from small non-adherent portions of the secondary groove, which lay in a level superior to the shut orifices of the sacs of all the milk-teeth, and of the tooth in question—the first permanent molar. In reference to its function, however, as the most efficient grinder in the adult mouth, we must consider it as a permanent tooth. It is a curious circumstance, and one which will readily suggest itself to the surgeon, that, laying out of view the wisdom-teeth, which sometimes decay at an early period from other causes,* the anterior molars are the permanent teeth, which most frequently give way first, and in the most symmetrical manner, and at the same time, and frequently before the milk set.

On the Tardy Development of the Superior Incisive Teeth.— A reference to the first section of this paper will show that at the ninth week, when the papillæ of the superior incisives are quite distinct, those of the inferior are with difficulty recognised. This is a fact which may be included under a law which will be more fully referred to afterwards—viz. that the dentition of the upper precedes, and is always in advance of, the same process in the lower jaw. A week or two later, however, when the papillæ of the inferior incisives are imbedded and hid in deep follicles, those of the superior are

* Bell, *Anat. etc. of the Teeth*, p. 133.

nearly in their original condition. Although the latter recover in some degree their lost ground, yet, as every one knows, the inferior central incisive almost always cuts the gum before the superior, and the lateral sometimes does so also. In order to explain this apparent exception to the law above mentioned, it will be necessary to go a little into the history of the intermaxillary bones, in doing which reference must necessarily be made to some of the other bones of the face and head.

When the superior portion of the large common nasal buccal and pharyngeal cavity is exposed in an embryo of the sixth or seventh week, by removing the lower jaw, we observe the boundary of the future palate to be defined by what has been denominated in a former section the horse-shoe lobe (c, Fig. 2). Attached to the posterior inner edges of this lobe two other lobes are seen. These grow from behind forwards, and from without inwards, and complete the palate by joining in the median line, being assisted in doing so posteriorly by two other smaller lobes behind the posterior extremities of the horse-shoe lobe. In the two first lobes become developed the palatine plates of the superior maxillary bones, and in the two smaller posterior the palatine plates of the palate bones.

The bar (h, Figs. 2 and 4), which ultimately coalesces below with the median line of suture of the four last mentioned lobes, is proved by development to contain the nucleus of the vomer.

The median lobule (m) and its two lateral and anterior appendages (n n) form the anterior division of the embryonal palate. Of these three, the two lateral are observed in the course of development to contain the nuclei of what are usually denominated the intermaxillary bones. With regard to the median it may be stated that, as all the other lobules which appear in the soft pulpy texture of the fœtal palate are proved by development to contain the nuclei of all the well-known bones of this region, I am inclined to consider it as indicative of the existence of the rudiment of a bone also, especially when the interesting antagonism, which I will show exists between it and the lateral lobules, is taken into consideration.*

As the object of this part of my paper, however, is not to discuss the osteogenesis of the human head, but to explain why the inferior incisive teeth, although later in their appearance, are yet more rapid in their progress than the superior, I shall now recall some circumstances formerly detailed regarding the development of the three intermaxillary lobules, immediately before and for some time after the appearance of the incisive papillæ.

During the seventh week the three lobules are equal, and there is no appearance of either the upper or lower incisive teeth.

During the eighth week the median lobule has increased relatively, and the laterals only absolutely; while as yet there is no appearance of either the upper or lower incisives.

During the ninth week the median has diminished relatively, and in the transverse direction; the laterals again have increased relatively and also in the transverse direction. This relative transverse increase of the lateral lobules is synchronous with the first appearance of the upper incisives. The inferior incisives are so indistinct at this time, as to be recognised with difficulty as slight bulgings on the floor of the dental groove.

During the next fortnight the relative size of the median

---

* A small cartilaginous body exists in the median intermaxillary lobule of the child at birth. It is situated in front of the inferior orifice of the nasopalatine canal, and between the mucous membrane and periosteum.

The median intermaxillary lobule exists in the adult palate, and may be felt behind and between the central incisives. Median intermaxillary bones and cartilages exist in certain of the lower vertebrata.

The bar-like vomer of the human embryo at the sixth and seventh week reminds the anatomist of the adult vomer of the lower vertebrata.

and lateral lobules remains the same, and there is no further development of the superior incisives. During the same period the inferior incisives have been rapidly increasing.

Afterwards the median undergoes much relative transverse diminution, while at the same time the laterals acquire a remarkable relative increase, which is accompanied by a corresponding development of the superior incisives ; but the inferiors have now got so much in advance as to retain their advantage ever after.

On the Laws which regulate the development of the Pulps and Sacs, and the period of appearance of each of the Tooth-Germs.—In the description which has been given of the earlier phenomena of dentition, it will be perceived that many of them range themselves under the laws recognised by MM. G. St. Hilaire, and Serres—viz. the law of symmetry (loi de symmetrie), the law of conjunction (loi de conjugaison), the law of balancing or antagonism (le balancement des organes), and the law of eccentric development (loi du developpement excentrique).

The primitive and secondary dental grooves, the follicles, the cavities of reserve, the osseous alveoli of the milk-teeth and their septa, are all formed originally of two halves, which ultimately join according to the laws of symmetry and conjunction.

The pulps of the milk-teeth* with their notched laminæ are productions from the external lip or ridge of the groove. The interfollicular septa, and the osseous alveolar septa, are also developed from without inward (loi du developpement excentrique).

I have already pointed out the beautiful example of

---

* It is a curious fact, that the first tooth-germs which appear—viz. those of the superior anterior and inferior anterior milk-molars—are not productions from the external lip of the dental groove, but bulgings on its floor.

antagonism which exists between the median and lateral elements of the intermaxillary system; and I may now point out, from among the facts formerly detailed, a few instances of the same kind, which must be referred to the same general expression (loi de balancement).

1. Before the tenth week the upper lip is full and prominent, but at that time it begins to recede and gradually to disappear anteriorly, so as to expose the follicles and papillæ of the incisive teeth. It afterwards begins to regain its former position and size, and at the fourteenth or fifteenth week it is as large as the inferior, which from the first has not changed its appearance.

At the tenth week, when the lip begins to recede, the maxillary palate advances its anterior extremity, so as to conceal in some degree the intermaxillary palate (median and lateral lobules). When the middle of the lip has disappeared, the maxillary has not only encroached upon the intermaxillary, but has also thrown itself into a bundle of irregular folds at its anterior part. As the maxillary palate retires, and the folds become regular crenated rugæ, the anterior part of the lip again appears, and at the fifteenth or sixteenth week, it is full and prominent, when the maxillary palate has retired to its proper position.

2. When the outer lip of the primitive dental groove sends off the laminæ, which constitute the greater part of each of the interfollicular septa, and the floor of the secondary groove, the lip itself almost disappears.

The inner lip, again, which contributes a very small share towards the accomplishment of this process, becomes so much enlarged as to cover the whole groove.

3. The external and internal lips of the primitive dental groove are, originally, equally prominent. The former, when it sends off the interfollicular septa, diminishes, while the latter increases. When all the follicles of the primitive groove have

been completed, the external lip begins to increase, and the internal to diminish. This increase of the external lip goes on after the closure of the secondary groove, until, at the fifth month, it becomes very prominent, and is divided into an incisive, a canine, and molar portion, each of which has a general similarity in shape to the acting portions of the corresponding divisions of the future tooth-ranges. As long as it remains in this condition it is employed by the infant as a masticating organ. During this period the internal lip has altogether disappeared, except a small portion posteriorly; but a short time before the milk-teeth appear, it again increases, and the raphe of the dental groove, instead of being hid behind the base of the external lip, is situated on the ridge of the dental arch, which now, as at first, is composed of two equally-developed portions. The raphe forms a little border in the situation just mentioned, and is familiar to the eye of the surgeon, who, by its disappearance at any particular point, can satisfy himself of the proximity of the milk-tooth under it.

Careful observation of the whole process of Dentition in man leads to the following conclusions:—

Milk Teeth.—1. The milk-teeth are formed on both sides of either jaw, in three divisions, a molar, a canine, and an incisive, in each of which dentition proceeds in an independent manner.

2. The dentition of the whole arch proceeds from behind forwards—the molar division commencing before the canine, and the latter before the incisive.

3. The dentition of each of the divisions proceeds in a contrary direction, the anterior molar appearing before the posterior, the central incisive before the lateral.

4. Two of the subordinate phenomena of dentition also obey this inverse law, the follicles closing by commencing at the median line, and proceeding backwards, and the dental groove disappearing in the same direction.

5. Dentition commences in the upper jaw, and continues in advance during the most important period of its progress. The first tooth-germ which appears is that of the *superior* anterior molar, which precedes that of the *inferior* anterior molar.

The apparent exception to this law in the case of the inferior incisive has already been explained.

Permanent Teeth.—6. The germs of the permanent teeth, with the exception of that of the anterior molar, appear in a direction from the median line backwards.

7. The milk-teeth originate, or are developed, from the mucous membrane.

8. The permanent teeth, also originating from mucous membrane, are of independent origin, and have no connection with the milk-teeth.

9. A tooth-pulp and its sac must be referred to the same class of organs as the combined papilla and follicle from which a hair or feather is developed—viz. bulbs.*

---

* An abstract of this paper was read at the last meeting of the British Association for the Advancement of Science.

Dr. Allen Thomson stated to me at that time, that he had no doubt that the fact of the *milk*-tooth sacs being at one period open follicles had been observed, but that, then, he could not inform me where I could find it mentioned. I saw Dr. Thomson in Edinburgh a few weeks afterwards, when, on looking into Valentin's work on Development (*Handbuch der Entwickelungs-geschichte des Menschen*), he pointed out to me the fact that Arnold had observed that the milk-tooth sacs were formed by a duplicature of the mucous membrane of the mouth, and had inserted a notice of the discovery in the *Salzburg Med. Chir. Zeitung*, 1831, p. 236. In order that Professor Arnold's discovery (which appears to have been altogether overlooked both in this country and in France) may be more generally known, I will give all his facts as he has recorded them. His notice occupies less than a page, and I am not aware that he has extended it elsewhere. At p. 236, *loc. cit.* he has observed, " In an embryo at the ninth week, we may perceive in both jaws, on the projecting edges of the gums, a proportionally pretty deep furrow, with ten depressions in it ; a little later we may see a flat surface, on which there are many openings, communicating with small sacs, into which fine bristles may be passed. At the third month the sacs of the second molars may be seen communicating with the cavity of the mouth by small holes. The openings of the remaining sacs are soon closed by the mucous membrane of the mouth.

"The sacs of the permanent teeth are also formed immediately from the mucous membrane of the mouth, partly at the fourth month of fœtal existence, partly towards the end of that period, partly at birth. Once only, in a new-born child, I observed behind the most prominent edge of the gums several openings which led to the sacs of the incisives and canines, and which are usually already obliterated before birth."

These are all the facts Arnold has recorded, and from them it appears that he was acquainted at that time with the secondary dental groove, the ten milk-follicles, and the ultimate closure of the latter. So far as we can judge from his brief notice, he appears to have been unacquainted with the mode of formation of the permanent follicles, supposing them to be formed immediately (unmittelbar) from the mucous membrane of the mouth, an opinion which is very prevalent among the continental anatomists. I can only account for the openings he mentions in the new-born child by arrest of development, or by supposing that he had observed a few of the Tartar glands of Serres (Glandes dentaires, *Essai*, etc., p. 28), which are best seen at the period to which he alludes.

Having now mentioned all the facts which Professor Arnold has published, I may be allowed to state that I had made out all the facts detailed in this paper before I was aware that any of them had been on record; that I had given an account of them at the last meeting of the British Association, before I knew of Professor Arnold's notice; and that this paper was in the hands of the Editor of the *Edinburgh Med. and Surg. Journal* before I had an opportunity of seeing the Salzburg periodical.

I had also demonstrated the principal facts in the follicular stage of dentition, in 1835, to Mr. Nasmyth, to whom I am deeply indebted for the information he has given me respecting the anatomy and surgery of these organs, and in whose cabinet I at that time deposited preparations illustrative of the facts.

II.—ON THE FOLLICULAR STAGE OF DENTITION IN THE RUMINANTS, WITH SOME REMARKS ON THAT PROCESS IN THE OTHER ORDERS OF MAMMALIA.

SINCE the meeting of the British Association in 1838, at which the paper on the development of the human teeth was read, I have detected the follicular stage of dentition in the pig, rabbit, cow, and sheep, but have not had an opportunity of examining it in those animals in which observations would have been most valuable. I have been able to verify, what was at that time stated as probable—viz. that all the permanent teeth, with the exception of the first molar, which does not succeed a milk-tooth, are developed from the internal surface of cavities of reserve, and that the depending folds of the sacs of composite teeth are formed by the lips of the follicles advancing inwards after closure of the latter. In tracing the progress of development of the pulps and sacs of the teeth in the cow and sheep, from their first appearance, as minute as possible, on the full surface of the membrane of the mouth, or on the internal surface of the cavities of reserve, till they have acquired their ultimate configuration, I have to announce the fact, that at an early period of the embryonic life of these animals they possess the germs of canine and superior incisive teeth ; the former existing as developed organs in two or three genera only of ruminants, the latter being found in the aberrant family of camels. These germs present themselves under the form of slight dimples in the primitive groove, and after the closure of the latter, they remain for a short time as opaque nodules imbedded in the gum, in the course of the line of adhesion. The existence of germs of canines and superior incisors in the cow and sheep is highly interesting, as it shows how general the law of unity of type is within certain limits. Geoffrey St. Hilaire was the first to announce the existence of tooth-germs in the fœtus of the *Balæna mysticetus*, a fact which has been verified by Dr. and Mr. Frederic Knox, in whose museum there is a preparation exhibiting the germs under the form of sacs and pulps. Although the germs never arrive at this stage of perfection in the cow and sheep, they are yet distinct enough to indicate their existence ; and I have no doubt that when embryos of other partially or wholly edentulous mammals have been examined, similar results will be obtained. The peculiar manner in which the sac of a ruminant molar, and probably of every other composite tooth, is formed, may be best seen in longitudinal or transverse sections of the sac and pulp of the fourth permanent molar of the sheep or cow. The internal surface of the cavity of reserve is seen to end in a fold or folds ; when these meet, they begin to curve towards the papilla, and to enter parallel to one another the cavity or notch which is simultaneously forming in the latter. As soon as the edges of the folds meet, the granular matter denominated enamel-pulp by Hunter (the formation of which was described in the human embryo, at the last meeting of the Association) begins to be deposited, cementing together the opposing folds, sealing up the new sac, separating it from the rest of the cavity of reserve, filling up the space existing between the pulp and sac, and ultimately assisting in the formation of the depending folds of the latter.

A distinction must be drawn between those permanent teeth which are developed from the primitive, and those which are developed from the secondary groove. I have been in the habit of dividing the teeth of these animals, the dentition of which I have examined, into three classes—viz. 1*st.* Milk or primitive teeth, developed in a primitive groove, and deciduous. 2*d.* Transition teeth, developed in a primitive groove, but permanent. 3*d.* Secondary teeth, developed in a secondary groove, and permanent. I hope that other anatomists may verify and extend this line of research, as the results appear to me not only confirmatory of certain great general laws of organisation, but as leading, by the only legitimate path, to the determination of the organic system to which the teeth belong (a subject exciting great interest at present), and as it may enable us in investigating the relations of dental tissue to true bone, to avoid the error of confounding, what there appears to be a tendency to do, analogy with affinity. In recapitulation of the principal facts it may be said :—1. In all the mammalia examined the follicular stage of dentition was observed. 2. The pulps and sacs of all the permanent teeth of the cow and sheep, with the exception of the fourth molar, are formed from the minor surfaces of cavities of reserve. 3. The depending folds of the sacs of composite teeth are formed by the folding in of the edges of the follicle towards the base of the contained pulp, the granular body assisting in the formation of these folds. 4. The cow and sheep (and probably all the other ruminants) possess the germs of canines and superior incisives at an early period of their embryonic existence.

III.—ON THE MODE IN WHICH MUSKET-BULLETS AND OTHER FOREIGN BODIES BECOME INCLOSED IN THE IVORY OF THE TUSKS OF THE ELEPHANT.—Plate II.

Musket-bullets are occasionally found inclosed in ivory, and every anatomical museum contains specimens of this kind. Why bullets should be so frequently met with in this situation it is not easy to say: the head of the elephant appears to be generally aimed at, and foreign bodies, when they enter the tusks, instead of being removed in the usual manner are retained by the process, an investigation of which is to form the subject of the present paper. My attention was directed to this subject by Mr. Syme, who submitted to me for examination some highly interesting specimens of bullets in ivory, presented to the Anatomical Museum of the University by Sir John Robison. Sir John has also kindly afforded me an opportunity of examining some remarkable examples of wounded ivory, and Sir George Ballingall has directed my attention to preparations in his possession, which have satisfied me of the truth of those opinions on the subject which I shall now have the honour of submitting to the Royal Society.

One circumstance was at once detected in all these specimens, and its importance was evident, as affording a clue to the explanation of the mode of inclosure. The circumstance to which I allude is, that in none of the specimens are the bullets or foreign bodies surrounded by regular ivory. They are in every instance inclosed in masses, more or less bulky,

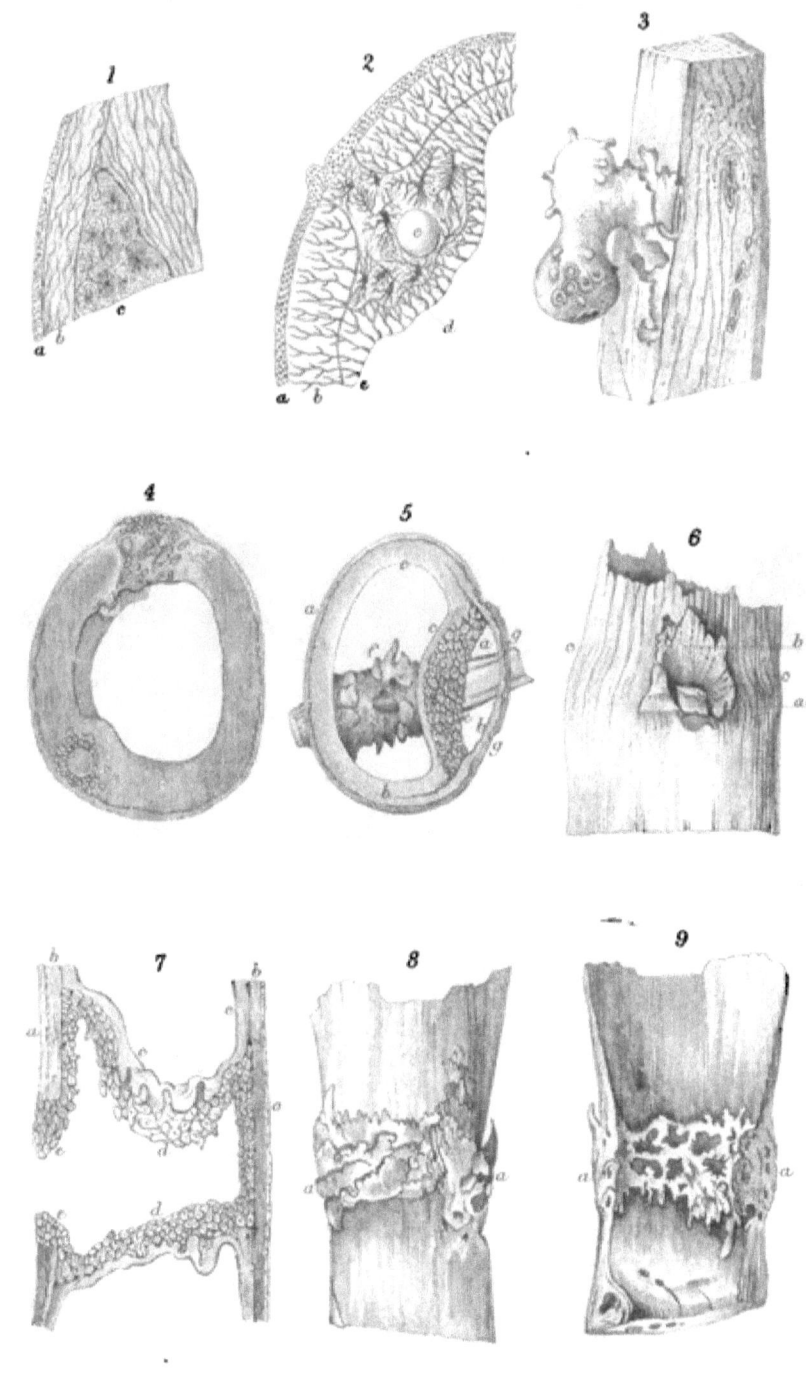

of a substance which, although abnormal in the tusk of the elephant, is nevertheless well known to the comparative anatomist as occupying the interior of the teeth of some of the other mammals, and usually considered to be ossified pulp. It was evident that the pulp had ossified round the bullet, as the first step towards the separation of the latter from it. In one specimen the bullet has become enveloped in a hollow sphere of this substance, on the surface of which the orifices of medullary canals are situated. In other specimens the irregular ivory, which surrounds the balls, had become smooth on its surface, the medullary canals had disappeared, and the regular ivory had been formed in a continuous layer over the surface of the mass. In one tusk a cicatrix was seen occupying the hole through which the ball had passed, a circumstance which, when seen in similar specimens, has greatly perplexed anatomists. It was observed, however, that in this instance the shot had passed through that part of the tusk which had been within the socket; and bearing in mind that the tusk is an organ of double growth, it appeared probable that the shot had been plugged up from within by the ossified pulp, and from without by the continued growth of cement, without any regeneration of the displaced ivory—a hypothesis which was afterwards verified by examination. Before proceeding to give a more detailed account of this interesting process, I shall state very briefly the opinions of those authors who have written on the subject, so as to ascertain how near they had approached to the truth, and to point out the fallacies which had led them astray.

Klockner mentions a ball of gold which was found by a turner of Amsterdam in the substance of an elephant's tusk. The longitudinal fibres of the tusk surrounded the metal in an irregular manner, and were separated from the sound ivory by a concentric chink situated at some distance from the ball.

Camper, in the *Description Anatomique d'un Elephant Male*, remarks that it is not unusual to see foreign bodies inclosed, or as it were soldered, into the substance of the ivory. The same anatomist also figures and describes a bullet which was inclosed in a very irregular mass of ivory, covered with long appendages, which were directed parallel to the axis of the tusk. The metallic bodies in question, he remarks, must have penetrated across the alveolus into the hollow of the tusk, and must have remained for a long time in the substance of the pulpy flesh which fills that cavity, because the ivory enveloped them on all sides, and would at length have carried them beyond the alveolus by the increase of the tooth. He supposes that the nodules which are formed around the balls and the very incomplete union of their fibres with the sound ivory, add weight to this conjecture. Ruysch, in his X. Thesaurus, Plate II., figures brass and iron bullets inclosed in isolated nodules of irregular ivory.

Blumenbach considers the tusks of the elephant to differ from other teeth, more particularly in the remarkable pathological phenomenon of bullets, with which the animal has been shot, being found, on sawing through the tusk, imbedded in its substance in a peculiar manner. He looks upon this fact as important in reference to the doctrine of a "nutritio ultra vasa." He mentions a tusk, equal in size to a man's thigh, in which an unflattened leaden bullet lay close to the cavity of the tooth, surrounded by a peculiar covering, and the entrance from without closed as it were by a cicatrix. From these facts Blumenbach concludes that the elephant's tusk, when fractured or perforated, can pour out an ossific juice to repair the injury.

Mr. Lawrence, in his notes to Blumenbach's *Comparative Anatomy*, overlooking these cases (one of which is given in the text of his author) in which cicatrices have been seen filling up the orifices produced by balls, explains satisfactorily enough those instances in which no such cicatrices exist, and concludes by denying the power of the ivory to throw out ossific matter, as asserted by Blumenbach.

The author of the *Ossemens Fossiles*, in his chapter on the Structure, Development, and Diseases of the Tusks of the Elephant, after stating that grooves and notches on the surfaces of the tusks never fill up, and only disappear from the effects of friction, allows that musket-balls are found in ivory without any apparent hole by which they could have entered. He does not believe that the holes are filled up with ossific deposition, as Haller and Blumenbach supposed; but maintains that they are never obliterated. He states that the ivory on the outside of the ball is natural, and that it is only the bone surrounding it which is irregular. The phenomena are to be explained, he says, by supposing the balls to penetrate the very thin bases of tusks in young elephants, so as to enter the pulps when still in a growing state.

There appear, then, to be two circumstances, regarding which great doubts still exist—first, whether a shot-hole is ever closed up; and, secondly, how this is accomplished in a non-vascular substance like ivory.

In proceeding to consider this subject, two facts must be borne in mind in reference to a tusk. The first is, that the two substances of which it is composed, ivory and cement, undergo no change of form or arrangement from vital action, after they are once deposited; the second, that it is an organ of double growth—it is endogenous as well as exogenous, the ivory being formed from without inwards, the cement from within outwards.

As there are certain processes which invariably commence when a foreign body passes through or lodges in the pulp, it will facilitate the conception of the mode in which a bullet is inclosed if these be described first. Recent researches have proved that the regular ivory of teeth is formed by the cells on the surface of the pulp becoming solid from the deposition of earthy salts in their walls and cavities. It is evident from this that when a portion of the surface of the tusk-pulp is destroyed by the passage of a ball, the formation of ivory at that spot must cease. But we know that the formation of irregular ivory commences, which indicates the existence of a healing process in the pulp. The mode in which the wounded pulp heals cannot be ascertained; but it is accomplished probably by effusion and subsequent absorption of blood, deposition of lymph, and regeneration of the peculiar tissue of the pulp. So far this process is conjectural, but the irregular ivory, formed by the regenerated pulp, is the subject of observation. When the ball passes quite across the pulp, the track heals, but does not necessarily ossify, except in the immediate neighbourhood of the ivory.

There are two exceptions, however, to the non-ossification of the track of the ball—namely, the ossification which takes place round the bullet, and that which occurs round the whole or any portion of the track, which may suppurate and form a sinus or abscess. In both these cases deposition of irregular ivory takes place, assuming the same characters as the irregular masses which appear at the two extremities of the track of the ball through the pulp.

The ossification round the ball generally assumes the form of a hollow sphere. Its surface exhibits a number of holes (which are the orifices of medullary canals), and these are occasionally prolonged through stalactitic-looking processes, which lie in the direction of the axis of the tooth. The ossification surrounding an abscess or sinus assumes the appearance of a shell of variable thickness, and directed towards one or both of the shot-holes.

When thin sections of this irregular ivory are examined under the microscope, it is seen to consist of a transparent matrix, in which exist numerous medullary canals, showing traces of dried pulp in their interior. From these canals, which correspond to the Haversian canals of true bone, secondary medullary canals, similar to those in the teeth of certain fishes, radiate. The sides and extremities of these secondary medullary canals send off numerous minute tubes, which are true Retzian tubes, and similar to those in the regular ivory, but not so closely set. These Retzian tubes have a general radiating direction, and proceed in irregular wavy bundles, which sweep past one another without mingling, but branching particularly at their extremities.

The great central medullary canals are very numerous, and each of them has its own system of secondary canals and Retzian tubes.

These individual systems, when seen in a mass of irregular ivory, appear globular or spindle-shaped; when viewed in section, they resemble circular or oval opaque spots with a hole in the centre. These individual systems, however, are not isolated; for they communicate, first, by means of the central canals, which constitute an inosculating system; and secondly, by the ramifying extremities of the Retzian tubes, which communicate through the medium of cells more or less minute, and which are more numerous in some places than in others.

The formation of the irregular ivory does not go on indefinitely; a limit is set to its increase, and the changes which ensue at this stage of the process are highly interesting. I have already mentioned the existence of the orifices of Haversian or medullary canals on the surface of the mass of irregular ivory When the further formation of this is to terminate, these orifices are gradually closed, and appear like imperforated projections on the surface. It is evident, therefore, that the enclosed vascular contents of the canals—that is to say, the ramified processes of the tusk-pulp in the irregular ivory—are cut off from the system. They dry up, and the formation of ivory in the interior ceases. The peripheral surface of the irregular ivory is now, in reference to the general pulp, in the same relation as the whole internal surface of the irregular ivory of the tusk. The pulp, therefore, becomes converted into ivory, not only on the whole internal surface of the tusk, but also on the surface of the newly-formed mass. The cause of the formation of the irregular ivory to a limited extent only, when it exists as an abnormal structure, I have not been able to ascertain; but its mode of development and limitation is highly interesting, and forms a leading distinction between a tooth and a true bone under similar circumstances.

From this description it is evident that the abnormal ivory in the elephant's tusk strongly resembles, if it be not identical with, the peculiar substance which fills the pulp-cavities of the tusks of the walrus and the teeth of the cetacea, first announced as a distinct species of dental tissue in a paper read before this society five years ago by Dr. Knox, and since minutely described by Retzius, Owen, and Alexander Nasmyth.*

This identity of a diseased structure in one animal with a normal structure in another is remarkable, and must be looked

* Cuvier described this species of dental tissue in the tusk of the walrus, and compared it to pudding-stone. Dr. Knox, in the paper to which I have referred in the text, affirmed that, in addition to the cement, enamel, and ivory, a fourth substance—namely, the substance described by Cuvier—entered into the formation of many teeth. He stated that, in the teeth of certain fishes, this substance, or a tissue closely allied to it, constituted the greater part of their mass; the other three elements having disappeared or become greatly diminished in bulk or importance. Retzius has accurately described the microscopic structure of this class of dental substances as existing in different animals. Mr. Owen has extended and confirmed the observations of Retzius. Lastly, to Mr. A. Nasmyth belongs the merit of having pointed out the resemblance which this kind of substance (which he denominates ossified pulp) bears to diseased ivory in the tusks of the elephant, and still more closely to the substance which fills the pulp-cavity of the aged human tooth. In ignorance of Dr. Knox's previous observations, he announced this kind of ivory as a fourth dental substance.

upon as another instance indicating the existence of a system of laws regulating the relations between healthy and morbid tissues—laws which have been speculated upon, but have never been sufficiently investigated by anatomists.

Having now given the anatomical characters of the abnormal ivory which invariably surrounds musket-bullets and other foreign bodies which lodge in the pulps of the tusks of the elephant, I shall proceed to state the various conditions under which these enter the organ, and the changes which ensue.

Foreign bodies enter the tusk in three ways—first, through the free portion of the tusk; secondly, through that part of the organ which is contained in the socket; and thirdly, from above through the base of the pulp.

First. When the ball hits the free portion of the tusk, if it only penetrates to a certain depth of the ivory, no change whatsoever can take place. Neither the cement nor the ivory can be reproduced. In course of time the hole may be obliterated, the ball may be got rid of by wearing down of the ivory, and the ivory under the hole may be strengthened by the formation of new substance. When the ball is detained by the ivory, but penetrates so far as to wound the pulp, the latter ossifies around it, and the ossified portion sooner or later becomes enveloped in new ivory. If the ball penetrates the pulp, the latter ossifies round it, and becomes attached to the hole in the ivory. If the tusk is growing rapidly, and the nucleus of pulp-bone does not speedily adhere to it, the ball will ultimately be situated above the hole. The ball may also pass across the pulp, and become at last enveloped, along with its bony envelope, in the ivory of the opposite wall.

Second. In the second class of wounds, in which the ball enters the pulp-cavity through the socket and side of the tusk, the consequent changes seem to be the following:—First, ossification of the pulp surrounding the ball, and the ultimate application of the mass to the hole in the ivory, and, as the latter is necessarily at this part of its extent very thin, the hole is closed; second, the application to the hole in the ivory and to the surface of the ossified pulp in it, of cement formed by the internal surface of the tusk-follicle. For although the ball may have removed, or at least torn, the follicle opposite the hole in the ivory, yet, as the tooth advances in the socket, the ball will in time arrive at a sound portion of the latter. One of the specimens exhibited to the Society proves that the wounded portion of the follicle may perform this duty sufficiently well. In it the external surface of the cement exhibits a longitudinal fissure, with smooth rounded edges, resulting from the defective formation of cement in the situation of a longitudinal rent or wound in the membrane of the follicle, through which the ball had entered the ivory. The hole in the ivory then being plugged up externally by cement, and internally by ossified pulp, the case proceeds as in the last class of wounds—the ossified portion of the pulp surrounding the ball becoming enclosed in true ivory.

Third. When the foreign body enters from above, without wounding the tusk, the pulp ossifies round it, and true ivory envelopes the mass in the usual manner. I have not seen any morbid ivory which could be referred to wounds of the class now under consideration; but a very interesting account is given by Mr. Comb in the *Philosophical Transactions*, 1801, of a tusk in which a spear-head was found, and which could only have entered the cavity from the base of the pulp. Mr. Comb describes and figures the ossified portion of the pulp, and the manner in which it had attached itself to the ivory, and become covered by it, so as to obliterate partially and to alter the relative width of the pulp-cavity.

The description I have now given of the changes which

ensue on wounds of the tusks of the elephant explains many curious appearances in ivory, and the difficulties anatomists and physiologists have had in understanding them.

It explains the drawings and descriptions of Klockner, Ruysch, and Camper; does away with the necessity of supposing, with Blumenbach, that true ivory is regenerated, or that it can throw out ossific juice to produce cicatrices; and leads us to believe that Cuvier, in denying the possibility of the obliteration of a shot-hole, had allowed himself to be deceived. All difficulties are got over and contradictions reconciled by bearing in mind the different circumstances insisted upon in this paper, namely—

1. That a tusk is an endogenous as well as an exogenous organ.

2. That the pulp forms irregular ivory round foreign bodies, and at wounds on its surface.

3. That the membrane of the follicle is an important agent in closing up the holes produced by foreign bodies which penetrate a tusk through the socket.

IV.—ON THE SUPRA-RENAL, THYMUS, AND THYROID BODIES.—Plate III.

While engaged, two years ago, in observing the structure of the lymphatic glands, my attention was directed to the thymus, thyroid, and supra-renal bodies; and I was led to frame a hypothesis, which, although afterwards requiring some modification, has, I conceive, nevertheless enabled me to detect, if not the real physiological, at least the morphological signification of these apparently anomalous organs.

My hypothesis was, that the thyroid, thymus, and supra-renal bodies are the remains of the blastoderma; the thyroid being a portion of the original cellular substance of the germinal membrane grouped around the two principal branches of the omphalo-mesenteric vein; the supra-renal capsules, constituting other portions grouped around the omphalo-mesenteric arteries; and the thymus, the intermediate portion of the same membrane arranged along the sides of the embryonic visceral cavity.

Subsequent observations have satisfied me that this hypothesis is essentially correct, with the exception of that part of it relating to the thyroid, which body I have now ascertained to be a portion of the membrana intermedia of Reichert, which remains in connection with anastomosing vessels between the first and second aortic arches, or carotid and subclavian arteries.

In the embryo of the sheep, while the branchial clefts are still open, and for some time afterwards, there is a quantity of

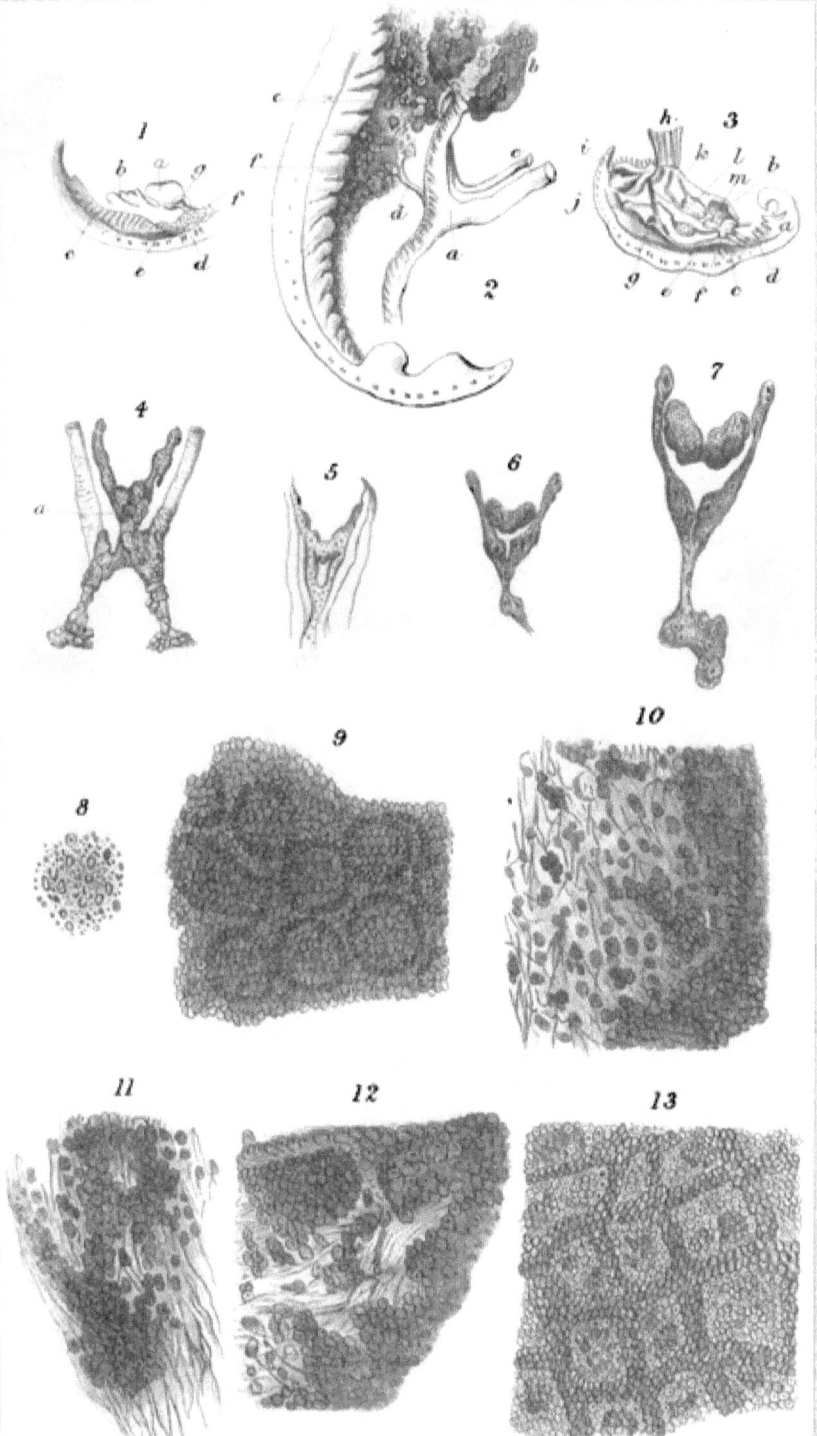

blastema arranged in minute lobular masses around the anterior parts of the cardinal veins of Rathke, surrounding the jugular veins and ductus Cuvieri for a short distance behind the forepart of the Wolffian bodies. Immediately in front of the Wolffian bodies these lateral masses of blastema are narrow, being scarcely perceptible on the coats of the cardinal veins; but around the ductus Cuvieri they are larger, and differ from the general texture of the embryo, in having a darker colour, in containing no fibres, in separating readily from the surrounding parts, and in their lobulated appearance. They extend forwards nearly to the base of the cranium, and are not connected across the median plain. They are broadest at the sides of the heart, and when the pericardium is opened, are seen through its posterior wall occupying the future situations of the lungs, which at the period stated exist as two small lobulated white bodies, projecting from the intestinal tube, behind and below the heart.

These two lateral masses are the only remaining portions of the membrana intermedia: the posterior portion on each side, on the inner aspect of the anterior extremity of the Wolffian body, becomes the supra-renal capsule; the enlarged middle portion and the outer part of the cervical portion become the thymus; while the internal anterior part resolves itself into the thyroid body. These three organs are therefore at this period continuous with one another on each side of the middle line, no isthmus having yet been formed. They are also continuous with the Wolffian bodies; these bodies, the supra-renal capsule, the thymus, and the thyroid, forming a continuous mass, situated in the elongated angular channel, which stretches from the cranium to the coccyx on the outside of the intestinal or mesenteric laminæ, and between them and the visceral laminæ.

The Wolffian bodies are the last organs formed out of the membrana intermedia, which assume a special structure. The supra-renal capsules, the thymus, and thyroid, retain throughout their existence the original texture of the blastoderma.

Proceeding therefore in the order of formation as well as of position from the Wolffian body, I shall state very briefly what I have observed concerning the mode of development of the supra-renal capsules, thymus, and thyroid.

In the embryo of the sheep, in which the branchial clefts are still quite open, the omphalo-mesenteric vessels well developed, the liver consisting of an equal-sized lobe on each side of the intestinal tube, the Wolffian bodies well formed, the allantois beginning to protrude from the abdomen, and the umbilical vessels already apparent, there may be seen between the internal anterior part of the Wolffian bodies and the aorta at the origin of the omphalo-mesenteric arteries, and also around the omphalo-mesenteric vein, where that vessel is passing forward into the liver, a mass of blastema spread over the internal surface of the fore-part of the Wolffian body, and arranged in one or more masses between that gland and the aorta.

In embryos rather more advanced, these masses of blastema become less distinct, apparently from their increased bulk causing them to be applied more uniformly over the anterior extremities of the Wolffian bodies. They may always be detected by their whiter appearance, and by being destitute of the cross-markings produced by the ducts of the Wolffian glands.

It is not till the testes, ovaries, and kidneys have appeared, that the supra-renal capsules are recognised as distinct organs; and their progress after this period need not be considered further at present.

The cardinal veins of Rathke pass forward along the posterior and lateral part of the Wolffian bodies; after passing beyond the blunt anterior extremities of these bodies, each vein carries with it, or is covered by a thin layer of the blastema already alluded to as forming at its posterior part the supra-renal capsule. This portion of the blastema becomes much larger at the side of the heart, round the ductus Cuvieri, behind the lateral parts of the pericardium, and in the future situation of the lungs, which have not yet left their median position. Each lateral portion of the blastema stretches from the heart forwards along the internal side of the jugular vein, par vagum, and carotid arteries. These two anterior portions of the lateral blastema, from the narrow portion forwards to the skull, are the lateral portions of the thymus and thyroid, which have not yet joined across the middle line.

In embryos a little further advanced, the two portions of blastema join across the trachea in a line extending from the base of the heart to the lower end of the larynx, which has now appeared as an oblong oval swelling behind the tongue. Previous to, and also contemporaneous with, this cross junction, a change has occurred in the position of the lungs and of the ductus Cuvieri.

As the lungs proceed in development, they pass in a direction from behind forwards and from within outwards, moving from their original median position to a lateral one: they at the same time increase both absolutely and relatively. At the same time, a somewhat similar change takes place in the two ductus Cuvieri. They pass forward so as to appear to enter the anterior instead of the posterior extremity of the auricle, becoming in this way the anterior venæ cavæ, this change of position being produced apparently by a semi-revolution of the whole heart, coinciding with its elongation and the altered arrangement of the bulbous aortæ.

Coincident with this change in the ductus Cuvieri is a corresponding change in the position of the lateral masses of the blastema. These pass forward, become grouped around the auricles and anterior venæ cavæ, and join across the middle line as already stated; but a narrow portion, particularly along the left side, still passes downwards and backwards along the cardinal veins, which have now become the azygos veins.

While these changes in the veins and blastema have taken place, the lungs have increased in size, and their roots have taken up their proper position. In consequence of this change in the position of the pulmonary roots and of the ductus Cuvieri, the cardinal veins arch over the root of the lungs in the same manner as the azygos vein of the adult does.

At the same time the blastema of opposite sides unites, as has been stated, across and in front of the base of the heart and root of the neck.

Shortly after this period, the posterior part of the blastema, which has now advanced, as already stated, from the sides of the chest to the front of the heart, becomes separated by a narrow neck from the cervical portion. The posterior part has now become the thoracic portion of the thymus, and in the embryo of the sheep is largest on the left side, corresponding in this respect to the large size of the left vena azygos and left vena cava at this period.

The cervical portion of the blastema now begins to exhibit a separation into the thyroid and cervical portion of the thymus. This is effected by the absorption of a portion of the blastema, of a triangular form, a little behind the larynx, the apex looking backwards, the concave base forwards, so that the future thyroid presents a crescentic form, its sides being as yet united to the anterior horns of the thymus, which pass along the jugular veins.

The thyroid now separates more completely from the thymus, by the prolongation forwards of the absorption previously mentioned from the anterior angles of the triangular portion, so as to separate the thyroid from the anterior horns of the thymus; at the same time the posterior angle of the absorbed portion passing back so as almost again to separate the cervical portion of the thymus into two lateral portions.

As development advances the thyroid becomes more completely separated from the thymus, and the lateral portions of the cervical part of the latter are united only by the narrow portion which connects them with the thoracic lobe of the organ.

At this stage a distinction may be observed, with low magnifying power, in the texture of the two organs. The thyroid is more opaque and homogeneous, the thymus consists of minute granular masses imbedded in a semitransparent matrix. The component elements of the textures of the two organs is however identical—namely, simple nucleated cells grouped around dark points, which I am inclined to regard as centres of nutrition. In the thyroid, these groups are separated and connected by a more or less dense highly vascular areolar texture. In the thymus this texture is weak or deficient.

After this period no great change occurs in the thyroid and thymus of the sheep; the anterior extremities of the horns of the thymus on each side presenting two bulbous enlargements near the base of the skull, close to the ganglions of the vagus.

Four minute white cords may now be seen passing into the superior, and two into the inferior border of the thyroid. These are the inferior and superior thyroid arteries, branches respectively from the first and second branchial arteries.

From these observations it would appear that the supra-renal capsules, the thymus, and thyroid, are persistent portions of the membrana intermedia of the germinal area of the ovum, retaining throughout their existence the original simple cellular constitution of that portion of the germinal membrane.

I shall now endeavour to explain in how far the observations just detailed appear to me to enable us to trace the functional import and anatomical peculiarities of these organs.

During the first stage of the development of the animal ovum, digestion and respiration—the absorption and preparation of nutriment—are carried on by the blastoderma, a structure consisting of nucleated cells and of vessels.

The cells, of which the blastoderma consists, are the progeny of that previously occupying the germinal spot of the ovum, and are continually reproduced and increased in numbers by the production of others from the nutritive centres, or secondary germinal spots distributed over it.

Materials for the nutrition of the blastoderma are derived from the subjacent yelk. The matter resulting from the solution of a certain number of the secondary blastodermal cells—that is, of the progeny of the primary blastodermal cells, or *nutritive centres*—is employed by the nutrient matter of the remaining secondary or proper blastodermal cells. In this way " pabulum " is afforded for two purposes—the growth of the blastoderma, and the growth of the embryo itself.

During the early period of the existence of the blastoderma, before the circulation has been established, the product of solution of the elder is at once absorbed by the younger cells. During the later periods, the product of solution drops into the incipient loops of the blood-vessels, and so circulates for purposes of nutrition. This is an instance of primary lymphatic absorption, and differs in no essential particular from the same process in the animal further advanced. We may consider the blastoderma in fact, during the first period of its circulation, as containing very numerous lymphatic ducts, instead of a few, as in the more perfect animal.

In the blastoderma, the process by which nutrient matter passes into the circulation, or the act of absorption, as it is usually called, is reduced to its most simple form, being contemporaneous and also identical with the formation of the imperfect capillary network. In the more advanced animal, when the capillary network is consolidated, the product of solution of the textures passes or drops into the intercellular or textural lacunæ, which appear to be the radicles of the lymphatic system; a system which in the adult communicates with the blood-vessels only at a few places in the neighbourhood of the trunks of the original blastodermal veins.

The blastoderma may be considered therefore not only as the first form which the being assumes after the commencement of development, and as a basis out of and in which its higher structures are to be raised, but also, as has been already stated, the organ of primary digestion—that is, of the appropriation and elaboration by the individual of nutritive matter already prepared, to a certain extent, by another individual or organ.

All the principal organs and parts of the future being are formed in, and out of, portions of the blastoderma. The laminæ dorsales, the cerebro-spinal axis, the visceral laminæ, the intestinal tube, heart, and liver, derive their origin from this source. Their original relation to this part is soon lost sight of from changes in their positions, but principally from the increased development of their original blastema, and its change into the various textures, and from the various arrangement of these textures in the organs.

There are three organs, however, which still retain their primitive structure after all the other parts of the animal have undergone their complete development, so as finally to exhibit no trace of their original simple texture and arrangement. These organs are the supra-renal capsules, the thymus, and thyroid.

The structure of each of these three organs is essentially the same: they consist of masses of nucleated cells. These cells are grouped around numerous germinal spots arranged throughout the mass, and which may be supposed to act as centres of origin and of nutrition, each for its own group. The mass of the organ is supplied with blood-vessels to convey the blood to and from the part, and with lymphatics which receive the product of solution of the cells, and convey it back again into the general circulation, whence it was originally derived.

The account of the structure of the thymus given by Sir Astley Cooper is so far incorrect, as this organ contains no reservoirs or cavities in its substance. The cavities exhibited by Sir Astley Cooper in his drawings and preparations are the results of modes of preparing. They are artificial cavities formed by distension, between the somewhat smooth, highly vascular, and slightly adhering outer surfaces of contiguous lobules; the whole organ being at the same time bound together by a stronger external areolar texture. No milky fluid is found naturally in these interlobular spaces. Indeed, Sir Astley Cooper says, that "the best mode of obtaining it is by cutting the gland into very small pieces and placing them upon gauze, which being squeezed, the solid is separated from the fluid part, and the latter escapes through the gauze."

The thymus, from the time it assumes its most perfect structure till it begins to degenerate into fatty substance, consists of lobes connected by areolar fibres, without cavities or ducts, formed of nucleated cells grouped around germinal spots, deriving matter for the formation of their cells from arteries passing into it, and being relieved of its venous blood by returning veins, being plentifully supplied with lymphatics, which do not communicate with the supposed reservoirs, as has been suggested, but appear to take their origin, as in other parts, by intercellular lacunæ, in which the walls seem gradually to lose themselves, as the ducts of the liver are lost among the secreting cells of that organ.

The thyroid body possesses a structure which is essentially the same as that of the thymus. It differs from the thymus in not being divided into lobules, in having the groups of cells of which it consists separated from one another by moderately strong capsular membranes, and in being more vascular, the anterior and venous trunks being much larger.

The supra-renal capsules also consist of nucleated cells grouped round germinal spots, and arranged, not in lobules, but in columns passing towards the surface of the organs; an arrangement corresponding to the radiating direction of the veins, and the converging arteries of these parts. The supra-renal and thyroid bodies are more vascular than the thymus from being developed around large arteries, while the thymus is in connection with smaller trunks, the former being developed in connection with the first and second aortic arches and the omphalo-mesenteric vessels; the latter in connection with the internal mammary arteries and other small thoracic and cervical branches. The greater density of the areolar capsule of the thyroid may probably be explained by this increased vascular supply.

That portion of the membrana intermedia which is separated from the rest of the membrane, and included in the body of the embryo by the umbilical constriction, and which has not already been devoted to the formation of the heart, liver, pancreas, and external portion of the intestinal canal, is found massed along the trunks of the primitive venous system, the sides of the arches of the aorta, the terminal portion of that vessel, and the origins of the omphalo-mesenteric arteries.

The portions of the membrana intermedia which are last of being converted into special organs, the Wolffian bodies, are the parts which project one on each side of the aorta, along the posterior part of the cardinal veins of Rathke, between the intestinal plates and visceral laminæ.

The portions of the membrana intermedia which remain between the upper extremities of the Wolffian bodies and the heart and liver, and which surround the origins of the omphalo-mesenteric arteries, do not become converted into organs of special structure, but retain during life the original constitution of the membrana intermedia of the blastoderma, and increase rapidly in the embryo, constituting the supra-renal capsules. Whatever doubt may be entertained as to the exact functional import of these bodies, the identity of their anatomical constitution with that of the blastoderma is sufficiently evident, and their morphological signification appears to be equally so.

That portion of the membrana intermedia which is situated between those two aortic arches, the extremities of which become the carotid and subclavian arteries, remains during life as the thyroid body. It receives its blood from the first and second aortic arches by two large trunks on each side, the superior and inferior thyroid arteries.

That portion of the membrane which passes in two parts from near the base of the cranium back as far as the ductus Cuvieri and anterior portions of the veins of Rathke, and which are united and concentrated in front of the heart by passing from behind forwards, in harmony with corresponding motions of the neighbouring part, becomes the thymus.

The structure of these three organs is identical with that of the blastoderma. Their probable function—namely, to prepare by the action of their nucleated cells, and to throw into the vascular system, a matter necessary for the nutrition of the animal during the period of its active growth—a function which the observations and opinions of the majority of physiologists have assigned to them—is also essentially the same with that of the blastoderma.

The question as to the exact or intimate nature of the function of these organs can only be answered by further inquiries in chemical physiology. It appears to me to be sufficient at present to insist that their function, as deduced from their structure and anatomical relations, is similar to that performed by the blastoderma, whatever the exact nature of that function may be.

I have therefore been led to consider the supra-renal capsules, the thymus, and thyroid, as organs essentially similar in structure; as developments of the remains of the blastoderma, being formed of a continuous portion of that part situated along each side of the spine, from the Wolffian bodies to the base of the cranium, the supra-renal capsules being developed in connection with the omphalo-mesenteric vessels, the thymus to the jugular and cardinal veins, and ductus Cuvieri; and the thyroid to the anastomosing branches of the first and second aortic arches, as organs performing functions, whatever these may be, analogous to those of the blastoderma, differing from them only in this, that the blastoderma not only elaborates nourishment for the embryo, but absorbs it also from without—that is, from the yelk; whereas the three organs in question only elaborate the matter which has already been absorbed by the other parts, and is now circulating in the vessels of the more perfect individual.

V.—ON THE MORPHOLOGICAL RELATIONS OF THE NERVOUS SYSTEM IN THE ANNULOSE AND VERTEBRATE TYPES OF ORGANISATION.*

THE term annulose is employed provisionally, and in a morphological sense, as including all animals possessing a ganglionic nervous collar and axis, and presenting, at the same time, more or less distinct indications of a segmented structure of body.

Physiologists appear generally inclined to consider the central portions of the annulose and vertebrate nervous systems as modified forms of the same arrangement. These forms are held to possess a general similarity of structure, and correspondence in function; and the ganglionic collar and axis of the annulose are assumed to be homologous either with the cerebro-spinal axis, or with the series of ganglions on the posterior roots of the spinal nerves, or with the system of sympathetic ganglions of the vertebrate animal.

In my own examination of this subject I have been strongly impressed with the necessity of determining the morphological character of the œsophageal collar, and the opposite positions of the so-called brain and abdominal ganglionic cord, before any satisfactory advance could be made in ascertaining the relations of the two forms of nervous system. The apparent morphological difference between

---

* This and the two following papers were read to Section D at the Cheltenham Meeting of the British Association, Aug. 5-12, 1856, and were published in abstract in the *Edinburgh Philosophical Journal*, Jan. 1857.—EDS.

them does not appear, in the estimation of physiologists generally, to present that obstacle to a satisfactory comparison which its essentially fundamental character would lead us to expect. The difficulty has, however, been clearly stated by Professor Owen, who, in discussing the relations of the endo- and exo-skeletons in his *Lectures on Fishes*, page 21, ed. 1846, says—" Geoffroy St. Hilaire thought it needed but to reverse the position of the crustacean—to turn what had been wrongly deemed the belly upwards—in order to demonstrate the unity of organisation between the articulate and vertebrate animal. But the position of the brain is thereby reversed, and the alimentary canal still intervenes in the invertebrate between the aortic trunk and the neural canal."

I must here premise, that while I hold the general morphological relations of the annulose and vertebrate nervous systems to be identical, I do not consider these two types of organisation to be mutually reducible. On the contrary, they are fundamentally distinct, presenting differences which demand careful consideration. It is, nevertheless, incumbent on the morphologist to ascertain in what respects they correspond, so as to determine their distinctive limits.

My earlier conception of the morphology of the annulose nervous system was based on that of Carus. I conceived that each segment of the annulose animal contains potentially an annular nervous arrangement, set in a plane at right angles to the axis of the segment, or longitudinal axis of the animal; that the only complete nervous ring is that one through which the œsophagus passes; that the ganglions on this ring are arranged in the various forms of superior, lateral, and inferior œsophageal masses; that the nervous rings in the postcephalic segments are all incomplete above, and have their ganglions united into a single or double mass below; and that all the rings are united by a series of longitudinal abdominal commissures. According to this view, the œsophageal collar, with its superior, lateral, and inferior ganglions, is homologous with each pair of segmental nerves, and the corresponding abdominal ganglionic centre; the œsophageal collar being in a plane parallel to those in which the post-cephalic ganglions and their pairs of nerves are situated, but at right angles to the line of the series of abdominal ganglions.

I first recognised what I believe to be the real morphological relations of the annulose nervous system during the delivery of a course of lectures on Invertebrate Anatomy in 1849; but more fully and completely during courses on the Anatomy of the Mollusca in 1850, and on the Anatomy of the Crustacea in 1851.

I now perceived that the fundamental difference between the morphological relations of the annulose and vertebrate nervous systems, consists in the position of the mouth.

I saw that the entire axis or central portion of the nervous system extends along the neural aspect of the body in both types of organisation; but that while, as is well known—although its morphological importance does not appear to have been perceived—the vertebrate mouth opens into the hæmal, the annulose mouth passes through the neural aspect of the body.

In the annulose animal, therefore, the buccal entrance interferes with the nervous axis—passing up between the two lateral halves of one of its longitudinal commissural or interganglionic cords, so as morphologically to divide the continuous axis into a *pre-stomal* and a *post-stomal* portion.

These relations are most satisfactorily seen in the crustacea, in which the so-called brain, or supra-œsophageal ganglion or nervous mass, is actually in front of the mouth, and not above it.

In insects, annelids, and mollusca, the bulk of the buccal mass, and other necessary modifications of the oral apparatus, elevate the so-called brain, curving upwards the morphological axis of the body of the animal.

By comparing the indications of segments in front of the mouth, and their corresponding diverging appendages, with the arrangement and distribution of the nerves given off from the so-called brain, it appears very evident that this brain is the aggregate of the segmental nervous centres in front of the mouth.

In like manner indications afforded by the segments, and their appendages immediately behind the mouth, enable us to determine whether the so-called sub-œsophageal ganglionic mass is a single segmental ganglion, or an aggregate of anteroposteriorly united segmental ganglions.

In this way I was enabled to perceive that the axis of the nervous system of the annulose animal does not consist of a supra-œsophageal mass, of an œsophageal collar, of a sub-œsophageal mass, and a continuous sub-intestinal ganglionic chain; but of a continuous line of connected and serially homologous ganglions situated in the mesial line of the neural aspect of the body.

The annulose, like the vertebrate animal, is developed with its nervous axis turned away from, and its hæmal axis applied against, the vitellary mass.*

* From the passage in his lectures already quoted, Professor Owen would appear to consider the dorsal heart, with its anterior and posterior arterial trunks in the decapod crustacean, and consequently the dorsal vessel in the insect, arachnidan, and annelid, as corresponding to the thoracic, abdominal, and caudal aortic trunk of the vertebrate animal. On this supposition only can we understand his assertion, that when the so-called belly of the crustacean is turned upwards, its alimentary canal is still interposed between the aortic trunk and the neural canal. Embryology, comparative anatomy, and physiology, appear to me, however, to afford ample proof that the cardiac-arterial dorsal trunk of the annelid, crustacean, insect, or arachnidan, is homologous, not with the sub-spinal aorta of the vertebrate, but with the pri-

G

But, in the course of development, the mouth of the vertebrate opens through the surface applied against the vitellary mass, whilst that of the annulose animal passes through the aspect turned away from it. The vertebrate mouth is hæmal, the annulose mouth neural.

Rathke formerly described the pituitary body as originating in a diverticulum passing up from the pharyngeal mucous membrane through the basis of the embryo skull. I at one time conceived it to be probable that the pituitary body, and the mucous tube, in which, according to Rathke, it originates, might be indications in the vertebrate of a structure which, in the annulose animal, is converted into the mouth. This presumed neural alimentary passage may be conceived as passing up between the bodies of the anterior and posterior sphenoid bones into the Sella Turcica, along the course of the infundibulum to the third ventricle of the brain, and through the cavity of that organ to its upper surface behind the cerebellum, thus leaving the origins of the nerves of smell and vision in the pre-stomal portion of the organ, while the origin of the nerve of hearing would remain in the medulla oblongata or post-stomal portion of the cephalic nervous mass. The arterial circle of Willis, and other peculiar arrangements at the base of the skull and brain, appeared to support the view taken. I shall not, however, pursue this hypothesis further, because, from the observations of Reichert, we know that the base of the cranium is not perforated in the embryo, and that the supposed canal or diverticulum was an incorrect interpretation of the peculiar appearances pro-

mordial cardiac-arterial tube in all the forms of the embryo vertebrate, and, consequently, with the heart and trunk of the branchial artery of the fish. If this, then, is the real homology of the "aortic trunk" of the crustacean, and if its "brain" is in fact only a *pre-stomal* portion of its nervous axis, the French anatomist was quite correct in his general morphological statement, although he was not legitimately entitled at the time to employ the illustration.

duced by the curvature **downwards of the** early Mammalian head.*

If I have determined aright the morphological relations of these two forms of nervous system, we shall have advanced a step in our conceptions of the anatomico-physiological relations of the annulose and vertebrate animals, and this without losing sight of the fundamental differences, developmental and structural, between them. The researches of Milne-Edwards, and of Newport and others, on the annulose nervous axis may thus be physiologically associated with those of Wagner, Schroeder Van der Kolk, Owsjannikow, Jacobowitsch, and Kupffer, on the cerebro-spinal axis; and we may now legitimately employ the annulose animal in the morphological investigation of the vertebrate skeleton.

Omitting, for the present, the consideration of the mode in which the nervous systems in the Tunicata, Rotifera, and Entozoa, are reducible to the typical annulose form, I proceed to make some general morphological statements, based to a certain extent on the principle indicated in this, and introductory to the two following communications :—

1. The morphology of any one organic system in the annulose or vertebrate animal, cannot be safely or satisfactorily investigated, without constant reference to the others. That it must be so is evident from the fact, that all the organic systems are dependent on one another, in the constitution of the organism.

2. All sound morphological inquiry demands constant reference to the series of embryo, as well as of adult forms.

3. As morphology deals with forms and relations of position, it demands a careful selection of terms, and a methodised

* I have introduced the hypothesis of a vertebrate neural mouth (cast aside in the course of my examination of the subject), because I believe it will be found to involve relations of importance in the anatomico-physiological investigation of the pre-stomal and post-stomal portions of the vertebrate and annulose cephalic nervous masses.

nomenclature. All terms involving more or less than their morphological application demands, must be avoided. Terms derived from other departments of the science, and having therefore an established technical meaning, have invariably produced misconception, when transferred for morphological purposes.

Influenced by these considerations, and satisfied that the annulose and vertebrate types of organisation, although fundamentally distinct, present parallel forms of structure, and must consequently be closely linked together in morphological inquiry, I have to suggest a more extended and precise system of nomenclature for this department of the science.

In the annulose and vertebrate types of organisation, the body of the animal consists of a linear series of segments. To the constituent segment, with its diverging appendages, I apply the term *somatome* (σῶμα, τέμνω).

For the purpose of avoiding circumlocution, and of supplying a term for a generalised conception, and thereby facilitating morphological description, without encroaching on zoological nomenclature, I denominate a segmented animal, whether annulose or vertebrate, an *entomosome*—an entomosomatous animal (ἔντομος, σῶμα).

As the constituent somatomes are invariably arranged in groups, in each of which they are more or less modified in form, or fused together, I find syssomatome (σύν, σῶμα, τέμνω) a convenient designation for such a group. A typical crustacean presents a cephalic, a thoracic, and a caudal syssomatome, in each of which there are seven somatomes—twenty-one in all.

The constituent somatomes lie in planes at right angles to the *morphological axis* of the body, and are symmetrical in the transverse, but unsymmetrical in the perpendicular direction. They are, however, not only unsymmetrical in their upper and under surfaces, but the surfaces so named in the annulose are morphologically distinct from those similarly designated in the vertebrate animal. The annulose animal moves on the surface which was turned away from the vitellary mass during development; the vertebrate animal moves on the surface which was applied to it during development. As the axis of the nervous system is formed at the surface turned away from the vitellary mass, and the axis of the vascular system is formed at the surface applied to it in both types of organisation, I employ, as morphological designations, the term neuropod (νεῦρον, πούς) for an annulose, and hæmapod (αἷμα, πούς) for a vertebrate animal.

The mouth of the entomosomatous animal is invariably situated between two somatomes, so that a certain number of somatomes are interposed between it and the anterior termination of the body. As the mouth is only one of a number of openings situated between somatomes, I find such openings conveniently distinguished as *metasomatomic.*

The mouth of the neuropod is a neural, that of the hæmapod a hæmal metasomatomic opening.

As the somatome exhibits in its structure corresponding segments of certain or of all the organic systems, I have found the following morphological terms extremely convenient in referring from the segment of one organic system to the corresponding segments of the others.

For the entire framework of an entomosome, whether this framework be developed in its integument or in its interior—whether it be fibrous, cartilaginous, or osseous—I employ the term *sclerome* (σκληρός, with the termination of completeness). To a segment of the sclerome I apply the designation *sclerotome* (σκληρός, τέμνω). An aggregate of more or less modified sclerotomes I name a *syssclerotome* (σύν). Making use of my former illustration, the sclerome of a typical crustacean consists of twenty-one sclerotomes grouped in three syssclerotomes.

Again, the sclerome of a mammal consists of a number of sclerotomes, grouped into the cephalic, cervical, thoracic, lumbar, sacral, and caudal syssclerotomes.

For the muscular system I employ the terms *myome, myotome, symmyotome;* for the nervous system, *neurome, neurotome, synneurotome;* for the vascular system, *hæmome, hæmatome, synhæmatome;* for the morphologically as well as physiologically important digestive system, with its segments, and groups of segments, *peptome, peptatome,* and *synpeptatome,* etc.

Till very lately, I had not met with any indication of the actual morphological character of the so-called supra-œsophageal ganglion in the works of British or foreign physiologists. I have now found, in an obscure corner of Von Baer's works, sufficient evidence that he had recognised its pre-stomal character. His statements are contained in a single paragraph, which forms an episode in the middle of the second corollary of the fifth scholium of his work on the development of the chick *in ovo*. Von Baer holds, with E. H. Weber and Treviranus, that the nervous axis of the neuropod is homologous with the series of ganglions on the posterior roots of the spinal nerves of the hæmapod; and he considers the "supra-œsophageal" ganglion to be the homologue of the Gasserian ganglion; but he adds, "Peculiar stress is laid on this, that it (the supra-œsophageal ganglion) lies above (über) the mouth. This appears to me to be a false view of the matter; it lies, in fact, in front of (vor) the mouth." He gives a diagram of the arrangement, and proceeds: "The following sketch will make it evident that the so-called brain of the insect has the same signification as the posterior ganglions; and the œsophageal ring is only a secondary formation, dependent on the breaking through of the mouth, permitted by the symmetry of the structure, and the necessary connection of the ganglions."

It is somewhat remarkable that no one even of Von

Baer's own countrymen, has, so far as I know, made any allusion to this passage. Indeed, **he does** not appear to have been himself **aware of the value of** the observation, as he adduces **it** merely in the form of an argument in illustration of another subject, and does not again recur to it. For my own part, having ascertained, on independent grounds, and publicly taught and illustrated for some years, the principle stated in this communication, I feel gratified in having this **opportunity of rescuing from** temporary oblivion, and of **adducing in support of** my own statement of the principle, the **original** announcement of it, made twenty-eight years **ago**, by **one of the most** philosophic of modern anatomists.*

* I accidentally discovered, a few weeks ago, that Professor Huxley had published translations of portions of Von Baer's works in the *Scientific Memoirs* for 1853. This judicious selection contains the passage referred to in my paper. (Dec. 4, 1856.)

VI.

ON THE MORPHOLOGICAL CONSTITUTION OF THE SKELETON OF THE VERTEBRATE HEAD.

In an abstract which professes to give only the general results of my own investigations, I cannot enter into such critico-historical details as would be necessary were the corresponding or opposite results obtained by other inquirers to be in every instance brought forward. I am therefore obliged at present to state, in a somewhat dogmatic form, the results which I conceive I have obtained, and the views I have been induced to take of a subject in itself extensive and difficult, and one to which so many distinguished anatomists have devoted themselves.

Nature of the Subject.—The framework of the vertebrate head is a syssclerotome—that is, a group of sclerotomes variously modified, and more or less connected, so as to form a distinct whole. The points to be determined are the number and modifications of the sclerotomes in the various forms of vertebrate head. There are, however, some preliminary questions which must be briefly examined.

The Source and Mode of Origin of the Sclerome in the Vertebrate Embryo.—The knowledge we at present possess of the source and mode of origin of the vertebrate sclerome is the result of the successive researches more particularly of Pander, Von Baer, Rathke, Reichert, and Remak, on the development of the blastoderma.

Von Baer, while he adopted the doctrine of Pander regarding the so-called "serous" and "mucous layers," took a somewhat modified view of the "vascular layer," and directed attention more particularly to the "dorsal" and "ventral folds" of the blastoderma, in connection with the "corda dorsalis," as fundamental embryological characteristics of the vertebrate type of organisation.

Among the numerous results of the researches made by Rathke in every department of embryology, there are two which bear particularly on the present subject. These are his early discovery of the so-called branchial clefts; and his later recognition of the fact that the series of quadrilateral bodies on each side of the "corda dorsalis," instead of being the rudiments of vertebræ, contain potentially the germs not only of these bones, but of the dorsal muscles, and "probably" of spinal nerves.

Reichert supplemented the previous observations of Rathke on the development of the "branchial" or "visceral laminæ," and of the nasal and maxillary portions of the face.

Finally, Remak has ascertained, on independent grounds, that each pair of the dorsal quadrilateral bodies, usually considered as the rudiments of vertebræ, becomes developed superiorly into a right and left muscular plate, and inferiorly into a pair of spinal nerves, with their ganglions, along with the rudiments of a vertebra and pair of ribs, the nerves being in front of the sclerous elements. In the course of development a change takes place in this "primordial vertebral system." The rudiments of the vertebral arch and ribs move backwards, from their original site under the posterior margins of the overlying muscular plates, to the anterior margins of the pair of muscular plates immediately behind, and become united to both pairs. A transverse division takes place at the same time in the rudimentary central masses of each of the primordial vertebræ. These changes constitute a new order of parts—the order or arrangement of the "permanent vertebral system." Thus, the products of the development of a single primordial vertebra are—1. A pair of spinal nerves, with their ganglions; 2. The vertebral arch and pair of ribs immediately behind this pair of nerves; 3. The anterior part of the body of the vertebra to which this arch and ribs are attached; 4. The intervertebral disk in front of it; 5. The posterior part of the body of the vertebra in front; and, 6. The group of spinal muscles between these two vertebræ. The bones, muscles, and nerves of the abdominal and thoracic wall are formed by an extension downwards, and adhesion of the lower or costal portion of the "primordial vertebral system" to the inner surface of the external of the two layers into which the "primary abdominal wall" divides. This outer or adherent layer of the "primary abdominal wall" becomes the areolar layer of the integument, and enters into the formation of the limbs. The inner layer, separated from the outer by the pleuro-peritoneal space, forms, with its fellow of the opposite side, the Wolffian bodies, reproductive glands, spleen, permanent aorta, mesentery, and the muscular and serous covering of the alimentary tube.

From these remarkable observations of Remak, it would appear that the sclerome of the hæmapod, from the anterior part of the neck backwards, originates as a series of independent sclerotomes, and that, contemporaneously with each sclerotome, a corresponding myotome and neurotome take their rise in a common primordial segment of blastema.

The cephalic portion of the early vertebrate embryo is peculiar, more particularly, according to Remak, in the non-appearance of distinct "primordial vertebræ," and of the subsequent changes which result from their development. The great divisions of the brain and of the cerebral nerves indicate, indeed, the segmented character of the entire structure, but I am inclined to believe that, in the present state of the subject, these indications are not to be depended on for the determination of the segments of the embryo or adult head. It appears to me that the segmented structure of the brain is to be looked for, not in its greater masses—those developments on its upper surface in which it differs from the spinal cord, and by the possession of which it becomes a brain—but in the series of groups of ganglion-cells, the nervous centres of the cerebral nerves, whatever the typical number of these may be, arranged along its base, and strictly homologous with the groups of ganglion-cells which undoubtedly constitute the morphological segments of the spinal cord.

The "visceral" or "branchial laminæ" afford, in the present state of the subject, a more secure embryological basis for the determination of the segments of the head. The so-called "first visceral lamina," the one in which the mandibular arch is developed, and the two succeeding "visceral laminæ," those in which the anterior and posterior segments of the hyoid of mammals and birds are formed, must be looked upon as embryological indications of three cephalic segments.

On the under-surface of the forepart of the embryo head, in front of the so-called "first visceral lamina," there are five processes, in which are developed the palate and pterygoid, the maxillary, malar, and lachrymal, the intermaxillary and nasal bones. The first of these processes on each side extends obliquely forwards from the "first visceral lamina" towards and under the eye. It is the so-called "superior maxillary lobe." The second process on each side—the "lateral frontal process" of Reichert—passes down in front of the eye, the eye being situated in the cleft between it and the former process. The fifth process is situated in front, and in the median line. It is the "anterior frontal process" of Reichert. The clefts or notches between this process and the "lateral frontal process" are considered by Rathke and Reichert to be the external nostrils.

Now, in regard to the so-called "superior maxillary lobes," it is clearly established that the palate and pterygoid bones are formed in them, but there is no sufficient evidence that they contain the germs of the superior maxillary bones. No traces of the superior maxillary bones appear until these so-called "superior maxillary lobes" have extended forwards, and united with the "lateral frontal processes" and the "nasal process," and until the maxillary margin has become considerably extended. I am, therefore, of opinion that the "lateral frontal processes" of Reichert are, in fact, the real maxillary lobes, and contain not only the germs of the lachrymal, but those also of the maxillary and malar bones. This view of the place of origin of the superior maxillary is in accordance with the adult relations of these bones. The position of the superior maxillary is in front of the eye; the orbit being, in fact, an expanded cleft between it and the palate bone.

Again, the nasal bones of the mammal are formed in the upper part, and the intermaxillary bones in the lateral angles and palatal lobes of the "anterior frontal process." The notch or cleft on each side of this process cannot therefore become the external nostrils, for these are not situated in the mammal behind the intermaxillary bones, but in front of them. From these circumstances, I am inclined to consider the external nostrils of the mammal to be formed by the transverse union of the palatal lobes of the "anterior frontal process," and by the formation of the cartilages of the external nose in the mesial portion of the free margin of that process.

Embryologists generally consider the so-called superior maxillary lobes to be the upper portions of the "first visceral laminæ" bent forward, and the "lateral" and "anterior frontal processes" to be superadded structures in no way related to the "visceral" or "branchial laminæ." It appears to me, however, that the general aspect, the relations, and the changes undergone by them in development, prove these parts to be serially homologous with the "visceral laminæ," and to be, like them, indications of the segmented structure of the head in front of the so-called first visceral arch. The so-called superior maxillary lobes indicate a segment of which the palate and pterygoid bones are elements. The "lateral frontal" indicate a second segment, containing the maxillary, malar, and lachrymal bones. The external margins and angles of the "anterior or frontal processes" indicate an intermaxillary segment; and the development of the mesial part of the same process into the cartilages of the nose indicates a segment probably only fully developed in the mammalian head.

In addition, therefore, to the "visceral laminæ" behind that one in which the mandibular arch is formed, there would appear to be a series of less developed "visceral laminæ" in front of it, all of which, in addition to other structures, give rise to hæmal arches of the sclerome, and indicate a number of corresponding sclerotomes.

Of the Primary or Fibrous Sclerome.—The bones and cartilages to which, from their palpable character, the attention of anatomists has been hitherto chiefly directed, are parts only of the vertebrate sclerome. They are imbedded in a continuous fibrous matrix, which, variously modified, binds them together, and co-operates in their general economy and functions. This matrix forms a more extensive, and, in some respects, a more important element of the sclerome in the lower than in the higher vertebrata; and if viewed in the former in connection with its early stages of development in the embryo, it will be found to be arranged on the plan of the "primordial vertebral system." It is most satisfactorily studied in the fish, and particularly in those forms in which the bones and cartilages are feebly developed. The fibrous element of the sclerome forms the sheath of the "corda dorsalis" in the lancelet, and envelopes the column formed by the bodies of the vertebræ in other fishes. It then bounds the neural and hæmal cavities, and from these cavities passes in the mesial plane above and below to the neural and hæmal margins of the body. Corresponding cartilaginous and osseous parts are imbedded in these fibrous neural and hæmal laminæ. From the right and left sides of this deep or central system of fibrous laminæ, other laminæ extend outwards between the myotomes, and are connected to the deep fibrous layer of the integument. The bones usually distinguished as "additional ribs," "upper ribs," "epipleural spines," "diverging appendages," are imbedded in these metamyotomic laminæ; and as the class of radiating bones to which these so-called additional ribs belong may be conveniently distinguished as actinapophyses (ἀκτίς-ῖνος), I apply the term actinal to the metamyotomic fibrous laminæ of the sclerome. As those dermal bones or plates which, from their histological as well as their teleological characters, certainly constitute elements of the sclerome, are formed in the layer of the integument to which the actinal sclerous laminæ are attached, this integumentary fibrous structure must be considered as constituting a dermal sclerous lamina, and so completing the fibrous portion of the sclerome.

The sclerome thus consists fundamentally of a fibrous structure, which surrounds the "corda dorsalis," bounds the neural and hæmal cavities, forms a mesial septum above and below, separates the myotomes from one another, and, under the integument, envelopes the deeper parts.

The Development of Cartilaginous and Bony Elements in the Fibrous Sclerome.—The immediate development of certain bones from or in a fibrous matrix, and of others in cartilage previously formed in it, has given rise, among other questions, to one as to whether the former are to be included in the vertebrate system of bones. Now, while I admit the importance of the embryological and histological facts which the discussion of this question has afforded, I am inclined to think that a histological bias has influenced both the views which have been taken of it. Why certain bones originate in a fibrous matrix, why others originate in cartilage which has been previously formed in the same matrix, are questions of undoubted importance, but which at the same time cannot legitimately be put in opposition to the unity of the fully-developed sclerome.

Of the Cartilaginous and Bony Elements, and of the general Morphological Constitution of the Sclerotome.—A sclerotome is, fundamentally, a segment of the fibrous sclerome, and the series of fibrous sclerotomes is indicated by the actinal laminæ, each of which, for reasons to be afterwards stated, ought probably to be considered as potentially double—that is, as consisting of two layers, one belonging to the sclerotome behind, the other to the sclerotome in front.

The fully developed hæmapod sclerotome is therefore a fibrous structure, in which all the cartilaginous and osseous parts are formed and imbedded. With regard to these cartilaginous or osseous elements, I shall at present only direct attention to certain points which bear on the constitution of the sclerotomes of the head. In doing so, I must bear testimony to the general applicability and convenience of the terms employed by Professor Owen to designate the elements of his typical vertebra, venturing to suggest modifications in their application only where I am compelled to differ from him in regard to the relations of the elements themselves.

The term "centrum" is highly useful as a designation for the cartilaginous or osseous mass formed around the "corda dorsalis," whatever the constitution of that mass may be.

The neurapophyses or hard parts developed in the lateral neural laminæ are "typically" two at least on each side. Not only are there two on each side in the trunk sclerotomes of certain cartilaginous and probably osseous fishes; but there are two on each side in certain cephalic sclerotomes in at least fishes and reptiles. Professor Owen admits one neurapophysis only on each side of his typical vertebra. He accounts for the additional pair in the spine of the sturgeon on the principle of "vegetative repetition," while the additional elements in the neural arches of certain cephalic vertebræ he at one time considered as parapophyseal, and latterly as diapophyseal elements. But it appears to me that the principle of "vegetative repetition" is out of place in a morphological question; and a parapophysis cannot, according to Professor Owen's archetype, be intercalated between a neurapophysis and a neural spine, nor can a diapophysis become an independent element.

The superior or posterior spinous process, "neural spine," or (as a more convenient general designation) metaneurapophysis, is developed in the mesial neural fibrous lamina. As this element is situated in the mesial plane, it is potentially double, and its right and left halves become depressed and more or less flattened out in the cephalic sclerotomes. With the neurapophysis it completes the neural arch.

The cartilaginous or osseous elements developed in the lateral and mesial hæmal laminæ of the fibrous sclerotome constitute the hæmal arch. The fundamental character of the inferior or hæmal arch, as I understand it, consists in this, that its constituent elements take their rise at or close to the inner surface of those "ventral laminæ" or "folds" in the embryo, which form the lateral and inferior walls of the visceral chamber. Every hæmal arch, therefore, within the antero-posterior range of the alimentary tube must, according as it is more or less developed, necessarily inclose that tube more or less completely. Accordingly, no arch within the range of that tube, if it excludes the tube, can be considered as a hæmal arch, merely because it incloses great blood-vessels. Again, before any arch beyond the range of the alimentary tube can be considered as a proper hæmal arch, its development must have been ascertained, or its relations to those muscular, vascular, but more particularly nervous elements, which constitute in their respective systems the arrangements corresponding to the hæmal arch in the sclerotome, must have been determined.

I must confess therefore my inability to discover the precise view of the hæmal arch taken by Professor Owen. Judging from his diagram of the "ideal typical vertebra," and from his general treatment of the subject, a chevron bone in the reptile or mammal, or that portion of the cervical vertebra in certain birds which completes the canal beneath the centrum, represents the primary typical form of this arch. It would also appear to follow from his doctrine that the expanded form of hæmal arch, provided for the lodgment of the central organ of circulation, and presented by the thoracic segments, is a secondary formation—the result of the removal of the primary hæmal arch from its "typical" position under the centrum, and its intercalation between the elongated pleurapophyses. But this doctrine appears to me to involve embryological contradictions. The relations of these primary and secondary forms of hæmal arch in the neck and throat respectively are not explained by it. The so-called hæmal arch under the cervical vertebra of the pelican is undoubtedly hæmal in function; but as it excludes the œsophagus and trachea, it cannot be the real or morphological hæmal arch. In other words, this so-called hæmal arch cannot have been formed in the "ventral folds" of the embryo neck.

Again, it is difficult to conceive how the pleurapophyses and hæmal arch of Professor Owen's "ideal typical vertebra" can be developed together in the "ventral folds" of the embryo. For, according to the doctrine of Professor Owen, a pleurapophysis may, in different instances, present two sets of relations. In the thorax it is attached by opposite ends to adjoining sclerous elements, and lies in the wall of the hæmal chamber. In the neck and tail it is connected to its own vertebra at one end only, and does not lie in the wall of the hæmal chamber. The mode in which the continuously-arranged elements of the costal arch of a bird—the "pleurapophyses," "hæmapophyses," and "hæmal spine"—are developed in the embryo is known. But it is difficult to conceive how the detached and peculiarly-arranged "pleurapophyses" and "hæmal arch," as represented in the "ideal typical vertebra," or exemplified in a proximal caudal vertebra of a reptile or perenni-branchiate amphibian, have assumed the positions they occupy, if they belong to the same group of elements—that is, if they all spring from or originate in the wall of the visceral chamber.

Is the pleurapophysis a fundamental or primary element of the hæmal arch? In other words, is it originally developed in the wall of the visceral cavity, and in certain instances afterwards extruded from it? or is it merely a secondary element in the hæmal arch—that is, formed externally to, or away from it, and only intercalated into it in certain vertebræ?

As a rib, so far as its development has been traced in the series, appears to be formed in the inner layer of the "ventral fold;" and as it is previously connected or continuous with the diapophyseal portion of the neurapophyses, its head and neck being secondary formations, I am inclined to consider the caudal transverse processes in the mammal, lizard, and amphibian as lying in the position of the original "ventral folds," and that, therefore, the feebly-developed "pleurapophyses" of this region are the only representatives of its hæmal arches, while the chevron-bones have no title to this morphological distinction.*

* In dissecting lately a large crocodile, I found that an aponeurotic membrane extended outwards and curved downwards on each side from the extremities of the caudal transverse processes. These aponeuroses met one another in the mesial line below the tail, and were there joined by a mesial aponeurosis which extended down from between the chevron-bones. A layer of fat one-third of an inch in thickness lay on the outside of the lateral apo-

The processes which complete the canal under the posterior cranial and anterior trunk centrums in certain fishes, and of the cervical centrums in certain birds, are probably of the same nature as the chevron-bones, which, according to Joh. Müller, appear to be developments of the inferior pair of constituent pieces of the centrum.

We are entitled, then, to require that every part to which the pleurapophyseal or hæmapophyseal character is attributed, should have been proved, by direct observation or otherwise, to have been developed in the "ventral folds."

It appears to me very doubtful whether there are sufficient grounds for limiting the number of morphological elements in the hæmal arch to one pair of " hæmapophyses " and a " hæmal spine ;" or to a pair of " pleurapophyses," a pair of " hæmapophyses," and a " hæmal spine ;" while an increase in the number of sclerous pieces is accounted for by the principle of " vegetative repetition," or " teleologically." While I admit the grouping of the elements of the more com-

---

neuroses, and, embedded in it, the hæmal divisions of the spinal nerves extended outwards, downwards, and backwards, like a series of intercostal nerves. The lateral muscular mass of the tail arranged in myotomes with metamyotomic fibrous laminæ, nearly as distinct as in the fish, lay on the outside of the layer of fat. Each of the lateral aponeurotic cavities was occupied by the "fémoro-péronéo-coccygien" muscle of Cuvier, which arose from the under surfaces of the transverse processes, the sides of the chevron bones and mesial aponeurosis, and passed out of the cavity through a space left in its outer wall behind the ischium to be inserted into the thigh-bone. The mesial membrane divided above, its two laminæ corresponding to the limbs of the chevron-bones, and passing in front into the walls of the pelvis.

This arrangement appeared to me to indicate that the transverse processes, the lateral aponeuroses, and the hæmal divisions of the spinal nerves, were in the position of the proper hæmal arches of the tail ; that the two aponeurotic chambers constituted in fact, together, the abdominal or visceral cavity, divided by the mesial lamina, and occupied by a pair of muscles, referable to that group of muscles which in the trunk lie on the inner surface of the visceral chamber, and that therefore the chevron-bones are not real hæmal arches, but subcentral developments.

plex hæmal arches into an upper and a lower series, I am compelled on philosophical grounds to deny that the subdivision of a "pleurapophysis" or of a "hæmapophysis," is beyond the range of morphological law; or that morphology and teleology are distinct in the sense that the latter principle provides for what the former is insufficient. Morphology and teleology are merely opposite, because, in the present phase of science, necessary anthropomorphic aspects of the same Divine principle evinced in the laws of organisation.

Until, then, we know more than we do at present of the laws which regulate the number of "centres of chondrification and ossification," and until the constitution of the inferior vertebral arches in the embryo and adult series has been more fully analysed, I cannot give my assent to the expression for a hæmal arch involved in Professor Owen's osteological doctrine.

I must here allude to a point which does not appear to have attracted that attention which it deserves. None of the hæmal arches of the head inclose the hæmal axis. If we are to consider the so-called median and lateral frontal with the superior maxillary lobes as visceral laminæ, then, as such, they have no primordial relation with the hæmal axis, which, under the form of the cardiac-branchial tube, extends forward as far only as the so-called "first visceral lamina." After the hæmal arches have been formed in "the first and other visceral laminæ," usually so called, of the head, the hæmal axis is found to be excluded from them. It is in consequence of this remarkable developmental arrangement that the heart, branchial artery, and its branches, in the fish and amphibia, are situated below and external to the skeleton of the branchial apparatus.

Before pointing out what appear to me to constitute certain of the developmental conditions on which this peculiar relation of the hæmal arches of the head to the hæmal axis is dependent, I must direct attention to another relation, in which the cephalic hæmal arches are peculiar. The hæmal arches of the head are in immediate contact with the alimentary tube; they are lined by the mucous membrane, which is also in contact with their centrums. There is, in fact, no extension of the peritoneo-pleuropericardiac space into the head. The cephalic portion of the primary abdominal wall (Kopfseitenplatte of Remak) becomes from the first united to the corresponding portion of the cephalic primordial vertebral system (Kopfurwirbelplatte); and the former, instead of dividing into two layers—one for the wall of the alimentary tube, and another for the wall of the visceral cavity, with a serous space between them as in the trunk—becomes, in conjunction with the latter, perforated by the branchial clefts.

The hæmal portion of the head, therefore, is distinguished from the corresponding portion of the trunk, in presenting metasomatomic clefts, in having no serous cavity, and in having the hæmal axis external to the hæmal arches of its sclerotomes. We are not yet in possession of sufficient data to explain these various peculiarities of the head in the hæmapod. I must direct attention, however, to the following facts, which bear upon the cephalic exclusion of the hæmal axis. The anterior portion of the primordial alimentary tube, from the cul-de-sac in which it terminates in front, back to its vitellary margin, consists essentially of two parts; a cephalic portion, terminated by the cul-de-sac, is bounded laterally by the "visceral laminæ," from the so-called first pair of laminæ backwards, and becomes developed into the pharynx; and a cervico-thoraco-abdominal portion, bounded laterally by the anterior portion of the primordial vertebral system of the trunk and the corresponding portions of the primary ventral wall. The primordial hæmal axis (heart and branchial artery) is formed within the pericardiac space, on the inferior aspect of the posterior or trunk portion of the tube from which are afterwards developed the œsophagus, stomach, duodenum, liver, pancreas, and lungs. The heart and pericardium are at first comparatively large, project downwards, and only pass backwards at a comparatively late period into the interior of the hæmal arches of the thoracic sclerotomes in reptiles, birds, and mammals. The cephalic portion, or pharyngeal cul-de-sac, on the other hand, does not present originally any traces of the development of the hæmome. This may be to a certain extent explained by the great comparative development of the cephalic portion of what would have been formerly considered the "serous layer" of the blastoderma. The extremities of the so-called "first visceral laminæ" have in fact approached one another below, before the apex of the cardiac tube has advanced so far forwards as to communicate with them. The precise conditions, however, which determine the formation of the sclerous elements of the mandibular, hyoidean, and branchial arches on the inside of the corresponding vascular arches, remain to be ascertained by future inquiry. At present I can only conceive of these conditions as in some way dependent upon the developmental relations to which I have alluded.

These relations of the hæmal arches of the head must be taken into consideration in determining the signification of the branchial arches of the amphibian and fish. The division of the sclerous system into dermo, neuro, and splanchno skeleton was first systematically carried out by Carus. I was early brought, by the study of the works of the philosophical and ingenious Dresden anatomist, to adopt this threefold division of the skeleton. I have latterly, however, been induced to reject as untenable the doctrine of a splanchno-skeleton. I believe it may be confidently asserted that no structure referable in any way to the skeleton is developed in or around any portion of the mucous layer of the vertebrate alimentary tube beyond that part of it which belongs to the head; in other words, beyond the pharynx, or part perforated by the branchial clefts. The mandibular, hyoidean, branchial, and pharyngeal arches, the cartilages of the larynx, trachea, bronchial tubes, and lungs, are all primarily developed in immediate relation to the cephalic portion of the alimentary tube.

It is remarkable that those who refer the branchial and pharyngeal arches to a splanchno-skeleton have not adduced the external position of the hæmal axis to these arches as an argument in support of their opinion. On this ground, however, the hyoidean, and, I believe, the mandibular arch also, as internal to the first, or to the first and second aortic arches, would be also thrown into the system of the splanchno-skeleton. Carus has accordingly done so in the case of the hyoidean arch; but Professor Owen, overlooking the fundamental embryological relations which indissolubly connect all these arches as serially homologous, holds the hyoidean to be a "strong, bony, persistent arch of the true endo-skeleton;" while, on grounds which appear to me altogether secondary, he refers the branchial and pharyngeal to the splanchno-skeleton, and thus relieves himself of the onus of determining their "homologies." From the view I have been led to take of this subject, I am under the necessity of considering these arches as true hæmal arches, and as certainly referable to the endo-skeleton as the mandibular arch itself. I also, for the same reason, conceive that the complete morphology of the skeleton of the head includes the homologies of the cartilages of the larynx, trachea, and lungs.

The cartilages and bones developed in the actinal fibrous laminæ are most important elements in the sclerome. In the head they are variously modified and arranged, not only for the protection of organs, but also as a system of props to afford additional security to the fundamental parts of the skeleton. In the trunk they are chiefly subservient to the myome. They thus exhibit their highest development in the framework of the limbs, for the entire constitution of which they alone, I believe, supply the elements.

The bony rays developed in the metamyotomic laminæ of fishes exhibit the most elementary forms of actinapophyses. Here again I must differ from Professor Owen, who limits the number of these "diverging appendages" to one—generally attached to the pleurapophysis—on each side of the vertebra. This "epipleural element" he considers to be a part of the endo-skeleton, while the additional radiating bony filaments he refers to the exo-skeleton, and recognises in them a manifestation of the principle of "vegetative repetition." While I admit that the so-called "epipleural spines" are the most constant of these bones, yet, as the others are developed in the same fibrous membrane, which has, moreover, no primary relation to the dermal system, I cannot see on what grounds they can be excluded from the endo-skeleton. As, again, I cannot avail myself of the principle of "vegetative repetition" in a morphological inquiry, and as I find all of these "additional ribs" connected with important modifications of the myome, I account for their presence teleologically, and hold, therefore, that they must also be explicable morphologically.

The question as to the typical number of actinapophyses in a sclerotome cannot, it appears to me, be determined in the present state of the science. Their existence and general morphological relations having been ascertained, the conditions which determine their position and number must remain for future inquiry.

On these grounds I cannot, with Professor Owen, regard the branchiostegal rays on each side collectively as a single "diverging appendage." I not only recognise on each side of the hyoidean arch of the osseous fish one series, but a double series of actinapophyses. This double arrangement of the branchiostegal rays has not, so far as I know, been recorded. One series of these rays is attached along the outer, and therefore morphologically anterior surface, and the other along the inner, and therefore posterior surface of the cerato-hyal;

but as the two series are attached, the one to the upper, the other to the lower part of the bone, they form together a single range for the support of the branchiostegal fold.

I recognise a similar but more developed form of this double arrangement of actinapophyses in the variously-modified cartilaginous or semi-osseous double styles or plates which are attached to the convexities of the branchial arches for the support of the respiratory membrane of osseous fishes. These branchial actinapophyses also exhibit that jointed or multi-articulate structure so generally presented by the rays of the mesial and bilateral fins.

This leads me to observe that I have not been able to satisfy myself of the truth of the doctrine at present generally held, that the inter-spinous bones and rays of the mesial fins belong to the dermo-skeleton. I admit that, in certain instances, these fins present more or less dermal bone in their composition ; but I cannot see how fin-rays, from which the skin and subcutaneous texture may be stripped, can be considered as portions of the dermo-skeleton. These rays can scarcely, I conceive, be referred to the dermo-skeleton in the cartilaginous fishes ; and as the rays of the bilateral fins resemble those of the mesial in their histological as well as in their general relations, they ought to be placed in the same category. The rays of the mesial, as well as of the bilateral fins cannot, therefore, in my opinion, be consistently excluded from that portion of the sclerome usually denominated neuro- or endo-skeleton ; but like other elements of the endo-skeleton which approach the dermal sclerous fibrous lamina, they may coalesce with dermal bone.

I have been led to consider the inter-spinous bones and mesial fin-rays as actinapophyseal elements. With reference to the mesial position and characters of these bones, I would remark, that it appears to me to be quite permissible, on morphological grounds, to look upon each inter-spinous bone, with its corresponding fin-ray, as consisting of a right and left actinapophysis mesially united—that is, to consider the right and left halves of which they consist in the young fish as fundamental elements of opposite sides of the body. This view of the actinapophyseal character of the bones of the mesial fins appears to be supported by the occurrence of double anal and caudal fins in monstrous fishes, and also by the so-called urohyal bone. The relations of this bone appear to me to indicate that it is not referable to the basohyal elements of the arch, but to the actinapophyseal. I recognise it as consisting of two of these elements fused together at the mesial plane.

I am further supported in the view which I take of the actinapophyseal character of the inter-spinous bones and mesial fin-rays, by the well-known and hitherto unexplained antero-posterior duplicity which they exhibit in certain fishes. In the Pleuronectidæ, for instance, the inter-spinous bones are attached in pairs, one bone in front and another behind each spinous process. In these instances I conceive we have examples of mesial anterior and posterior actinapophyses in each sclerotome. The corresponding fin-rays are, it is true, alternate, but this does not affect the general principle, when we keep in view the remarkable antero-posterior movements of certain elements of the sclerome discovered by Remak in the embryo, and the highly-important observations of Professor Owen with reference to the alternations of some of the elements of the spine in certain reptiles and birds—alternations undoubtedly referable to movements of the kind discovered by Remak.

In the head actinapophyseal elements are generally bar-like, or more or less flattened from without inwards. From the peculiar forms assumed by these elements in the head, an anterior actinapophysis of one sclerotome may meet a posterior one from the sclerotome in front, so as to form together a bar-like or flattened bridge, or buttress, between the two. These bridge-like connections of neighbouring sclerotomes are not unfrequently completed by the fibrous basis of the sclerome. In birds, and the typical lacertians, indeed, in which the actinapophyseal elements exhibit remarkable adaptations, the fibrous matrix in which they are imbedded, and by which they are connected, forms an essential feature of their arrangement.

The actinapophyseal elements of a sclerotome are to be distinguished as hæmal and neural—those attached to the hæmal and those connected with the neural arches. The hæmactinapophyses are the most usual and numerous, and have hitherto been alone recognised as such by anatomists. I shall therefore at present only remark, in reference to the neuractinapophyses, that I consider as such the neural range of "additional ribs," the interspinous bones and rays of the dorsal fins, and of the neural half of the caudal fin in cartilaginous fishes, and also the inter-neural cartilages, to which attention was first directed by Joh. Müller. In the cephalic sclerotomes, the neuractinapophyses constitute the so-called "sense capsules" and the system of "muco-dermal bones." The so-called "muco-dermal bones" have been latterly referred by the continental anatomists to the dermo-skeleton. I am, nevertheless, inclined to believe, that when the general morphological relations of these bones, and their existence in at least reptiles and birds, are taken into consideration, they will be admitted as elements of the endo-skeleton. They are not the only bones in the head of the osseous fish which are traversed by mucous tubes; but from their superficial position they generally are so, and from the same circumstance are frequently overlaid by dermal bone. Professor Owen has adopted the doctrine of the muco-dermal character of these bones, and includes the lachrymal among them. Believing the lachrymal to be a cephalic neuractinapophysis, I cannot assent to the rejection of this bone from the endo-skeleton, and more particularly to referring the perforation which generally characterises it to the system of dermal mucous canals. The lachrymal canal is a metasomatomic opening. It is the remaining portion of the cleft between the maxillary and palatine visceral laminæ. The lachrymal bone is situated at the upper end of this cleft, at the extremity of that metasomatomic space in which the eyeball is situated—viz. the orbit. The lachrymal bone is therefore grooved or perforated by an integumentary canal, which, as a portion of one of the original clefts in the wall of the face, is retained in the adult as a passage for the secretion of the lachrymal gland.

The most important cephalic neuractinapophyses are those fibrous, cartilaginous, or osseous structures which support and protect the nose, eye, and ear. They exhibit their fundamental character most distinctly in the cyclostomatous and plagiostomatous fishes, in which they consist of sessile or pedunculated cartilaginous cups or capsules attached to the outer margins of the cranium. In the other vertebrata these "sense-capsules," variously modified in form and texture, become more or less involved in the wall of the cranium. In their fundamental form they must be considered as parts of the endo-skeleton, homologous in the hæmapod with those parts of the dermo-skeleton of certain neuropods, such as the crustacean, which carry the organs of sense, and are serially homologous with its masticatory and ambulatory limbs.

Professor Owen refers the "sense-capsules" to the splanchno-skeleton. But the organs of hearing, vision, and smell, are developed not from or in connection with the mucous layer of the blastoderma, but from the so-called "serous layer"—that is, from that superficial layer which produces the skin, its appendages, the cerebro-spinal axis, and the primordial vertebral system. It appears to me that it would have been more natural to refer the sense-capsules, as De Blainville did, to the dermal system; but their histological, embryological, and general relations, indicate, I believe, their real nature as parts of the neuro-skeleton.

The most complex and important development of the actinapophyseal elements of the sclerome are those arrangements which constitute the framework of the limbs. As, however, I find myself compelled to dissent from Professor Owen's determination of the anterior pair of limbs as the hæmal arch and "divergent appendages" of the occipital vertebra; and as I also dissent from his general doctrine of limbs, I shall reserve my observations on the subject for a separate communication.

The osseous formations in connection with the subintegumentary fibrous lamina constitute collectively the dermal portion of the sclerome. As the constitution of the exo-skeleton does not immediately bear on the object I have in view, I shall merely observe, in reference to it, that a more extended and systematic investigation of its structure and morphology is at present very much to be desired.

From the statements already made, it will be observed that I consider that the most general conception we can at present reach of a vertebra or sclerotome, is a somewhat expanded or detailed form of Von Baer's ideal transverse section of the vertebrate animal, which is based on the original neural and hæmal foldings of the blastoderma from the sides of the corda dorsalis. With reference to the further development of the idea, I venture to express my decided opinion, that formally to announce the archetypal number of elements in a segment of the skeleton is a premature attempt at generalisation, and that a dogmatic statement on a subject of this kind must have a greater tendency to check legitimate induction the higher the authority from which it emanates.

The modifications which occur in the Sclerotomes towards or at the front of the Head.—It is generally admitted, that in tracing backwards the series of sclerotomes in a vertebrate animal, they become modified in form in proportion to the withdrawal of the other organic systems, until at last the sclerotome may become a mere nodule or filament. Although it is also generally admitted that a certain amount of deterioration takes place in the sclerotome towards the anterior part of the cranium, the nature and extent of the change has not hitherto been precisely determined. I find that it presents, according as the nasal fossæ are, or are not present, two forms.

First general form of Deterioration.—The deterioration is much less in the first form than in the second. The first form may be best observed in the mammal, in which alone the nasal cavities are complete. The nasal fossæ of the mammal are bounded below by a series of at least four hæmal arches, the palatine, maxillary, intermaxillary, and ali-nasal, which, along with the soft parts, form collectively the palatal vault of the mouth, with the upper lip and under surface of the external nose; these three continuous surfaces forming in fact the anterior part of the sternal or hæmal aspect of the head, the palatal portion being inclosed within the mouth in consequence of the elongation of the lower jaw. If now the sclerotome, of which the intermaxillary bones constitute the hæmal arch, be examined, it will be found to present superiorly the two nasal bones, as its neural elements; but which, instead of bounding, along with their corresponding centrum, a neural space, assist the intermaxillary bones in forming two spaces, which are completed, and at the same time separated from one another by the centrum, which, no longer separating a neural from a hæmal space, separates a pair of lateral neurohæmal spaces, or nostrils, from one another. This modification of the sclerotome depends, primarily, on its not being required to enclose a segment of the neural axis; and, secondarily, on its co-operating in the formation of the nostrils. This form of sclerotome, in which the centrum passes from above downwards, I denominate *catacentric*, to distinguish it from the ordinary form in which the centrum passes across, which, therefore, I also occasionally find it convenient to indicate as the *diacentric* form of sclerotome. The passage from the diacentric to the catacentric form is exemplified in the ethmoidal sclerotome, the hæmal arch of which, consisting of the pair of maxillary bones, enters into the formation of the nasal passages. The centrum of this sclerotome has assumed the form of a more or less compressed plate, which, while it retains its lateral connection with the neurapophyses, extends at the same time more or less upwards into the neural space, and downwards between the nostrils, which, under this sclerotome and the one behind, consist of a mesially bisected hæmal cavity.

The anterior terminal sclerotome in the non-proboscidian mammals is cartilaginous and catacentric. Its neuro-hæmal chambers are closed in front by the junction of the anterior margins of its neural and hæmal elements. In consequence, too, of the position of the external nostrils, which, as metasomatomic openings, are situated between the hæmal elements of this sclerotome and those of the sclerotome immediately behind, its hæmal elements are tilted forwards, so that towards their junction with the neural elements their sternal margins are continuous with the dorsal line of the nose. In the more developed forms of this sclerotome, from one to three hæmactinapophyses on each side enter largely into its arrangements.

In the proboscidian mammals, instead of being greatly developed, as might naturally be expected, this sclerotome is, on the contrary, much simplified. In the tapir the hæmapophyses have disappeared, while in the elephant the neurapophyses alone exist in a comparatively undeveloped form. I believe, however, that it will ultimately be admitted, that the proboscis is not a mere elongation or development of the external nose, like the pseudo-proboscis of the bear, racoon, and coati, but a syssomatome.

Second general form of Deterioration of the Sclerotome at the front of the Head.—The character of this form of deterioration may be best observed in the intermaxillary or vomerine sclerotome of the osseous fish. Instead of being reserved for the purpose of forming portions of nostrils, the neural space no longer required for the lodgment of a segment of the neural axis disappears entirely, the neurapophyses being at the same time generally absent. The centrum may also disappear, or may exist in the form of a cartilaginous nodule; a pair of neurapophyses may therefore form the entire sclerotome. These hæmapophyses generally extend outwards and downwards from one another, or from the centrum if it exists at the mesial plane. They form together, therefore, an arch suspended at its centre, with its piers unsupported. The hæmapophyses of the two sclerotomes immediately behind form respectively two arches, the maxillary and palatal, suspended by their centres from the base of the skull. The centres of these two arches are, however, morphologically their approximated piers, the actual centres; their sternal or hæmal conjunctions are not completed in the osseous fish, in consequence of the non-formation of the nasal fossæ. These three incomplete hæmal arches retain their embryonic form of imperfect visceral laminæ. They do not bridge across to form a palate, and therefore the first complete hæmal arch in the osseous fish is the mandibular. The palate in it is, therefore, like that of the mammal, morphologically a portion of the external surface of the animal. But they differ from one another in this respect, that the palate of the fish is a primary, that of the mammal a secondary surface.

Number of Sclerotomes in the Vertebrate Head.—It has tended not a little to throw discredit on the vertebral theory of the skull, that its advocates have differed much as to the number of its constituent vertebræ. I am inclined to think that these discordant views are the result of a tendency in later inquirers to be influenced by that *à priori*, or "transcendental" method, characteristic of those German and French anatomists with whom the subject originated. For my own part, so far from coinciding in the received opinion, that the number of segments in the vertebrate head is the same in all its forms, I believe that it varies. I shall state in the sequel the grounds on which I hold the number of sclerotomes to vary slightly in the heads of the ordinary forms of vertebrata. I am, however, inclined to believe that there are indications afforded by embryology and comparative anatomy, of the existence in certain forms of vertebrate head of a considerably greater number of sclerotomes than has been generally supposed. I base this conjecture, first, on the system of cartilaginous nasal segments in the cyclostomes ; and, secondly, on the circumstance that if the head is to be distinguished embryologically from the trunk, by the presence of "visceral laminæ" separated by clefts, then not only the cyclostomes, but the still more remarkable branchiostoma indicate a number of cephalic segments, and a form of vertebrate structure, of which, in the present state of the science, it can only be said that such a form is deducible from the vertebrate type.

I recognise in the head of the fish, exclusive of the cyclostomes, six sclerotomes ; in that of the amphibian and reptile also six ; with the exception of the crocodiles, in which the seventh is feebly developed ; in that of birds, six ; and in that of mammals, exclusive of the proboscidians, seven.

I find it more convenient to examine these sclerotomes from before backwards ; and I distinguish them provisionally by the following designations :—

1. RHINAL.
2. VOMERINE.
3. ETHMOIDAL.
4. PRE-SPHENOIDAL.
5. POST-SPHENOIDAL.
6. TEMPORAL.
7. OCCIPITAL.

Keeping out of view, therefore, the cyclostomatous fishes and the proboscidian mammals, which present indications of a greater number, the vertebrata generally possess all the sclerotomes enumerated above, except the rhinal, which exists only in mammals and crocodiles.

On a Fundamental Difference between the Cranium of the Mammal and that of the Bird, Reptile, Amphibian, and Osseous Fish.—In my earlier attempts to unravel the intricacies of this subject, I found myself opposed by difficulties in passing from the mammalian to the lower form of cranium, and *vice versa*. I afterwards discovered that this mainly depended on the reciprocal development and atrophy of the meta-neurapophyseal elements of four sclerotomes in the two forms. In consequence of this, we had been hitherto confounding the frontal bone, or meta-neurapophysis of the ethmoidal sclerotome of the mammal, with the so-called "proper frontal bone," which is in fact the meta-neurapophysis of the pre-sphenoidal sclerotome of the bird, reptile, amphibian, and osseous fish, an element of which there are, and this only in rare instances, faint or doubtful traces in the former; and *pari passu*, we had been confounding the parietal bones, the double meta-neurapophysis of the post-sphenoidal sclerotome of the mammal, with the so-called parietals, the largely-developed meta-neurapophyses of the temporal sclerotome of the bird, reptile, amphibian, and osseous fish, elements which are much reduced in size, and masked in the former. Among other important organic relations indicated in the existence of these two forms of cranium, I would here more particularly note their bearing on the encephalon. Of the two forms, that of the fish, reptile, and bird, while it adheres to the common type, is modified mainly in relation to the organs of smell, sight, and hearing. That of the mammal, also adhering to the common type, is modified in relation to the cerebrum proper—to that nervous structure superimposed upon the series of ganglionic masses at the base of the brain which are serially homologous with the spinal cord.

RHINAL SCLEROTOME.—*In Mammals.*—The principal parts of the cranium which remain unossified in the mammal are the nasal septum and the cartilages of the nose. Of these, the unossified portion of the nasal septum is the anterior prolongation of the basal portion of the so-called "primordial cranium." It is consequently a continuous mass of cartilage, but is nevertheless referable to three sclerotomes ; its superior portion completing the centrum of the ethmoidal ; its lower portion the centrum of the vomerine ; and its anterior that of the rhinal sclerotome.

The rhinal sclerotome in the mammal is fibrous, cartilaginous, and catacentric. Its centrum, formed by the anterior portion of the nasal septum, extends from its neural to its hæmal margin. Its right and left neural elements are the so-called superior or triangular cartilages of the nose. They may be continuous with or merely attached to the neural edge of their centrum. The anterior margins, or angles of these cartilages, and the corresponding point of the septum or centrum is the absolute anterior termination of the animal, or more precisely of its morphological axis. The ridge of the nose downwards and forwards to that point is neural or dorsal ; beyond it, although continued in the same line, the ridge is hæmal or sternal.

The two alar cartilages are the hæmapophyses of this sclerotome. Variously modified in form, they are more or less firmly attached to the lower margins of the upper cartilages. In front they are attached to the septum, to which also they are more loosely connected round the tip of the nose, being frequently folded in on the ridges of the septum. In the fibrous membrane occupying the sides of the space between the posterior margins of the alar cartilages which together constitute the hæmal arch of their sclerotome, and the anterior margins of the intermaxillary bones which form the hæmal arch of the succeeding sclerotome, there are generally a number of variously modified cartilaginous pieces. These pieces are teleologically highly important elements of the rhinal sclerotome. Morphologically they are actinapophyses. When fully developed, they are three on each side attached to the alar cartilage. In the ox and other ruminants, the superior actinapophysis is an irregular lamina, which, imbedded in the fibrous membrane, assists in supporting the wall of the nostril. The second is a thick, short bar, articulated to the alar cartilage in front, and jointed behind to the corresponding element of the vomerine sclerotome, by which arrangement it is immediately connected with the inferior turbinal bone, which is an actinapophyseal element of the ethmoidal sclerotome. The third or inferior rhinal actinapophysis is a crutch-like cartilage, articulated to the alar element by its stem, which is bent inwards, then downwards, and outwards to the margin of the nostril, which it supports by its curved transverse portion. In the bear, racoon, and coati, the two superior actinapophyses are much developed, and, along with the neurapophyseal, form the cartilaginous wall of the trunk-like nose, or pseudoproboscis. In the phacochoer the acuminated nasal bones curve down toward the intermaxillary, so as to separate the neural elements of the rhinal sclerotome from one another. The rhinal centrum is therefore much diminished in extent; but is, at the same time, strengthened for the support of the nasal buckler by a deposit of bone. The hæmapophyseal and actinapophyseal elements are thus pushed outwards, along with the nostril, so as to produce that breadth for which the snout of this pig is remarkable. In man the rhinal actinapophyses are reduced to the sesamoid cartilages. In the solipeds they disappear altogether. The so-called semilunar cartilage of the horse is, in fact, the alar cartilage itself, the internal inferior angle of which, much elongated, supports the inner margin of the nostril, as the transverse limb of the crutch-like inferior actinapophysis of the ruminant supports the outer margin of the orifice.

The Rudimentary Rhinal Sclerotome in the Crocodiles.—In the crocodiles, as in the mammalia, the vomerine sclerotome is traversed by the nasal fossæ, which open therefore in front, instead of behind it, as in the other reptiles and in birds. It is evident therefore, that if the crocodiles do not possess, like the mammalia, a rhinal sclerotome, their external nostrils must present an exceptional arrangement; for, instead of being metasomatomic, they must be terminal. I find, however, that in the alligator the hoods which extend from the anterior inner margins and septum of the osseous external nostrils consist of dense fibrous tissue, covered by the muscles which act upon them. This double fibro-muscular hood is so arranged on each side as to have the oblique slit-like nostrils situated between their outer margins and the intermaxillary edges. If a plate of cartilage were developed in the margin of each hood, the whole arrangement would occupy the position and exhibit the relations of an ali-nasal cartilage—a rhinal hæmapophysis, or neurapophysis, as in the elephant.

VOMERINE SCLEROTOME.—*In Mammals.*—In the mammal the vomerine is a perfect catacentric sclerotome. The nasal bones are its neural elements, as they occasionally run together, and are evidently, as has been generally admitted, serially homologous with the frontals and parietals; they must be viewed as metaneurapophyses, the neurapophyses being absent in the absence of a nervous centre. The intermaxillaries meeting below form the hæmal arch, and the centrum consists of the vomer, with a corresponding portion of the cartilaginous nasal septum.

The vomer is a bone peculiarly mammalian. It may be said to make its appearance as a developed element, along with the completed nasal fossæ. But its development in the mammalian series is not only dependent on the nasal fossæ, but on the intermaxillaries, with which, as will be shown in the sequel, it is invariably connected. Its passage backwards under the centrum of the ethmoidal sclerotome to abut against that of the pre-sphenoidal, is, as will also appear, a mammalian peculiarity, and an instance of that antero-posterior elongation and of that overlapping arrangement so frequent in the adaptation of the cephalic centrums to one another.

When the inferior turbinal bone, an actinapophysis of the ethmoidal sclerotome, is highly developed, as in the ruminants, a strong flattened bar of fibro-cartilage is attached to the inner aspect of the ascending process of the intermaxillary, and widening out into a soft curved cartilaginous plate, completes the fore part of the inferior turbinal, connecting it at the same time to the second actinapophysis or turbinal process of the ali-nasal cartilage. I look upon this appendage as a hæmactinapophysis of the vomerine sclerotome; and serially homologous with the second or turbinal hæmactinapophysis of the rhinal, and with the turbinal hæmactinapophysis of the ethmoidal sclerotomes. These hæmactinapophyses have all of them been enclosed within the nasal chamber during development; having passed in through the metasclerotomic clefts, instead of forming parts of the nasal wall, or projecting from its outer aspect.

Vomerine Sclerotome in the Crocodiles.—It is remarkable that the familiar fact of the peculiar position of the external nostrils of the crocodiles should not hitherto have attracted attention. They open in front of the intermaxillaries as in the mammals; whereas, in the typical lacertians, and in the extinct plesiosaurs, ichthyosaurs, and pterodactyles, in the ophidians, amphibians, and birds, they open behind these bones. On this peculiarity in the crocodiles depends the very perfect development of the anterior part of the nasal septum. Along with the complete and pervious intermaxillary arch, we find a complete although cartilaginous vomer. Of that part of the extended nasal septum of the crocodiles, corresponding to the mammalian nasal septum, the only ossified portion is an elongated single or double slip along the lower edge of its ethmoidal region, and continuous with the elongated presphenoidal centrum. Professor Owen considers this slip of bone as the vomer. I will only observe at present that, holding the vomer to be invariably in relation to the intermaxillaries, I can only conceive, as the vomer in the crocodile, that elongated cartilaginous portion of the nasal septum which extends beneath the elongated nasal bones to the intermaxillary suture.

Vomerine Sclerotome in Typical Lacertians.—In the proper lizards this sclerotome is imperforate. The intermaxillaries not only close in at the palate, but in front also; the more or less elongated and combined ascending processes joining the united or distinct nasal bones. The centrum is represented by the anterior part of the cartilaginous septum. The two bones, usually described as the double vomer of the lizard, belong, as I shall endeavour to show in the sequel, to the succeeding sclerotome—the ethmoidal.

Vomerine Sclerotome in Birds.—The vomerine sclerotome of the bird consists principally of the intermaxillaries, but partly of the persistent anterior portion of the primordial cranium. The intermaxillaries speedily unite below and in front, so as to form the first and principal part of the beak. Their united ascending processes extend up to the so-called "principal frontal bone," and separate completely the so-called nasal bones. In the sequel the evidence will be adduced on which I found my belief that the bone called in birds the "frontal," or "principal frontal," is not the frontal of the mammal; but that the two so-called nasal bones in the bird are the two halves of that bone which in the mammals is called frontal. If so, where are the nasal bones of the bird?

as the ascending processes of their intermaxillaries, which occupy the proper position of the nasals, have not been observed as separate centres of ossification; and as the greater number of chelonian reptiles want these bones, and resemble birds in the general character and horny covering of their beaks, I am inclined to believe that the nasal bones are deficient as ossified elements in the bird. In young birds, after boiling or maceration, the osseous elements of the beak may be removed, and the anterior part of the primordial cranium brought into view. In the fore part of its septum we again recognise the vomerine centrum, but more or less deficient in certain birds from the septal perforation peculiar to them. The upper margin of the cartilaginous septum, where it is in contact with the ascending processes of the intermaxillaries, flattens out into a lamina, which partly roofs over the external nostril on each side. These marginal processes of the cartilaginous vomerine centrum extend down in front, so as to line the fore and under part of the nasal fossæ, projecting somewhat behind the intermaxillary margin of the external nostril. The broad projecting upper portion of the cartilaginous septum occupies the position of the nasal bones, while the inferior portions project from behind the intermaxillaries, like opercular actinapophyses. In the chick the part of the primordial cranium just described as belonging to the vomerine sclerotome presents an opaque aspect and fibro-cartilaginous structure, contrasting with the hyaline cartilage posterior to it—a peculiarity pointed out by Reichert as characteristic of certain portions of the primordial cranium. It will be observed that I do not consider the bone or bones usually called "vomer" in the bird as correctly designated. In the sequel I shall indicate the grounds on which I hold these bones to be the upper elements of the palatine arch.

The Vomerine Sclerotome in Chelonian Reptiles.—The intermaxillaries in the chelonian, united below, complete the front of the palate, alveolar margin, and floor of the nasal fossæ. The only trace of ascending processes which they present is a compressed spine, which projects upwards at their junction in the median line of the nasal opening of the cranium. The lateral margins of that opening are formed by the maxillaries alone; its upper margin by the so-called pre-frontals, except in Hydromedusa and certain fossil forms. The cartilaginous septum of the nasal fossæ extends up from the intermaxillary suture to that of the pre-frontals.

Is the chelonian vomerine sclerotome modelled on that of the crocodile, or of the bird? The chelonian presents the first stage in the remarkable development of the nasal passages exhibited by the crocodiles. But the general deficiency of the nasal bones, the indications of ascending processes of the intermaxillaries in the mesial plane, the formation of the posterior margins of the external nostrils by the maxillaries, appear to me to show that in the construction of its vomerine sclerotome, the chelonian differs from the crocodiles, and resembles the typical lacertians, the ophidians, amphibians, and the birds. The cartilaginous lining of its nasal fossæ, a remnant of its primordial cranium, projects, in general, a little beyond the margins of the osseous nostrils, as in birds; but in Trionyx and Chelys, the projecting margins run forward together in the form of a double cartilaginous proboscis.

The Vomerine Sclerotome in the Osseous Fishes.—I have already described the general constitution of the vomerine sclerotome of the osseous fish, as one form of deterioration of the fore part of the cranium. Its centrum, the vomer, when it is present, is merely a cartilaginous nodule in the longitudinal axis of the basis of the cranium, in front of the bone usually described as the "vomer," but which I believe to be the centrum of the ethmoidal sclerotome; the neural elements are those scale-like bones, which Cuvier recognises, I believe correctly, as the nasals. Professor Owen considers these bones to be the turbinal divisions of the olfactory "sense-capsules;" and, according to his doctrine of the sense-capsules, elements of the splanchno-skeleton. If Professor Owen understands by the turbinal divisions of the olfactory sense-capsules, bones homologous with the inferior turbinated, or even the so-called ethmoidal turbinated bones of the mammal, it is difficult to understand, on embryological principles, how, as splanchnic bones, and as developed in connection with the maxillaries, they come to be situated under the integument of the upper surface of the head. It is, moreover, questionable, whether the sclerous capsule of this, or of any of the special sense-organs, is ever divided, and its parts separated from one another, under such relations as those presented by the so-called "turbinals" and "ethmoidal" of the osseous fish.

The intermaxillaries form the principal and more peculiar elements of this form of vomerine sclerotome. The nasal fossæ being entirely absent, the merely fibrous olfactory sense-capsule is subcutaneous, or partly under cover of the nasal bones (turbinals); the vomer is not developed as a septum, but merely to supply a fulcrum for the intermaxillaries, which may even constitute the entire sclerotome, but are never united below, so as to form a complete hæmal arch.

THE ETHMOIDAL SCLEROTOME.—The ethmoidal sclerotome, and the presphenoidal immediately behind it, present, in the different forms of vertebrata, various remarkable modifications of their elements, partly dependent on the position of the olfactory lobes of the brain, partly on the position of the olfactory capsules themselves, partly on peculiar adjustments of the nasal fossæ, and on the arrangements subservient to mastication.

The withdrawal from behind forwards of the neural axis, in the course of development, from the posterior extremity of the neural canal, is accompanied by well-known changes in the evacuated but rapidly-increasing posterior trunk sclerotomes. Corresponding, but much more remarkable changes, to which attention has not been hitherto sufficiently directed, accompany the withdrawal from before backwards of the anterior part of the brain from the ethmoidal and presphenoidal sclerotomes. The neural portions of these sclerotomes assume more or less of the catacentric character—they become *demicatacentric*. The neural chamber of the ethmoidal sclerotome of the mammal, in addition to a portion of the cerebrum proper, lodges its homologous segment of the neural axis. In the bird the neural chamber of this sclerotome is completely evacuated by the neural axis, which not only leaves it, but withdraws in part also from the presphenoidal. The absence of the anterior extremity of the neural axis from the neural chamber of the ethmoidal sclerotome is accompanied by the division of that chamber into a right and left compartment by a mesially laminar centrum, the two compartments being occupied by the olfactory capsules. The olfactory lobes in the bird are not only withdrawn from the ethmoidal sclerotome, but retreat to a certain distance backwards in the neural chamber of the presphenoidal. To this extent the chamber becomes catacentric; but instead of its two resulting compartments being occupied by new structures, having only to transmit the olfactory nerves, their outer walls collapse upon the mesially laminar centrum, and very generally disappear almost altogether, so as to leave the nerves uncovered on the sides of the laminar centrum as they pass forward to the ethmoidal chambers. The neural chamber of the ethmoidal sclerotome of the bird, containing only the olfactory capsules, is so connected with the bones of the face and with the neural arch and centrum of the presphenoidal, as to be more or less movable along with the lower mandible. The ethmoidal in the mammal is thus seen to be the anterior cerebral sclerotome, while in the bird it becomes the posterior facial sclerotome.

In the reptile both the ethmoidal and presphenoidal (?)[*] sclerotomes are evacuated by the neural axis, the olfactory nerves alone passing along in the compressed tubular, partially-catacentric neural chamber of the latter—the olfactory capsules occupying the right and left chambers of the former. In reptiles, however, the very varied forms assumed by the bones of the face, and more particularly by those of the palatine arch, in relation to the nostrils, and the arrangements for mastication, produce numerous remarkable modifications of these two sclerotomes.

In passing from the reptile to the fish, the ethmoidal sclerotome may be said to gather together its scattered elements, and to present a centrum and neural arch frequently as compact as the human, but modified by the deficiency of nostrils, and by the withdrawal of the neural axis.

Ethmoidal Centrum and Neural Arch in the Mammal.— The human cranium, as the most perfect in the higher of the two forms of skull, will not unfrequently be found to afford a clue to the signification of bones which, being only applied to their final purposes in it, are more or less masked in the other mammalia, and apt to be misunderstood altogether in the fish, reptile, and bird. If we examine in connection the two bony masses, which, in the current nomenclature of human anatomy, are distinguished as frontal and ethmoid, they will be seen to constitute a ring, the space within which is greatly dilated behind, in consequence of the vast expansion, more particularly of the upper and lateral portions of the frontal, while it is diminished to a tubular chink in front, and is so indistinct towards the nasal fossæ that the older anatomists named it "foramen cæcum."(?) The development of this bony ring shows it to consist of five pieces. These are—the mesial plate, including the crista-galli of the ethmoid, the lateral masses of

---

[*] This and the succeeding marks of interrogation we have found in a copy annotated by the author.—EDS.

the same bone, including the corresponding halves of the cribriform lamina, and the two halves of the frontal. We have here, therefore, a centrum, a pair of neurapophyses, and a divided metaneurapophysis. The pair of olfactory nervous centres, which terminate in front the entire series of segments of the neural axis, are the segments of that axis, homologous with this neural arch and centrum. In the mammalia only is the upper part of this neural arch expanded and adapted for the protection of the more or less developed fore part of the cerebrum proper. In the central portion and lateral masses of the ethmoid, and in the frontal bones of the mammal, I recognise the centrum and neural arch of a sclerotome, which I provisionally distinguish as the ethmoidal.

Centrum and Neural Arch of the Ethmoidal Sclerotome in the Osseous Fish.—The more or less concurrent statements of Oken, Bojanus, Geoffroy, Cuvier, and Owen, as well as the relations of the bones themselves, leave no doubt as to the homology of the so-called pre-frontals of the fish. They are neurapophyseal elements, the lateral ethmoidal masses of the mammal in another form, and *minus* the ossified olfactory capsules. The median bone superimposed upon the "pre-frontals" of the fish, and which has been very generally held to be the united nasals, and the spine of the olfactory vertebra, must be homologous with the frontal bone of the mammal if its relations to the "pre-frontals" and olfactory nerves of the former are compared with those of the ethmoid and frontal bones, and the olfactory nerves of the latter. Professor Owen, while he adopts the determination of the superior median bone as the united nasals, also holds by the hitherto unanimous opinion of anatomists, that the median bone armed with teeth, situated below the pre-frontals of the fish, is the vomer. Guided by the ethmoid of the mammal, I cannot see in this bone aught else than the homologue of the central element of the mammalian ethmoid. The vomer is a mammalian bone;

if it appears in the fish at all, it is a cartilaginous or semiossified nodule between the intermaxillaries. That the centrum of the ethmoidal sclerotome in the fish, considered as the homologue of the central plate or bar of the mammalian ethmoid, should carry teeth in the fish, is not more remarkable than that one of the centrums of the cervical vertebræ in that class of animals should be so armed.

Hæmal Arch of the Ethmoidal Sclerotome in the Mammal and Osseous Fish.—I have commenced my account of the morphological constitution of this important sclerotome by pointing out the typical arrangement which its neural arch and centrum present in the mammal and fish. As the arrangement of these parts of this sclerotome becomes much and variously modified in birds, reptiles, and amphibia, in relation to the various forms presented by the organs of smell and the nostrils, it will be necessary, before proceeding further, to examine the constitution of its hæmal arch. Even in its most complex form, this hæmal arch, like those of the rhinal and vomerine sclerotomes, consists of two elements only, the right and left maxillary bones. In the osseous fish they resemble the "lateral frontal processes" in the embryo; they form only an incipient arch like that formed by the vomerine hæmapophyses in front of them. They do not invariably carry teeth. They are variously connected to the hæmapophyses before and behind them, and superiorly to the lateral and fore part of the centrum, neurapophyses, and metaneurapophyses of the neural arch of their own sclerotome.

The maxillaries of the mammal, more or less extended from before backwards, and increased in breadth and depth to adapt them to their functions in mastication; meeting one another below, to form a great part of the vault of the palate, and to assist in the formation of the nasal passages; hollowed out to combine lightness with strength; and buttressed by numerous connections with neighbouring bones, nevertheless retain their connection with the neural portion of their own sclerotome, being attached superiorly to the lateral masses of the ethmoid, and to the frontal. They are not articulated, as in the fish, to their centrum; but those connections to the neurapophyses and metaneurapophyses, which in fish are affected by ligaments, are sutures in the mammal. In the sequel it will be shown, that of the two connections of the maxillary—that to the frontal, and that to the lateral ethmoid —the former is the most constant; presenting in my opinion the fundamental discriminative character of the remarkably modified frontal of the bird, reptile, and amphibian.

The Ethmoidal Sclerotome in the Bird.—The ethmoidal sclerotome is remarkably modified in the bird. It forms no part of the cranium proper, but assumes the position and structure of a facial sclerotome. The bird, like the mammal, has two proper facial sclerotomes. In the former there are the vomerine and the ethmoidal; in the latter the rhinal and vomerine. In the majority of birds, also, the ethmoidal sclerotome, along with the vomerine, moves more or less freely on the presphenoidal. It is, moreover, peculiar in being chiefly devoted to the economy of the organs of smell; in having its metaneurapophyseal elements separated from one another by the passage backwards of the conjoined ascending processes of the intermaxillaries; in the feeble development of its hæmapophyses; and in its cavities being altogether neural, its neurapophyseal elements forming more or less of its palatal aspect.

The metaneurapophyses of the ethmoidal sclerotome of the bird are the so-called nasal bones. From their invariable connections with the maxillaries, I cannot see in these "nasal bones" aught else than the proper frontal bones—the frontals of the mammal. They are separated from one another by the ascending processes of the intermaxillaries; a circumstance which does not militate against their being the right and left halves of a metaneurapophysis. They are more or less elongated in the antero-posterior direction; and they bound the posterior margins of the external nostrils by the descending processes which connect them with their maxillaries. To distinguish them from the metaneurapophyses of the presphenoidal sclerotome, I designate them ethmoido-frontals.

The arrangement of the centrum and neurapophyses of this sclerotome in the bird appears to me to have been in a great measure overlooked, from having been examined in the macerated skull, in which these parts, as consisting principally of cartilage, are to a great extent absent.

The centrum consists of the posterior and greater part of the mesial cartilaginous lamina, the interior portion of which forms the vomerine centrum. The ethmoidal portion of this laminar mesial cartilage flattens out at its upper margin, in the same manner as the vomerine portion in front; and like the flattened upper edge of the so-called "ethmoid bone"—the centrum of the presphenoidal sclerotome behind. In the same manner as the flattened upper margin of the vomerine portion extends outwards on each side, so as to form a hood over the upper and fore part of the external nostrils, the flattened upper margin of the ethmoidal portion of the septum passes outwards on each side, under cover of the ascending processes of the intermaxillary, and under the ethmoido-frontal, extending down more or less to the level of the palatal plate of the maxillary, and then turning in towards the mesial plane, approaches or meets the lower margin of the mesial lamina itself. Posteriorly, these curved cartilaginous plates close in upon the posterior margin of the septum; which is not continuous with the anterior margin of the laminar septum of the presphenoid. They are each, however, perforated or notched for the transmission of the olfactory nerve; and they also leave on each side of the septum at their posterior inferior angles, a space for the posterior nasal orifice. The superior and middle turbinated folds of the nasal chamber on each side are also supported by turbinated cartilaginous projections from the internal surfaces of their plates.

I have already stated that the anterior fibro-cartilaginous portion of the persistent part of the primordial cranium of the bird enters into the structure of its vomerine sclerotome; it will now be observed that its posterior hyaline portion enters into the formation of the ethmoidal sclerotome. In the majority of birds the septal lamina continues cartilaginous, as well as the greater part of the curved lateral plates, with their internal turbinal projections. A more or less extended portion only of each curved plate becomes ossified when it extends inwards across the palate; and the ossified portion becomes anchylosed to the maxillary, or to the descending maxillary process of the ethmoido-frontal ("nasal"), and in many birds to the anterior extremity of the palate bone.

I recognise, therefore, the posterior part of the nasal septum as the centrum; the so-called "nasals" as the meta-neurapophyses; and the more or less ossified lateral and inferior walls of the olfactory chambers as the neurapophyses of the ethmoidal sclerotome of the bird. If it be objected to this determination, that the parts which I consider as neurapophyses are only portions of the olfactory sense-capsules, I would merely observe that these sense-capsules are in fact combined with the neurapophyseal portions of the ethmoidal sclerotome in the bird, as in the primordial cranium of the mammal, reptile, and amphibian, and as in cartilaginous fishes; but that this circumstance in no way nullifies the existence of the neurapophyseal element itself, either in the sclerotome with which the olfactory capsules, or in those with which the ocular and auditory capsules, are connected. I would also observe that I base my determination of the neurapophyseal character of these parts, not merely on their relations in the bird, but on the varied relations exhibited by their corresponding parts in reptiles.

The maxillaries or hæmapophyses of the ethmoidal sclerotome are feebly developed in the bird. Connected above, chiefly to the descending processes of the ethmoido-frontals, and more or less prolonged in the antero-posterior direction, the maxillaries do not invariably complete the hæmal arch. Their region, therefore, of the palate, is more or less completely occupied by the neurapophyseal plates of their own sclerotome.

The Ethmoidal Sclerotome in the Chelonian.—The connection of the maxillaries of the tortoises and turtles, by means of the ascending processes of these bones, with the so-called pre-frontals, appears to me to indicate that the latter are homologous with the ethmoido-frontals of the bird, or the frontals of Mammalia. I recognise in them the meta-neurapophyses of the ethmoidal sclerotome. Each of these bones sends down from its posterior margin a lamina, concave in front, and forming, with the concave under surface of the bone itself, the posterior superior hollow of the nasal fossa. The inner margins of these two descending laminæ give attachment to the anterior margins of the fibro-cartilaginous laminæ, which bound laterally the compressed pre-sphenoidal neural space, and form the so-called interorbital septum. The inner margins of the two descending frontal laminæ are, therefore, separated from one another above by the breadth of the fore part of the groove on the mesial part of the under surface of the combined so-called "frontals." If now the macerated skull of the turtle be examined, it will be found that a complex bony piece, the so-called "vomer," connects by its pair of short divergent upper processes the inferior extremities of the inner margins of the descending frontal processes, converting the space between them into a triangular orifice. This so-called vomer, after sending a horizontal plate backwards between the palatines to form the mesial portion of the common orbital floor, and to support the cartilaginous bar-like centrum of the pre-sphenoid, passes down as the osseous septum of the posterior nares, and terminates in the form of a pentagonal plate in the palate, between the palatines and maxillaries, and in some species in a hexagonal form, between the palatines, the maxillaries, and intermaxillaries. The relations of the ethmoidal neurapophyses to their meta-neurapophyses in the bird, and the presence of the former in the maxillary region of the palate, led me to suspect that the so-called "vomer" of the turtle is the combined neurapophyses of its ethmoidal sclerotome. But its posterior horizontal laminar process which supports the cartilaginous pre-sphenoidal centrum, as well as the process which forms the septum of the posterior nares, indicated the probability of the "vomer" being a still more complex bone. I have not met with the palatal plate as a separate bone in the turtle, although in longitudinal sections I have observed faint indications of its having been so. I find, however, that in certain tortoises, not only is the palatal plate connected by a distinct suture to the upper portion of the so-called "vomer," but it is divided by a similar suture in the mesial line of the palate into two halves. In these tortoises, therefore, the separation of the posterior nares, the junction of the descending processes of the ethmoidofrontals, and the support of the cartilaginous bar-like centrum of the pre-sphenoid, are affected by a distinct bone, which, including its connections to the palatines, presents all the characters of the so-called "vomer" of the bird. But I have already stated my belief that the bone so-called is not the vomer of the bird; and in the sequel I shall state the grounds on which I hold it to be the combined ento-pterygoids—the upper elements of the palatine arch.

Ethmoidal Sclerotome in the Crocodiles.—In the crocodiles proper, and the gavials, the lachrymal is interposed between the so-called pre-frontal and the maxillary. In the alligators the maxillary resumes its connection with the pre-frontal, which it had lost in the two other families on account of the elongation of the snout. The pre-frontals in all the crocodilians are separated from one another mesially by the passage backwards of narrow contiguous processes of the nasals, and by similar processes which pass forwards from the so-called "proper frontals"—in this respect resembling the so-called "nasals" of the bird, which are separated from one another by the ascending processes of the intermaxillaries.

Assuming the relations of the pre-frontals of the crocodilian to the maxillary arch as evidence of their being the meta-neurapophyses of the ethmoidal sclerotome—that is, collectively, the homologue of the mammalian frontal—the next elements of this sclerotome to be determined are its neurapophyses. At this point the type of ethmoidal sclerotome exhibited by the bird, and the modification of that type presented by the chelonian, indicate its character in the crocodilian. The descending processes of the pre-frontals of the crocodiles are connected inferiorly to the ascending processes of the so-called "palate-bones." Now, a bone connected to the homologue of the mammalian frontal cannot well be considered as the palate-bone, even although it be situated between and united by suture to the maxillary and pterygoid. But a bone with such relations, if viewed in the light of the corresponding relations of the ethmoidal neurapophyses of the bird, indicates its own real nature. The ethmoidal neurapophyses of the bird, connected above with the ethmoido-frontals, form below more or less of the palatine vault. The ethmoidal neurapophyses of the chelonians, pushed away forwards and downwards from the ethmoido-frontal by the ento-pterygoid, still form a part of the vault of the palate. (?) In like manner I recognise, in the so-called "palate-bones" of the crocodilian, the neurapophyses of its ethmoidal sclerotome. The ethmoido-frontals and neurapophyses of the bird, form, along with their cartilaginous septum or centrum, a complete catacentric neural ring. The interposition of the ento-pterygoid of the chelonian separates the meta-neurapophyses from the neurapophyses of the ethmoidal sclerotome, and at the same time separates the neural space into an upper portion, mesially divided by the cartilaginous septum or centrum for the passage of the olfactory nerves, and into an inferior, mesially divided by the ento-pterygoid itself for the right and left nasal passages. A similar but somewhat modified change is effected in the ethmoidal sclerotome of the crocodilian, by the interposition of the anterior extremities of its pterygoids—which anterior processes I believe to be, in fact, the ento-pterygoids. These anterior, generally mesially united, processes of the pterygoids of the crocodilian, were considered by Cuvier as representing the under portion of the mammalian vomer. He describes them as two osseous pieces fixed to the inner margins of the "palate-bones," in front of the "anterior frontals," and of that part of the pterygoid which covers the nasal canals. Professor Owen describes these pieces as the "vomer," and as being generally anchylosed to the fore part of the basi-sphenoid; but he adds the following very important observation, which I have verified, that they (the "vomer") form a distinct bone in a species of alligator, which passes so far forward and downwards as to appear in the form of a plate in the vault of the palate, in front of the palate-bones.

That this double bony splint is not a vomer, as Cuvier supposed, must be evident, if the vomer is to be considered as an element of the vomerine sclerotome. It cannot be, as Professor Owen states, a vomer united to the "basi-sphenoid;" because, in front of the elevated, laterally compressed, quadrilateral process which passes forwards and upwards from the centrum of the post-sphenoid, the real axis of the skull is continued forward in the form of a compressed cartilaginous bar, which is the centrum of the pre-sphenoid, and which passes in front into the cartilaginous nasal septum, which constitutes the ethmoidal and vomerine centrums. The crocodilian and chelonian skulls are, in fact, entirely destitute of ossified central elements in front of their post-sphenoidal centrums, the superincumbent framework in these forms of cranium being supported along the base, not by ossified centrums, but by greatly expanded and modified pterygoids, ento-pterygoids, ethmoidal neurapophyses, maxillaries, and inter-maxillaries, immediately above which series of bones lies the persistent central axis of the primordial cranium, as far back as the ossified centrum of the post-sphenoidal sclerotome. In the mesial antero-posterior section of the macerated skull of the *Crocodilus vulgaris*, a suture will be found commencing in front of the common orifice of the Eustachian tubes, and terminating at the lower part of the root of the laterally-compressed post-sphenoidal process already alluded to. In front of this suture, the section presents no traces of central elements, the pterygoids and so-called "palatals" taking their places. In a section of this kind in the Museum of the University of Edinburgh, the extremity of the anterior process of the pterygoid passes forwards and downwards, appearing in the suture between the two "palatines," about an inch from their anterior margins; the right and left portions exposed on the vault of the palate being separated from the "palatines" by surrounding suture, and forming together a narrow double surface, one-eighth of an inch in length. In the section to which I allude, and in similar sections, I observe traces of the line of anchylosis between these anterior processes and the pterygoids themselves. These lines run upwards and forwards, and appear to include the anterior and greater part of the pterygoidal portion of the nasal septum, and the thin plate which, on each side, passes up to be united to the descending process of the "pre-frontal." In disarticulating the skull of the crocodile the pterygoids generally remain attached to the post-sphenoidal centrum, so that the prolonged anterior processes of the former present the appearance of being elongations of the latter, which they in fact are not.

From the foregoing considerations, and on grounds to be explained in the sequel, when the palatine arch or hæmal arch of the pre-sphenoidal sclerotome comes to be examined, I recognise in the crocodilian vomer of Cuvier and Owen the proximal or upper element of the pre-sphenoidal hæmal arch—the same element to which, when existing in certain fishes, Professor Owen applies the sufficiently expressive term ento-pterygoid.

It will now be observed, that in consequence of the great development of the pterygoids, and of the ento-pterygoids in the crocodilian, the latter, extending forward into the neural space of the ethmoidal sclerotome, roof over the greater part, and provide a septum for nearly the whole of that extent of the nasal fossæ, the sides and floors of which are formed by the so-called "palatals" or ethmoidal neurapophyses, and abut against the descending processes of the "pre-frontals" or ethmoido-frontals, without entirely extruding the neurapophyses from these processes, as in the chelonian. There is another minor difference between these parts in the crocodilian and chelonian. In the chelonian, as has been already stated, the ento-pterygoids having pushed the ethmoidal neurapophyses from their natural connection with the descending processes of the ethmoido-frontals, complete, by means of their ascending divergent processes, the triangular space for the olfactory nerves. In the crocodilian, again, the descending processes of the ethmoido-frontals complete the space for the olfactory nerves, by means of a short process from each of them, which, passing inwards, meets its fellow of the opposite side a little above the junctions of the descending processes themselves with the ento-pterygoids. The space left between this transverse commissure above, the combined ento-pterygoids below, and the lower ends of the descending ethmoido-frontal processes laterally, is occupied by a prolongation forwards of the cartilaginous bar-like pre-sphenoidal centrum.

If the bones hitherto considered by comparative anatomists as the "palatines" in the crocodilian, are in reality the neurapophyses of its ethmoidal sclerotome, the question arises— Where are the actual palate-bones? This question comes to be examined in the sequel, when the hæmal arch of the pre-sphenoidal sclerotome, of which these bones are elements, is under consideration. At present I may state that the study of the crania of the bird, lacertian, and ophidian, has led me to recognise as the palate-bone that bone which Cuvier was induced to consider peculiar to the lizard and serpent, and named "os transverse" or "pterygoide externe;" and which Professor Owen also names ecto-pterygoid.

The Ethmoidal Neural Arch and Centrum in the Lacertians.—The maxillaries of the typical lacertians are invariably connected above to the so-called pre-frontals. These pre-frontals are widely separated from one another by the anterior extremities of the so-called "principal frontals," which pass forward, and bound laterally the divided or undivided nasals. The pre-frontals bound the anterior superior angles of the orbits, sending downwards on each side a plate which separates the orbit from the nasal cavity, is more or less intimately connected with the so-called "double vomer," and with the so-called "palatines." I shall, in the sequel, state the grounds on which I hold the "palatines" of the lizard, ophidian, and amphibian, to be its ento-pterygoids, and to be the homologues of the bone or bones which in the bird are considered as the "vomer." I believe the "transverse bones" of the lizard to be actually its palate-bones, pushed backwards and outwards by the greatly-developed ento-pterygoids, and of its so-called "vomer." The so-called "vomer" of the lizard consists of two bones, which form the floor of the nostrils, separated from, but at the same time connected to, one another by the lower margin of the cartilaginous nasal septum, abutting against the intermaxillaries in front, and the so-called "palatines" or ento-pterygoids behind, and leaving a space on each side, wider behind than before, between their outer margins and the maxillaries, for the posterior nares. In some lizards the posterior extremities of the two halves of the "vomer" are separated from the transverse descending plates of the "pre-frontals" by the interposition of the anterior extremities of the ento-pterygoids, but in others they articulate with the pre-fronto-lachrymal. Anatomists appear to have been induced to look upon these two bones in the lizard as the two halves of the vomer, by the same circumstance which has induced them to consider the ento-pterygoids of the bird as its vomer—viz. their position between the posterior nares. But the general relations of the so-called double "vomer" of the lizard indicate that its two halves are homologous with the ethmoidal palate-plates of the chelonian, with the so-called "palatines" or ethmoidal neurapophyses of the crocodilian, with the corresponding cartilaginous or osseous pieces in the bird, and with the lateral masses of the ethmoid in the mammal. It appears to me that the ethmoidal neural arch and centrum form a catacentric arrangement, the two compartments of which constitute the greater part of the nasal fossæ, the olfactory nerves entering through the mesially divided space between the descending or orbito-nasal processes of the meta-neurapophyses; and the posterior nares passing off on the outer sides, and between the neurapophyses and the maxillaries.

The Ethmoidal Neural Arch and Centrum in Ophidians.— The maxillaries of the serpent are articulated or connected to the "pre-frontals." The latter are separated from one another mesially by the elongation of the nasals back to the "principal frontals." Each of the "pre-frontals," comparatively large and anchylosed to the lachrymal, sends down a transverse orbito-nasal plate, notched on its inner margin for the olfactory nerve, but separated from its fellow of the opposite side by the pre-sphenoidal processes of attachment of the " palatines." The space roofed over by the **nasals and "pre-frontals"** is mesially divided above by the contiguous mesial descending laminæ of the nasals, and below by the cartilaginous nasal septum. It is floored by the double "vomer," the two halves of which, connected by the lower margin of the cartilaginous septum, extend from the intermaxillaries in front to the centrum of the pre-sphenoidal sclerotome behind, being separated from the orbito-nasal processes of the "pre-frontals" by the pre-sphenoidal processes of the "palatines."

From what has already been stated with reference to the corresponding parts in the bird, the chelonian, and saurian reptile, it will now be seen that I hold the so-called "pre-frontals" of the serpent to be its actual frontals or ethmoido-frontals; its so-called double "vomer" to consist of the right and left neurapophyses, as the "pre-frontals" are the two halves of the meta-neurapophyses; and the cartilaginous nasal septum the centrum of its ethmoidal sclerotome.

The Ethmoidal Neural Arch and Centrum in the Amphibians.—The view which I take of these parts in the Amphibia will at once appear from the foregoing statements, and may be illustrated by the structure in the frog. As in the bird, the basis of the ethmoidal neural arch and centrum consists of that portion of the persistent primordial cranium which is situated behind the intermaxillary region, and immediately in front of the "os a ceinture." The mesial portion of this mass of cartilage forms the centrum of the sclerotome, as the posterior part of the nasal septum. The posterior portions of the nasal fossæ are hollowed out on its sides. Its upper surface is covered by the so-called "pre-frontals," which are, in fact, ethmoidal-frontals, or the two halves of the divided meta-neurapophyses. Its lower surface is supported by the two triangular bones, covered with teeth, and which are the neurapophyseal ethmoidal elements, already examined in the other Vertebrata. The posterior nares are situated behind, between the outer margins of these so-called vomerine bones and the maxillaries. The latter are, as usual, connected to the ethmoido-frontals.

Of the Views which have been hitherto taken of the Ethmoidal or Nasal Vertebra, or Sclerotome.—I am precluded in an abstract from entering upon the important but tangled morphological history of the nasal segment of the cranium. I shall only, therefore, on this department of the subject, make a few observations, in deference to the authority of Professor Owen, and in explanation of those points on which I find myself at variance with his doctrine. I have already so far stated, and in the sequel shall more fully state, the grounds on which I dissent from the doctrine of Oken and Bojanus, adopted by Professor Owen, that the nasals and vomer are respectively the neural spine and body of the nasal vertebra. What I intend more particularly to notice at present is that part of Professor Owen's doctrine which relates to the neurapophyseal elements of the nasal vertebra.

Professor Owen considers the middle plate of the mammalian ethmoid to be the coalesced pre-frontals, and the two halves of the cribriform plate, the ethmoidal cellules, and turbinated laminæ, to be collectively the greatly-developed olfactory capsules. If the latter are kept out of view, as not entering, according to his doctrine, into the formation of the ethmoidal or nasal neural arch, the doctrine necessitates the conversion of the laterally-placed "pre-frontals" of the fish and reptile into a single mesial laminar bone. Here I would observe that, overlooking for the present the adoption by Professor Owen of the current statements as to the identity of the "pre-frontals" of the fish with the "pre-frontals" of the reptile, I cannot conceive how the "pre-frontals," either of the fish or reptile, can be homologous with a mesial bone. Embryologically, I cannot understand how the olfactory nerves, which in the fish and reptiles are situated mesiad of the "pre-frontals," can become placed in the mammal on their outer aspects. The pair of "pre-frontals" in the crocodile or turtle can be legitimately enough conceived as coalescing mesially into a single bone; but this change presupposes the withdrawal or obliteration of the olfactory nerves; for, otherwise, two conditions must be admitted, both of which are embryologically untenable—first, that the olfactory lobes of the mammal are at one period in its development mesiad to the right and left halves of its central ethmoidal plate; and secondly, that the nervous and sclerous structures change places, the former passing outwards through the latter, or the latter meeting in front of the former, and passing backwards between them. But the actual facts are these:—The mesial plate, or bar, of the mammalian ethmoid is mesial from the first; and the olfactory bulbs, or nerves, are situated from the first on its lateral aspects. The mesial plate is the prolongation forward of the central bar of the primordial cranium; it is a true vertebral centrum, and is continued onwards and downwards into the vomerine portion of the cranial axis. The cribriform lamellæ are the only parts, therefore, of the mammalian ethmoid which present in their embryo and adult conditions all the characters of neurapophyseal elements; connected below with their centrum, and laterally or above with their frontal meta-neurapophyses, they, along with the latter and the centrum, close in the fore part of the encephalic portion of the cranial cavity, and enclose the olfactory lobes of the brain. That the olfactory, like the fifth nerve of the mammal, leaves the encephalic cavity by more than one orifice, and that the olfactory "sense-capsules" are united to the corresponding neurapophyses, are circumstances which afford no arguments against this determination, but, on the contrary, are in accordance with the union of the auditory capsules with their corresponding neurapophyses, and the exit of the auditory nerve from the encephalic cavity in divisions. It must also be observed, that if we are to look, with Professor Owen, upon the central lamina or bar of the mammalian ethmoid as the result of the mesial union of a pair of "pre-frontals," we must assign a morphological reason for the co-existence of a mesial cartilaginous septum with divided "pre-frontals" of the reptile and fish.

I am also obliged to dissent from Professor Owen's determination of the so-called "ethmoid" of the bird as the mesially-united neurapophyses of its nasal vertebra. Apparently influenced by its usual designation, and restricted to his own view of its homology by his determination of the "basi-sphenoid" as consisting of the connate centrums of the "mesencephalic" and "prosencephalic" vertebræ, Mr. Owen has in the bird, as in the mammal, arranged this portion of his morphological system in opposition to embryological facts. The two olfactory nerves of the bird pass forward on each side of the so-called "ethmoid" in shallow grooves; in certain instances only do they pass through notches or complete orifices formed by osseous development from the two surfaces of the bone. The two nerves in no instance pass forwards between the plates of the bone in any part of their extent. At no period during development are the olfactory nerves of the bird situated mesiad of any part of this bone; for it is originally a mesial cartilaginous plate, a portion of the axis of the primordial cranium, extending forwards and upwards from that part of the primordial axis which, when ossified, constitutes the anterior or acuminated extremity of the centrum of the post-sphenoidal sclerotome. In the sequel I shall have to point out that this bone in the bird, which anatomists have hitherto looked upon as the "ethmoid," is, in fact, the body or centrum of the pre-sphenoidal sclerotome converted into a mesial plate extending up to and flattened out at the upper surface of the cranium, in accordance with the catacentric character of the neural arch of the sclerotome, of which it is an element. Its corresponding neurapophyses are the pre-sphenoidal wings—the "orbito-sphenoids" of Professor Owen—which not only bound laterally the orifices for the optic, but also those for the olfactory nerves. The so-called "ethmoid" of the bird is not therefore formed by the coalescence of a pair of "pre-frontals," but is a mesial element belonging to another sclerotome. The bird already possesses distinct or "divided" "pre-frontals," with all the characters of the "pre-frontals" of the reptile in its so-called "nasals."

Dugés considered the "os en ceinture" of the frog to be the ethmoid, from its giving passage to the olfactory nerves by two funnel-shaped orifices at its anterior extremity, and from its intimate connection with the nasal cartilage in front. Professor Owen, on the same grounds, while he holds the posterior part of this bone in the *Rana boans* to consist of the "orbito-sphenoids," looks upon its anterior part as the confluent "pre-frontals." But as the "os en ceinture" of the common frog originates in a centre of ossification on each side of its fundamental portion of the primordial cranium; and as Professor Owen does not state the grounds on which he holds the "orbito-sphenoids" to be confluent with it in the bull-frog; as I can find no trace of such confluence either in the bull-frog or common frog, and as the fore part of the bone is divided by a mesial septum,—I look upon it as consisting of a single pair of neurapophyses and a catacentric septum. As this "os en ceinture" is situated upon the upper surface of the anterior acuminated portion of the centrum of the post-sphenoid, as in the bird, and as it is covered above, and in the common frog is united with the anterior portion of the so-called "parieto-frontal," it appears to me to constitute the neural arch and centrum of the pre-sphenoidal sclerotome, of which the orbito-sphenoids are the neurapophyses. The proper "os en ceinture" of Cuvier is in fact the homologous structure in the aneurous batrachian with the so-called "ethmoid," and the orbito-sphenoids collectively in the bird; the centrum being principally developed in the latter, the neurapophyseal elements in the former. On these grounds, and also because I hold, with Cuvier, the "nasals" of the frog to be its "pre-frontals," I cannot assent to Professor Owen's doctrine that the "os en ceinture" exhibits a stage in the mesial coalescence of a pair of "pre-frontals," the final effect of which is the formation of a mesial ethmoidal plate, or mesially-united nasal neurapophyses.

On the Actinapophyses of the Ethmoidal Sclerotome.—As the radiating elements of the ethmoidal segment of the skull are numerous and important, and as their elucidation requires a more extended reference to corresponding elements in the succeeding sclerotomes than can be made before the examination of these has been entered upon, I shall at present make only a general statement on the subject.

In the mammal we find a series of sclerous elements arranged from above downwards on each side of the ethmoidal sclerotome. On its upper or neural portion are the olfactory "capsule" and the lachrymal bone. On the lower or hæmal portion, the cartilages of the eyelids, with the inferior turbinated and malar bones. If the secondary antero-posterior elongation of the maxillary be kept out of view; and if it be conceived in its fundamental developmentary form as a rib-like bone, the convexity of which is inclined outwards and backwards; and if, at the same time, the possibility of a double arrangement of actinapophyseal elements in each sclerotome be borne in view, it will be seen that the malar extends outwards and backwards from the anterior or outer; the inferior turbinal from the posterior or inner aspect of the bone. I have already stated that the actinapophyseal elements of the cranium are generally flattened or extended so as to abut against one another, and against the other bones of the skull. Thus the malar passes backwards in the fibrous membrane which extends across the orbital opening, and which covers in the temporal fossa. The final purpose of the malar is to afford an abutment against the squamosal so as to strengthen the flank of the mammalian head. The malar, therefore, in many instances sends secondary processes upwards and inwards to abut against other bones. While I gladly avail myself of Professor Owen's term "squamosal," and fully agree with him as to the bone itself being a "radiating" element of the cranium; and while I more particularly assent to his very beautiful determination of it as the "quadrate jugal" of the bird, I must, nevertheless, contend for the much greater probability of its being a radiating element of the mandibular than of the maxillary arch. Its intimate connection with the quadrate bone in the development of the chick, and the disunion of it and the malar in certain Mammalia, appear to me to indicate that they belong to distinct sclerotomes.

The extended attachment from above downwards of the inferior turbinal to the inner aspect of the maxillary of the fœtal ruminant, a form of attachment which is repeated in the lachrymal process of the bone in the human subject, indicates the primary actinapophyseal form of the bone. Its elongation backwards on the inner aspect of the palate-bone, and its prolongation forward to abut against the cartilaginous actinapophysis of the vomerine hæmal arch, are secondary processes in the development of the bone, and steps towards the completion of that antero-posterior system of serially homologous actinapophyses which constitute what may be termed the inferior turbinal system. The inferior concha is peculiar to the nasal fossa of the mammal. The sclerous elements, which constitute its skeleton, in its most fully developed form, are posterior or inner actinapophyses of the rhinal, vomerine, and ethmoidal hæmal arches. These actinapophyses become included in the nasal fossa by the closure of the metasomatomic clefts; and, as they subsequently elongate, they abut against one another in the antero-posterior direction.

I shall, in the sequel, show that the more or less defined space termed orbit, at the side of the mammalian cranium, is fundamentally the metasomatomic fissure between the ethmoidal and pre-sphenoidal sclerotomes. The upper part of this fissure continues permanently open as the lachrymal canal, and drains away the secretion which bathes the front of the eyeball, while that organ, supported by the sclerotic, which is a pre-sphenoidal neuractinapophysis, and surrounded by its accessory structures, is lodged in its dilated portion. From the upper, anterior, and lower orbital margins, which are formed by elements of the anterior of its two bounding primary sclerotomes, a fibrous membrane extends backwards, covered externally by the orbicular muscle, and closing in the contents of the orbit, with the exception of the front of the eye, exposed through the palpebral fissure. This fibrous membrane is a metasomatomic or actinal lamina, extending very obliquely outwards and backwards like an operculum over the orbit. The succeeding metasomatomic membrane assumes the form of the tissue which separates the orbit from the temporal fossa, and which, passing backwards external to that fossa, forms the temporal fascia which constitutes an operculum to that space. The temporal fossa itself is the upper portion of the metasomatomic fissure between the pre- and post-sphenoidal sclerotomes, occupied by the muscles of mastication and the homologous nerve; the lower part of the fissure on each side remaining permanently open as the mouth, or more correctly as the anterior opening of the isthmus of the fauces. By the extension of ossification from neighbouring

L

bones into the anterior and external portion of this fibrous layer, the orbit may be more or less shut off from the temporal fossa.

The cartilaginous laminæ which support the eyelids of the mammal are developed in the fibrous layer which constitutes the operculum of the orbit, and lie in the same morphological plane as the malar and lachrymal bones. Their histological, as well as morphological relations appear to me to indicate not only that the palpebral cartilages are actinal elements of the endo-sclerome, but also that they are anterior or external hæmactinapophyses of the ethmoidal sclerotome. This view of the morphological relations of the malar bone, palpebral cartilages, and opercular membrane of the orbit in the mammal, is borne out by the corresponding arrangement in the bird. A fibrous membrane extends backwards over the orbit, from the posterior extremity of the feebly-developed maxillary, and from the posterior margin of the descending process of the ethmoido-frontal. In the lower part of this membrane the malar is imbedded; across its centre the palpebral cartilage; and at the antero-superior angle of the orbit, the lachrymal bone. These have all distinct actinapophyseal characters, which, in the case of the lachrymal, enables us to perceive more clearly how the mammalian lachrymal, having become intercalated between its corresponding hæmapophysis and neurapophysis, retains only so much of its actinapophyseal character as is indicated in the anterior margin of its groove, the remainder of the bone being a secondary expansion.

The lachrymal bone of the bird may extend into the orbital membrane along the outer margin of the so-called "principal frontal," or sphenoido-frontal, and become attached to that bone without losing its connection with the ethmoido-frontal. It may thus also form a union with the supra-orbital bone, when that bone is present, as in the hawks. The lachrymal may, moreover, extend backwards under the eye to the post-frontal process, and may have a branch of communication with the antero-inferior projection of the mastoid, as in certain parrots. It may also extend down to the malar, and may be connected in this direction with the transverse projection of the so-called "ethmoid," or pre-sphenoidal centrum. The infra-ocular bony arch in the maccaws and certain other birds is not a zygomatic arch, although consisting like it of actinapophyseal elements. The proper zygomatic arch, as consisting of the malar and squamosal, exists in all birds; the infra-ocular arch is ossified in comparatively few.

The reference of the lachrymal and the other bony formations round the orbit in birds to a muco-dermal system by the continental anatomists and by Professor Owen, appears to me to be disproved by their relation to the soft parts. They are all developed in aponeurotic bands, which enter into the formation of the orbital fascia already alluded to. In a band extending along the margin of the sphenoido-frontal, the supra-orbital bone takes its rise, which may thus become connected with the lachrymal, when that bone, which is developed in the anterior extremity of the band, extends backwards in it. A second band extends downwards and backwards from the lachrymal to the malar, forming a ligament between the two bones, and along which ossification may extend. A third band extends from the post-frontal process downwards and forwards to the quadrate-jugal or squamosal, along which ossification may extend from above. In all birds a band connects the lachrymo-malar with the post-fronto-squamosal band, thus forming an arch below the under eyelid. The extension of ossification into this commissural band, probably from both extremities, completes the infra-orbital bony arch, and may approximate or unite it to the squamoso-jugal or proper zygomatic arch. A fibrous band, which extends downwards and forwards in the temporal fascia from the anterior process of the mastoid, becomes ossified in some birds; and it is an extention of this ossification which appears to form the mastoidal limb, or attachment of the infra-ocular arch of the maccaw. I shall, in the sequel, state the grounds on which I regard as actinapophyseal all the bones developed in the opercular membrane of the orbital of the bird. I regard the lachrymal bone and the supra-orbital bone or bones of the saurians, as referable to the same morphological category; and as due to arrangements in the fibrous operculum of the orbit, similar to those in the bird; as also the connection between the malar and the post-frontal of the crocodilian, as well as the change in the direction of the jugal, and the peculiar position of the squamosal in the typical lizards.

The supra-orbital bone or cartilage, with the infra-ocular bony arch, appears in various forms in the osseous fish; and the arrangements presented by this form of cranium clearly indicate that these orbital bones are parts of a system of actinapophyseal elements referable respectively to the ethmoidal, pre- and post-sphenoidal, temporal, and occipital sclerotomes, peculiarly modified and connected in front for the protection of the orbit, and behind for the suspension of the pectoral girdle.

THE PRE-SPHENOIDAL SCLEROTOME.—*Its Centrum and Neural Arch.*—It has been already stated that this sclerotome is peculiar in the mammal, in the absence of its metaneurapophyses, while this mesial element is more or less fully and largely developed in the other forms of Vertebrata. When the cerebrum proper is developed, the sphenoido-frontal bone is absent; when the cerebrum proper is a mere film, as in birds and reptiles, or is absent altogether, the sphenoido-frontal is present. As the evidence on which this statement is based is derived from the consideration of the varied relations of all the primary elements in the different forms of cranium, I am compelled, in this preliminary abstract, to refer those who are desirous of weighing that evidence to what has been already adduced with regard to the ethmoido-frontals, and to the statements to be afterwards made in regard to the meta-neurapophyses of the post-sphenoidal and temporal sclerotomes. In the meantime, I shall confine myself to a general exposition of the arrangement as I regard it.

The anterior part of the body of the human sphenoid, and the corresponding pre-sphenoidal piece in the Mammalia generally, constitute an undoubted centrum, to which the lesser, anterior, or orbito-sphenoidal wings, are the corresponding neurapophyses.

How far we may be entitled to assume the frequent "triquetral" bones in the coronal suture in the human, and in certain other mammalian crania, and the separately-developed antlers of the giraffe, as indications of the missing bone, remains to be determined. I would only observe at present, that the great extent and permanency of the anterior fontanelle appear to be connected with the deficiency in question.

I have already stated that I regard the so-called "principal frontal" of the bird as the missing frontal of the mammal. Distinguishing it as sphenoido-frontal, it is the divided meta-neurapophysis corresponding to the feebly-developed "orbito-sphenoids," which, bounding the optic and olfactory orifices, constitute the neurapophyses, and to the so-called "ethmoid" as the centrum of the pre-sphenoidal sclerotome. Assuming for the present the signification I have attached to the "principal frontals," and holding the neurapophyseal character of the orbito-sphenoids as incontestable, I would only add a few remarks regarding the central element. The determination of the "ethmoid" of the birds as the centrum of the pre-sphenoidal segment of the cranium, while it does not require Professor Owen's hypothesis of connation of this element with the centrum behind, presents the element under a form similar to that exhibited by the ethmoidal and vomerine centrums. It resembles these in being an ossified portion of the primordial axis of the cranium, in being flattened into a horizontal plate at its upper margin, in extending down to the line of the base of the skull, and in thus presenting a catacentric relation to its neural arch. The passage of the anterior acuminated extremity of the centrum behind beneath the lower margin of the pre-sphenoidal centrum, so as to support it, is merely an example of that longitudinal obliquity in the setting of cranial centrums against one another, which may be considered as the rule rather than an exception. The posterior margin of the bone is oblique from below upwards and forwards; gives attachment to the orbito-sphenoids, or to their membranous neurapophyseal substitutes, which bound or give passage to the orbital and olfactory nerves. The obliquity of this margin of the bone corresponds with the similar obliquity of the fore part of the basis of the brain of the bird, a remarkable feature in its configuration. The flattened upper edge of the bone may be more or less exposed on the upper surface of the cranium; and when the intermaxillaries, ethmoido- and sphenoido-frontals are removed, this flattened margin is found to be similar to and continuous with the flattened upper margin of the ethmoidal and vomerine cartilaginous septum. The anterior margin may be nearly perpendicular, but is generally oblique from below upwards and forwards, concave or concavo-convex, sharp, and generally free, being connected to the posterior margin of the ethmoidal cartilaginous septum by membrane, thus permitting, more or less, movement of the upper mandible—that is of the combined ethmoidal and vomerine sclerotomes on the pre-sphenoidal.

In the majority of birds a laminar process projects outwards and downwards from the lower and fore part of this bone. This process, variously developed, forms, along with the descending process of the lachrymal, the anterior wall of the orbit, separating it from the nasal space, and permitting the passage of the olfactory nerve through a notch or hole in its upper edge. I regard this process on each side of the presphenoidal centrum as of the same nature as the process which will be found projecting from each side of the lower part of the ethmoidal septum or centrum, and which, abutting against the descending process of the ethmoido-frontal, forms a wall or rampart across the floor of the nasal passage, extending nearly half-way up to its roof, immediately behind the external nostril, thus converting that part of the nasal chamber in front of it into a vestibule. This process is largely developed in the ossified ethmoido-vomerine septum of the hawks and owls.

I would here observe that the "os en forme de cuiller" of Cuvier, which he considers as the inferior turbinal of the lizard, and which forms the fore part of the floor of the nostril on each side, and the convex anterior part of which stretches like a buttress across the cavity, between the septum and the maxillary, immediately behind the external nostril, appears to me to be, with its fellow of the opposite side, merely the ossified lower portion of the ethmoidal centrum. These so-called "cornets inferieurs" of the lizard form the floor, and do not, therefore, project from the outer wall of the nasal passage in the manner of the inferior turbinals; and I believe anatomists will, in reviewing the subject, admit that the inferior turbinal accompanies the fully-completed maxillary arch, and only exists, therefore, in the mammal.

I regard these lateral processes of the ethmoidal and presphenoidal centrums of the bird as homologous with the pterygoid processes of the post-sphenoidal centrum, and generally with those processes which, under various forms, project downwards from the sides of the lower or hæmal aspects of the occipital and succeeding centrums in certain fish, or with those processes termed "hypopophyses" by Professor Owen.

Before dismissing the consideration of this important centrum in the bird, I would direct attention to certain interesting modifications which it may undergo. In the first place, it may, like many other bones in the cranium of the bird, become greatly dilated and altered in form by the development of air-cells in its interior. The pneumatic openings are two in number, one on each side of the anterior margin below the superior horizontal plate. The pneumatic excavation and dilatation extends backwards more or less in certain species; and in some owls the bone presents the form of a cubical cellular mass. This peculiarity of form might be adduced in support of Professor Owen's doctrine of the formation of this bone from the coalescence of the pre-frontals; but then it will be observed that the increased breadth of the bone is not due to incomplete mesial fusion of lateral parts, but to expansion from the mesial plane, for the olfactory nerves still run forwards in grooves on its lateral aspects, although these may be deep in front, and posteriorly their margins may overlap the nerves. The expansion of the pre-sphenoidal centrum also produces a remarkable separation of the optic foramina. As explanatory of this effect, I would observe, that the development of this bone in the chick shows that it forms the posterior border of the common optic foramen by means of a pair of processes which project from its posterior inferior angle like the limbs of the letter Y. When, therefore, the bone takes on transverse dimension, the single optic chasm separates into two optic foramina, which, in *Strix flammea* are three-eighths of an inch asunder.

The separation of the optic foramina from the pneumatic expansion of the pre-sphenoidal centrum leads me, in the second place, to observe, that the characteristic separation of these orifices in the extinct forms Dodo, Dinornis, Palapteryx, did not depend entirely on pneumatic expansion of the pre-sphenoidal centrum, nor on such width of that bone as might be attributed to incomplete mesial fusion of a pair of "prefrontals," but on the remarkable prolongation backwards on each of its sides of the neurapophyseal walls of the ethmoidal olfactory chambers.

Professor Owen, in his series of graphic and valuable memoirs on these three extinct forms, and in his memoirs on Apteryx, assuming the pre-frontal doctrine regarding the bone in question, and directing special attention to the more or less complete passage backwards of the nasal chambers to the anterior or inferior wall of the cranial cavity, and to the passage of the olfactory nerves into these by a number of orifices, apparently recognises in Apteryx, for instance (although he does not directly make the statement), a completed mammalian ethmoid. Now, recalling attention again to the embryological considerations from which the formation of neither the mammalian ethmoidal septum, nor the so-called ethmoid of the Ostrich, Dinornis, Dodo, nor Apteryx, can be conceived as resulting from coalesced pre-frontals, I would remark, that the arrangement of the nasal fossæ in Apteryx, instead of being mammalian, presents the peculiar ornithic character of its parts, fully brought out; all the phases in the development of which may be observed in the series of birds. In all birds, the posterior extremities of the cartilaginous pouchlike ethmoido-neural, or olfactory chambers, approach or encroach upon the sides of the pre-sphenoidal centrum; so that the membrane, which connects its anterior margin to the cartilaginous nasal septum, and a certain extent of both its surfaces, separates the two pouches from one another. The laminar or hypopophyseal process on each side of the bone, variously modified in form, limits, posteriorly and inferiorly, the olfactory portion of the lateral surface of the bone, and, folded over the pouch, walls it in more or less from below; while the lachrymal from above passes down on its outer side. The gradual environment of the pouch may be traced in the series of birds; and I find in the Asiatic Cassowary, the stage immediately preceding the completion of the process in Apteryx. In this bird, the pair of deep fossæ in the interior of the skull, which lodge the olfactory lobes, are separated from one another by the posterior margin of the pre-sphenoidal centrum, which here represents the crista galli. The plate of bone which forms the floor of each fossa, instead of being cribriform, as in Apteryx, is perforated by a single star-like foramen, a form due to the partial shooting across of bony processes from its margin.

In the Chelonian.—The neural arch and centrum of the chelonian are represented in the dry skull by the pair of bones usually considered as the "proper frontals," but which I regard as sphenoido-frontals. In the recent condition the centrum appears in the form of a compressed cartilaginous bar, continuous posteriorly with the compressed anterior part of the post-sphenoidal centrum, resting below on the conjoined pterygoids and ento-pterygoids, continuous in front with the cartilaginous ethmoidal septum or centrum, and thus presenting all the relations of the pre-sphenoidal centrum of the bird. It is continued upwards, and represents the orbito-sphenoids, or neurapophyses, in the form of a double fibro-cartilaginous membrane, the two laminæ of which separate to unite with the posterior margins of the orbito-nasal processes of the ethmoido-frontals, with the two parallel descending ridges of the sphenoido-frontals, and with the anterior margins of the peculiar descending processes of the so-called "parietals." The olfactory nerves pass forwards between these neurapophyseal laminæ above; and the optic, with the other orbital nerves, perforates them.

In the Crocodilian.—In the crocodiles, the sphenoido-frontals have coalesced; but the cartilaginous centrum and neurapophyseal interorbital laminæ present exactly the same relations as in the chelonian; the only difference being the result of the union of the orbito-nasal processes of the sphenoido-frontals near their lower extremities, and the consequent space left between this bony bridge and the deep furrow formed by the inclined upper surfaces of the ento-pterygoideal portions of the pterygoids.

In the Lacertians.—In the lizards, the sphenoido-frontal is again double. In consequence of the mesial separation of the ento-pterygoids ("palatals") and pterygoids, the elongated fibro-cartilaginous centrum and neurapophyseal interorbital laminæ, are left unsupported below; to which circumstance is probably due the formation in the interorbital laminæ of a pair of delicate triradial osseous neurapophyses, which pass off from the upper margins of the optic foramina.

In the Ophidian and Batrachian.—Leaving the further consideration of the special homology of the anterior sphenoidal wing in the reptiles, and more especially in the crocodiles, until the posterior sphenoidal wing, and the so-called "petrosal," have been examined, I would observe, that the grounds on which Professor Owen distinguishes the "os en ceinture" of the frog, from that segment in the python which includes the so-called "frontals," appear to me somewhat arbitrary. This segment in the serpent consists of a pair of neurapophyses, or orbito-sphenoids, which are distinct, as cartilages at least, in the embryo; of a double meta-neurapophysis (sphenoido-frontals), which not only occupy on each side the positions of the neurapophyses, but extend the fore part of their inner margins downwards, back to back, in the mesial plane, on the sides of the compressed centrum; which thus, along with them, divides the neural chamber in front, for the transmission of the olfactory nerves. The sides of the "os en ceinture" are formed by neurapophyses; while the so-called "frontals" of the serpent occupy the greater part at least of the sides of their segment; in other respects, their relations are similar. They are both catacentric; the centrum, in both, resting, as in the bird, on the upper surface of the anterior acuminated extremity of the post-sphenoidal centrum, and in the plane of the ethmoidal centrum in front. I regard, therefore, the "os en ceinture" in the Batrachian, along with the anterior segments of its "parieto-frontals," as consisting of the centrum, neurapophyses, and **meta-neurapophyses of the** pre-sphenoidal sclerotome ; and, therefore, also as homologous with that segment in the ophidian which includes its "frontals," but exclusive of the elongated anterior prolongation of the post-sphenoidal centrum.

The Pre-sphenoidal Centrum and Neural Arch in the Fish.—The bone which predominates over every other in the cranium of the fish is the so-called "principal frontal;" which, however, as already stated, I do not regard as the frontal or ethmoido-frontal of the mammal, but as a sphenoido-frontal. It is the pre-sphenoidal meta-neurapophysis of the fish, presenting all the relations of the corresponding bone or bones in the bird, chelonian, and lizard, except that the ethmoido-frontals anterior to it have coalesced in the middle line ; while the ethmoidal neurapophyses have become so much developed, exposed, and connected to it laterally, as to assume the position of the so-called "nasals" and "pre-frontals" in the bird and reptile. The enormous development of this bone in the fish and bird appears to depend on the great bulk of the organs of vision. There is, therefore, in both, an extended interorbital space to be filled up. In the fish, as in the bird, this is variously effected by means of fibro-cartilage and bone. The extreme forms of the interorbital arrangement may be illustrated by the gadoid and cyprinoid fishes. In the cod the greater part of the so-called interorbital septum consists, as in the chelonian and lizard, of a double fibrous membrane, which extends upwards from the anterior prolongation of the post-sphenoidal centrum to the margins of the mesial grooves on the under surface of the sphenoido-frontal. The two laminæ of this membrane thus bound the sides of the compressed neural space, along the upper part of which the olfactory nerves pass forward. In the posterior superior part of each of these neurapophyseal fibrous laminæ, a comparatively small plate of bone is developed, while the centrum consists of the bar of persistent cartilage, which extends along the grooved upper surface of the anterior portion of the post-sphenoidal centrum, and terminates above the ethmoidal centrum ("vomer"). The optic nerves pierce the membranes so far back as to notch very deeply the anterior margins of the post-sphenoidal neurapophyses, or post-sphenoidal wings.

In the carp, again, the interorbital space is occupied above by a considerable descent of the margins of the sphenoido-frontal groove; in front, by complete ossification of the fibrous membranes, which thus become pre-sphenoidal neurapophyses; behind, by the passage forwards of the post-sphenoidal wings ("ali-sphenoids"), through which, during development, the optic nerves have passed back, to be lodged in notches in their posterior margins; and below, by the bar of semi-ossified cartilage situated upon the upper surfaces of the posterior sphenoidal and ethmoidal centrums.

Of the Hæmal Arch and Hæmactinapophyses of the Pre-sphenoidal Sclerotome.—The palatine arch, between which and the mandibular the mouth is situated, and which terminates therefore posteriorly the prestomal series of hæmal arches, may be presumed to undergo very varied modifications in connection with the olfactory, the respiratory, and the digestive functions. In the present instance, as in many others, the anatomy of the human body, instead of leading astray by complexity and extreme modification of its parts, supplies the key for their morphological solution, by affording an example of the employment of the fundamental type of structure for the fulfilment of the most complex functional purposes.

The human pre-sphenoidal centrum, hollowed out by nasal air-cells, as in certain birds, is bounded below and in front by a pair of separate triangular-curved bony plates, which, limiting the size of the right and left **pneumatic orifices**, brings these into communication with the posterior ethmoidal air-cells or sinuses. These "sphenoidal turbinated bones," or "bones of Bertin," in contact along their outer margins, and outer part of their inferior aspects, with the sphenoidal processes of the palate-bones, constitute the upper elements or suspensory extremities of the inverted arch, completed by the meeting of the palate-bones themselves in the posterior part of the mesial line of the palatal vault. The right and left pterygoids are attached, as a pair of actinapophyses, to this arch. They pass off backwards and outwards from the posterior margins of the perpendicular plates of the palate-bones, and abut in the embryo against the upper and fore part of the mandibular arch, retaining in the tympanic processes of their adult form indications of their early connection with that arch. The most important secondary connection of the pterygoids in the human adult is with the pterygoid processes of the post-sphenoid; and it is this sphenoidal connection which is most frequently repeated in the animal series.

I shall not enter at present into the question of the probable existence of "bones of Bertin" in the Mammalia generally; nor inquire whether the separate orbital pieces of the palate-bones in the herbivorous Cetacea, according to Cuvier, and the separate anterior portions of the pterygoids of the young dolphin, as described by Meckel and Rapp, may be indications of the upper elements of the palatal arch; but pass on to the consideration of the palatal arch in the lower Vertebrata, in which the two elements of which it appears to consist on each side are distinctly developed.

The Palatal Arch and Pterygoids in the Bird.—The bone hitherto considered by all anatomists as the vomer of the bird, is a more or less elongated narrow plate, the margins of which are bent upwards so as to convert its upper surface into a groove, which is applied against the under surface of the acuminated anterior extremity of the post-sphenoidal centrum, which is therefore interposed between it and the pre-sphenoidal centrum. This bone, more or less compressed or extended laterally, separates the posterior nostrils from one another. Its anterior extremity reaches the anterior limits of these orifices, or, passing forwards into the palate between the ethmoidal neurapophyseal and maxillary palatal laminæ, and concealed more or less by them, may terminate on the surface of the palate between the intermaxillary palatal plates. When this bone is much compressed it is single throughout; when flattened, it is more or less extensively divided in the mesial line.

The palate-bones of the bird, more or less elongated, extend anteriorly under the maxillary palatal laminæ, to which in general they are only slightly connected, forward to the intermaxillary palate-plates, with which they are anchylosed or articulated, separated from one another in front, to form the lateral boundaries of the posterior nares, the palate-bones become broader posteriorly, approach one another, and are either attached to, or anchylosed with, the posterior extremity of the so-called "vomer." Their posterior extremities are provided with facets for articulation with the bar-like pterygoids, which extend from them, outwards and backwards, to articulate with the quadrate bone on each side. The pterygoids of certain birds have also secondary connections; they articulate with processes which project from the post-sphenoidal centrum in some part of its extent; and on which their shafts glide, rotate, or vibrate.

The reciprocal relations of the so-called "vomer," the palatines, and pterygoids of the bird, are extremely interesting and important. At present, I can only direct attention to those relations which bear upon my subject. When the palate-bones are greatly developed, the "vomer" diminishes.

When, again, the "vomer" is much developed, the palatines are in an atrophied condition. The pterygoids present phases of development dependent on the variations of the palatines and pterygoids. The two extremes may be observed in the parrots and the struthious birds. In the former, the palatines are enormously developed, while the "vomer" has disappeared. In the latter, the "vomer" is greatly elongated and developed, while the palatines present the relation, and exhibit the form, of the "transverse" or "adgustal" bones of the reptile.

The Palatal Arch and the Pterygoids in Reptiles and Amphibians.—The three bones on each side, which form the palatal system of the ordinary lizard, present the same relations, and almost the same form, as the "vomer," palatines, and pterygoids of the struthious birds. The pterygoids are in every respect similar. The "transverse bones" of the lizard are also, in relations and almost in form, like the palatines of these birds. The so-called "palatals" of the lizard, while they exhibit all those relations to the "transverse" and pterygoids, which the "vomer" of the bird presents, differ from that double bone in this respect, that although in contact at the mesial line, they are comparatively so much broader, occupying so much of the comparatively narrow palatal space that they touch the maxillaries by their anterior external angles. They bound, therefore, the internal nares posteriorly ; but, like the so-called vomer in the bird, separate them from one another, passing forward like that double bone to the ethmoidal neurapophyseal plates, which constitute the so-called "vomer" of the lizard. In the monitors, these so-called "palatines," like the pterygoids, are evidently separated in the middle line, and forced backwards along the inner margin of the maxillary towards the transverse bones, by the development and elongation of the ethmoidal neurapophyseal elements. In the crocodiles, again, the full development of maxillary palatal plates, and more especially of the ethmoidal neurapophyses, has forced backwards and towards the middle line, not only the bone called "palatal" in the lizard, but also the pterygoids; and as the latter also exhibit that remarkable tubular development, various phases of which are perceptible in the Chelonians, Birds, and Mammalia, the former again presents the ornithic vomerine aspect.

In the Ophidia the two halves of the palatal system are widely separated at the middle line. The so-called "palatals," elongated forwards into the ethmoidal region, articulated by ascending processes to the pre-sphenoid, slightly attached externally to the maxillaries, as in the lizards, bound as in these reptiles, the nostrils posteriorly, but do not separate them mesially.

In the frog, the so-called "palatals" extend transversely outwards from the "os en ceinture" to the maxillaries, being also connected at their outer extremities with the pterygoids. The latter are articulated posteriorly to the post-sphenoid and to the quadrate bone. The "os transversum" has disappeared at the junction of the so-called palatal, pterygoid, and maxillary.

The modifications presented by these bones in reptiles and Amphibia are much too numerous to be followed in detail at present. I have therefore selected those which are essential for the elucidation of my subject; and shall sum up the conclusions I draw from them, by a comparison of them with the corresponding elements in chelonians.

The chelonians, we are told, have no "transverse bone." They are distinguished in this respect from all the other reptiles. But if we examine the skull of a tortoise, we shall find all the elements which enter into the formation of the palatine aspect in that of the crocodile. In front are the intermaxillaries, immediately behind which, in the median line, is the double bony plate, which is usually described and figured as the fore part of the so-called "vomer," but to which

M

I have already directed attention as the combined ethmoidal neurapophyseal elements. In the turtles the maxillaries meet across the palatal vault in front of the united ethmoidal neurapophyses, so that the latter are pushed backwards, and are in contact laterally with the palatals in the vault of the palate; while in the tortoise the latter want entirely the palatal processes, consisting, as Cuvier expressed it, only of their upper portions, and extending outwards on each side from the outer margins of the so-called "vomer," and of the pterygoids, to the inner margins of the maxillaries. Now, let the base of the skull of a tortoise, a turtle, and a crocodile, be examined side by side. In all three we shall find the intermaxillaries in front. The maxillaries, although they do not meet across the palate of the tortoise, do so in that of the turtle, and thus, as in the crocodile, bound posteriorly the intermaxillary segment of the palate. The transverse union of the maxillaries, in the turtle and crocodile, pushes back the ethmoidal neurapophyses (which are in contact with the intermaxillaries in the tortoise), but to such an extent in the crocodile that the ethmoidal neurapophyses, also themselves much elongated, carry back the pterygoids, so that the latter almost entirely conceal the post-sphenoidal centrum. The outer margins of the pterygoids, already curved downwards in the tortoise and turtle, pass downwards and inwards in the crocodile, so as to meet again in the mesial line of the palatal vault. The bony septum of the pterygo-ethmoidal portion of the nostrils of the crocodile is at the same time seen to be the result of the extension downwards in the mesial plane of the middle ridge of the so-called "vomer" of the tortoise or turtle, and of the connection of the anterior part of that double bone with the ethmoidal neurapophyses. It will thus be observed, that if the maxillaries of the tortoise were united across the palate, in front of its ethmoidal neurapophyses, to a considerable extent backwards; if the ethmoidal neurapophyses were also elongated in the same direction; and if the outer margins of the pterygoids, below the palatines, were to meet in the mesial line, the latter would be forced backwards and outwards; so that, still retaining their connections with the pterygoids and maxillaries, but leaving those with the "vomer" in front and internally to abut against the malar behind and externally—the palatal aspect of the skull of the tortoise would present the arrangement of the corresponding region in that of the crocodile, the palate-bones assuming the form and relations of "transverse bones."

If to the skulls of the tortoise, turtle, and crocodile, those of a serpent, a lizard, a frog, and an ostrich be added, it will be observed that the palate-bones have disappeared in the frog; that they have assumed the form and relations of "transverse bones" in the lizard, crocodile, and serpent, that they are essentially "transverse bones" in the struthious bird, while in the tortoise, but especially in the turtle, they present the mammalian (?) character and form. It will also be observed, that the bones in the turtle, tortoise, crocodile, and bird, hitherto denominated "vomer," are the same bones which in the frog, lizard, and serpent, are named "palatals," the term "vomer" being applied in these animals to those two bones collectively, which are situated under the ethmoidal portion of the skull. It will also be noted that the bones called "vomer" in the* crocodile and bird, and the bones called "palatals" in the frog, lizard, and serpent, are related to the others, along with which they have been examined, exactly as the "bones of Bertin," in the human cranium, are to the palate-bones and pterygoids.

The Pre-sphenoidal Hæmal Arch and Hæmactinapophysis of the Fish.—In the osseous fish a fibrous membrane extends outwards and downwards on each side from the suborbital bar-

---

* In the annotated copy the words turtle and tortoise, which appeared in the original memoir, were deleted.—(EDS.)

like portion of the basis of the cranium. In most fishes there will be found in this membrane, where it passes off from the pre-sphenoidal portion of the cranium, a more or less elongated scale-like bone on each side. This is the "pterygoïdien interne" of Cuvier, the "hérisséal" of St. Hilaire, the "ento-pterygoid" of Professor Owen. The palate-bone, connected by the same fibrous membrane to the outer margin of the ento-pterygoid, extends forwards to the side of the so-called "vomer," or to the ethmoidal centrum and neurapophysis, to which, as also to the maxillary and intermaxillary, it is variously attached directly and indirectly. The corresponding actinapophyseal element or pterygoid in the fish is firmly connected in front to the palate-bone, and less intimately to the ento-pterygoid, and, extending backwards, downwards, and outwards, abuts against the anterior margin of the "hypo-tympanic" and "pre-tympanic" bones, as the pterygoid of the bird and reptile does against the so-called "quadrate," or "tympanic" bone. If, then, the basal aspect of the cranium of the osseous fish is placed in series with those of the bird, lizard, serpent, tortoise, and frog, it will be observed, that while its palatals and pterygoids may be at once associated with the corresponding bones, as already determined, in the bird and reptile, the ento-pterygoid of the fish presents all the relation of the double bone, usually called "vomer" in the bird; of the posterior or horizontal portion of the bone called "vomer" in the tortoise; and of the bones called "palatals" in the lizard, serpent, and frog. It will also be observed, that while the toothed bone, called "vomer" in the fish, has, from a catacentric change, disappeared from the under aspect of the cranium in the bird, reptile, and batrachian, the two bones, called in the fish "pre-frontals"—its ethmoidal neurapophyses —present the same relations to its ento-pterygoids as the ethmoidal neurapophyses of the bird to its so called "vomer," and as those of the tortoise to the posterior portion of its so-called "vomer," and as those of the lizard, serpent, and frog to the bones hitherto called "palatal" in these three forms. I therefore apply provisionally the term ento-pterygoid to the so-called "vomer" of the bird, to the posterior part of the so-called "vomer" of the chelonian, to the corresponding bony piece in the crocodiles, to the so-called "palatals" of the ophidian, lacertian, and batrachian, to the "bones of Bertin," and their representatives in the mammal.

The Constitution of the Nasal Fossæ, and the Relative Positions of the External and Internal Nares.—The details necessary for the morphological examination of the rhinal, vomerine, ethmoidal, and pre-sphenoidal sclerotomes, have involved a number of facts connected with the varied constitution of the nasal fossæ in the different vertebrate forms. As, however, the constitution of these fossæ has important bearings on the morphology of the entire cranium, I shall briefly direct attention to the subject.

The only perfect form of nasal fossæ is that presented by the mammal. They consist of the entire neuro-hæmal cavities of the rhinal and vomerine, combined with the hæmal cavities of the ethmoidal and pre-sphenoidal sclerotomes. That portion of the combined nasal fossæ which consists of the cavities of the rhinal and vomerine sclerotomes, is divided in the mesial plane by the centrums of those sclerotomes; while the dependent portion of the ethmoidal centrum, and the posterior portion of the vomerine centrum, divide in the same manner that part of the combined fossæ which consists of the hæmal cavities of the ethmoidal and pre-sphenoidal sclerotomes. The mammalian nasal fossæ are therefore bounded in front by the walls of the neuro-hæmal chambers of two catacentric sclerotomes; and posteriorly by the catacentrically divided hæmal chambers of a demicatacentric and diacentric sclerotome.

As the hæmal portions of the cephalic somatomes are separated from one another in their early embryo condition by metasomatomic clefts, we may expect to find traces of these clefts in the walls of the adult nasal fossæ.

The first or anterior pair of metasomatomic clefts of the embryo head, that is the clefts between the rhinal and intermaxillary lobe of the "median frontal process," are retained in the adult as the external nares. These openings in the non-proboscidian mammal, are situated therefore between the ali-nasal cartilages and the intermaxillary bones. In the proboscidian mammals, they are probably situated between the ultimate and penultimate, or, at least, between two of the distal somatomes of the proboscis.

The second pair of metasomatomic clefts, situated between the external angles of the median frontal process and the lateral frontal processes, may disappear entirely in the course of development; but they occasionally remain under the form of Stenson's ducts, which pass obliquely through the so-called "incisive spaces," or "foramina," from the mouth to the nasal fossæ, between the intermaxillaries and maxillaries. The mucous walls of the canals of Stenson are supported by cartilaginous tubular folds, which are continuous superiorly with cartilaginous laminæ, which, passing off laterally from the lower margin of the nasal septum and vomer, cover more or less of the floor of the nasal fossæ, upper part of the incisive fissures, and spaces between the intermaxillaries and maxillaries. The "organs" or "sacs of Jacobson," supplied by the olfactory and fifth nerves, lined by glandular integument, sheathed by a continuation of the cartilaginous laminæ already alluded to, and opening into the canals of Stenson, when these are present, are, whatever their function may be, morphologically connected with the second pair of metasomatomic clefts.

The next pair of metasomatomic clefts, situated between the lateral frontal processes and the so-called "superior maxillary" deflection of the "first visceral lamina," continue pervious in all the Mammalia except the Cetacea. The lachrymal canals which connect the anterior pouches of the conjunctivæ with the nasal fossæ, consist of the persistent upper portions of these clefts. Their outer or lower portions are obliterated, but the corresponding inter-sclerotomic space, much dilated, constitutes that part of the orbit formed by elements of the ethmoidal and pre-sphenoidal sclerotomes, while the spheno-palatine and posterior palatine foramina and fissures are also enclosed portions of the space between these two sclerotomes, retained for the passage of vessels and nerves.

The posterior nares are not meta-somatomic openings, they are merely the communications between the catacentric hæmal space of the pre-sphenoidal, and the corresponding but undivided hæmal spaces of the succeeding somatomes.

The mouth is the persistent and developed form of the great cleft between the pre- and post-sphenoidal somatomes. It is situated therefore morphologically in the same transverse plane as the posterior nares. Its fundamental or morphological relations are retained and represented by the posterior isthmus of the fauces. The buccal chamber is a vestibule superadded to the alimentary tube, by the anterior elongation of the lower jaw, and by the development of the floor of the mouth and of the tongue, with the consequent inclusion of the vault of the palate; so that the latter, instead of forming the anterior portion of the hæmal or sternal aspect of the head, becomes apparently a portion of the wall of the visceral tube.

The complete development of the vomer, characteristic, as already stated, of the mammalian head, is also a characteristic feature of the nasal fossæ in the mammal. As the centrum of that sclerotome, of which the intermaxillaries are the hæmapophyses, it extends back from them to abut against the presphenoidal centrum, forming a beam which adds to the anteroposterior strength of the entire arrangement, and which supports the more feebly-developed ethmoidal and rhinal portions of the nasal septum. All these relations of the vomer are retained in the remarkably-modified nasal passages and snout in the Cetacea.

The seat of the olfactory sense is limited to the upper part of the ethmoidal portion of the nasal fossæ. However complex the arrangement of the ethmoidal turbinal laminæ may be, they invariably present the general character of folded laminar neuractinapophyses, connected to their corresponding neurapophyses, after the type of the cartilaginous sessile olfactory cups in the plagiostomes.

As already stated, the so-called inferior turbinals consist of an antero-posteriorly arranged series or system of mutually abutting hæmactinapophyses, enclosed during development within the nasal fossæ. The inferior turbinal system is peculiar to the mammal, and consists of elements which, in developed forms of the system, are derived from, and attached to, the rhinal, vomerine, and ethmoidal hæmapophyses. The palate-bone, or distal pre-sphenoidal hæmapophysis, supports the posterior extremity of the turbinal system, but I have not had occasion to observe any turbinal element supplied by it.

As the rhinal sclerotome has disappeared in the bird, the neuro-hæmal chambers of the vomerine sclerotome become closed in front, and the external nostrils are supplied by those metasomatomic clefts between the vomerine and ethmoidal sclerotomes, which in the mammal form the "incisive foramina," the "canals of Stenson," and the "organs of Jacobson."

As the anterior nares are removed one somatome back in the bird, so the posterior nares are removed one somatome forwards. They are situated between the maxillary and incomplete palatine arches, the ento-pterygoids separating them, while the palatines are on their outer sides. The posterior nares, instead of being directed backwards in a plane at right angles to the axis of the alimentary tube, open downwards in the plane of its upper wall. This direction of the posterior nares is due to the following circumstances:—1. That the intermaxillaries, although completing their arch below, are principally developed upwards and backwards; 2. That the maxillaries, even when they meet partially across the middle line, have the space which they enclose occupied by the neurapophyses, centrum, and sense-capsules of their own sclerotome—in other words, they are in contact with the central and neurapophyseal aspect of their own sclerotome; 3. That the palatines do not form an arch at all, but lie in the horizontal plane of the under surfaces of the centrums of the cephalic sclerotomes behind them.

The bird, in fact, does not possess nasal fossæ in the same sense as the mammal—that is, it does not present nasal chambers, formed by the completed hæmal arches of a certain number of sclerotomes. Its nasal fossæ consist only of the catacentric-hæmal or neuro-hæmal spaces of the vomerine sclerotome, and of the combined neural and "sense-capsule" spaces of the ethmoidal sclerotome, which occupy the space enclosed by its hæmal arch. They differ therefore from the mammalian nasal fossæ, not only in wanting rhinal compartments, but also in the deficiency of ethmoidal and presphenoidal hæmal spaces. The palate of the bird, instead of being, like that of the mammal, situated in a plane inferior and parallel to that in which the vertebral column lies (?), is in the plane of the latter, like that of the fish. The palate of the fish is in the horizontal plane of the vertebral column, because its nasal fossæ are absent, the constituent hæmal arches being all incomplete; and because the cavities of its olfactory capsules open externally. The palate of the bird is in the horizontal plane of the vertebral column for reasons already stated, and also because the olfactory capsules, instead of being situated external to the cavities of their sclerotome, as in the fish, or in its hæmal cavity, as in the mammal, have become involved in, or have taken the place of, its neural chamber, and have therefore their inner orifices or posterior nares directed downwards, on the central aspect.

The mode in which the walls and cavities of the olfactory capsules of the bird become involved or lost in its ethmoidal neural chamber and walls, may be morphologically conceived, if the structure is compared with the corresponding segment of the cranium of a ray. The cranium of the plagiostome is modelled on the form of the "primordial cranium" of the mammal and bird. The laterally projecting sessile cartilaginous olfactory cups communicate each by a wide orifice with the cranial cavity. If the orifices be conceived as much enlarged, and the walls of the capsules as withdrawn into, or becoming continuous with, those of the cranium; or if the latter be conceived as disappearing, while the former take their places, the general arrangement of the ethmoidal section of the persistent "primordial cranium" of the ray will be seen to be similar to that sclerotome in the bird's skull which retains most of the primordial character. The development of the imperfect maxillaries in contact with the lower aspect of the slightly-ossified inferior wall of the combined capsular and neural mass, and the formation of the ethmoido-frontals in the perichondrium which covers its upper surface, would reduce the entire arrangement to the type of the corresponding parts in the bird.

By a similar process, the sessile cartilaginous auditory capsules of the cyclostome may be conceived to become buried in the temporal portions of the cranial wall in the plagiostome, while in the osseous fish, after the primordial cranium has become enveloped in the bony plates, which are formed in its substance and in its fibrous covering, the auditory capsules pass into the cranial cavity, having been enclosed by the neurapophyseal and meta-neurapophyseal bony pieces of their own and neighbouring sclerotomes.

The external nostrils of the lacertian, ophidian, and amphibian, are situated, as in the bird, between the vomerine and ethmoidal sclerotomes ; the intermaxillaries being closed in front and below. The so-called nasal fossæ in these vertebrate forms are also, as in the bird, merely olfactory chambers, occupying the neural space of the ethmoidal sclerotome. The posterior nares, too, open as in the bird, between the ethmoidal and pre-sphenoidal sclerotomes, but with the following subordinate differences :—In the lizard they are separated by the anterior extremities of the ento-pterygoids, and are bounded behind by the maxillary processes of these bones, and externally by the maxillaries themselves. In the ophidian they are separated by the free margin of the ethmoidal catacentric plates ; anteriorly by the posterior margins of the ethmoidal neurapophyses, externally by the anterior projecting portions of the ento-pterygoids, and behind by the pre-sphenoidal attachments of the latter. In the frog they open between the ethmoidal neurapophyses ("vomer"), the ento-pterygoids ("palatals"), and the maxillaries.

We again approach the mammalian type of nasal fossæ, through the tortoises, turtles, and crocodiles.

It has been already stated that the anterior nostrils of the Chelonian appear to possess more of the ornithic than mammalian conformation. The primordial cartilaginous lining of the olfactory fossæ projects in some turtles through the anterior nasal opening of the cranium in the form of a double proboscis. The posterior nares in the tortoises are separated by the combined ento-pterygoids (upper and back part of the "vomer"), and are bounded by the maxillaries and the palatines, the latter remaining open or ununited across the vault of the palate. In the turtles, the vault of the palate and the posterior nares present more of the mammalian aspect, although still formed essentially on the type of the corresponding parts in the bird. This is effected by the ethmoidal neurapophyseal plates (palatal plate of the "vomer") which lie somewhat above the level of the vault of the palate in the tortoises, passing down into, and forming an area of it in the turtles, extending from its posterior margin half-way, or quite up to the intermaxillary palate-plates. In the latter arrangement the ethmoidal area is hexagonal, and separates the palatal plates of the maxillaries from one another. In the former it is pentagonal; and the palatal maxillary plates meet in the mesial line in front of it. The palatal plates of the palatines are more or less developed in the turtles; and many approach one another at the free margin of the vault, but are always separated by the posterior or free margin of the ethmoidal area.

The arrangement of the vault of the palate in the turtles, and the peculiar chelonian configuration of the pterygoids, lead to the very remarkable combination of ornithic and mammalian structure presented by the nasal fossæ and palatal vault of the crocodiles. The mammalian characteristics are the full development of the intermaxillary and nasal bones, with the extensive, although cartilaginous, vomer. The vomerine sclerotome of the crocodile is not closed anteriorly as in all the other lacertians, in the ophidians, amphibians, and birds, but presents a completely perforated catacentric arrangement. This complete form of the vomerine necessitates a rhinal sclerotome, which, accordingly, feebly represented in the crocodiles and alligators, appears to be more fully developed in the gavials. The extensive and complete crocodilian palatal vault is only apparently mammalian, it is partially ornithic or chelonian in its constitution. As in the mammal, the anterior extremity of the vault is formed by the pair of fully formed palatal inter-maxillary plates. Except in the alligators, in which there is a slight intrusion of the ento-pterygoids, the palatal plates of the maxillaries, meeting along the mesial line, form the second and most extensive area of the palatal vault. The next area of the vault consists, as in the turtles, of the ethmoidal neurapophyses (the so-called "palatals"), united along the mesial line, and much elongated backwards. The posterior margin of the combined ethmoidal neurapophyses of the turtle forms the central part of the free margin of the palate; but the completion in the crocodile of the deflected outer margin and central ridge of the pterygoids into a double tube, or pterygoidean prolongation backwards of the nasal fossæ, produces a corresponding elongation of the palatal vault, which accordingly presents, behind its ethmoidal, an extensive and broad pterygoidean area, which thus completes the vault behind, as in certain Cetacea and Edentata. The great elongation backwards of the combined maxillary palatal plates, the corresponding elongation of the combined ethmoidal neurapophyses, and the great breadth of the pterygoidean area, have displaced the palate-bones so far backwards and outwards, that, separated from the ento-pterygoids and the ethmoidal neurapophyses by a wide chasm, but retaining their connections with the maxillaries and pterygoids, and coming into contact with the malar, they are, in fact, extruded from the walls of the nasal fossæ, and from the palatal vault, and, thus disguised, have been hitherto known only as "transverse bones," "adgustal bones," "pterygoïdes externes," "ecto-pterygoids."

The Nasal Passage of the Cyclostomous Fishes.—The cyclostomes differ from all other fishes in possessing a tubular passage, which, opening externally above the oral disk, passes backwards to the combined olfactory capsules, and behind which it terminates in a *cul-de-sac* in the lamprey, but in the myxine and bdellostoma communicates with the alimentary and respiratory tract.

The form and arrangement of the cartilages, which enter into the formation of the walls of this tubular passage, have been figured and minutely described in the classical memoirs of Joh. Müller, on the "Cyclostomous Fishes." It becomes a point of much interest to ascertain the morphological character of this tubular passage, and to determine the morphological relations of its cartilaginous elements.

The olfactory capsules of the myxine, bdellostoma, and lamprey, are completely fused into one another at the mesial plane, so as to form a single chamber, situated immediately in front of, and in a line with, the cranial cavity. The common olfactory chamber communicates with the cranial cavity by two orifices perforated in the fibro-cartilaginous transverse septum, for the passage forwards of the olfactory nerves. The olfactory chamber opens below into the naso-pharyngeal passage. In the lamprey this passage is membranous throughout, the portion in front of the olfactory chamber lying above the posterior superior oral shield; its posterior portion passing back between the base of the cranium and the central part of the palatal cartilage, terminates in a *cul-de-sac* at its pharyngeal extremity. In the myxine and bdellostoma the posterior portion of the passage is a membranous canal situated between the base of the cranium and the mesial palatal cartilage, and opens posteriorly into the pharynx. That portion of the naso-pharyngeal passage in front of the olfactory chamber is supported above and laterally by a series of ten cartilaginous rings, incomplete below—the entire arrangement closely resembling a mammalian trachea. The membranous floor of this part of the passage is supported by the anterior portion of the central, and the transverse junction of the lateral palatal cartilages, and in front by the mesial and transverse superior oral cartilages.

The morphological constitution of this remarkable nasal skeleton appears to be similar to that of the nasal fossæ of the higher Vertebrata. The olfactory capsules have passed inwards, as in the bird and reptile, so that, instead of projecting from the sides of the cranium, like the auditory capsules, they occupy the space of the corresponding cranial segment. The incomplete cartilaginous rings of the nasal tube, viewed in their relations to the cranium and conjoined olfactory capsules, are in the position of a superadded series of neural arches, similar to the neural portions of the rhinal and vomerine mammalian sclerotomes, destitute, however, of centrums, but supported below by the peculiarly-developed palatine and maxillary elements which have passed forward beneath them. The entire arrangement presents the general characters, or is developed on the plan of the nasal fossæ of the reptile, bird, and mammal, with the additional peculiarity of an increase in the number of constituent segments, similar to that which apparently exists in the proboscidian mammals.

POST-STOMAL CEPHALIC SCLEROTOMES.—*Their Central and Neural Elements.*—As the discrimination of the constituent central and neural elements of the three post-stomal segments of the skull demands a constant reference from the one segment to the other, I shall examine them together. Of these three segments—the post-sphenoidal, the temporal, and the occipital—the second has not hitherto been recognised except by Carus, whose system includes a temporal intervertebra.

My attention was directed to the temporal segment of the cranium by the remarkable indications of it presented by the human skull. The human occipital bone, in addition to that upper angular portion of its squamous plate, which presents the relations of the interparietal, exhibits all the characteristics of a vertebral centrum, in combination with neura- and meta-neurapophyses. The inferior articular processes of this cranial segment are largely developed, in relation to the atlas. But it has not been hitherto noted, that the so-called jugular processes are in fact its upper or anterior pair of articular processes; and that, consequently, the jugular processes on the posterior margins of the petrosal portions of the temporals must be the zygopophyses of the succeeding cranial segment. These occipital and temporal jugular articular processes, like the corresponding processes in the column below, present distinct cartilaginous articular facets, and are contiguous to the "foramina lacera posteriora" or "intervertebral foramina," formed by the conjunction of the temporal and occipital jugular fossæ, and which transmit, as in the spine, vessels and nerves. But the petrous portion of the human temporal bone has, in addition, a pair of distinct pro-zygopophyses. They are situated on the anterior margins of the petrous portions, where these margins form the angles with the squamous portions, in which are situated the openings of the Eustachian tubes. The articular surfaces of these processes are perpendicularly striated, and are applied against corresponding surfaces of the so-called styloid processes of the sphenoid at the posterior angles of its great wings. These "styloid processes" are therefore the zygopophyses of the post-sphenoidal sclerotome. The pro-zygopophyses of the post-sphenoidal and the zygopophyses of the pre-sphenoidal may be observed at the fore part of the pterygo-palatine groove in the fœtal bone, but are more remarkably developed in the young ruminant; in which also may be observed the zygopophyseal connection of the pre-sphenoidal with the ethmoidal neurapophyses.

We have, therefore, in these zygopophyseal connections distinct evidence of five cranial segments—an ethmoidal, pre-sphenoidal, post-sphenoidal, temporal, and occipital—in addition to the vomerine and rhinal.

For the further development of this subject, the cranium of a cyprinoid fish should next be selected. If the lateral wall of the cranium be examined, either from the external or mesial aspect, five serially-arranged neurapophyseal plates will be recognised, connected to one another by four distinct zygopophyseal articulations. These plates are, from before backwards, the so-called " pre-frontal," the " cranial ethmoid," the " orbito-sphenoid " of Owen, the " ali-sphenoid " of Owen, and the lateral occipital. I have already stated the grounds on which I believe we must look upon the " pre-frontals " of the fish as the neurapophyses of the ethmoidal, and the " cranial ethmoid," as the combined neurapophyses of the pre-sphenoidal neural arches. If so, then the succeeding plate must be the " ali-sphenoid," and not the " orbito-sphenoid," as Professor Owen considers it to be; and therefore, as there has never been a question regarding the lateral occipital, the plate interposed between the latter and the former, as it has all the characters of a neurapophysis, indicates the existence of a cranial segment between the post-sphenoidal and occipital. I shall not at present allude to the various opinions entertained regarding this plate, but shall merely distinguish it as the inferior temporal neurapophysis.

Proceeding now to the consideration of the centrums corresponding to this series of neurapophyses, it must be observed that in no osseous fish in any stage of development have more than three osseous pieces been observed in the basis of the cranium from the so-called " vomer" to the " basi-occipital" included. The assumed " connation " of the centrums of the pre- and post-sphenoids, as held by Professor Owen, has at present no support from embryology; the missing centrum or centrums must therefore be accounted for otherwise than by a hypothetical division of the " basi-sphenoid." Professor Owen appears, indeed, to a certain extent to admit this, for in certain fishes he considers the symmetrical Y-shaped ossicle marked in his diagrams 9^1, and superimposed on the pre-sphenoidal process of his basi-sphenoid, as the central part; while that process itself he holds to be the capsular portion of the ossified notochord.

That mutual elongation and overlapping of the cranial centrums formerly alluded to is strongly marked in fishes, the sphenoidal centrum being dovetailed into and elongated beneath the occipital behind, and above the ethmoidal ("vomer") in front. The manner in which the anterior elongated portion of the post-sphenoidal centrum of the bird elevates and carries on its upper surface the compressed pre-sphenoidal centrum has already been stated; and I must again observe that it appears to me that the pre-sphenoidal centrum exists in certain fishes only in the form of a bar of cartilage—a portion of the "primordial cranium" situated on the upper surface of the anterior prolongation of the post-sphenoidal centrum, and terminating on the upper surface of the ethmoidal centrum or so-called "vomer," and that in fishes with an "ossified orbital septum" or "cranial ethmoid," it is to be recognised in the half-ossified cartilaginous mass which unites the right and left plates of that "septum," and which have been already indicated as its corresponding neurapophyses. The pre-sphenoidal is an undeveloped centrum in the fish, retaining more or less of its "primordial" texture and form, and elevated, therefore, above, or carried inwards, so as to be covered by the fully-developed ethmoidal and post-sphenoidal centrums.

I am acquainted with no example of a fully-developed temporal centrum. It is represented in the "primordial cranium" by the quadrilateral cartilaginous plate, bounded laterally by the ear-capsules, behind by the portion corresponding to the cartilaginous lateral occipitals, and in front by the part in which the post-sphenoidal centrum first appears. In all vertebrate animals this portion of the basis of the primordial cranium is of great comparative extent, and is encroached upon by the advancing ossification of the occipital and post-sphenoidal centrums in modes which vary in the different vertebrate forms. In mammals, the occipital advances into it at the expense of the post-sphenoidal centrum. In birds and fishes the post-sphenoidal passes more backwards. In the reptiles the two centrums appear to share it equally.

In all the forms, I believe that traces of the intermediate or temporal centrum may be detected, either in the cartilaginous or osseous condition. In fishes, more or less of the primordial cartilage remains above the junction of the occipital centrum, post-sphenoidal centrum, and temporal neurapophyses ("petrosals"), and covered more or less internally, or towards the cranial cavity, by the internal prolongations of the occipital centrum, and of the temporal and post-sphenoidal neurapophyses. The peculiar canal for the muscles of the orbit existing in certain fishes, and which is roofed over principally by the "petrosals," or temporal neurapophyses, appears to be hollowed out principally in the primordial temporal centrum, and to be lined by its constituent cartilage. The peculiar Y-shaped bone met with in the pike, perch, and salmon, marked 9^1 by Professor Owen, and * by Hallman, and considered by the former as that portion of the pre-sphenoidal centrum which results from the ossification of the corresponding central portion of the notochord, appears to me to be a central element, but referable rather to the post-sphenoidal or temporal than to the pre-sphenoidal segment. For, in the first place, it may be questioned whether the corda dorsalis of the fish reaches the region of the pre-sphenoid; and, in the second place, if I am correct in my determination of the post-sphenoidal and temporal neurapophyses of the fish, the two ascending limbs of this bone abut against these latter elements, and are not at all connected with the pre-sphenoidal neurapophyses. As, moreover, these ascending limbs of the bone in question are more intimately connected with the bones which Professor Owen considers to be the ali-sphenoids, but which I must hold to be the inferior temporal neurapophyses, I am inclined to conceive it an ossified portion of the temporal centrum.

With regard to the bone termed by Hallman os innominatum, which is small but well marked in the carp, and larger in the perch, and which Professor Owen considers to be the petrosal, I quite agree with him. But while I do so, I make a distinction between an ossified portion of the auditory capsule and the bone which constitutes the corresponding neurapophysis, in the same manner as I find myself compelled to admit the independent existence of the ethmoidal neurapophysis and the olfactory capsules, whether fibrous, cartilaginous, or osseous, and the corresponding independent existence of the variously-modified sclerotics and the orbito-sphenoids.

Proceeding now to the examination of the remaining elements of the post-stomal neural arches in the fish, I would observe that if we put aside those conceptions of the constitution of the arches in question, derived from previous study of the cranium of the mammal, the constitution of the corresponding arches in the fish which naturally suggests itself is the following :—

1. Over the occipital centrum the lateral occipitals and the external occipitals—as two pairs of neurapophyses, and the superior occipital—as a single meta-neurapophysis.

2. Over the position of the temporal centrum, the bones termed petrosals by the continental anatomists, but by Professor Owen petrosals in the cod, and ali-sphenoids in the carp, and over these the mastoids, these "petrosals" or "ali-sphenoids," along with the mastoids—as two pairs of neurapophyses, and the contiguous or separated bones usually termed "parietals," as a divided meta-neurapophysis.

3. Over the great basi-sphenoid, the bones termed by Professor Owen orbito-sphenoids in the carp, and ali-sphenoids in the cod, with the post-frontals—as two pairs of neurapophyses, the meta-neurapophyses being absent.

Before making any statements in support of this view of the constitution of the post-stomal neural arches in the cranium of the osseous fish, I would direct attention to the corresponding parts in the other Vertebrata from the same point of view.

In the bird, the occipital neural arch wants the ex-occipitals. The temporal arch possesses no centrum, but the petrosals, mastoids, and parietals are placed one over the other as two pairs of neurapophyses and a divided meta-neurapophysis. The post-sphenoidal centrum is surmounted by the post-sphenoidal wings and the feebly-developed post-frontals—as two pairs of neurapophyses, while the meta-neurapophysis is deficient.

In the crocodiles, the occipital arch, as in the birds, has lost the upper pair of neurapophyses. The temporal centrum is not developed, but the two pairs of neurapophyses, and an undivided meta-neurapophysis—the petrosals (ali-sphenoids of Owen), mastoids, and so-called parietal—form a continuous arch. The post-sphenoidal centrum is again found to carry two pairs of neurapophyses, the great sphenoidal wings (orbito-sphenoids of Owen), and the post-frontals. The meta-neurapophysis is missing.

In the chelonians, the occipital arch consists of one pair of neurapophyses and a meta-neurapophysis surmounting a centrum. The temporal centrum is not developed. The inferior pair of neurapophyses, the so-called ex-occipitals, abut externally against the mastoids, and are thus connected with the largely-developed so-called "parietals." These "parietals" not only form a large part of the cranial and temporal vaults, but send down laminæ to rest on the pterygoids, and thus enter into the formation of the lateral walls of the cranial cavity in front of the post-sphenoidal wings. Above the post-sphenoidal centrum, the post-sphenoidal wings and the post-frontals rise in connection with one another as two pairs of neurapophyses, but the meta-neurapophysis is again wanting.

In the ophidians, the occipital centrum is again surmounted by one pair of neurapophyses and a meta-neurapophysis. The temporal centrum has disappeared behind the basi-sphenoid ; but the well-developed so-called "petrosals," the ali-sphenoids of Professor Owen, are surmounted by the elongated and nearly extruded mastoids; while the single meta-neurapophysis, the undivided "parietal," is so largely developed, that, passing down as in the chelonian to the basis of the cranium, it rests upon the post-sphenoidal centrum over a great extent in front of its own neurapophyses, so as altogether to obliterate the post-sphenoidal wing. The post-sphenoidal centrum is there cut off from the post-frontals, which constitute the only remaining elements of its neural arch.

In the lacertians, the occipital centrum, with its pair of neurapophyses and single neurapophysis, is followed by a temporal arch, without a centrum, but with two pairs of neurapophyses, "petrosals," and mastoids, and an undivided meta-neurapophysis or "parietal," generally single in front, but projecting backwards, with the mastoids on each side behind. The post-sphenoidal centrum is not surmounted by ali-sphenoids, except the parietal columella represents these elements. The post-frontals again appear; but without a corresponding meta-neurapophysis.

In the frogs, the occipital centrum and the corresponding meta-neurapophyses have disappeared; a single pair of neurapophyses constituting the sole osseous elements of the arch. The temporal centrum appears in the primordial cartilage, which extends across on the upper surface of the posterior part of the much-elongated "basi-sphenoid," and between the cartilaginous auditory capsules. The latter are intimately connected to the inferior temporal neurapophyses, the ali-sphenoids of Professor Owen, with which feebly-developed mastoids or superior neurapophyses are conjoined; the whole being surmounted by the greatly-developed antero-posteriorly elongated so-called "parietals," which dip down slightly at their margins, in front of the temporal region towards the "basi-sphenoid," as in the chelonians and ophidians. The portions of the post-sphenoidal wings and the post-frontals are occupied by fibrous texture; the "basi-sphenoid" or post-sphenoidal centrum extending forwards below; and the "parietals" taking the place of the deficient meta-neurapophyses.

The preceding view of the arrangement of the centrums and neural arches of the post-stomal sclerotomes of the lower forms of cranium, is that which would appear naturally to suggest itself to a mind uninfluenced by the arrangement of the corresponding region of the mammalian skull. It is assumed throughout that there are more or less complete cartilaginous or osseous auditory capsules in addition to corresponding neurapophyses; and that these neurapophyses are not post-sphenoidal but temporal, as evinced by their zygopophyseal connections in the human cranium. No reference has been made to the relations of the contested "petrosals" and ali-sphenoids" to the fifth nerve, because, while the fundamental relation of that nerve to the post-sphenoidal sclerotome is admitted, the divisions of the nerve exhibit the same tendency to vary in their points of exit, as is presented by the other cerebral nerves; moving backwards more or less across the corresponding neurapophyses, and notching or perforating the neurapophyses behind. In fact, until a more minute investigation of the development of the cranium in its relations to the cerebral nerves has afforded some explanation of the varied relations of these parts in the series, we cannot, in my opinion, attach much weight to the determination of a "petrosal" or an "ali-sphenoid" by means of their relations to the trigeminal nerve.

Proceeding now to the examination of the post-stomal centrums and neural arches of the mammalian cranium, let the human skull be selected for examination. The occipital centrum is surmounted by a pair of neurapophyses and a double meta-neurapophysis. But again, surmounting the meta-neurapophyses there is a double piece, which occasionally remains permanently separate from the "occipital bone."

This double piece, or pair of bones, presents the relations of the interparietal bones in lower Mammalia. They may extend laterally to join the "mastoids," or they may be connected to the latter by a more or less continuous chain of "triquetral bones" in the line of the lambdoidal suture.

The zygopophyseal attachments of the "petrous portions of the temporal bone" indicate these masses to be neurapophyses enveloping the ossified auditory capsules. Keeping out of view the "squamous," "tympanic," and "styloid" portions of the "temporal bones," the "mastoidal portions" become early and intimately connected with the "petrous portions." Commencing with the "petrous portions," as an inferior pair of temporal neurapophyses, they are surmounted, as in the lower Vertebrata, by the "mastoidal portions" as a second pair of neurapophyses, while the arch is closed by the double element which forms the upper angle of the "occipital bone," as a meta-neurapophysis. There are well-marked indications of a temporal centrum in the human cranium. The irregularly-truncated apices of the "petrous portions," directed obliquely forwards and inwards, are continuous, by means of the fibro-cartilaginous remains of the basis of the "primordial cranium," which occupy the "foramina lacera media," with the inclined plate of bone which, in the plane of the "basilar process of the occipital" or occipital centrum, forms the back part of the "body of the sphenoid," including the "posterior clinoid processes." This plate of bone is frequently surrounded by a deep groove, the posterior part of which lodges the "transverse venous sinus," and I have seen it nearly detached.

The feebly-developed post-frontals in the bird have disappeared in the mammal, so that the post-sphenoidal centrum is surmounted by the "ali-sphenoids," as a single pair of neurapophyses; and by the enormously-expanded double meta-neurapophysis in the human subject, or the less developed form of parietals in the Mammalia generally.

The fundamental facts on which the preceding determination of the comparative constitution of the post-stomal neural arches of the cranium depends, are the zygopophyseal connections of the human "petrosals." If the "petrosals" even in one species can be proved to present the characters of neurapophyses, the sclerotome to which they belong must exist in addition to those to which the "ali-sphenoids" and "orbito-sphenoids" are referable. The existence of temporal neurapophyses explains the existence of interparietal, in addition to parietal bones in the mammal; both of these meta-neurapophyses taking part in the protection of the developed cerebrum; while the non-appearance of the anterior or spheno-parietal in the bird, reptile, and fish, accords with the complete development of the posterior or temporo-parietal, repressed in the former by the influence of the cerebrum, and by the full development of the ethmoido-frontal. I base my determination of the separate existence and reciprocal development of ethmoido-frontals and spheno-frontals, of spheno-parietals and temporo-parietals, not only on my analysis of the bones themselves in the series, but also on the evident reciprocal influence which the superimposed cerebral mass in the mammal, and the bulky organs of sense and uncovered sense-ganglions of the lower Vertebrata have on the cranial neural arches. I believe also, that in this, as in other departments of inquiry, we are apt to look for greater simplicity and uniformity in details than actually exist. The simplicity of natural law consists in the comprehensiveness of its general principles. In tracing these principles into details, the complexity is found to be infinite.

The Hæmal Arches of the Post-stomal Cephalic Sclerotomes.—The clue by means of which we can alone be safely guided to the morphological constitution of these arches, in the midst of the varied complexity which they present to the comparative anatomist, is afforded by embryology. The hæmal arches of the post-stomal sclerotomes are developed each in the corresponding pair of "visceral laminæ." By endeavouring to ascertain, therefore, in which of these post-stomal "visceral laminæ" the sclerous elements of the varied forms of the post-stomal hæmal arches are originally formed, the morphological constitution of the individual hæmal arches may reasonably be anticipated. If, again, I am correct in my determination of the constitution of the pre-stomal sclerotomes, the allocation of the individual post-stomal hæmal arches to their proper centrums and neural arches follows as a matter of course.

From the observations more particularly of Rathke and Reichert, the formation of the osseous elements of the post-stomal hæmal arches in the "visceral laminæ," is preceded in each by a more or less distinct and continuous cartilaginous streak or band. Rathke found seven pairs of these cartilaginous streaks loosely connected to the basis of the embryo head of the *Blennius viviparus*, and corresponding to the mandibular, hyoidean, first, second, third, and fourth branchial and pharyngeal arches. In the adder the same indefatigable embryologist and comparative anatomist found a cartilaginous style, with a process directed forward in the position of the maxillary, palate, and pterygoid bones, embedded in the first visceral lamina, and its "superior maxillary process," and attached to the side of the basis of the primordial cranium in front of its auditory region; a similar style lay in the second visceral lamina, and was firmly attached to the base of the cartilaginous cranium behind, and external to the auditory capsule; a third style lay in the third visceral lamina, and was also firmly attached like a rib to the occipital region of the primordial cranium. Similar primordial hæmal arches have been found by Reichert in the visceral laminæ of the mammal and bird, and by numerous observers in the Amphibia. It is important to observe again at this point, that the relations of all these seven pairs of primordial hæmal arches are similar. Firstly, all the visceral laminæ in which they are developed appear to consist of the serous, vascular, and mucous layers united; secondly, the cartilaginous streaks are formed towards their inner surfaces, under the mucous layer; thirdly, the heart and vascular arches are on their exterior, under the serous layer.

First Post-stomal Hæmal Arch.—The constitution of this arch must be determined by the examination of the development of the first post-stomal visceral lamina. It has been already stated that the process usually considered as the upper part of the so-called "first visceral lamina" is, if its general relations be taken into account, the posterior pre-stomal visceral lamina in which the pre-sphenoidal hæmal arch is developed.

The cartilaginous streak in the first post-stomal visceral lamina of the mammal divides into two portions. The superior and smaller of the two becomes the incus. The long inferior portion is the cartilage of Meckel; around the lower part of which the corresponding half of the lower jaw is developed; the upper part forms the slender process and the head of the malleus. As the Eustachian tube, the tympanum, and the external auditory passage, consist of the persistent upper portion of the first visceral cleft, the cartilage of the Eustachian tube, and the tympanic bone, which are continuous with one another, and form the floor of these three spaces, are developed in blastema deposited near the upper extremity of the cleft. This blastema also forms the membrane of the tympanum, into which the handle of the malleus shoots. It is to be observed that this lower jaw and tympanic bone do not originate in the primordial cartilaginous streak, but in blastema deposited around it. The tympanic bone forms at first an inverted arch across the visceral cleft, or a ring incomplete above, which supports the membrane of the tympanum on the outer side of the attenuated portion of Meckel's cartilage, which connects the malleus to the inner side of the jaw. It then extends inwards, so as to form the floor of the tympanum and Eustachian tube, folding up before and behind, and thus, inclosing the incus and malleus, leaves the latter connected to the jaw through the tympanic fissure.

The development of the first post-stomal visceral lamina appears, therefore, to indicate at least four elements on each side of the mandibular hæmal arch in the mammal. The tympanic element is probably complex; the mandibular consists of at least two portions, one on the outer, the other on the inner side of the corresponding portion of Meckel's cartilage.

In the bird the omoid and palate bones are formed like the pterygoid and palate bones of the mammal, in the so-called "superior maxillary process." In the proper first post-stomal visceral lamina, the primordial cartilaginous streak divides, as in the mammal, into two portions. The upper and smaller of the two becomes the quadrate bone; the lower and longer portion—Meckel's cartilage—becomes enveloped in the corresponding half of the lower jaw; but instead of the upper end of this portion forming the slender process of a malleus, it remains as the peculiarly-formed articular piece of the jaw itself. The original intimate connection of the rudiment of the pterygoid bone, in the so-called "superior maxillary process," with the upper or incudal portion of the primordial cartilaginous streak of the first post-stomal visceral lamina of the mammal, speedily diminishes; but in the bird, not only does the pterygoid or omoid bone rapidly increase in relative size and configuration; but the quadrate portion of the first visceral streak does so likewise. The latter also exhibits, attached to its outer side, as the omoid is to its internal process, a styliform ossicle, the rudiment of the quadrate-jugal bone, which again is connected anteriorly to the jugal.

Reichert, who has minutely described and figured the development of this visceral lamina in the bird, makes no allusion to the remarkable indication which it affords of the signification of the quadrate bone, and articular piece of the lower jaw. It affords, as it appears to me, sufficient evidence that the quadrate bone of the bird is the homologue of the mammalian incus, and that the articular piece of its lower jaw is the homologue of that ossified portion of the upper end of Meckel's cartilage, which in the mammal forms the slender process of the malleus.

The quadrate bone has been hitherto considered as the homologue of the tympanic bone in the mammal, not only from the proximity of the latter to the condyle of the jaw, but chiefly from its presumed absence in the skull of the bird. But there appears to me to be sufficient evidence of its existence, not only in the fibro-cartilaginous frame which connects the margin of the tympanic membrane to the mastoid, lateral occipital, and basi-sphenoid, but more particularly in the thin well-defined lamina of bone, which, apparently united to its fellow of the opposite side, forms the floor of the tympanic cellular space in the broad posterior portion of the basisphenoid. As these apparently united laminæ are continuous with the single cartilaginous Eustachian tube, below the single or double osseous Eustachian orifice, I am induced to believe that they will turn out to be the feebly-developed representatives of the tympanic bones of the mammal.

By a very beautiful analysis Professor Owen has proved that the quadrate-jugal bone of the bird is the homologue of the squamous portion of the mammalian temporal. I cannot, however, give my assent to his determination of its special homology, as a portion of the subdivided radiating appendage of the maxillary arch. Its relations in birds and crocodiles, in which it presents all its fundamental connections, appear to me to show that it is an anterior actinapophysis of the mandibular arch; passing forwards to abut against the malar, which I have already stated to be a posterior actinapophysis of the ethmoidal hæmal arch, or as in the lacertians against the post-frontals. The squamous portion of the quadrate-jugal bone is a mammalian superaddition, to adapt it to the part it takes in the formation of the cranial wall. It is withdrawn therefore from the quadrate or incudal portion of the mandibular arch (which portion diminishes relatively), and passes—as the entire bone does in the lizards—upwards to be connected with the cranial wall. The development of the first post-stomal visceral lamina in the bird appears therefore to afford evidence that the mandibular hæmal arch in the bird and mammal includes a tympanic element, a quadrate or incudal, a malleal or articular, and the elements of the corresponding side of the lower jaw.

On the same grounds I am inclined to believe that the articular piece of the lower jaw of the reptile and amphibian is malleal like the corresponding piece in the bird, and not the homologue of the condyle of the mammalian jaw. They are all malleal portions of Meckel's cartilage retained in connection with the jaw. In like manner, I am inclined to believe that the so-called tympanic bone of the reptile and amphibian, like the quadrate or so-called tympanic bone of the bird, is not the homologue of the tympanic bone of the mammal, but of the incus. The incus of the mammal has been set free from its fundamental quadrate-jugal and pterygoid connections to co-operate with the similarly released malleus in the economy of the ear. The absence of proper tympanic bones in the reptile and amphibian is explained by the absence or feeble development of the tympanic cavity. I am inclined to think, however, that traces of them may be detected under and between the basi-sphenoid and occipital of the crocodile, in the walls of those canals which connect, as Professor Owen has shown, by a common tubular communication, the Sella Turcica and the tympanic cavities with the basis of the cranium.

The tympanic systems and lower jaw of the osseous fish

form together a well-marked hæmal arch, developed in the first post-stomal visceral lamina of the embryo. From what has already been stated regarding the sclerous elements which result from the development of this visceral lamina in the other Vertebrata, Professor Owen's view of the tympanic system of the osseous fish, as the teleologically-divided homologue of the quadrate bone of the bird, and tympanic bone of the reptile, would appear to require additional evidence. We are not yet in possession of materials for a rigorous determination; but it appears extremely probable that the tympanic bones of the osseous fish are morphological, as well as teleological elements. If the articular piece of the lower jaw be assumed as the malleal portion of the persistent cartilage of Meckel, the hypo-tympanic occupies the position of the incudal element, connected, as usual, with the pterygoid. The epi-tympanic is in the position of the proper tympanic element of the mammal, while the pre-tympanic, in its relations to the hypo-tympanic and pterygoid, closely resembles the quadrate-jugal or squamosal.

The opercular bones form on each side of the mandibular arch a series of actinapophyseal elements, which, from the view already taken of such elements, would appear to be posterior, as the quadrate-jugal or squamosal is anterior in relation to the sclerotome. With regard to any traces of these opercular or actinapophyseal elements in the mandibular hæmal arch of the higher Vertebrata, I must agree with Carus in considering the cartilages of the external ear in the Mammalia as homologous with them. The objection of Rathke to this determination of Carus—that the cartilage of the concha is attached to the tympanic bone so as to be situated at the back of the auditory foramen—that is, at the posterior margins of the first visceral cleft—appears to me to be met by taking into account the peculiar curved form which the tympanic element assumes in passing from before backwards across the cleft.

The allocation of the mandibular hæmal arch to the postsphenoidal or first post-stomal sclerotome follows from the analysis already made of the pre-stomal sclerotomes.

The Second and Third Post-stomal Hæmal Arches.—As the researches, more especially of Rathke and Reichert, on the development of the first visceral lamina, afford a clue to the constitution of the corresponding hæmal arch, so do the labours of these observers in like manner indicate the nature of the second and third arches. These arches are developed in the second and third visceral laminæ, and, from the varied forms which they present in the series, could only have been determined by an appeal to embryology.

In the mammal the primordial cartilaginous streak in the second visceral lamina, and which is attached superiorly to the auditory region, divides into segments, the uppermost of which becomes the stapes; while the succeeding become, in succession with the intermediate soft portions, the "stapedius muscle," the pyramid and its prolongation downwards, the styloid process, the stylo-hyoid ligament, and the series of sclerous elements which terminates below in the anterior horn of the hyoid.

The primordial cartilaginous streak in the third visceral lamina is attached to the occipital region, breaking up into four segments; the two upper disappear; the two lower become respectively the posterior horn and corresponding half of the body of the hyoid.

In the second visceral lamina of the bird, in like manner, the auditory columella is developed superiorly, and the feeble anterior horn of the hyoid below, while the elements of the suspensory or posterior horn of the hyoid are formed in the third visceral lamina. The fibrous septum of the tongue and the epiglottis of the mammal make their appearance in the line of junction of the second and third visceral laminæ. The respective share taken by these two laminæ in the formation of the so-called basi-glosso and uro-hyals in the bird remains to be determined.

The precise observations of Rathke have shown that the lateral halves of the feebly-developed hyoid of the ophidian are formed by the lower portions of the primordial cartilaginous streaks of the second pair of visceral laminæ, while the auditory columellæ are formed in their upper portions. Rathke also found that the primordial cartilaginous streaks of the third pair of visceral laminæ, and which are attached to the occipital region, disappear altogether.

There are no embryological observations in sufficient detail to indicate the morphological relations of the more or less complex hyoid apparatus in the chelonian and lacertian. The so-called hyoid, or suspensory arch of the branchial apparatus in the Amphibia, is developed in the second pair of visceral laminæ. The corresponding arch in the tadpole, and the anterior or suspensory horn of the so-called "hyoid" of the frog, are also developed in this pair of visceral laminæ. The suspensory arch of the branchial apparatus is attached to the quadrate, or so-called "tympanic" piece of the mandibular arch, and not to the base of the cranium. Rathke had observed a filament extending between the auditory region of the cranium and the quadrate cartilage of the tadpole. He found that the so-called "malleus and incus" are developed in this filament. According to Reichert, this filament appears to be the upper part of the second primordial cartilaginous streak, which, in consequence of the peculiar manner in which it curves forward superiorly towards the quadrate cartilage (a curvature of the same kind towards the quadrate bone has been observed by Rathke in the adder), becomes attached to it. In consequence of this attachment, the hyoidean arch becomes suspended to the quadrate portion of the mandibular; and the upper portion, between the quadrate cartilage and the auditory region of the skull, becomes converted into those elements in the frog which have their homologues in the stapes of the mammal, and the columella, with its cartilaginous extremities, in the bird and reptile.

As the cartilaginous branchial arches of the tadpole, and of the other Amphibia, are formed in the succeeding visceral laminæ, it would appear to follow, as a necessary consequence, that the suspensory or hyoidean arch of the amphibian, with its inferior mesial element, and along with the auditory ossicles, is homologous with the anterior or suspensory part of the hyoid, along with the stirrup-bones in the mammal, and with the corresponding structures in the bird and serpent; and that the first branchial arch of the amphibian, with its corresponding inferior mesial elements, are homologous with the posterior horns and body of the hyoid in the mammal, and with the posterior or suspensory horns, with the corresponding inferior mesial elements of the hyoid in the bird. The so-called posterior horns of the hyoid of the frog cannot, therefore, be the homologues, as Professor Owen's statements might lead us to infer, of the posterior horns of the hyoid of the mammal or bird. The posterior horns of the hyoid of the frog are the remains of its posterior pair of branchial arches, or enlargements of the posterior angles of its basi-hyals. They are developed therefore in its posterior visceral laminæ; while the posterior hyoidean horns of the mammal and bird are developed in the third pair of visceral laminæ.

As the skeleton of the hyoidean and branchial apparatus of the fish is developed in the form of a series of inverted arches in the corresponding visceral laminæ, from the second inclusive, we are obliged to conclude that its hyoidean arch is the homologue of the stylo-hyoidean arch, with the stirrup-bones—or second post-stomal arch—in the mammal; and of the corresponding portion of the hyoidean apparatus in the bird, with the columellæ; and of the entire hyoid in the serpent, with the columellæ; and that the first branchial arch in the fish is the homologue of the corresponding arch in the amphibian; of the posterior horns of the hyoid, and their associated elements in the bird; and of the posterior horns and body of the hyoid in the mammal.

It has not yet been determined upon what developmental change the suspension of the hyoidean arch of the fish to its mandibular arch depends. It is probably of the same nature as that which occurs in the tadpole, with this difference, that the upper portion of the hyoidean arch disappears in the fish, without developing a stapedial ossicle; while its lower portion remains permanently connected to the mandibular arch, instead of regaining an attachment to the cranium.

The hyoidean and branchial arches of the fish are provided, as has been already stated, with a well-developed double series of actinapophyses, for the support of the branchiostegal membrane and the branchial laminæ. These actinapophyses in the fish are foreshadowed in the tadpole by the tubercular margins of its branchial styles.

The question may now be put—if we are brought by reference to the development of the parts to allocate to the three post-stomal sclerotomes, hæmal arches, consisting respectively of the sclerous parts developed in the three anterior post-stomal visceral laminæ, to what sclerotomes are we to refer the potential or actual hæmal arches in the remaining visceral laminæ? For reasons already stated, they cannot be disposed of by referring them to a splanchno-skeleton, because in that case the hyoidean arch or arches, and apparently the mandibular arch also, must be referred to the same category. Neither can they be referred to any of the cervical, or trunk sclerotomes; because it would appear that the visceral walls of the head are alone perforated by clefts. We are not yet prepared to answer the question. It involves, as it appears to me, the investigation of a residual quantity, the solution of which will require some information in reference to certain points, regarding which we cannot at present be said to possess any. First, the development of the cyclostomes, but more especially of branchiostoma; secondly, the mode in which the trunk sclerotomes increase in number and become arranged in groups; thirdly, the mode in which the same changes proceed in the cranium; fourthly, the determination of the series of cephalic nervous centres, with their corresponding nerves (neurotomes), more especially in the medulla oblongata, with the causes which determine the grouping and order in which the cerebral nerves pass through the walls of the cranium.

If there appear to be no sufficient developmental grounds for making a distinction between the branchial arches of the amphibian and fish, as belonging to a splanchno-skeleton, and the hyoidean and mandibular as referable to the neuro- or endo-skeleton, it becomes important to determine the signification of the sclerous elements of the larynx, trachea, and bronchial tubes. Without presuming to anticipate the minute observation of the development of the parts themselves necessary for the solution of a question of this kind, I would venture to suggest that the proper cartilages of the larynx are developed from the inferior or mesial extremities of certain of the visceral laminæ; and that the cartilages of the trachea and bronchial tubes are a pair of highly-developed actinapophyseal systems, referable to one of the posterior visceral arches.

Post-stomal Neuractinapophyses.—In addition to the auditory capsules, I recognise as post-stomal neuractinapophyses more particularly those ossicles attached to the post-frontals, mastoids, and external occipitals of fishes. Those attached to the post-frontals may enter into the formation of the infra-ocular bony arch. Those, again, which are developed on the temporal and occipital sclerotomes are modified so as to co-operate in the cranial suspension of the scapular girdle.

In conclusion, Goethe was the first to indicate the intermaxillaries, the maxillaries, and palatals, as elements of three distinct cranial segments. In the course of my investigation into the development of the teeth, I became early aware of the correctness of Goethe's views on this subject, and have found myself, therefore, unable to coincide with the doctrine of Professor Owen as to the constitution of his palato-maxillary or nasal hæmal arch.

VII.—ON THE MORPHOLOGICAL CONSTITUTION OF LIMBS.

CARUS, maintaining generally the doctrine of cephalic limbs, originally propounded by Oken, has at the same time given much greater precision to the conception of the skeleton of a limb, by viewing it as a system of elements radiating from the exterior of a costiform arch. Professor Owen, while he rejects, with British and the majority of foreign anatomists, the fantastic doctrine of Oken and his immediate followers with regard to cephalic limbs, has adopted the general doctrine of the skeleton of the limb as propounded by Carus, and has developed and applied it with much ingenuity to the illustration of actual structure. Professor Owen, has, however, at the same time, by his allocation of the scapular girdle to the occipital segment of the cranium as its hæmal arch, and by the view which he takes of the opercular and branchiostegal elements, actually reproduced the doctrine of cephalic limbs in another form. I do not propose in this communication to examine in detail the grounds on which Professor Owen's general doctrine of limbs is based, but shall merely state categorically those considerations which appear to me to render it untenable.

1. It is highly improbable that the sclerous elements of a limb should be derived from one, or at most two, sclerotomes; while its other elements, and more especially its nerves, are supplied by a greater number of somatomes.

2. It appears to be highly improbable that the bones which enter into the structure of an arm or leg, or that the

corresponding sclerous parts in the lower animals, should be the result of teleological subdivision of a single " diverging appendage" or "archetypal element." Professor Owen virtually admits that these "teleological" elements have a morphological value when he institutes an inquiry into their "special" and "serial homologies."

3. It appears to me that the scapular girdle cannot be the hæmal arch of the occipital segment of the head—firstly, because that segment is already provided with a hæmal arch in the series of transitory and persistent sclerous elements developed in the third pair of visceral laminæ; secondly, because the scapular girdle is invariably found to be developed at or in the immediate neighbourhood of that part of the trunk of the animal where it is ultimately situated; and, thirdly, because it is improbable that the exceptions to a general law should be more numerous than the instances in which it is adhered to.*

The germs of the limbs make their appearance when the ventral laminæ of the primordial vertebral system are passing down towards the hæmal margin. At first they resemble lappet-like projections of the inferior margins of these laminæ; they extend along at least four or five of their segments, and are situated in those regions of the body to which the future limb is attached—viz. in the pelvic and posterior region of the neck, except in the fish, in which the pectoral lappets are situated close behind the head. As the ventral laminæ extend downwards, the lappets retain a position more or less elevated on the side of the trunk. At this stage they also

* It is somewhat remarkable that the only embryological evidence which Professor Owen adduces in support of that portion of his Doctrine of Limbs, in which the anterior limb is assumed to be developed at or close to the head, is a reference to a passage in Rathke's *Entwickelung der Schildkröten*, in which the author adduces the *fundamental position* of the bones of the shoulder—viz. the posterior region of the neck—as a circumstance tending to explain their ultimate passage into the thoracic cavity.

begin to exhibit a change in their form and position. They become first sessile, then pedunculated, and the peduncle then indicates by an angle at its centre the formation of the central joint of the shaft of the future limb—the elbow or knee-joint. At the same time, what I term the plane of the limb is changed. The lappet was originally developed in a plane, which is coincident with the axis of the corda dorsalis. This is the primary or fundamental plane of the limb; and when in this plane the lappet presents its radial or tibial margin forwards towards the head, and its ulnar or fibular margin backwards. When the limb leaves its primary position, it lies in its secondary plane, which cuts the corda dorsalis more or less obliquely, so that the radial or tibial margins of the limb are directed more or less forwards and inwards, and the ulnar and fibular backwards and outwards. The permanently-sessile pectoral lappets or fins of the osseous fish exhibit a peculiar modification of the same movement; they rotate on a transverse axis, so that their anterior or radial margins are directed downwards and their ulnar margins upwards. In the sharks and rays the pectoral and abdominal fins continue permanently in the primary plane.

While the lappet is still in its primary plane, the rudiments of the girdle of the future limb may be detected under the integumentary covering, and therefore external to the proper mass of the visceral wall of the body. In the primordial condition of the lappet of the wing of the chick, Remak has detected four parallel streaks running to its outer margin, and continuous internally with the rudimentary nervous structures of the four primordial vertebræ, with which the attached margin of the lappet is connected.

Guided by embryological facts and conclusions, to the more important of which I have just alluded, I have endeavoured to detect, more particularly in the osseous fishes, plagiostomes, amphibians, and reptiles, the principle which lies at the basis of the morphology of limbs. The view which this inquiry has induced me to take of this subject I shall, in conclusion, state very briefly.

1. A limb does not necessarily derive its elements from one somatome—about fifty segments of the trunk appear to contribute towards the structure of the great pectoral fin in the ray.

2. The nervous elements of the limbs appear, as in other parts of the vertebrate animal, to indicate most distinctly the morphological constitution of the sclerous elements. About fifty spinal nerves contribute the greater part of their hæmal divisions to the pectoral fin of the ray; and there are about one hundred fin-rays—a pair of fin-rays to each nerve, and derived from each sclerotome. This correspondence does not apparently exist between the fin-rays and nerves of the osseous fish; but it may be fairly assumed that when we have detected the developmental circumstances which induce the attachment of the pectoral girdle of the osseous fish to its cranium, as well as those peculiarities exhibited by its anterior trunk sclerotomes, this discrepancy will be explained. A more careful analysis than we yet possess of the number of spinal nerves which supply branches to the limbs of the higher Vertebrata is still a desideratum in this department of the subject; but it appears to be extremely probable, that in the Mammalia at least five spinal nerves transmit filaments to the five distal divisions of the limb. It would appear, too, that, notwithstanding their plexiform arrangement at the attached end of the limb, the greater number of the filaments of each nerve reach their own morphological district at the distal part of the limb. The radial and the ulnar nerves are formed principally by the upper and lower roots of the human brachial plexus—that is, from the nerves of the upper and lower primordial segments with which the embryo

limb was connected, and from which it derived its various elements.

3. The nerves supplied to a limb are not the inferior or hæmal divisions of the spinal nerves, but radiating or actinal branches of these divisions. The intercostal nerves are not the nerves serially homologous with the roots of the brachial plexus. The thoracic nerves, serially homologous with these roots, are the intercosto-humeral and the succeeding middle intercosto-cutaneous.

4. Each sclerotome supplying elements to the structure of a limb supplies as a sclerous element a single actinapophysis; or, as in the rays, an anterior and a posterior—that is, a pair of actinapophyses.

5. From the structure of the mesial and lateral fin-rays of the fish, the actinapophyseal elements of a limb may be assumed as primordially segmented.

6. The fin-rays in the fish, and the phalangeal, metacarpal, and metatarsal bones of the higher Vertebrata, are more or less persistent conditions of the distal segments of the primordial actinapophyseal elements of a limb.

7. By atrophy, or otherwise, one or more of the segments in the successive transverse rows of actinapophyseal elements disappear, so as to leave in man, *e.g.*, four elements in each carpal row; two in the fore-arm, one in the arm, two in the next row for the coracoid and clavicle, one in the proximal row for the scapula.

8. The nature of the subsequent changes which the elements of the limb undergo, up as far as the shoulder or hip, may be inferred from an examination of the paddle of the Enaliosaur or Cetacean.

9. A careful application of the hypothesis to the limb-girdles of the cartilaginous fishes, Amphibia, and reptiles, leaves me strongly inclined to believe that the coracoid is an actinapophyseal segment between the humerus and scapula,

prolonged downwards, towards the hæmal margin of the body; that the scapula is a proximal segment, elongated towards the neural margin of the body; that the clavicle is the only other retained segment in the same transverse row as the coracoid, in front of it, and elongated like it in the hæmal direction; and that the corresponding elements of the posterior limb have a similar morphological signification.

DIVISION II.

ANATOMY, PHYSIOLOGY, PATHOLOGY.

DIVISION II.

VIII.—ON THE EMPLOYMENT OF MATHEMATICAL MODES OF INVESTIGATION IN THE DETERMINATION OF ORGANIC FORMS.*

LECTURE I.

BIOLOGY, the science of which physiology and anatomy formed parts, had been hitherto advanced by the study of the structure of animals or vegetables, and the investigation of the functions or uses of the various parts of that structure. This was the object with which they sought to ascertain the uses and functions of the particular parts of animals and vegetables under examination, and to determine why the bones of any particular animal should be of a particular form. Biologists had

---

* The two Lectures on this subject formed the conclusion of Professor Goodsir's course of lectures on Comparative Anatomy, delivered in the University in the Summer Session, 1849. The Abstract appeared in the *Daily Mail* newspaper, July 31st and August 7th of that year. It had obviously not been furnished or corrected by the author, and contained not only many positive mistakes, but interpolations by the reporter. In the absence of any manuscript copy from which to correct it, we had some doubts at first whether it should be reprinted. But as it shows that the author's attention had been directed many years ago to a department of inquiry, which, though comparatively neglected, undoubtedly affords room for useful research, and in which, indeed, he was engaged up to within a few weeks of his death; as it is an attempt to illustrate that, the original form and law of growth of an organic body being known, its form at any future time may be made a matter of mathematical investigation, we have reproduced it, with the omission of such phrases and errors as were most obviously due to blunders on the part of the reporter.—EDS.

hitherto proceeded in this way; knowing the habits of the animals, and the form of the skeleton, and arrangement of the muscles which co-operate with it in performing the movements of the animals, they sought to determine what the particular economy of the animal, under certain conditions, required. It should be remembered that there was always a corresponding harmony between the shape and connections of the organs of the body and the motions peculiar to the animal. This involves the principle of final causes, which entered so largely into anatomical and physiological investigations. Upon this principle we determined what were the functions, because there was no other the parts were so well adapted to perform.

The wonderful progress of biology—the science comprehending the study of anatomy and physiology—or of comparative anatomy, was attributable to this; it owed its greatness to this study of final causes—that of the remarkable adaptation of structures to particular functions.

The application of the doctrine of final causes was not, however, the most fertile mode of procedure in physical investigations. It was only with respect to organised bodies that it had enabled men of science to advance human knowledge. It was very different in regard to chemistry, mechanics, etc., where no progress had been made till men of science had thrown aside the consideration of final causes. But although physical science did not advance till the introduction of the inductive philosophy, and till final causes had been laid aside, still the principle of final causes pervaded all nature. Take in illustration the sun. But for the peculiar arrangement of the sun in regard to the relations which he holds towards the earth and other planetary bodies, his shape, and manner of moving on his axis, we could have neither heat nor darkness, which the economy of animals and vegetables rendered absolutely necessary. Thus we might reason of the sun and earth, etc., from final causes, and might explain why the sun was so constituted. But the natural philosopher, admitting all this, arrived at his conclusion by another path altogether; and, after he had reached it, ascertained that a final cause was at work here also.

It was interesting to inquire why, in physical and chemical science, the progress had been so slow, by the application of final causes, whereas anatomy had made great progress by that means? though after all, they were only at the threshold. It was difficult to say why. It probably had connection with the difference betwixt organised and inorganised bodies. Every plant or animal formed a system in which every part was related to some common centre, and the whole completely organised. In the study of any given organised body, we had the whole of it before us. We take into consideration its physical conditions, temperature, medium, etc., yet each individual organism forms a system; we may refer all its parts, configuration, and phenomena, to a principle residing in no other but individuals of the same species. We are thus enabled to take the whole system into consideration; to enter upon its examination as a whole, and to consider the relations of any part to any other given part; we thus see the reason why all its parts are adapted to each other.

It is different with regard to inorganised bodies, such as the sun, whose parts, although constituted with reference to the wellbeing of parts of our own system, have yet reference to others. There is some common principle which governs all these; and this must be ascertained before we can reason on the forms or uses of the parts of inorganic nature, and see how all these parts are related. If it were possible to get the whole system of the universe under the eye for examination with our telescopes and microscopes, we should then have the inorganic world before us in the same position as the animal or vegetable world, and should then see the reason for its adaptations.

Although biology had hitherto made great, decided, and certain advances by the superficial method of inquiry, chemical and mechanical philosophy had gone far beyond it. Motions, forms, and weights are now subjected to geometrical analysis, and treated in the abstract, a result which had not yet been attained in anatomical and physiological science, but which in time would be so.

Without trenching upon the important considerations connected with soul or spirit, or inquiring into the nature of the spiritual organs, if any, of the animal or vegetable—philosophical questions, with which physiology and anatomy had nothing to do, yet questions which should not be allowed to lie uncultivated—an acquaintance with the principles of philosophy in their applications to the physiological sciences ought to be gained. These constituted a set of sciences based upon altogether different principles : 1st, on the internal analysis of their own feelings, their own minds, and the principles originally implanted within them, by consideration of which, sound moral and intellectual conclusions were arrived at; and, 2d, an inquiry into the mental phenomena, or whatever they might choose to call them, presented by the lower animals. This they might perform either by reasoning from their own intellects downwards, just as they reasoned in regard to their fellowmen, only passing down the scale; or they might compare the mental phenomena of the lower with those of the higher animals—thus building up a comparative psychological science which would become simplified as they passed down the series, and complex as they passed upwards. The study by the anatomist and the physiologist, and by every medical man, as far as the bent of his own mind admitted, of these results of psychological science, was most important.

Anatomy had been hitherto advanced by the study of the animal form and of the exact harmony under which only the animal could exist. But there was another view that might be taken. Was it not possible, by ascertaining the accurate shape, the form and proportion between the parts, organs, and whole body of any animal, to advance the study geometrically? Suppose the anatomist gave the exact curvature of the surface, the volume and proportions which different parts of the organs might bear—what their formal geometry was might become matter of calculation. He might begin, by the lengths, and breadths, and volumes of the different parts, by ascertaining whether they have a correspondency, and exhibit a mathematical relation, spherical or spheroidal curves, etc. These once ascertained, he would become certain of the geometrical construction, and could reason as to the probable forms of other parts.

Impossible as it might appear, this had been effected in certain instances, and especially in a most beautiful manner in regard to shells of molluscous animals, by the Reverend Professor Moseley, late of Cambridge,[*] who had made an exact geometrical examination of shells, and especially of the Turbines, which were possessed of a spiral curve wound round a central axis, which curve had been found to be logarithmic, and from it had been framed a series of *formulæ*, by which the other conditions of the shell could be predicted and found to exist.

By a very accurate measurement of the shell, mathematically, it was found that its spires increased in breadth in an exact successive series, each one of which was a multiple, in a certain ratio, of another. Thus there was a mathematical principle arrived at, which could be carried out—the shell must possess this form, and could possess no other. It had a spiral curve, and the properties of that curve pointed it out to be a logarithmic curve, one which would reproduce itself; a curve formed by a thread wound off the exterior, would trace the form of its operculum; and the mouth of the animal was remarkable for geometrical symmetry. As

---

[*] *Philosophical Transactions*, 1838, p. 351.

the shell was formed by the soft parts of the animal—those parts, though not possessed of the rigidity of the outer shell, yet, if we measured their textures, their relative proportions and rates of increase, we should also find that they were formed according to a mathematical law. It was impossible, therefore, they should not form a general harmony! How rapidly science advances! A few years ago it was supposed that the capillary vessels would model anything, and that parts were formed by the extremities of these. But if we admitted absorption, and the death of precise parts, we might expect to ascertain the mathematical law of the body. The period was not far distant when this subject would embrace a much greater number of mathematical rules. No subject could better employ those possessed of mathematical talents than the application of modern analysis to organised bodies. They must begin with the Mollusca. Professor Moseley had examined only the turbinated and discoid shells. The logarithmic curves varied in different shells. But it would come to this at last, that instead of the naturalist describing these bodies by a long roundabout enumeration of their colours, sizes, etc., he would just give the mathematical curves which indicated them. This was already done in crystallography, where crystals were classified according to certain geometrical relations.

By Professor Moseley's investigations matter had been added to the stock, and something had been done towards the investigation in this manner of animals and vegetables. Professor Moseley, by mathematics, had ascertained that a process must go on, which other naturalists had not discovered —namely, by the revolution which the operculum of the shell must make. It was easily conceived that the operculum made a revolution round its axis. The mouth was of a particular figure. Cut any part in a certain direction (the direction of the plane of its axis), and every section would give a form exactly similar to the form of the mouth. The form of a turbinated shell was produced by the revolution of the perimeter of the figure round the axis of the shell. In the Nautilus the figure was that of an ellipse, which revolves round its minor axis, and increases in geometrical progression without ever changing its form as it revolves. A turbinated shell revolving round its axis shows the figure carried forwards along the axis of revolution, from the apex of the spire to its termination. They might do this by cutting a piece of paper to the figure of the turbinated shell. It would be found that the figure was always the same, but increased. Professor Moseley ascertained this in two ways—1st, after the curve had been ascertained; and 2dly, by a very curious investigation of the operculum. He had ascertained that the spiral possessed the peculiar properties of a logarithmic spiral; hence the operculum was found to form a very convenient measure of the shell itself and all its parts. The operculum being fixed, as the shell increased in size it underwent a gradual increase— the size of the mouth gradually increased with the size of the operculum. Now, if the operculum were merely pushed forward by the animal, one of two circumstances would occur —it would either require new calcareous shelly matter (but it was not so), or there would be, as indeed was the case, a much more precise method of extension by the deposition of additional matter along the lower margin of the shell which formed the tangent of the curve.

There were other examples of a similar kind. Take one of the Goniums, a little animal or vegetable structure existing amongst the polygastria, and consisting of four cellules in a square plate, as also the Sarcina Ventriculi. The Goniums and others were rectangular forms. They were all squares. And why? They reproduced themselves in a geometrical progression, and that because each individual consisted of four cells, and four only, until it was reproduced by other four. The law of its reproduction was by a geometrical series multiples of four, in extreme rapidity. Four cells would always represent a flat figure, and recur in the form of a plate; all the angles might not in every case be alike, but it would always be in laminæ. The reproduction of the confervæ was also by the multiplication of cellules. Certain silicious polygastric animals—the Diatomaceæ, and some others—existed in two halves, reproducing each into two. These would always form a line, or linear series, increasing in length, and not in breadth. The line might form a curve, but this linear form was a necessary consequence of the mode of reproduction.

This was a sketch of what might be done; and it ought to be done by a mathematical investigation of the animal body, its masses and organs, or what was of more importance, its ultimate atoms. This was a difficult process, but we should not despair of arriving at it. Suppose the science were so far advanced that we could obtain the formal mathematical expression of forms, the same as astronomers did before the time of Newton, when they ascertained the motions of the planets in their orbits, and the curves that bounded these bodies. Newton, from the geometric forms, made out THE LAW OF THE FORCE.

We have merely to ascertain *the law of the force*. This can never be done till we have got the mathematical forms. We are probably far from this. But meanwhile science makes great progress on the principle explained at the beginning of this lecture. There is room to get into another inquiry naturalists have never dreamed of, probably from not having had a mathematical education. Those of them who had such, and a taste for biological studies, would do well to carry out the mathematical study. What the chemical and other forces had to do in the animal economy could only be made out after the forms of matter were found out. It by no means trenched on the other department—the mental and spiritual—although the two went together.

Lecture 2.

Professor Moseley's paper contains the germ of what would yet form a new epoch in natural science, though known only to a few mathematicians, who probably considered it merely as a curious and ingenious memoir.

As a very remarkable coincidence, Newton had shown in his *Principia* that if attraction had generally varied as the inverse cube instead of as the inverse square of the distance, the heavenly bodies would revolve, not in ellipses but in logarithmic spirals, rapidly diffuse themselves, and rush off into space. It would be curious that if the law of the square were the law of attraction, the law of the cube might therefore prove to be the law of production. He did not say that this was the case. But if this law of force were admitted, and cellules grew by a certain law, we could thereby explain how all cellules passed off from one another, and how all form was produced—namely, in a rapidly-increasing geometrical ratio, instead of revolving round an axis. Probably the logarithmic spiral would be found to be the law at work in the increase of organic bodies.

Another remarkable confirmation of the possibility of carrying out the principle of geometrical investigation where we would least expect to find it; in reference to the forms of the most highly-organised bodies with which we are acquainted, but which had yet been found to be bounded by geometric figures, has recently been pointed out.

For the examination of the geometric outline of the human body we are indebted to Mr. D. R. Hay.*

By the geometrical construction of a diagram, we should now be enabled to trace the outline of the skeleton; and all the leading parts of the body would come out exactly as they ought to be.

---

* *On the Human Figure*, 4to, 1849; *Natural Principles of Beauty*, 1852; *The Science of Beauty*, 1856.

In order not to involve what was undeniable in Mr. Hay's theory in any hypothesis—and those who had studied Mr. Hay's works would know that much in them was based on harmonical theories—these last should be kept out of view. What might be shown was, that the artist accustomed to draw the outline of the figure could do so, and would thereby find his figure better proportioned, nor would he be liable to commit those glaring blunders, which, however good figures might be artistically, were offensive to the critical anatomical eye.

The first diagram in Mr. Hay's book* was that of a female figure seen in front with the arms by the side. Mr. Hay first drew a line which represents the full height of the figure. From the upper extremity of this line he drew lines making with it respectively angles equal to 1-3d, 1-4th, 1-5th, and 1-6th of a right angle; and from the lower extremity a line making 1-8th of a right angle. The point in which the two last lines, making respectively 1-6th and 1-8th of a right angle, intersect one another determines the semi-breadth of the figure. Passing through the upper extremity of the vertical line, a circle and three ellipses were described—the line which joins the extremities of the axes major and minor of the first ellipse being the first of the lines above drawn, and that which joins the extremities of the axes of the second being the third of the said lines. These give the skull, face, and neck. A third ellipse, similar to the first of these, but larger, represents the body. The other lines are few and simple in their relations, the characteristic being that they make an angle of 1-3d and 1-5th of a right angle with the vertical line. It will be seen that the ruling feature in Mr. Hay's theory is that *position is determined by direction, not by distance.*

The diagrams show how, in the very simplest way, by integral divisions of a right angle, a succession of lines had been attained which corresponded precisely to the position of

---

* *Natural Principles of Beauty*, Plate I. Figs. 1 and 2.

the symphysis of the lower jaw—the lower part of the chin; the upper part of the dorsal vertebræ; the tip of the shoulder—upper end of the humerus (showing also the breadth); the upper part of the sternum—and average position of the upper parietes; the middle of the dorsal region—sixth and seventh dorsal vertebræ; the nipple in the female; the upper part of the lumbar, and lower part of the dorsal region; the exact position of the elbow-joint; the upper part of the pelvis—the haunch-bones; the lower edge of the last lumbar vertebræ; the upper part of the sacrum; the line so long familiar to artists as dividing the body and corresponding with the upper part of the pelvis; the tip of the longest finger—a remarkable feature in drawing the body; and the upper end of the tibia, one-fourth of the body.

Undoubtedly, in all organic bodies, as they had seen in a few examples, certain geometrical principles would be discovered, and though Mr. Hay's diagram was artificial and empirical, because it had been used empirically in the meantime, yet it gave correctly all the parts.

Mr. Hay had at first proceeded by following theoretical views. He believed the human body to be beautiful, and to give pleasure artistically because it included certain symmetrical and geometrical forms.

His investigations were limited at first to the human head, the anterior part of which he had found to be spheroidal, and the posterior, seen from the side, from above, and from below, to be included in a sphere and oblate spheroid, formed by the revolution of a circle and an ellipse. These figures enclosed certain triangles. The triangle of the circle was a right-angled isosceles triangle; the triangle of the ellipse a right-angled scalene. They varied, according to their peculiar character, within certain limits.

With these views he had been able, by continuing the system of geometrical construction, which he had found successful in the geometrical analysis of the head, downwards through the thorax and body, and by a series of measurements of individuals, to construct triangles and figures in combination, enclosing within them the great outlines of the body.

In the first place, dividing the figure into five parts, on each of which an equilateral triangle was produced or formed, doubling the right-angled scalene triangle, whose angles were 30°, 60°, and 90°, he got the breadth of the shoulders and various points of the figure. A remarkable confirmation of Mr. Hay's views was arrived at by the division of the body into five, which might be effected by continuing downwards the equilateral triangle contained within the second oval of the head in a succession of figures. By this succession they had also the breadth of the figure.

The angles of the first right-angled equilateral triangle were 45°, 45°, and 90°; those of the second, or scalene, being half of the equilateral triangle, 30°, 60°, and 90°; and those of the third, or right-angled triangle, being the primary angle of the pentagon, as seen at the neck, 18°, 72°, and 90°. The ratio of the angles in the right-angled equilateral triangle was as 1 to 2, in the scalene as 1 to 3, and in the third right-angled triangle as 1 to 5. The angles of the other triangles were 22° 30′, 67° 30′, and 90°; and 11° 15′, 78° 45′, and 90°, and their ratios 1 to 4, and 1 to 8; whilst the angles of the remaining triangle were 15°, 75°, and 90°—the angle at the apex bearing a ratio to the right angle of 1 to 6.

They would thus find that, in regard to the various angles, Mr. Hay had arrived at them partly on theoretical views. He was just as much entitled to theorise as any other man of science. No discovery had ever been made without hypothesis. He had started, expecting to find in the proportions of the human frame a musical harmony; and, by continual measuring, had at last been able to construct a figure, **partly hypothetically, but which was found to correspond with nature.**

Having arrived at these conclusions in a legitimate manner, he found the tonic repeated thrice, the dominant twice, and the mediate once. The ratios, which they would perceive the angles of the triangles bore, as laid down, were ratios which held in the musical chord. By simply prolonging the transverse lines of the diagram, a perpendicular line would be intersected in a series of fractional parts, all of which were indicated in the musical scale. If this perpendicular were a musical string set a-vibrating, it would vibrate, for instance, first as a whole string, then as two halves or octaves, then as third parts or fifths; another set of vibrations repeated the octaves—viz. fourth parts or double octaves; another series of vibrations divided the chord into fifth parts or thirds, etc.

This was certainly very remarkable. The artist who drew as Mr. Hay directed would produce a figure infinitely more correct than by the mere eye or a prolonged study of figures. It was remarkable that the angles which he had attained by correcting himself, by careful measurement, and by preserving a certain ratio of one to another, should repeat themselves at intervals representing musical intervals.

In the female figure the common or primary chord of music, where 2, 3, and 5 were the leading numbers, was indicated. The male form differed essentially and materially from the female. Mr. Hay had begun his researches with the female form. It was necessary for him also to construct a diagram of the male; and he had made trials, but not at random, from which he thought it probable that the male differed from the female in harmonic ratio. By making the figure on a dominant triangle, for which, instead of 30°, he took 33° 45′ (and this related to the dominant angle in the female, in the mathematical ratio of 9 to 8, or, to express it musically, as a major tone to a minor tone), he was enabled to construct a diagram for the male into which you can't draw a female figure! It comes out a male! It would be remembered that the breadth of the pelvis was less, and the outlines of the thigh-bones were situated closer together, in the male than in the female; that also in the female the knees were brought together. Besides these distinctive marks, Mr. Hay had, moreover, of himself, brought in the female elbow and bent out the wrist; although he was not aware, till he (Professor Goodsir) had told him, of the difference in this respect between the sexes—for in a well-made man the arm was always perfectly straight. This showed that, however artificial the system, the artist might depend upon it for giving to the figure the correct anatomy in its great leading features. The breadth of the thorax from side to side had been ascertained by the general angle, which gave the breadth of the male thorax ($33°\ 45'$), and so increased in like proportion. In regard to the depth, by assuming the angle $30°$ again, and taking the average depth of both male and female; on the harmonic hypothesis the angle for production of the equilateral triangle, half of which gave the depth of it in the female, would be $27°$. Now $33°\ 45'$ to $30°$ is as 9 to 8; whereas in the female, $30°$ is to $27°$ as 10 to 9—these being the ratios of the major and minor tones in the science of musical harmony.

This very ingenious piece of research was an approach to those principles indicated in the previous day's and this day's lectures. With regard to Mr. Hay's views, if they followed the directions in the diagram, they would be mechanically correct in filling up, which a little practice would enable them to do, for the male as well as for the female, the outline of a figure anatomically correct.

This was an extremely useful result. If they were to view it in no other light, artists were greatly indebted to Mr. Hay. This could not be denied. And, without involving himself or them in the hypothesis on which it depended—in the ratio of angles, or the number of times which they were repeated

—they were not to despise that hypothesis, because it was by working it out Mr. Hay had been enabled to frame this diagram. They could not deny that harmonic proportion was something, if they admitted the diagram to afford a correct anatomical outline; for it must exist in nature. This was something like an approach to a general geometrical inclusion of the surface of the body by the revolution of triangles, and the perimeters of certain figures, including certain masses of the body. If they included the general mass, there was reason to expect that the outline of the subordinate parts would be arrived at by a process of the same kind. They were all produced by some law, according to which the parts of the body were formed. If this law were complete, they should have a formal anatomy of the body— a geometrical outline, however complicated—a complex geometry—but they must believe in it. There were no parts of the body not injured—not even parts diseased—that were not geometrical structures, however complex. It was only after knowing these they could arrive at *the law of the force.*

He had not, in this hurried manner, been able to do that justice he was anxious to see done to Mr. Hay's not merely ingenious diagram ; but by the lecture of yesterday and to-day, although not yet in the exact scientific position reached with regard to the shell by Professor Moseley, yet he was desirous to show that the harmony and geometrical analysis of the human body, by continuing the research, would rapidly advance that department of biological knowledge.

IX.—ON THE HORIZONTAL CURVATURE OF THE INTERNAL FEMORAL CONDYLE; ON THE MOVEMENTS AND RELATIONS OF THE PATELLA, SEMILUNAR CARTILAGES, AND SYNOVIAL PADS OF THE HUMAN KNEE-JOINT.

ASSUMING the ordinary descriptions of the human knee-joint, and the more precise observations of the brothers Weber (*Mechanik der Menschlichen Gehwerkzeuge*, 1836), as presenting the present state of information on the subject, I shall proceed to explain the arrangement and use of the peculiar curvature at the fore-part of the inner condyle of the femur, as recently determined by Professor Meyer of Zurich (*Die Mechanik des Kniegelenks, Müller's Archiv.*, 1853); and the movements and relations of the patella, semilunar cartilages, and synovial pads of the articulation, as observed by myself.

Before entering on the peculiarities of the inner condyle, I may remind you that the knee-joint consists of two articulations, with a common synovial membrane, the patello-femoral, and the femoro-tibial, the latter being double. The articular surface of the femur is consequently divided into a trochlea for the former, and two condyles for the latter; the condyles being separated from one another by the intercondyloid fossa, and from the trochlea by two shallow oblique grooves.

Anatomists had not hitherto noticed that the so-called obliquity of the inner condyle of the femur is in fact, as Meyer has pointed out, a curvature of its anterior third, with its concavity directed backwards, outwards, and downwards. The two posterior thirds of the inner condyle pass backwards parallel to, and have the same general form and extent as, the entire outer condyle of the bone. The curved portion or anterior third of the usually so-called inner condyle may therefore be conceived as a part intercalated between the patellar trochlea and the proper inner condyle.

According to Meyer, the mechanical advantages which result from the peculiar antero-posterior curvatures of the femoral condyles, which the brothers Weber concluded, from their admeasurements, to be spirals, may be with greater simplicity assumed to consist, as his own admeasurements suggest, each of two circular segments, the posterior of 120°, the anterior of 40°, the radius of the former being to that of the latter as 5 to 9. The horizontal curvature at the fore-part of the inner condyle, or, more precisely, the oblique curvature, may, as Meyer states, be conceived as a segment of 60° of the margin of the base of a cone, the axis of which is directed at an angle of 45° downwards, outwards, and backwards, in front of the spine of the tibia, so that its apex is situated in the external condyle of that bone.

In flexion and extension, therefore, of the knee-joint, as long as these movements are confined to the outer condyle, and the two posterior thirds of the inner condyle of the femur with the condyles of the tibia, they take place round two transverse axes, which pass respectively through the centres of the posterior antero-posterior circular curvatures of the femoral condyles, and the centres of the anterior. To simplify the conception, however, of this part of the arrangement, Meyer assumes as sufficiently accurate a single transverse axis.

In the first third of flexion, and in the latter third of extension, the movements of the femur and tibia take place round the oblique curvature or anterior third of the internal femoral condyle; and involve, in addition to the completion and commencement of flexion and extension respectively, a movement of rotation of the tibia and consequently of the leg and foot inwards in the former, and outwards in the latter. These remarkable movements of rotation inwards and outwards, inseparable from the commencement of flexion and the completion of extension, take place round the axis of the ideal cone already alluded to. This axis Meyer denominates the oblique axis of the knee-joint.

These movements of rotation, combined with flexion and extension, must be carefully distinguished from those of which the joint is capable when considerably flexed. The latter, with which anatomists are already familiar, take place, in general terms, round a prolongation of the axis of the tibia. This axis Meyer denominates the rotation-axis of the knee-joint.

The most remarkable ligament concerned in the movements round the oblique axis of the joint is the external crucial, which becomes tightened in extension, as the movement round the oblique curvature of the inner condyle proceeds, and thus acts, from its obliquity, in a direction from below, upwards, backwards, and outwards, so as to guide the rotation of the tibia outwards.

The discovery of the oblique axis of the knee-joint has enabled Meyer to determine with greater precision the action of certain muscles of the thigh. The use of the peculiar mode of insertion, hitherto unexplained, of the sartorius, gracilis, and semitendinosus, becomes evident. Their tendons, passing down behind the inner side of the knee, curve forwards and outwards on the tibia; so that these muscles effect that rotation inwards which is a necessary accompaniment of the commencement of flexion. These muscles produce this rotation directly—that is, by an adaptation of their tendons to the purpose; but, according to Meyer, the proper flexors of the knee, the biceps and semimembranosus, only act indirectly as rotators, through the medium of the articular surfaces and ligaments. I conceive, however, that the latter may act directly in producing rotation inwards at the commencement of flexion; for its tendon, instead of being inserted, as is usually stated, into the back part of the inner tibial condyle, passes forwards and outwards round the head of the bone in a distinct groove, in which it moves, being kept in its place by prolongations of the internal lateral ligaments of the joint, and thus presenting the same general mode of insertion as the three muscles already alluded to.

The rotation outwards, at the completion of extension, is produced indirectly by the quadriceps-extensor; the form of the articular surfaces, and the tightening of the external crucial ligament, co-operating with the group of extensor muscles.

Meyer has detected a very beautiful adaptation of parts in connection with this latter movement, and has thus explained the characteristic enlargement, and the extensive attachment to the patella, of the vastus internus muscle. When the knee is extended, the ligamentum patellæ, instead of being perpendicular, will be found to pass downwards and outwards to its tibial attachment, which has moved outwards in the rotation of the leg. The lower portion of the vastus internus is enlarged, and the upper portion of its tendon is attached to the greater part of the inner edge of the patella, for the purpose of preventing that bone from being pressed against the outer part of the femoral trochlea during the rotation outwards of the leg, by drawing it inwards and upwards, and keeping its axis in the line of the ligamentum patellæ; while the lower portion of its tendon passes down to be attached somewhat obliquely to the inner side of the head of the tibia, and thus assists directly in rotating the leg outwards.

Meyer has also shown that, in standing quietly upright

on one or both limbs, the knees are not necessarily kept straight by continued action of the extensor muscles, for the ligaments of the patella may be slack. The continued extension cannot be the effect of the superincumbent pressure of the body, for the transverse plane, in which the common centre of gravity is situated, lies behind the transverse axes of the knee-joints. Two arrangements conduce to this remarkable example of economy in muscular action. When the foot is on the ground, and the knee extended, the inward rotation of the leg in the commencement of flexion cannot take place; and if the pelvis and trunk are kept erect, the reverse rotation of the thigh-bone outwards is prevented by the tightened condition of the ileo-femoral band of the hip-joint: but if the trunk and pelvis be inclined forwards, although the ileo-femoral band is relaxed, and the femur relieved, the tendency to flexion of the knee-joint is removed by the passage of the line of gravity to the front of the transverse axis of the articulation. The thick longitudinal band of the fascia lata on the outer side of the thigh, extending from the anterior superior spinous process of the ileum, and from the inferior attachment of the tensor vagina femoris to the fore part of the outer condyle of the tibia (ligamentum ileotibiale), is another arrangement for economising muscular exertion; for as long as the pelvis is kept erect on the heads of the thigh-bones by the glutei maximi muscles, it is evident that these ileo-tibial bands must tend to keep the knees extended, and transfer the action of the quadriceps-extensor to the great muscle of the hip.

The patella exhibits various interesting relations during the movements of the joint; and in addition to those observed by Meyer, others hitherto unrecorded may be pointed out. Meyer states that the under half of the patella is in contact with the femoral trochlea in extension, and the upper half in flexion; but if the bone is carefully examined, the following configuration and relation of its articular surface will be detected. Instead of two faces, a greater external, and a lesser internal, separated by a perpendicular ridge, as usually described, the surface presents, in every instance, six, frequently seven, facets, separated from one another by two perpendicular and two transverse ridges. The external perpendicular ridge is the one commonly described. The internal cuts off a small elongated perpendicular facet at the inner edge of the surface. The two transverse ridges only extend inwards to the inner perpendicular ridge, so as to separate from above, downwards, two superior, two middle, and one or two inferior facets, the external of the two latter being constant. The relations of the articular surface of the patella present four groups. In complete flexion, the internal or perpendicular facet is in contact with a remarkable crescentic facet, which bounds the oblique curvature of the inner condyle of the femur. In none of the other positions of the joint is this internal patellar facet in contact with an opposite cartilaginous surface, but is covered or sheathed by what may be denominated the internal patellar pad. At the same time, the external superior facet lies upon the fore part of the external condyle of the femur below and behind its bounding groove. These two facets are the only parts of the patella which come in contact with the proper femoral condyles. They do so only in complete flexion; and in this state all the remaining facets are in contact with the great infra-patellar pad, and the so-called mucous ligament.

In the second stage of extension, the superior internal and external facets are in contact with the inferior portions, respectively of the inner and outer halves of the femoral trochlea; the internal perpendicular facet being sheathed as before stated; and the remaining facets being in contact with the great infra-patellar pad.

In the third stage of extension, the superior internal and

external facets leave the femoral trochlea and become sheathed, and the space occupied partly by the supra-patellar, but principally by the supra-trochlear pads. The middle internal and external patellar facets now come in contact with the middle portions respectively of the inner and outer halves of the femoral trochlea; while the internal perpendicular and the two inferior facets are sheathed and padded as before.

In the fourth or last stage of extension, the middle internal and external facets also recede from the surface of the trochlea, and along with the internal longitudinal already sheathed, become applied against the fore part of the femur above its articular surface, the intervening space being stuffed by the supra-patellar, supra-trochlear, and upper pads, in the ascending cul-de-sac of the synovial membrane. In this last stage, the only portions of the patella in contact with the cartilaginous surface of the femur, are the inferior internal and external facets, or the latter, if one only exists. These slip somewhat abruptly upwards and inwards upon a narrow ledge or furrow, which terminates the femoral trochlea above, and forms a resting-place for the inferior facets of the patella in the complete extension of the joint.

Attention should be directed to the fact, that the patella, in complete flexion, lies so much to the outer side of the joint as to leave the inner condyle, with the exception of the crescentic facet, exposed in front. Meyer has pointed out that the external position assumed by the patella in complete flexion depends on the external patellar retinaculum, which consists of two oblique bands, extending from the outer edge of the bone to the anterior margin of the ileo-tibial band of the fascia lata already alluded to; and which, as it slips backward during flexion, drags the patella by means of the external retinaculum outwards.

In complete extension, again, the patella lies at the inner side of the upper end of the joint, with its long axis directed outwards and downwards. It assumes this position under the action of the lower portion of the vastus internus, which may now be considered as an adductor patellæ. It will be observed also, that the passage forwards of the lower end of the ileo-tibial band, and the consequent slackening of the external retinaculum, permits the bone to take up this internal position. In consequence, therefore, of the movements of the patella, in harmony with the oblique rotations of the knee-joint, the bone, under the influence of its external retinaculum, and of the lower part of the vastus internus, describes a curved path, the concavity of which is directed upwards and outwards. It is also guided in this path by the form and direction of the femoral trochlea, and particularly by its upper and outer portion, which, as is well known, projects considerably upwards, forwards, and inwards, so as to convey the patella to the inner side.

The spaces, which would otherwise be produced by the recession of certain parts of the cartilaginous surfaces from one another in the movements of some joints, are occupied by movable and yielding structures of two kinds—interarticular fibro-cartilages, and the so-called Haversian glands, which may be denominated synovial pads. The former occur when resistance to pressure is to be provided, the latter when space is only to be occupied. The semilunar fibro-cartilages of the knee belong to the former category; and the brothers Weber have pointed out generally how these elastic crescentic masses move backwards and forwards in the flexion and extension of the joint. But Meyer has indicated with greater precision their peculiar functions. The external semilunar cartilage must be viewed as an appendage to the external condyle of the femur, with which it moves backwards in flexion, forwards in extension. These movements are facilitated by its circular form, the approximation of its horns, its non-attachment to the anterior external lateral ligament, although the posterior external lateral ligament gives off a peculiar arrangement to support its posterior limb. The internal semilunar fibro-cartilage, again, must be regarded as an appendage to the internal condyle of the tibia, to which it is fixed by the two internal lateral ligaments. It resembles a curved, yielding, but elastic railway on the upper surface of the inner condyle of the tibia, along which the corresponding condyle of the femur rolls backwards and forwards.

The term of synovial pad may be applied to the mass of vascular fat covered by the synovial membrane, and usually called a **Haversian gland**, or synovial vascular fringe. Some years ago, I directed attention to the structure and relations of these bodies, as corroborating the opinion of Havers regarding their function (*Anat. and Pathological Observations*, p. 42*), and have now ascertained that, in addition to their probable function in supplying synovia, they act undoubtedly as movable stuffing-pads, which not only smear the synovia over the opposite cartilaginous surfaces, but steady the movements of the joints by passing into the spaces left between the surfaces during action. These pads are so constant in their form and relations as to indicate the general character of the movements the joint is capable of.

The principal structure of this kind in the knee-joint is the great infra-patellar pad—the mass in connection with the so-called alar and mucous ligaments. It presents a posterior free surface of a quadrilateral form, which is applied against the cartilaginous surface of the femur, principally in the extended condition of the joint; a superior free margin cut into two lobes, which fill up the variable angular space between the femur and patella, being forced upwards from below by the so-called flabelliform ligaments of the patella; an inferior free margin, also divided into two lobes, separated

* No. XXVII. of this volume.

from one another by the attachment of the mucous ligament, and which, in the nearly extended state of the joint, is pulled back into the angular space between the condyles of the femur and the tibial aspect of the articulation by the traction of the mucous ligament; and, in the flexed condition, is forced backwards by the pressure of the atmosphere.

The supra-patellar pad is adapted to a deep and characteristic notch, which exists between the upper end of the patella and the tendon of the quadriceps extensor. This would appear to adapt the tendon to the bone in the varied antero-posterior angular positions of the two parts during action.

The lateral patellar pad is the pouch-like fold which sheathes the internal longitudinal facet of the patella.

The great and the supra-trochlear pads are situated, the former at the upper and outer part of the great cul-de-sac of the synovial membrane; the latter, a larger external and smaller internal, towards the upper part of the outer face of the trochlea. These fill up the space between the patella and the fore part of the femur above the trochlea in complete extension.

I may conclude by adverting shortly to the remarkable facetted configuration of the articular cartilages of the knee-joint, a structure which has hitherto escaped notice. In a previous part of this lecture the facets of the patella have been described; which bone, from the variable projections of these facets, exhibits sometimes a concavity, sometimes a convexity, and occasionally a flat profile.

On the surface of the tibial condyles the following facets may be demonstrated:—a semilunar facet on each condyle, corresponding to the under surfaces of the semilunar fibro-cartilages, and separated by faint but distinct blunt ridges from a central femoral facet on each condyle, the latter in contact with the femoral cartilage.

On the femur, in addition to the trochlea separated from

the condyles proper by the oblique grooves, and presenting, particularly in aged and slightly-diseased examples, traces of **the three** successive stages in the position of the patella, there are on the condyles semilunar tibial facets separated by faint ridges, and in contact with the upper surfaces of the semilunar cartilages, and uncovered portions, or femoral facets of the tibia. On the inner condyle of the femur, and bounding the **oblique curvature,** is the important crescentic facet already **described.**

X.—ON THE MECHANISM OF THE KNEE-JOINT.*

THE physiology of the locomotory system, and especially that of the joints, has been hitherto much neglected. Even in Henle's elaborate *System of Anatomy*, now in course of publication, there is a lingering tendency to adhere to the formal method of description; and though presenting much freshness and minuteness of description in his account of the articulations, he has scarcely done justice to the results latterly attained by the physical physiologists in this department of the science.

The first step towards an anatomy of the joints adequate to the physiology of the locomotory system—that is, an anatomy based on details affording data for precise mechanical investigation—was taken by Ed. and Wilh. Weber.†

As bearing on my present communication, I shall merely indicate the more important results obtained by the Webers in their examination of the knee-joint, as these appear to me to involve the first germ of the correct conception of the mechanical constitution of the diarthrodial joints.

1. The knee-joint cannot be considered as a hinge-joint, inasmuch as it does not present a fixed axis.

2. The femoral condyles roll, and at the same time glide, like a wheel partially restrained by the drag, forwards in

---

* This paper was read in detail before the Royal Society of Edinburgh, January 18, 1858, but only an abstract was printed in the *Proceedings* of that date. As the essay was found in its complete form amongst the author's papers, we reproduce it here *in extenso*.—EDS.

† *Mechanik der Menschlichen Gehwerkzeuge*: Göttingen 1836.

extension, backwards in flexion, on the nearly horizontal surface of the tibia.

3. By a peculiar arrangement, certain ligaments become tightened when the knee is extended, and the column or shaft of the limb becomes rigid, and thus fitted more particularly for the mechanical support of the body in its erect position.

4. The arrangement by which these ligaments become alternately tightened and slackened, is the antero-posterior spiral curvature of the femoral condyles; the ligaments in question being attached above to the neighbourhood of the polar extremities of the curves, are consequently drawn up and put on the stretch in extension, let down and slackened in flexion.

5. The ligaments relaxed in flexion permit a rotation of 36° in the horizontal plane of the joint, during which the inner condyle of the femur is comparatively fixed, while the outer describes a curve, like the front-wheels of a carriage in passing round a corner. These observations of the Webers on the knee-joint were published in 1836, but have in no respect modified the current modes of viewing and describing this important articulation.

H. Meyer published, in Müller's *Archiv* for 1853, in the course of a series of memoirs on the mechanics of the human skeleton, his observations on the knee-joint. The most important features of this memoir are the observations on the curvatures of the femoral condyles and on the axis of the articulation. Viewing the patellar as distinct from the two condyloid portions of the joint, he pointed out for the first time a feature of the internal condyle of the femur which had previously escaped notice in its proper form. The two posterior thirds of this condyle are on the whole parallel to, and of the same length as, the entire external condyle. The previously-recognised greater length, and so-called obliquity, of the inner condyle, depends on the addition of a portion curved in a plane, oblique at once to the antero-posterior plane of the condyle and to the horizontal plane of the joint, and intercalated between the antero-posterior portion of the condyle and the patellar surface. This intercalated portion may, according to Meyer, be conceived as a segment of the base of a cone, the vertex of which, in the erect position of the limb, is situated in the external condyle of the tibia, with its axis directed from above forwards and inwards, to below, backwards and outwards. The curve extends over 60°, and the axis of the generating cone inclined 45° to the horizontal.

This axis he distinguishes as the oblique axis of the joint, and round it the leg and thigh are compelled to rotate, at the close of extension and the commencement of flexion, when the conical surface in question is in contact with the lateral internal and anterior part of the inter-condyloid spine of the tibia and the anterior crucial ligament.

Referring to the unsatisfactory character of the series of co-ordinates on which the Webers based their assumption of an equiangular spiral as the profile curvature of the femoral condyles, Meyer concluded from measurements procured from outlines of the curve made by means of a tracing-frame and a telescope, that its posterior and anterior portions may be safely assumed to be arcs of two circles, respectively 120° and 40°, the radius of the former being to that of the latter as 5 to 9. He conceives, therefore, that there are two transverse axes of rotation in the knee-joint, an anterior and a posterior; but holds that, in treating the subject, one transverse axis only need be assumed.

Whatever exceptions may be taken to Meyer's double transverse axis, and to his assumed circular profile curve of the femoral condyles, there can be no doubt of the general correctness and great value of his observations on the so-called oblique rotation of the joint, the corresponding arrangement of the inner condyle, the coadjusted movements of the patella, and the harmonised attachments of the related muscles. It is therefore somewhat remarkable that Henle, in his recent work, should have referred to Meyer's researches only to deny the specific character of the obliquely-curved portion of the inner condyle.

I may here be permitted to state that, having been in the habit, since I became a public teacher of anatomy, of explaining the researches of the brothers Weber on the knee-joint, I lost no time, after the appearance of Meyer's paper, in re-examining the subject. An abstract of Meyer's observations, with additional observations made by myself, were published in a lecture in summer 1855, an abstract of which appeared at the time.* I have since annually gone over the subject in the University, and as the results in question bear essentially on the more immediate subject of this communication, I shall briefly enumerate them.

I obtained, then, satisfactory evidence that, as stated by Meyer, the thigh and leg rotate in opposite directions at the close of extension and at the commencement of flexion, and that the co-ordinated arrangements for these movements, in the patella, the ligaments, and muscles, are such as described by him. But, in addition, I found that the cartilaginous surfaces of the patella, femur, and tibia, respectively, are not continuous but facetted surfaces.

The patellar surface presents seven facets, which are in no position of the joint, at the same time, all in contact with the opposite femoral surface, nor can be made to fit it throughout in any position of the opposite bones; but come into contact with that surface in a determined order of succession, *which is invariable*. The patellar surface of the femur, as has been more particularly pointed out by Meyer, is separated from the two condyloid surfaces by grooves; but in addition, I found that there are distinct marginal facets on the

* *Edinburgh Medical Journal*, July 1855; also No. IX. of this volume.

condyles corresponding to, and rolling upon, the semilunar fibro-cartilages; and distinct from their remaining or central portions, which are in contact with and roll upon the central cartilaginous facets of the tibial condyles. The oblique curved surface at the fore part of the inner condyle is a distinct facet, which at the close of extension and at the commencement of flexion moves upon and is in contact with the internal anterior cartilaginous surface of the intercondyloid spine of the tibia; and with the tibial attachment of the anterior crucial ligament; and in extreme flexion is then, and then only, in contact with one of the seven facets of the patella, which patellar facet, in no other position of the joint, touches any other cartilaginous surface, but is provisionally sheathed with a synovial fold.

The two tibial condyloid articular surfaces also present distinct semilunar facets, and central facets for the central facets of the femoral articular surfaces.

In consequence of this facetted configuration, and the peculiar curvatures of the opposite cartilaginous surfaces, the latter are in no position of the joint coincident throughout; but gape more or less in different parts of their extent.

In addition to the previously-recognised function of the semilunar fibro-cartilages as tough elastic structures for adapting the opposite femoral and tibial surfaces to one another, the so-called Haversian glands, in addition to their lubricating function, are arranged for a similar purpose. Every space or gap between the opposite surfaces of the patella, femur, and tibia, not provided for by the semilunar fibro-cartilages, is supplied, when it appears, with an invariable, vascular, fatty synovial pad, which is forced into the chink or pulled out again by special arrangements; and thus, not only do these pads support, and render steady, the movements of the joints, but lubricate the moving surfaces during action.

Since the publication of these results, I have annually

devoted much attention to the configuration, movements, and relations of the opposite cartilaginous surfaces of the diarthrodial joints. The details with reference to special articulations I shall reserve for future communications; at present I will merely refer to certain general results, which bear more particularly on the mechanism of the knee-joint.

In all diarthrodial articular surfaces there are facets, more or less pronounced, situated at the opposite extremities of the lines of movement. These may be conveniently designated terminal facets. They are not primarily engaged in guiding or conditioning the movements, although they frequently modify their initial and terminal portions. These terminal facets are essentially surfaces against which, and on which, the opposite bones come to rest.

The proper acting area in each of the opposite articular surfaces is, after eliminating the terminal facets, comparatively limited, and may generally be observed to present two facets. These opposite facets act in pairs (a pair consisting of one on each surface), acting together in the movement in one direction; the other pair in the opposite alternate movement. The pair of facets not in action break contact, or gape, during the action of the facets engaged; and the chink between them is occupied by synovia or by a fatty pad.

But even the acting facets, during their movements, are only partially in contact. They are only coincident when the facets approach or have reached the limit of their movement in their proper direction; that is, when the flexion-facets— as they may be conveniently termed—have completed flexion, or when the extension-facets have completed extension. In these latter stages of the movements of the acting facets, when they come into contact, the corresponding terminal facets close also. The acting facets may, even at the conclusion of their proper action, break contact, and the entire joint rest on the corresponding terminal facets.

The movements of opposite diarthrodial surfaces on one another appear to be in every instance a combination of gliding and rolling; the amount of gliding being directly, and the rolling inversely, as the coincidence of the opposite articular surfaces.

An important addition has recently been made to our conceptions of the mechanical constitution of joints, by the nearly simultaneous publication of memoirs by Langer and Henke, and of a report of these memoirs, with original observations on the same subject, by Meissner. As these new observations refer principally to the ankle and elbow-joint, and as I shall have afterwards to refer to them in detail, I shall at present only allude to such points as bear on the subject of this communication.

The important fact announced by these three observers is the screw configuration of the articular surfaces of the elbow, ankle, and calcaneo-astragaloid joints. The method of investigation adopted was to trace lines on one of the articular surfaces by means of a steel point passed a little beyond the opposite surface previous to putting the joint through its movements. These lines are termed "*ganglinii*" "go-lines," and in all the joints examined are arranged obliquely to their axes of rotation. Langer, acting on the happy idea of prolonging the screw, by uniting in one direction a number of plaster casts of the same articular surface, succeeded in forming continued screws from the upper articular surface of the astragalus in the horse, panther, and human subject.

Langer concludes that the "go-line" of the ankle-joint in all the Mammalia is a portion of a helix, and that therefore the astragaloid surface is a segment of a cylindrical or conical male screw, while the tibio-fibular surface is a segment of the corresponding female screw. The right ankle-joint is a left-handed screw combination; the left ankle-joint a right-handed. When, therefore, the foot is conceived to be fixed, the leg, in passing from a position of extension to flexion, moves laterally outwards along the axis of rotation, to an extent which is directly as the amount of rotation and the sine of the angle of inclination of the thread—that is, in proportion to the extent of flexion and the rapidity of the screw.

In attempting by Langer's method to develope these articular screw-models, I found, that when two casts were united, an apparently satisfactory helix was produced. But, in adding to the series, the spire diminished, and the helix closed on itself. It appeared that not only the angle of inclination of the thread, but also the radius of rotation, diminished. The surfaces of two casts of the same articular surface could not be accurately adapted to one another, even by placing them together in the mould in which they were both cast. I found that when one or the other of the lateral ridges which represent the thread of the screw was situated as a guide in joining the models, the helix closed in one or the other direction. In addition, I found that the models only fitted their moulds in one position—viz. that in which they were cast. This follows from what already has been stated regarding the forms of articular surfaces. The tibio-astragaloid articular surfaces cannot therefore be segments of a cylindrical series. It appears extremely probable that, abstracting the terminal facets, the acting areas on each surface consist each of a segment of a conical screw—the convex portions of these two screws being on the astragaloid, the concave on the tibial articular surface; the one screw coming into action in flexion, the other in extension.

In following up the subject, I was compelled to re-examine the knee-joint from this new point of view. It now occurred to me, that instead of attempting to procure co-ordinates by direct admeasurement of the articular surfaces, data for an approximate conception of the forms of these surfaces in any joint might be reached by tracing the path or locus of any distant point in one of the bones when in motion, or of the point of a rod prolonged from it. I was enabled leisurely to examine the path pursued by that point during flexion and extension as projected on a plane parallel to the transverse plane of the joint. The path described by the point of the rod was found to be the same in both movements, but presented a form which cannot be referred to the movements of the joint as hitherto conceived. It was a continuous curve, which crossed that perpendicular line in the field of view, with which the point of the rod in the extended position was coincident, before it again came to rest in it at the close of flexion. Supposing the leg to be fixed perpendicularly, whatever the nature of the profile curve described by the point of the rod fixed in the axis of the thigh-bone during flexion and extension—whether cycloidal, if the profile curve of the femoral condyles be circular, or some form of equiangular spiral, if the condyles possess that character, it appeared evident that the line projected on a plane parallel to the transverse plane of the joint must be a perpendicular line. It also appeared evident that if Meyer's rotation really occurred, the line projected on this transverse plane would be curved above and pass below into a straight line. I found, however, on viewing the point of the rod as projected in its course on this plane, that the line was a continuous curve, concave throughout towards the inner side in both the right and left lines.

It was evident, therefore, in the first place, that the upper part of the curve was due to Meyer's rotation, renewed in consequence of the obliquity of the shaft of the thigh-bone; and in the second place that the external condyle, and the two posterior thirds of the internal do not roll and glide in parallel planes, but along curved paths. But as the inner condyle is rolling while passing round Meyer's curve, it is clear that from first to last, in flexion and extension, the condyles of the femur roll and glide along curved paths.

This curve, being more leisurely examined by means of a plumb-line suspended between it and the eye, or through a cross-threaded frame, or with a telescope with parallel wires in the focus of its eye-piece, was found to be more rapid in its curvature at the upper and lower end, while in the intermediate portion of its extent it lay more in the direction of the plumb-line.

It was now observed, on examining the joint itself, not only that the condyles of the femur roll backwards and forwards in curved paths—a fact which has hitherto escaped notice—but that this curvature or rotation is as strongly marked at the flexion as at the extension extremity of the movement.

By fixing the joint in the horizontal plane, and setting up a series of rods from that plane to the point of the indicator fixed in the femur, at equal intervals in its course, I have procured a system of co-ordinates which enable me by the eye to trace more carefully the course of the curves on the three planes on which it is projected. By this rough method, altogether insufficient for precise results, the eye is nevertheless enabled to detect—1. That the line is a helix, with variable curvature, with a more rapid sweep at its upper and lower portions than in the intermediate distance, the upper sweep being the larger of the two; 2. That there are two breaks in its course, the first near its upper end at the commencement of the great sweep, and most perceptible in the mesial plane; the second is situated about the junction of the lower and middle third of the line, and consists of an angular bend, with a more rapid curvature on each side, observable in the mesial and transverse planes.

These peculiarities in the curve induced me to re-examine the curvatures of the femoral condyles, and I found that the upper break corresponded to the grooves between the patellar and condyloid surfaces, and also recognised what has also hitherto escaped notice, that a little behind the middle of the profile curvatures of the femoral condyles, and more particularly on the outer condyle, there is an angular break, in front of and behind which the curvature is more rapid. Tracing the posterior curvature backwards from the break at the outer edge of the external condyle, where its position is indicated by a tubercle about the middle of the popliteal notch, it passes backwards along the condyloid margin, and also obliquely backwards and inwards into the hitherto unnoticed prolonged superior posterior internal angle of the condyle. The portion of the inner edge of the outer condyle corresponding to the posterior part of the curve now in question is concave inwards, and is the margin of the space for the superior attachment of the external crucial ligament, as the outer margin of Meyer's curve limits the space for the attachment of the internal crucial ligament. Within these limits the curve of the posterior area of the condyle diminishes backwards, so as to give it the appearance of a conchoidal surface. The posterior area of the inner condyle and its curves are equally appreciable, but flatter and less distinctly marked.

The anterior area with its curve is most fully developed on the inner condyle. The outer part of this area is the facet previously mentioned in my reference to Meyer's oblique axis. It limits the attachment of the posterior crucial ligament, and its curvature diminishes from before backwards. The anterior area on the external condyle, like the posterior on the internal, is flatter, shorter, and less fully developed.

The helicoid character of the curve of movement appeared to me to indicate a screwed structure in the joint. The characters of the portions of the curve before and behind the posterior break, and the corresponding and remarkable peculiarity of the condyloid areas and their curves, taken along with what I had already observed in the ankle, led me to suspect that the movements of the knee-joint are combined gliding and rolling movements of conical screwed surfaces upon one another. To adapt this hypothesis to the structure of the joint and the general character of the curves, it was necessary to assume that the anterior areas of the combined femoral condyles are portions of a double-threaded conical nut; the anterior parts of the combined tibial condyles, and the corresponding part of the intercondyloid spine, with other structures to be afterwards mentioned, are portions of a corresponding double-threaded conical tap. It was also necessary to assume that the combined posterior areas of the femoral condyles are portions of a second conical nut, and the combined posterior portions of the tibial condyles and spine—the corresponding tap. The hypothesis, however, in addition required that the anterior screw-combination should be opposed to the posterior; if the anterior is a right-handed, the posterior must be a left-handed screw.

In the absence of numerical values for the co-ordinates of the curves (which, however, I do not despair of procuring), I cannot make a definite statement; but the general character of the curves observed, and the corresponding movements and structure of the joint, leave little doubt in my mind that the flexion and extension, combined gliding and rolling movements of the knee are performed between two conical double-threaded screw-combinations, an anterior and a posterior—the anterior being a left-handed screw, and the posterior a right-handed screw in the right knee-joint; the anterior a right-handed, and the posterior a left-handed screw in the left knee-joint.

The movements which take place round these two combinations are alternate—those round the anterior completing extension and commencing flexion; those round the posterior, completing flexion and commencing extension of the joint.

The movements round the anterior combination are more extensive and important than those round the posterior; and in the ordinary use of the joint are alone employed.

The result of these two combinations is, that in complete extension the anterior combination is screwed home, while the posterior is unscrewed. In complete flexion, again, the anterior combination is unscrewed and the posterior is home. For the purpose of understanding how the screw-movements of the femur and tibia round two axes alternately, both of which are only slightly, if at all, inclined to the axis of the limb, should result in the so-called flexion and extension at the knee, it is necessary to consider some of the properties of conical screws, and of the peculiar modification of them which is presented by the mechanism of the knee-joint. A conical screwed nut and tap, if both constructed of comparatively unyielding materials, do not coincide, and consequently do not afford any serviceable result as a screw-combination till they have been screwed home. Conical screw-combinations are consequently rarely employed in the arts; and when they are made use of, the male or female screw, more generally the latter, consists of a yielding, elastic, and tough material. The opposed threads of a conical screw-combination constructed of such materials are throughout congruent with one another; and that amount of friction consequently procured, which constitutes an element of the productive effect of a cylindrical screw-combination; and the total absence of which renders a conical screw-combination of unyielding materials inefficient till screwed home. In the knee-joint the concave screws on the articular femoral surface are comparatively unyielding; while the convex screws on the tibial surface are only partially cartilaginous, but mainly flexible, elastic, and tough. Their movements, therefore, are precise, and when screwed home the opposite elements of each combination become fixed. In screwing and unscrewing a conical combination of unyielding materials up to the completion of the one process, and from the commencement of the other, the concave and convex screws are non-coincident. Both processes may be conceived as being accomplished without any contact of the opposite surfaces up to the completion of the one and from the commencement of the other ; and the contact takes place simultaneously all over from base to vertex in the one case, and is as simultaneously broken in the other. However irregular the movements may be by which a conical screw-combination may be screwed on or off, there is one general direction by which the movements must be guided—namely, a rotation of one or other, or of both screws in opposite directions, round the common axis of the system. The amount of this rotation will be directly as the rapidity of the thread in any given combination; but, however rapid the thread may be in any such combination, there must always be a certain amount of rotation to admit of complete separation of the two elements. It is evident, therefore, that in the application of a conical screw-combination in the construction of a joint required to move in flexion and extension, the most advantageous direction in which the axis of the combination could be placed would be coincident with the axis of flexion and extension, and the most disadvantageous that which most nearly opposes the axis of the limb; for if coincident with that axis, there would be no apparent hinge-movement at all. We have exemplifications of the permissible limits of such an arrangement in the elbow and knee joints. In the former the axis of the screw is nearly at right angles to the axis of the limb; in the latter, nearly coincident with it.

The arrangements by which the screw-combinations at the knee-joint are adjusted for the general movements of flexion and extension are as follows :—The diameters of the fundamental cones considerably exceed their vertical height. They are double-threaded, deep cut, with an obliquity of thread so proportioned to the cone that they form little more than halfspires. The upper portions of the taps of these screw-systems consist of ligamentous texture (crucial ligaments), the basal portions of bone and cartilage (tibial condyles and spine), the lateral parts of fibro-cartilage and ligamentous texture (semilunar discs and lateral ligaments). The nuts consist of corresponding portions of the femoral condyles. There is actually retained, however, for the service of the joint, only so much of each combination as is necessary for the required movements. The base of the tap is connected to the vertex of the nut by the crucial ligaments, which form the apex of the former, and when the combination is screwed home these ligamentous bundles are in a state of tension. In the process of unscrewing, the ligamentous bundles of the tap become, on account of their mode of attachment to the vertex of the nut, successively relaxed from the point downwards; while this graduated relaxation of the ligaments provides for the tension necessary for the continued gliding screw-movement. The successive relaxations of those ligamentous bundles, which, having served their purpose, are no longer required, permit a movement to be superadded to this form of organic screw, which the artificial screw does not admit of. The relaxation of the vertex of the tap permits the two threads of the nut to roll as well as glide along. The nut rolls as well as glides on its convex condyloid surfaces. But as only a limited extent of the cartilaginous surface of the tap is adapted to the cartilaginous surface of the nut, the latter would speedily roll and glide off the former, if the latter were not prolonged in the required direction. The rolling movement of the convex margin of the nut is further provided for by the interposition of the tough and elastic semilunar discs; as, moreover, the rolling motion increases from the axis to the periphery of the combination, it takes place principally on these discs, while the gliding or proper screwing motion, increasing proportionally towards the axis, takes place chiefly between the opposite cartilaginous surfaces of the central part of the condyles of the two bones, and to the greater extent between the central margins of the femoral condyles and the surface of the spine of the tibia.

XI.—ON THE CURVATURES AND MOVEMENTS OF THE ACTING FACETS OF ARTICULAR SURFACES.*

1. The opposite gliding surfaces of joints employed by mechanicians are surfaces of revolution; and consequently all sections of these surfaces, at right angles to their axes of rotation, are circular arcs. In all uncompounded artificial joints, therefore, except those with spherical surfaces, the movements are limited to rotation in opposite directions round a single axis.

2. In organic joints, on the contrary, the opposite gliding surfaces are not surfaces of revolution; they are not cylindrical, conical, or spherical, in the geometrical sense of the terms. In no instance, as far as I have observed, is a section at right angles to the assumed or so-called axis of rotation, the arc of a circle; nor, as it appears to me, is it possible to associate the characteristic curvature of the path described by a given point in the bone or limb to which the joint appertains, with articular surfaces of revolution.

3. As stated in my former communication "On the Mechanism of the Knee-Joint,"† the opposed surfaces of organic joints are not continuous but faceted areas; and of the various kinds of facets indicated by me as existing on opposite articular surfaces, those termed "acting facets" determine the movements of the bones to which the joint appertains, and

---

* This memoir had evidently been carefully prepared for publication, but had not been sent to press. It is now published, therefore, for the first time.—Eds.

† *Proc. Royal Soc. Edinburgh*, Jan. 18, 1858; and No. X. of this volume.

are consequently the **fundamental facets** of the articular areas.

The object of the present communication is to put on record the general result of the observations I have made on the configuration and movements of central articular facets since the date of the paper above referred to; and to submit a theory of their probable geometrical character.

4. The central facet on one articular area of a joint is adapted to a corresponding central facet on the corresponding opposite articular area of that joint. The surface-curvatures of the two facets are similar, so that the facets themselves may be considered reciprocally as cast and mould of one another. I shall have occasion hereafter to employ the term *articular couple* to designate collectively two opposite corresponding facets of any kind; and the individual facets of such couples I shall term twin-elements.

5. The twin elements are not invariably developed to the same extent, one of them being generally only a portion of the entire facet, the deficient portion being supplied by yielding and elastic structure, and which may be replaced in the examination of certain joints by a cast in wax or plaster of the corresponding portion of the opposite facet. This restriction or curtailment of one of the twin elements is referable to that principle of constructive economy which is evinced in the arrangements of organic mechanism, in the midst of their general complexity; and it will, moreover, appear in another section of this communication that the retention of the whole of both the twin elements is not essential to their peculiar mode of action. I find it convenient to employ the terms *reserved* and *restricted* to distinguish the articular elements in these respective conditions.

6. If the two elements of an articular couple be observed during action, they will be seen to glide past one another in two directions in such a manner that, assuming both of them

to be complete—i.e. *unrestricted*—and therefore congruent or in contact throughout at the commencement of action, the congruence becomes a minimum at the close of action; and the twin elements may even be completely separated from one another in the subsequent movements of the joint. The two movements are simultaneous, so that the *actual movement is their resultant*.

7. The two movements determine the contours of the facets. The most extended movement, which determines the length of the facets, I shall term the *primary movement*, or (for reasons to be afterwards stated) the movement *along the thread*. The two extremities of the facets will be referred to as *proximal* and *distal*. The other movement I shall term secondary, or the movement *across the thread*. This movement determines the breadth of the facets and their two margins respectively; subject, however, like the lengths and extremities of the facets, to the *restrictive* modification of the two margins of each element respectively, the one has a higher teleological import than the other. I shall refer to the former as the *proximal*, to the latter as the *distal*, margin.

8. When, therefore, the elements of a couple are in their fundamental positions—*i.e.* when they are in contact throughout—their extremities and margins are also coincident respectively; but in consequence of the frequent restriction of portions of one element, the corresponding portions of the other are not in contact with correlative portions of surface, but with synovia, synovial pads, or elastic menisci.

9. The lines of *the thread*, or of primary movement, which extend from the proximal to the distal extremities of the facets, are curves of double curvature of a helical form. The curvature of these lines, while maintaining its general character throughout, diminishes in extent or sweep, appearing more rapid as it approaches the proximal extremities of the facets; and therefore I distinguish the proximal extremity of

a facet by the more limited sweep and apparently greater rapidity of its longitudinal curvature.

10. It is evident, therefore, that these helical lines of curvature cannot be conceived as developed on a cylindrical surface; they must lie in some surface of a conical form. The lines may, however, be provisionally assumed as conical helices of a given curvature.

11. The lines of movement *across the thread* are also curves of double curvature. The curvature of these transverse lines, like that of the longitudinal, while it maintains its character throughout, is more limited in extent, with less sweep, and therefore apparently more rapid as it approaches the proximal margins of the elements. The transverse lines also have their centres of curvature towards the proximal extremities of the facets. The concave margin also is of less extent than the convex, and the proximal extremity narrower than the distal.

12. It also follows that the margins of the twin-facets must be concave towards the centres of longitudinal curvature—*i.e.* the marginal outlines of the two facets respectively must be, as they are in fact, concave on one side, convex on the other.

13. As already stated, the actual movement of the twin-elements of an articular couple is the resultant of their primary and secondary movements. This resultant movement may be effected by either of the two elements on the other, or by both simultaneously. The resultant or actual movement of an articular couple occurs alternately in opposite directions along the same path; when completed in one direction the articular elements are in a maximum of contact; and when the movement is repeated in the opposite direction, they are in the position of minimum contact. I find it convenient, in treating of the movements of joints, to employ the terms *positive* and *negative* for the two opposite relative posi-

tions of maximum and minimum contact of their constituent articular couples. *In the positive position, an articular couple is in a state of stable equilibrium. In the negative position it is in the condition of unstable equilibrium.*

14. If the successive relative positions of the twin-elements of a couple are examined in series from their positive to their negative phase, it will be observed that as the proximal extremity of the one element glides towards the distal extremity of the opposite element, the corresponding margins of the opposite elements glide past one another; so that when the negative phase is attained it will be found that the proximal portion only of the distal extremity of the one element remains in contact with the distal portion only of the proximal extremity of the other element. During the return movement from the negative to the positive phase, the series of successive relative positions is reversed; thus the opposite extremities and margins glide towards one another, so that at the close of the movement the proximal portion of the distal extremity of the one element, which in the negative phase is in contact with the distal portion only of the proximal extremity of the other element, now resumes its original positive position, while the margins have also become coincident, and the twin-elements consequently congruent. The movement is thus of such a kind that in the passage from the positive to the negative phase the corresponding extremities and margins of the twin-elements recede from one another, until at last the proximal part of the distal extremity, and the contiguous part of the proximal margin of the one element, coincide with the distal part of the proximal extremity and the contiguous part of the distal margin of the opposite element.

15. As already stated (13), when the couple is in the positive phase its elements are in stable equilibrium; so it may now be observed that the only mode in which they can

pass from the positive to the negative phase without losing entirely their stability is by a **combination** of the primary and secondary **movements**—for any **attempt** to glide the one element over the other, except by the double movement, immediately destroys the congruence of the couple. It will also be observed that the twin-elements, when in their positive position, are *fixed* or adjusted in their proper localities ; and that *the successive extents of congruence during the action of the couple are directly as the approximation to the positive, and inversely as the approximation to the negative phase.*

16. The successive extents of congruence appear to be determined by the *successive adaptation of corresponding portions of curvature on the opposite elements*, as these elements pass through their opposite movements ; for it appears as if the gliding of the twin-elements across the thread not only successively accommodates their transverse, but also their longitudinal lines of curvature as they respectively meet one another.

17. During the gliding in the lines of the transverse curvatures in passing from the positive to the negative phase, the two bones on which respectively the twin-elements are situated gradually incline on one another towards that side of the articular couple on which the proximal margins of the elements are situated. As it will appear in the sequel that in some couples the proximal margins are on the concave, but in others on the convex sides of the couple, the inclination of the two bones will be to the concave side in the former, to the convex side in the latter.

18. During the gliding in the lines of longitudinal curvature in passing from the positive to the negative phase, the two bones incline towards the distal extremity of the couple if that couple has a concave proximal side, and towards the proximal extremity of the couple if that couple has a convex proximal side.

19. From what has now been stated, it is evident that the two bones return to their original positions as the couple resumes its positive phase. We may, therefore, assume a straight line passing through the surfaces of the couple, or a parallel to such a line, as representing the two bones in their relative positions to one another in the positive phase of the couple. At the commencement of the passage to the negative phase, the line separates into two portions at the point where it passes through the twin-surfaces; and these two portions thenceforward to their negative position assume a series of relative positions determined by the resultant movements of the twin-elements. These series of relative positions must be similar, but necessarily in inverse order, during the return to the positive phase.

20. As already stated, the longitudinal and transverse lines of curvature of the twin-elements are curves of double curvature; and as the resultant movements of the elements themselves must be helical, it follows that the two halves of the line representing the two bones must pass through a series of positions of such a kind that, during action, any given and corresponding point in each of these lines will describe a helical path of similar but opposite curvature.

21. The geometrical character of the generative curves of an articular couple can only be finally determined by means of numerical data. As, however, the forms and movements presented by the twin-surfaces exhibit throughout these strongly marked already described distinctive characters, it becomes a matter of importance to inquire whether the conditions of these characters are fulfilled or supplied by any one geometrical curve.

22. With this object in view, it is to be observed that during the double gliding of the elements upon one another in their alternate passages from their positive to their nega-

tive, and from their negative to their positive positions, a progressively diminishing or increasing extent of congruence appears to be provided for *by the successive gliding into apposition, and therefore into congruence, of geometrically-similar, as well as linearly-equal portions of curvature not previously coincident.*

23. In other words, the geometrical arrangement of the surfaces of the opposite elements appears to be such as will provide, not only for *their perfect congruence when in their positions,* by means of *geometrically-similar and linearly-equal longitudinal and transverse lines of curvature fitted into one another in the opposite elements,* but also for *an alternating series of progressively diminishing and increasing extents of congruence,* by means of *corresponding series of geometrically-similar and linearly-equal portions of longitudinal and transverse curvatures on the opposite elements,* and *increasing or diminishing in accordance with the positive or negative direction of the movements.* These successive coincidences of these similar and equal portions of longitudinal and transverse curvature being brought about by *corresponding gliding movements in the negative and positive directions.*

24. The equiangular spiral, in its more general form as a curve of double curvature, is the only geometrical curve which fulfils the conditions of the successive movements and adaptations of articular curvatures now under consideration. A characteristic property of this spiral, and one which peculiarly adapts it for generating the curvature of the surfaces of organic joints, is the geometrical similarity of all portions of any given example of curve which subtends the same polar angle, however different their linear dimensions may be; so that, if the spiral be conceived as revolving round its pole, in the plane of two lines diverging from the pole, the lines will intercept an infinite number of geometrically-similar portions of the curve, but which become infinitely smaller or greater as

the curve advances in the direction of its pole or away from it.

25. Now we may conceive the opposite, similar, and equal curved surfaces of an articular couple to be generated simultaneously by a given equiangular spiral. This spiral, in successive stages of development, represents corresponding successive transverse lines of curvature of the twin-elements; its primitive extent or dimension being assumed as equal to that of the first opposite transverse lines at the proximal extremities of the elements. The proximal extremities of the transverse lines of curvature, which collectively constitute the proximal margins of the elements, are assumed as representing the polar portion of the generating curve; while the distal extremities of the transverse lines of curvature, which collectively constitute the distal margins of the elements, are assumed as representing the anti-polar portion of the generating curve. The primitive dimension of the given curve having been assumed equal to the first proximal transverse curvature on each element, the successive greater transverse curvatures are geometrically conceivable as being produced by successive rotations of the generating curve round its pole and in the direction of the pole, so that successive additions are made to its anti-polar extremity, and consequently to the distal extremities, of the transverse lines of curvature of the anti-polar elements.

But it is evident, on inspection of the articular surface of an acting couple, that the transverse lines of curvature are arranged in series along the lines of longitudinal curvature, and that the series therefore sweeps in a helical or screwed direction round a central axis of the entire combination. We must assume, therefore, in addition, that the generating spiral, while increasing its dimensions by revolving round its pole in the direction of that pole, also revolves tangentially round a fixed axis, while it glides along that axis in the direction of its length. If, now, the generating spiral increases its dimensions, so that each linear increment corresponding to a given angular increment shall vary as the existing dimensions of the spiral itself, then the longitudinal curvatures of the surfaces developed—that is, the lines of curvature resulting from the revolution of the continually-increasing generating spiral round, and the gliding of it along, the fixed axis, must also be equiangular spirals, with a constant ratio determined by that of the generating spiral.

26. The opposite surfaces, thus simultaneously generated, would evidently be congruent screwed surfaces, representing respectively the concave and convex elements of a conical screw-combination. The curvature in the direction of the thread of such a screw-combination would possess the character of the equiangular spiral; while the curvature across the thread would possess corresponding characters.

27. It is evident that the concave and convex elements of a screw combination of this kind would be fully congruent when in apposition, and that their axes would be coincident. It is also clear that any attempt to unscrew a combination of this kind, while the axes of its two elements are retained in a right line, would at once render its entire opposite surfaces incongruent, in fact separate them from one another. If, on the other hand, it were possible to diverge the axes of the two elements from one another at the same time that the elements are unscrewed, then there would result from these combined movements a gliding of the opposite surfaces upon one another over a succession of extents, which would diminish in area in terms of the constant ratio of the generating spiral, until finally a minimum of contact of congruence would obtain—that is, to use the terms already employed, the screw-combination would be in its negative phase, and its elements in their negative positions. On reversing the combined movements—that is, on screwing the combination into

its stable or positive phase—the two elements would glide on one another over successive extents of congruence or contact, which would increase in dimensions in terms of the constant ratio of the generative spiral, until both surfaces become congruent throughout—*i.e.*, until the elements are again in their positive positions.

28. The combined movements—*i.e.*, the movements along the thread, and the inclination and consequent divergence of the axis of the elements, or, what is equivalent, the movement across the thread—are only possible under the condition that the structure of the combination shall consist of rigid materials, along a limited extent only of a single spire or whorl, so that the movements on that side of the whorl shall not be counteracted by those on the opposite side. It is this condition of applicability which determines the comparatively small extent of whorl in the greater number of articular couples, and more especially in their restricted elements.

29. The combined movements being thus provided for, the successive longitudinal and transverse adaptations must occur in the following order :—The elements being in their positive phase, it is evident that during the passage to the negative phase successive transverse curvatures in the one element must pass off and become unscrewed at the proximal extremity of the couple; while at the same time successive transverse curvatures of the opposite element must be left uncovered at the distal extremity of the couple. With regard to the mode of adaptation of those successive portions of the elements still in contact or covered by one another, it is to be borne in mind that the successive transverse curvatures are successive developments of a given extent of a given equiangular spiral; they are all, therefore, geometrically dissimilar, as well as linearly unequal; but from the law of the equiangular spiral, every greater development of a given extent of curve contains a portion geometrically similar and

linearly equal to every lesser development of it. And as all these geometrically-similar and linearly-equal portions of curvature are, from the assumed relations of the generating spiral, necessarily collocated in a regular series along the two elements of the couple, it follows that *in the passage from the positive to the negative phase, each greater transverse curvature, when it advances on the next opposite lesser curvature, cannot coincide with it as a whole, but by the transverse gliding, as much of its polar extremity as is geometrically similar and linearly equal to that next opposite lesser curvature will coincide with it, while the remaining portion of its antipolar extremity projects uncovered beyond the antipolar extremity of the lesser.* The same relations subsisting between all the other greater transverse curvatures of the one element, and those next lesser transverse curvatures on the opposite element, all the remaining transverse portions of linear coincidences go on diminishing, in terms of the common ratio of the generating curve, until the negative phase is reached, or loss of contact occurs. On reversing the combined movements during the passage from the negative to the positive phase, portions geometrically similar, and linearly equal transverse curvatures, increasing in terms of the common ratio, successively coincide; while the proximal and distal extremities of the twin-elements respectively approach one another, and their distal margins approximate till complete congruence is again attained.

30. It is evident that the principle, which provides for a succession of progressively diminishing, or increasing, portions of similar and equal transverse curvature, involves a corresponding series of progressively diminishing or increasing similar and equal portions of longitudinal curvature, and consequently a resultant series of progressively diminishing, or increasing, similar and equal areas of curved surface for contact on the opposite elements of the articular couple.

31. It is also evident that we may assume the generating

spiral, as it simultaneously glides along and revolves around the axial line, to do so with its polar extremity directed either towards or away from that axis. In the former case, the proximal or polar margins of the resulting elements will constitute the concave side of the couple, which will be consequently directed towards the axis. In the latter case, the polar or proximal margins of the resulting elements will constitute the convex side of the couple, and will therefore be turned away from the axis. These two forms of articular couples are therefore also respectively distinguished by the direction of their secondary or transverse gliding; when the polar side of the couple is concave, or towards the axis, the transverse gliding of the elements, during their passage from the positive to the negative phase, is such as that the inclinations of the two portions of a right line passing perpendicularly through the couple will be towards the axis, and away from it on the return from the negative to the positive. When, on the other hand, the polar margins of the elements are on the convex side of the couple, the elements glide in such a manner that the two halves of the perpendicular line incline away from the axis, and towards it on the return to the positive phase. As the collocation of these two forms of articular couples constitutes an important feature in the construction of certain joints, and as they demand therefore distinct designations, I shall employ the term *axial* to indicate a couple the proximal side of which is towards the axis, and the term *antaxial* to indicate a couple the proximal side of which is convex.

32. In certain joints, each articular couple acts in concert with a second articular couple, which is developed around the same axis, but on the opposite side. For this arrangement I shall employ, as in my former communication on the knee-joint, the term *articular combination*. If we assume, as I have done throughout the present communication, that the

generating curve of articular couples is in each instance a special equiangular spiral, we may conceive the two constituent couples of an articular combination to be simultaneously generated by two similar and equal equiangular spirals placed tangentially on opposite sides of a common axis, but with the polar extremity of the one, and the antipolar extremity of the other, in contact with it, so that all tangentially-corresponding parts in the generative curves of the two couples shall be parallel, while they at the same time glide along the axis and revolve around it in the same direction, increasing their dimensions by successive increments in a given ratio at their antipolar extremities, by revolving round their poles in the direction of these poles. The two couples thus generated would be respectively *axial* and *antaxial*, the former having the pole of its generative spiral towards, the latter turned away from, the common axis. During the passage of a combination of this kind from its positive to its negative phase, the opposite elements of both of its couples would respectively glide in the same direction along their threads, because the proximal and distal—*i.e.*, the polar and antipolar—extremities of the couples are symmetrical. But as by construction the one couple is axial, and the other antaxial, their margins are not symmetrical, for the polar margins of the axial couple are on the concave, those of the antaxial on its convex side. But this asymmetrical arrangement of the margins of the two couples of the combination necessarily co-ordinates their gliding across their threads. Their combined movements across their threads and their inclination in relation to the axis being simultaneous, and all their geometrical relations being similar and equal—*e.g.*, all tangents of corresponding points in their curvatures being parallel, as the same relations obtain during the passage of the combination from its negative to its positive phase—it follows that a combination of this kind could be screwed and unscrewed with increasing and diminishing series of contacts, and in the same manner as a single couple; but with this advantage, that while the single couple, in its negative phase and in its minor degrees of contact, is supported on one side only of the axis, an articular combination is supported by two equal contacts on opposite sides of the axis. An articular combination is in fact equivalent to a double-threaded screw, as a single articular couple may be conceived as a single-threaded screw.

33. The theory of the geometrical development of articular surfaces, which I have endeavoured to express in this communication, necessarily involves the possibility of *dexiotrope* and *scæotrope*—i.e., *right* and *left-handed* articular couples and combinations. The two forms depend upon the direction in which the generative curve revolves around the axis, moving with the hands of a watch to the right in a dexiotrope, against the hands of a watch in a scæotrope couple or combination. We find accordingly that the corresponding articular couples and combinations on opposite sides of the body are opposed to one another in the direction of their winding. Thus, for example, it was pointed out in my former communication (p. 242) that the anterior articular combination in the knee-joint is left-handed in the right knee and right-handed in the left, and that the same relations obtain in the posterior articular combinations of opposite knee-joints. In succeeding communications I will point out that articular combinations with opposite windings, on opposite sides of the body, similar to those in the knee-joint, exist in the ankle and tarsal, and in the elbow and carpal joints; and that the hip and shoulder joints consist of single-threaded couples, but also with opposite windings on opposite sides of the body.

34. The nature of that more or less marked restriction or curtailment of one or both elements of a couple, already adverted to in paragraph 5, may now be more fully examined. This restriction or curtailment consists essentially in the

elimination or removal of such portions of one or both of the elements in their typical form (that is, in the forms which they would possess in virtue of their completed geometrical construction), as are not absolutely essential to their efficient action. Thus, for example, as one essential condition of efficiency of an articular couple is the provision of a sufficient extent of perfect contact in the negative phase, an articular couple would act efficiently, although the whole of the proximal margin of one of the elements were removed, along with as much of the remaining portion of that element as would retain in reserve enough of the proximal extremity of its distal or antipolar margin for contact, during the negative phase, with the distal or antipolar portion of the polar margin of the opposite element; or, expressing the matter in less precise but more direct terms, the couple would act efficiently as regards its passage to its negative phase, although only the polar or proximal extremity of one of its elements were reserved, and the place of its removed portion supplied by soft, yielding, or elastic textures. It is obvious, however, that if only the polar portion of one of the elements be retained, a certain extent of the opposite element may be dispensed with—namely the distal and antipolar portion of its distal margin. Both elements of a couple may, therefore, be more or less restricted; but as, however much the polar margin of the one element may be curtailed, the corresponding margin of the opposite element must be reserved, I employ, as stated in paragraph 5, the term *restricted* to designate the element with the curtailed, and the term *reserved* to designate the element with the retained, polar margin. As the object of the present communication is to record the general principles involved in the inquiry, I reserve for succeeding communications on special points all details relating to articular elements, couples, and combinations, as well as their relative adjustments by means of ligaments, fibro-cartilaginous menisci, and synovial pads.

35. It appears necessary, however, at this point to anticipate so far by recording a few observations on the teleological relations or final purposes of these peculiar principles of construction which characterise organic joints.

From the peculiar character of the curvature which obtains in organic joints, all points of their opposite surfaces come successively into and then break contact, so that these joints perform a maximum of work with a minimum of surface-contact; while, at the same time, that weakness which is entailed by diminution of surface-contact on the organic as well as on artificial joints, is compensated for by muscular action in the former during its movements to and from its negative position, whereas the latter must in all its positions support itself. Both the organic and the artificial joints derive advantage from diminished surface-contact, for their deterioration is lessened by the diminished amount of pressure and friction. But the deterioration of the materials and structure of an organic joint during action may be assumed as proportionally greater than that of an artificial joint, for in addition to the actual injury to structure sustained, there is, during action, a suspension more or less complete of those nutritive processes on which the ulterior integrity of the organic joint surface depends. The artificial joint surfaces consist of materials which may be assumed as not subject to deterioration of their molecular constitution, but only in their configuration during action from pressure and attrition. This deterioration cannot be remedied by the economy of the joint, but accumulates with duration of action, and ultimately demands the interference of the mechanician. The organic joint surfaces again not only suffer from pressure and attrition, but in their molecular constitution as well, and as this molecular deterioration diminishes the efficiency of their ulterior action, the organic joint is subjected to more speedy injury in the performance of its function than the artificial.

But this liability of the acting surfaces of an organic joint to molecular deterioration during action, while it would subject the joint to greater injury from a given amount of work than an artificial joint, is compensated for by the curvature of its articular surfaces, which provides for that amount of time necessary for successive restorations in the intervals of successive contacts. For to whatever extent the opposite surfaces of an artificial joint may be diminished, there must always remain a certain extent of its opposite surfaces in contact; and from the circular form of the transverse section, the successive amounts of contact, corresponding to a series of equal changes in angular position during rotation, must be in arithmetical progression. But in the organic joint the successive amounts of contact, corresponding to successive equal increments of angular position, will be in geometrical progression, during which the work done will be inversely as the intervals of time in which each portion of it is performed.

If we assume, therefore, that the deteriorating effects of friction are diminished in both forms of joints by an increase of the rapidity of movement during a given amount of work, the advantage which is gained by the organic joint in time saved is greater than that gained by the artificial joint. For time is an essential condition in the restoration of organised matter, deteriorated by functional action. This condition of time determines that alternation or rhythm which characterises all the phenomena of organised bodies. The alternate intervals of action and inaction, of fatigue and repose, of deterioration and renovation, of waking and sleep, of life and death, are not solely due to the recurrent cosmical conditions under which organisation subsists, but essentially depend on the organic character of organised matter itself. Every portion of organised mechanism is constructed on principles which co-ordinate it with the peculiar molecular constitution of organised matter. It therefore appeared to be essential, that not only the structures and phenomena recorded in this communication should be recognised as in accordance with the principles of organisation, but also that the generalisation of these structures and phenomena, as apparently determined by the law of the equiangular spiral, should be found to supply the requirements of these principles.

36. The principle involved in the gain of time provided for repose after functional activity in organic structure is still further illustrated by an arrangement in organic joints, first indicated in my former communication on this subject. All organic joints consist of at least two articular couples, or of two articular combinations. The two couples or two combinations are so arranged that during the full action of the joints—*i.e.*, during the performance of its two opposite movements—the one couple or combination performs the work during the first half of the first movement and the last half of the second movement, while the other couple or combination performs the work during the last half of the first movement and the first half of the second movement. The effect of this arrangement is, that each of the two couples or combinations is alternately in action and out of action. While the one couple or combination is doing work and undergoing deterioration, the other couple or combination is relieved from functional activity, and engaged in its own necessary reparation—that is, in its own nutritive actions.

XII.—ON THE RETINA.

The anatomical elements of the retina are most satisfactorily examined in microscopic sections made at right angles to the surface of the membrane, after maceration in dilute solution of chromic acid. Viewed in this manner, the retina exhibits, from the peripheral to the central margin of a successful section, a series of strata, which may be distinguished as the bacillary, white cellular, grey cellular, filamentary, and limitary layers.

The bacillary layer consists of two kinds of bodies—the rods and cones. The rods are cylindrical or prismatic, with extremities transversely truncated, transparent, and of extremely delicate texture. The cones only differ from the rods in having their inner third, or two-thirds, pyriform. These are arranged close together at right angles to the outer surface of the retina, with their external extremities applied against the inner surface of the choroid. Throughout the greater part of the retina the rods predominate, the cones being uniformly interspersed. In the neighbourhood of the yellow spot, the cones become more frequent; and in the spot itself, they alone constitute the bacillary layer.

The transversely truncated inner extremity of each of the rods is connected with the deeper structures of the retina, either by a conical appendage, which tapers inwards in the form of a filament, or by an ovoidal appendage, which also transmits a filament inwards. The inner extremity of each of the cones is terminated by a pear-shaped appendage, containing a nucleus, and having its stalk prolonged inwards, like the filaments of the rods.

The white cellular layer is composed of three strata—an outer, an intermediate, and an inner. The outer consists of the ovoidal nucleated appendages of the cones; of the ovoidal appendages of the rods which have such bodies attached; and of similar bodies in which the conical appendages of the other rods terminate. The intermediate presents a semifluid granular basis, through which numerous filaments pass from the outer into the inner stratum, in a direction perpendicular to the surfaces of the retina. These filaments, which issue from the outer stratum, are, firstly, the prolongations of the filaments which proceed from the nucleated appendages of the cones; secondly, the prolongations of the filaments which proceed from the ovoidal appendages of the rods possessing such; and, thirdly, filaments proceeding from the inner extremities of the ovoidal bodies, which are connected with the filamentary terminations of the conical appendages of the other rods. The inner stratum also consists of two sets of ovoidal bodies, each of the first connected with some one of the prolongations of the filaments of the cones, and giving off, at its opposite end, a similar filament; while those of the second set, similarly formed and provided, are connected with the prolongations of the filaments of the rods.

Towards the circumference of the retina, many rods may be found, connected by the filaments proceeding from their ovoidal bodies with a single filament passing into the inner stratum. This connection never occurs between the filaments of the cones, which are thus invariably independent of one another.

There may generally be found a branch passing obliquely inwards from some part of the filament of the cone and rod, in its passage through the intermediate stratum, or from the ovoidal bodies of the inner stratum.

The grey cellular layer consists of a fine granular basis,

such as may be seen in many parts of the brain; of numerous cellules, with distinct nuclei, nucleoli, and two, three, or four radiating and branching prolongations, as in the cerebrospinal axis; of numerous blood-vessels; and of prolongations of the filaments of the rods and cones, passing inwards to the inner surface of the retina. It is extremely probable that the nucleated cellules of this layer are connected by certain of their prolongations to the filaments of the rods and cones; the prolongations of the former being continuous with the branches of the latter in the white cellular layer. It may also be confidently stated that, by means of others of their prolongations, the nucleated cellules of this layer are connected with the ultimate filaments of the optic nerve, which form the next layer of the retina.

The filamentary layer is composed essentially of the ultimate filaments of the optic nerve. These filaments, as soon as they pass off from the spot, enter the retina, lose their medullary sheath and dark margins, and assume a delicately transparent grey tint, and somewhat varicose form. They radiate in gradually diminishing anastomosing bundles all round; but, on the outer side of the optic nerve, they sweep in curves from above, and from below to a line which passes from the centre of the nerve outwards through the yellow spot, converging at the same time somewhat towards that spot. The terminations of the constituent filaments of this layer are probably all continuous with certain of the radiations of the nucleated cellules of the grey cellular layer. The meshes formed by the bundles of this layer afford passage inwards to the continued prolongations of the filaments of the rods and cones.

The limitary layer completes the retina on the inner side. It is an extremely thin, perfectly transparent membrane, which, although continuous throughout, can only be detached in minute portions, in connection with the terminal attachments of the filaments of the rods and cones, which terminate on its outer surface by expanding into conical brushes, or still more minute threads, which would almost appear to constitute the membrane itself.

At the entrance of the optic nerve, the bacillary, white cellular, and grey cellular layers, are necessarily absent; the limitary membrane alone covering the inner surface of the mass of nervous filaments, which, with the arteries, spreads out on all sides.

Over the macula lutea the bacillary layer consists of cones alone, the filaments of which do not reach the limitary layer, at least at the fovea centralis, but terminate in the white cellular layer. The latter exists, except at the fovea. The grey cellular layer is distinct throughout; but towards the centre, and at the fovea, its granular stratum is deficient, the nucleated cellules being crowded together under the limitary layer. The filamentary layer is deficient as a lamina, over the entire macula lutea; but its constituent filaments may be detected in the midst of the nucleated cellules of the spot. The peculiar yellow pigment is diffused through all the textures, with the exception of the bacillary layer.

The structure of the retina is so delicate, and its investigation so difficult, that much remains still to be determined regarding the precise connection of its different elements. The structure of the bacillary layer having been more particularly examined by Gottsche and Hannover, and the white cellular layer by Bowman, Pacini traced the filaments inwards from the rods and cones into the white cellular layer. The discovery of the filaments themselves, and their passage inwards to the limitary layer, is due to Heinrich Müller, by whom, along with Kölliker, the general anatomical connections of the microscopic elements of the retina have been more particularly traced. According to H. Müller and Kölliker, the rods and cones are connected by what may now be denominated the Müllerian filaments to the limitary membrane; the various bodies which constitute the white cellular layer being connected with these filaments in the manner already described. The branch which proceeds from each of the Müllerian filaments in its course through the inner stratum of the white cellular layer becomes continuous with one of the radiations of one of the nucleated cells of the grey cellular layer; all the cells of this layer therefore being connected with all the rods and cones of the retina. The remaining radiations of the cellules of the grey layer, passing inwards, form the commencements of the ultimate filaments of the optic nerve in the filamentary layer of the retina.

In reference to those parts in the structure of the retina upon which that impression is made, which, when conveyed to the sensorium, terminates in the perception of light, it may be stated, that the non-sensibility of the retina at the entrance of the optic nerve, and its perfect sensibility at the macula lutea, as well as other considerations, prove that this function is not performed by the filaments of the nerve.

Kölliker concludes, by exclusion of the other elements, that the rods and cones, with the Müllerian filaments, are the structures on which objective light first impresses itself. He believes the seat of this impression to be in the rods and cones, and also probably in the inner ends of the Müllerian filaments. He has examined with great care the chemical and structural characters of these bodies, and has satisfied himself that they are nervous structures.

Brücke and Hannover conceive the rods and cones of the bacillary layer to be structures which reflect the light back again from the outer surface of the retina against the filamentary layer, on which it is thus impressed. Helmholtz, again, who does not admit the sensibility to light of this layer, believes the reflected light to act upon the grey cellular layer.

Having carefully examined the retina since these observations and views have been published, I have succeeded in verifying the majority of the structures and relations described by Müller and Kölliker; but cannot coincide with the latter in opinion that the rods, cones, and Müllerian filaments are nervous structures. They have neither the general aspect nor the anatomical relations of mere nervous textures. Each rod or cone, with its Müllerian filament extending inwards to the limitary membrane, with the ovoidal bodies developed on it, would appear referable rather to the class of structures to which the touch-corpuscles and Pacinian bodies belong. They are structures developed around the extremities of the ultimate filaments of the optic nerve, for the purpose of placing those extremities in the necessary position and circumstances for being impressed by the rays of light. The ultimate nerve-filament enters the Müllerian stem of the rod or cone as it passes through the white cellular layer. This filament is probably, as has been stated, a radiation from one of the grey cells, which if they be collectively connected to all the rods and cones, as well as to the filaments of the optic nerve, may safely be considered, as Kölliker has pointed out, to be a retinal ganglion, intermediate between the sentient points of the retina and the sensorium, as well as between the corresponding points of its own and of the opposite eye. The ultimate nerve-filament, as it enters the Müllerian stem obliquely outwards, probably terminates towards or at the extremity of the rod or cone, so as to have its transverse section directed outwards at right angles to the axis of the rod or cone. Let it now be assumed that a ray of light cannot impress an ultimate optic filament, except it impinge upon the free extremity in the axis—that is, at right angles to the transverse section; and let it also be admitted, with Brücke and Helmholtz, that it is by light reflected from the bottom of the eye that vision is affected, then the theory of the retina in primary vision becomes more consistent. The divergent pencil of light which proceeds from any visible point to the eye, becoming convergent after having entered the refractive media, passing through the perfectly transparent retina, is probably brought to a point at the surface of the choroid or outer part of the bacillary layer of the retina, and is not entirely absorbed there, but is reflected as a divergent pencil. In passing towards the point of reflection, the rays of the pencil cannot impress any part of the retina, because they cannot impinge on any of its nervous elements in the only manner in which these can be affected—viz., against their free extremities at a right angle. Certain of the rays, however, of the reflected pencil—viz. those which pass along the axis of a rod or cone in the bacillary layer—will impinge in the proper direction on the contained nerve, and produce the luminiferous impression. No confusion, therefore, can result from the multitude of convergent and divergent rays which is passing through the chamber of the eye, and through the retina, for those only are capable of impressing which are reflected along the axes of the cones and rods. The human sensorium receives from the retina the impression of a picture, which is not continuous, but made up of detached points ; as in the vision of the insect, which only sees an object by as many points as can transmit rays along the axes of its eye-tubules.

The bacillary layer of the retina belongs morphologically to the transparent humours of the eye. The original bulb of the eye, whether it be a mere process of the brain, or partly a pulp developed on the tegumentary membrane, forms over its entire free surface transparent (cuticular) structures. That portion of the free surface of the pulp which is directed towards the orifice of the eye-follicle, developes the lens, the cornea, and the vitreous humour. That portion again, in contact with the inner surface of the follicle, and which becomes choroid, developes the bacillary layer with its rods and cones. As the lens and vitreous humour increase in size, the pulp or retina becomes cup-shaped, and intermediate between the two portions of the transparent structure developed from its original spheroidal surface.

XIII.—ON THE MODE IN WHICH LIGHT ACTS ON THE ULTIMATE NERVOUS STRUCTURES OF THE EYE, AND ON THE RELATIONS BETWEEN SIMPLE AND COMPOUND EYES.*

SINCE the publication, in 1826, of Joh. Müller's *Vergleichende Physiologie des Gesichtssinnes,* physiologists have admitted three fundamental forms of the organ of vision. 1*st,* The eye-spot, organised for the mere perception of light; 2*d,* The compound eye, in which the picture on the nervous surface is a mosaic; 3*d,* The simple eye, in which the retinal picture is continuous. The difference between the simple and compound eye, as explained by Müller, and since generally admitted, consists in this, that the formation of the picture in the simple eye is the result of the convergence of all the pencils diverging from the visible points of the object on corresponding points of the retina, by means of the lenticular structures of the organ; while, in the compound eye, the picture is formed by the stopping off, by means of the constituent crystalline columns of the eye of all rays except those which pass in or near the axes of the columns. The extent of surface of any object, and the number of separate parts of such surface, represented on the nervous structure of a compound eye, will vary, therefore, in terms of the distance of the object, the curvature of the superficial ocular surface, the corresponding inclination of the crystalline columns to one another, the size of their individual

* Read before the Royal Society of Edinburgh, April 6, 1857.

transverse sections, and their lengths. The continuous retinal picture in the simple eye is psychically interpreted as a continuous image. If, therefore, the possessor of a compound eye perceives a continuous image of an object, it must be the result of a more complex psychical operation, in virtue of which the separate portions of the ocular mosaic picture are psychically combined, and interpreted as a continuous whole.

The successive researches of Treviranus, Gottsche, Hannover, Pacini, H. Müller, and Kölliker, have determined the existence and general structure of close-set rods or columns, which extend between the inner and outer surfaces of the retina, in the midst of the nervous and vascular textures of that membrane. The outer extremities of these rods present a crystalline columnar aspect, and constitute, collectively, the external layer of the retina, usually termed Jacob's membrane. The ultimate filaments of the optic nerve, after being connected in a plexiform arrangement in the ganglionic layer of the retina, terminate each independently in the more perfect portion of the retinal field, by passing into, or becoming continuous with, the inner end or side of a rod. Kölliker considers these rods as nervous structures—that is, as terminal portions of the nerve-filaments themselves ; and holds that they constitute the parts of the nervous structure of the eye on which objective light primarily acts.

Having myself carefully examined the structure to which I have now alluded, I have been able to verify the more important anatomical details, as described by their discoverers, and agree with Kölliker in considering the rods as the primary optic apparatus. I cannot, however, coincide with this distinguished observer in holding these rods as modified nerve-filaments. I hold them to be special structures appended to the extremities of the ultimate nerve-filaments, and referable to the same category as the Pacinian bodies, touch-corpuscles, rods of Corti, etc. ; and, moreover, so far am I from coinciding with Kölliker in his speculations as to the part of the rod on which the objective light acts, that I have found myself compelled, not only from the consideration of the structures themselves, but also from the development of the eye itself, and the arrangements of the compound eye, to conceive the rays of light as acting upon the retina, not as they impinge upon it, or pass through it from before, but as they pass backward again out of the eye after reflection from the choroid.

The general aspect of the rods, and more especially of those portions termed Müllerian filaments, where they collectively amalgamate in the limitary membrane of the retina, indicate, as I believe will be generally admitted, that they consist of a modification of connective tissue, enveloping and supporting the extremities of the ultimate nerve-filaments in such a manner as to form special structures, which, from their functions, may be termed *photæsthetic bodies.*

That special structures are required for the initiation of action in the filaments of the optic nerve by objective light, appears to be established by the facts, that the nervous filaments of the retina, and the cut extremities of these filaments on the stump of the optic nerve, are not affected by it, although irritation of the same filaments by electrical or other means produces subjective luminous phenomena. Subjective sounds may be produced by various modes of irritation ; but actual sonant vibrations can only excite the acoustic filaments through the medium of the rods of Corti, or the corresponding terminal structures in the vestibule. Corresponding terminal structures are in like manner appended to the tactile, olfactory, and gustatory nerves, apparently for a similar purpose, to provide the necessary conditions of the initial excitement of the nervous current by those secondary properties of external bodies to which the organs of touch, taste, and smell, are related.

When the attention of anatomists was directed, a few years

ago, to the structure and physiological signification of the columns of the retina, by the observations of H. Müller and Kölliker, I became satisfied that those structures are not, as the latter asserted, nervous structures, properly so called, but special structures, of the same nature as the Pacinian bodies and the tactile corpuscles. I stated and explained my opinion of the nature of these bodies in a lecture on the retina delivered and reported in 1854.* But I had generalised these relations of nervous filaments to special terminal exciting structures, still further, in the zoological lectures which I delivered in 1853, for my late distinguished colleague and preceptor, Professor Jameson. I also expounded it at considerable length in my course of lectures last winter (1855-6). I shall now state the doctrine in general terms, not only because it is necessary for the elucidation of the distinctive characters of the simple and compound forms of eye; but also because I am anxious to put on record, by submitting it to this Society, a generalisation which appears to me of primary importance in the general physiology of the nervous system. I assume, as established the doctrine of Du Bois Reymond, that a nerve-filament is capable of propagating the nervous current equally well in both directions; and that the physical and physiological characters of this current differ in no respect, are in fact identical in the so-called motor and in the so-called sensory filaments, whether special or common. I also assume as established that the specific manner in which a centripetal nerve-current is converted at the central extremity of the filament—that is to say, is physiologically reflected into the motor filaments, or psychically interpreted as sensation—depends upon the physiological or psychical endowments of the different portions of the nervous centre with which the filaments are connected. These two positions being assumed, then, I hold that, although the ultimate nervous filament may have

* *Edinburgh Medical Journal*, p. 377, 1855; and No. XII. in this volume.

its functional current (that is, the common nervous current) excited or initiated by electrical or other physical or chemical agencies, yet this current can only be initiated or excited, for the special functional purposes for which each nervous filament is provided in the economy, by the structure or tissue with which such filament is connected peripherally. If so, then not only are the individual filaments of the nerves of special sense provided with current-exciting structures at their peripheral extremities, by means of which alone the objects to which they are related can initiate the nerve-current; but also centripetal nerve-filaments of whatever kind are provided, in their connection with the textures from which they proceed, with arrangements by means of which alone their functional currents can be initiated.

From this point of view every particular structure in the organism from which nervous filaments proceed to the nervous centre may be considered, with reference to the nervous system, as a peripheral nervous organ—that is, an organ capable of exciting or initiating centripetal nerve-current; which is physiologically converted, or psychically interpreted, at the corresponding central organ, according to the special endowments of that central organ.

After this preliminary statement, I am in a position from which I can explain the mode in which I understand the structure and actions of the rods of the retina in the simple, and the columns in the compound eye.

1. *In the Simple Eye.*—A ray of light can only impress an ultimate retinal nervous filament under certain conditions. These conditions are, that it should impinge upon the distal extremity of the filament in, or parallel to, the axis of that filament, or within a certain angle to that axis.

All rays impinging on the distal extremity of an ultimate retinal nervous filament under the conditions stated I term *photogenic* rays. Rays impinging upon, or passing through, the filament in any other direction, may be termed *aphotogenic*. The distal portion of the ultimate retinal nervous filament I distinguish as the *photæsthetic surface*.

In order that the ultimate retinal nervous filament may be subjected to the rays of light under the required conditions of vision, its distal extremity or photæsthetic surface is inclosed in a peculiar structure, consisting of a so-called *rod* or *cone* (which I distinguish as the crystalline column), and its appended Müllerian filament, with its nuclear enlargements. This structure constitutes a specific kind of peripheral nervous organ, which, from its function, I term a *photæsthetic body*.

A photæsthetic body consists of a distal segment, or dioptric portion, elongated, cylindrical, or club-shaped, homogeneous, transparent, and highly refractive, usually termed the rod or cone; and a proximal segment or peduncle, with its nuclear enlargements, into which the ultimate nervous filament passes, and within which it apparently terminates, probably at its outer end.

The entire aspect and arrangement of these photæsthetic bodies, their predominance over the other parts of the retina at the axial spot of the eye, and the direct continuity of their stems with the nerve-filaments at that spot, appear to me to indicate not only the nature of their functions, but also the general features of the mode in which it is effected. It appears to me that the rays which act upon the nervous filaments must be such rays as the arrangement permits to pass from behind forwards in the axes of the photæsthetic bodies. It has now been ascertained, that the quantity of light reflected, and consequently irregularly dispersed within the eyeball from the choroid and bacillary layer, etc., is very considerable; and it consequently becomes a very important question, to determine in what manner this reflected and irregularly-dispersed light is prevented from affecting the retina. The view which I have already given of the structure and probable mode of action of the photæsthetic bodies affords the basis of a hypothesis which meets all the conditions of the question, and is in full accordance with the comparative anatomy and development of the organ of vision. I cannot interpret the functions of the structure of the retina as now determined, except by assuming that the photæsthetic columns are impressed not by the light as it enters the eye, or as it is more or less irregularly reflected and dispersed in its interior, but only by those rays which, in their passage backwards to the pupil, pass along, or nearly in, the axes of the crystalline rods or columns of the photæsthetic bodies, so as to reach the photæsthetic spots under the required conditions. No confusion, therefore, can result from the multitude of convergent and divergent rays which pass through the chamber of the eye, and through the retina. By this means, the numerous rays not necessary for vision, are as it were eliminated from the operation, the eye being blind to them, and affected only by such as are reflected backwards to the pupil along the axes of the crystalline columns.

2. *The Crystalline Columns of the Compound Eye.*—As stated in my lecture on the retina, formerly alluded to, I conceive the crystalline columns in the eye of the insect or crab to act in the same manner as the retinal rods in the spheroidal or simple eye. That they do so may be held as established by the researches of J. Müller on the laws of vision in the compound eye. Müller even refers to the columnar structure of the retina, as presenting a certain similarity to the structure or arrangement of the compound eye. F. Leydig, in an elaborate memoir published in Müller's *Archiv.* in 1855, on the structure generally of the Arthropoda, examines minutely the structure of the simple and compound eyes, and arrives at the conclusion that the crystalline columns of their compound eyes, as well as the corresponding structures in their so-called simple eyes or ocelli, are of the same nature

as the so-called rods and cones—that is, the photæsthetic bodies which I have already described in the retina of the vertebrate eye. But Leydig entirely loses sight of a fact, which, if unexplained, vitiates his conclusion as to the physiological identity of the bodies in question. In the annulose or molluscous eye, whether in its so-called simple or compound form, the crystalline columns are directed, like the tubes of so many telescopes, towards the object, the corresponding nervous filaments passing to them from behind; whereas the crystalline rods of the vertebrate retina are directed away from the object—that is, towards the back of the eye—are in contact, in fact, with the choroid, while their nervous filaments are connected to them in front—that is, between them and the object.

On the other hand, if I am correct in holding that the vertebrate eye is acted upon by those rays only which are reflected from its choroidal surface, I have not only explained physiologically why its retinal columns are reversed, but I am legitimately entitled, as Leydig is not, to consider them as the homologues of the crystalline columns of the annulose and molluscous eye.

But the teleological explanation of the opposite arrangement of the corresponding structures in the vertebrate and invertebrate eye, is, in the present phase of the science, insufficient. The difference must be explained morphologically. This explanation is afforded by the different modes in which the vertebrate and invertebrate—that is, the simple and compound—eyes are developed.

In the compound eye the primordial ocular papilla or convexity, which is only slightly protuberant, has its cutaneous or superficial surface immediately converted into the crystalline columnar structure, the individual columns of which are connected with the filaments of the subjacent optic nerve. The columns are all therefore directed to the object.

The primordial cerebro-cutaneous spheroidal protuberance

or papilla of the simple refracting or vertebrate eye, is speedily hollowed out in front by the development in or upon it of the lens and vitreous humour, so that from a spheroidal convex surface, the primordial protuberance assumes the form of a cup, with its mouth directed forwards, and its cavity occupied by the refracting media of the organ. This cup-shaped mass is the retina; the crystalline rods are not developed on its concave surface, but on its outer or convex surface, as they exist on the convexity of the compound eye—that is, in the direction of the radii of the sphere, but directed backwards, on account of the nearly spheroidal surface.

In conclusion, I may state what appears to be the physiological superiority of the simple over the compound eye. As the simple eye is acted on by reflected light only, it cannot be disturbed by rays not required for the definition of the image. It is also arranged so as to admit of a much more delicate or minute mosaic representation of the object, from its microscopic and reversed photæsthetic bodies being in contact with the reflecting choroidal surface on which that image is formed. It moreover combines the advantages of the contiguous image, formed by the lenticular structures, and the mosaic image, which results from its crystalline rods.

XIV.—ON THE LAMINA SPIRALIS OF THE COCHLEA.

THE lamina spiralis of the cochlea, instead of being, as hitherto supposed, a single layer, osseous in the inner, and membranous in the outer portion of its extent, is a double structure, with numerous complex arrangements in its interior.

The osseous and membranous portions of the lamina spiralis, as hitherto understood, may be considered as the basis of the entire complex structure as it is now ascertained.

The osseous portion of the lamina contains the cochlear nerves in closely-arranged canals, which, at its outer margin, coalesce in a chink or fissure, which contains the ganglion recently discovered by Corti, and affords exit to the nervous filaments.

The membranous portion of the lamina consists, as discovered by Todd and Bowman, of a membrane which, except at its outer and inner margins, is closely streaked in the direction of the radius of the cochlea, and hence denominated zona pectinata. The outer margin of the membrane is attached by means of a fibro-nucleated texture to the accessory spiral lamina of Huschke, and to the neighbouring groove. This fibro-nucleated structure is the cochlear muscle of Todd and Bowman—the spiral cochlear ligament of Kölliker. The inner margin of the membrane is attached to that lip of the fissure of the osseous lamina which is next the apex of the cochlea, but so as to leave numerous orifices or more or less oblique canals, through which, as Kölliker has ascertained, the extremities of the cochlear nerve-filaments pass to the vestibular surface of the membrane. The cochlear nerves, therefore, instead of being distributed, as has hitherto been supposed, on the tympanic aspect of the lamina spiralis, pass through it to its vestibular aspect; its entire tympanic surface, and the nerves in their transit across that surface, from the fissure in the osseous to the orifices in the membranous portion, being covered by the fibro-serous lining membrane of the osseous labyrinth. It thus appears that all the complex structures in connection with the lamina spiralis, usually so called, of the cochlea, are situated on its vestibular aspect.

These structures are—1. The habenula sulcata, situated chiefly on the osseous lamina, and discovered by Todd and Bowman; 2. The habenula denticulata, situated on the membranous lamina, discovered by Corti, and latterly ascertained by Kölliker to be connected with the cochlear nerves; 3. The membrane of Corti, covered on its vestibular surface by the serous lining membrane of the osseous labyrinth, first partially recognised by Corti, but latterly more fully described by Claudius; 4. Large vesicular cells which occupy the space between the membrane of Corti and the lamina spiralis, usually so called, first recognised by Corti, but more precisely determined by Claudius.

The habenula sulcata is a structure of cartilaginous aspect, which, rapidly increasing in thickness as it advances to the outer margin of the osseous lamina, inclines over and beyond that margin so as to form the sulcus spiralis of Huschke. It consists of columns, which at its thin inner edge are set perpendicular to the surface of the subjacent bones, and therefore expose their free extremities on its vestibular aspect. Towards its thick or outer edge the columns become more and more inclined, so as to expose more and more of their sides, and at the edge itself they form a series of elongated, slightly clavate and flattened, clear glistening teeth, which project over the groove of Huschke. Some of the columns divide, others unite together, as they pass outwards to form these teeth; which are termed "teeth of the first series." In the grooves between the columns are numerous nuclei, which resist acetic acid, while the former swell up, and become somewhat striated under its action.

The habenula denticulata consists of a series of apparently jointed rods, laid on the surface of the membranous portion of the so-called lamina spiralis; each rod in the series lying in the direction of the radius of the cochlea. The first or inner segments of these rods form a series of compressed laminæ, attached across the bottom of Huschke's spiral groove, with narrow chinks between them, which are, in fact, the orifices through which the cochlear nerve-filaments pass, as already stated. These central segments are the "dents apparents" of Corti. The second segment, or portion of each rod, is also compressed, and lies flat on the membranous spiral lamina, and is loose and movable, except at its inner end, where it presents an enlargement like a nucleus, which was supposed by Corti to be the joint by means of which the rod is attached to and moves on the membrane; but which Kölliker has discovered to be the point at which one or more of the ultimate filaments of the cochlear nerves become connected with the rod, after they have passed through the orifices already mentioned. The series formed by these second segments of the rods are the so-called "teeth of the second order." The terminal segment is connected with the second by means of two short quadrilateral segments, the "coins articulaires" of Corti. The terminal segment is elongated and compressed. To its upper surface three pyriform bodies, each of which contains a nucleus, are attached by short peduncles, so as to be laid over one another, from within outwards. Corti and Kölliker describe the outer extremity of this segment as somewhat expanded and forked, and also as free or loose. But Claudius has ascertained that the expanded extremity is attached to the lamina pectinata, so that the rod cannot move to and from the membrane, as Corti has supposed.

It must here be observed, that the first or inner segments of the rods, the "dents apparents" are attached throughout, and from their position and relations belong rather to the structure of the habenula sulcata, than to that of the habenula denticulata. The latter consists, then, essentially of the second and terminal segment described above, connected together by the short "articular" portions. The cochlear rod, properly so-called, consists therefore of two principal segments, the inner segment being connected with one or more ultimate nerve-filaments, and the outer fastened at its external end to the membrane on which it lies.

Corti has described a thin membrane covered by the epithelium of the labyrinth, and extending from the prominent surface of the habenula sulcata somewhat beyond the habenula denticulata. The space between this membrane and the "dents apparents," and also the spiral groove of Huschke, are occupied, according to him, by large transparent nucleated vesicles. Similar vesicles, conceived to be epithelial by their discoverer, occupy the space between the membranous lamina spiralis and that portion of Corti's membrane which extends beyond the habenula denticulata. The rods of the cochlea, therefore, according to Corti, move like a series of hammer or pianoforte keys, in a space included between the membrane discovered by him, and the lamina spiralis, usually so-called. Claudius, however, has shown that Corti's membrane extends out to the external wall of the cochlea; and that the entire space between it and the lamina spiralis, usually so-called, is occupied by vesicular structure.

The following are the results of observations made for the purpose of verifying the descriptions of Corti, Kölliker, and Claudius. The membrane of Corti extends, as Claudius has stated, to the outer wall of the cochlea, and the large cells between it and the lamina spiralis have extremely thin walls, and transparent contents, so that they resemble, when pressed together, an areolar network. Portions of the rods were also occasionally seen curled up, and as observed by Claudius, attached by their expanded extremities, in series, to the membrane on which they lie. The detection by Kölliker of the connection of the nerve-filaments with the rods is, after the discoveries of Corti, the most important recent addition to our knowledge of the structure of the cochlea. Even in the ordinary view of the structure from the vestibular aspect, the nerve-filaments may, without much difficulty, be observed to disappear at or in the central extremities of the rods. Their inner extremities do not correspond, as Kölliker has correctly observed, to the outer ends of the "dents apparents," but to the intervals between the latter. Kölliker holds, on chemical as well as anatomical grounds, that the rods of Corti are true terminations of the cochlear nerves—peculiar forms of the ultimate nerve-fibre. He believes Corti's opinion to be erroneous, that they are developments from the membrane on which they lie, and that they constitute a physical apparatus. Notwithstanding Kölliker's opinion, it may be safely asserted that the rods of Corti present a configuration and aspect which distinguish them in the most marked manner from any form of the nerve-filament. The peculiar flattened articulated form, the variable breadth, and, as pointed out by Claudius, the alternate arrangement of the proximal and distal segments of neighbouring rods; and, lastly, the elasticity, slight, though marked, which they possess, indicate that they are not true nerve-structures. Without stating the nature of the function he supposes them to perform, Corti believes that the rods move like a series of hammers. Harless conceives that they act as dampers by pressing on the membrane during vibration. Kölliker, again, believes that from the almost mathematical regularity with which they are arranged along the vestibular surface of the lamina spiralis, these peculiar terminations of the cochlear nerves are the structures which distinguish the pitch, timbre, and strength of sounds, through the medium of the water of the labyrinth and the fenestra ovalis.

From comparative anatomy it would appear that the vestibule is that part of the organ by means of which any sound, or series or combination of sounds, is heard merely as *noise*. The simplest form of ear, which consists of a vestibule only, probably enables the sensorium merely to become cognisant of sound, irrespective of the pitch or harmony of its constituent tones.

In regard to the semi-circular canals, it appears probable from their intimate connection with the vestibule, that they, like it, have to do with sound merely as *noise*, and that their function, therefore, is of secondary importance in the higher forms of the organ.

Dr. Thomas Young, with his usual sagacity, considered the cochlea as a "micrometer of sound." Kölliker, as already stated, has put forward a similar idea, based on his knowledge of the structures just described. His conception, however, appears to be so far unsatisfactory, inasmuch as he considers the rods of Corti to be merely the extremities of the cochlear nerves; and it wants that completeness which it would have, had he been able to admit those rods to be a series of acoustic arrangements, as they are believed to be by their discoverer.

The hypothesis presents a more satisfactory form if we assume that each of the rods of Corti, or that groups of these rods are so organised and arranged as to act or vibrate as acoustic apparatuses appended to the extremities of the cochlear nerves. Each rod, or group of rods, may be so constituted as alone, among all the others, to act or vibrate, when the note or harmonic chord, for which that single rod, or that group of rods, had been provided, passes through the cochlea in the form of sonant vibrations of a correspondent physical value. If this be the case, we can understand how, by the instrumentality of a cochlea, the physical value of each tone, or harmonic combination of tones, may be detected by the ear, and impressions of correspondent value transmitted along the nerve-filaments to the seat of sonant sensation in the brain. It must be borne in mind, however, that the æsthetic perception of the sensations produced by the instrumentality of the cochlea, its nerves, and the sentient centre, is a psychical function, and a result of the pre-established harmony between the mental and corporeal elements of the animal constitution on the one hand, and external nature on the other.

XV.—ON THE ELECTRICAL APPARATUS IN TORPEDO, GYMNOTUS, MALAPTERURUS, AND RAIA.

THE electrical apparatus in fish consists of three parts—the battery, the nervous centre, and the internuncial cord.

The following would appear to be the general expression for the structure of the battery—a very large number of laminæ, consisting of vascular nucleated texture, largely supplied with centrifugal nerve-fibres, distributed on one of their surfaces only; so arranged in reference to one another, and to thin intervening layers of fluid, as to constitute a uniform series, in the order: nerve-surface—cellulo-vascular surface —fluid, nerve-surface—cellulo-vascular surface—fluid, etc. etc.

The nervous centre consists of a portion of the cerebro-spinal axis developed in relation to the large **nerves** distributed to the battery; and so organised, as to be capable, not only of excito-motory action, but also of being subjected to the influence of the will.

The internuncial cord is a centrifugal nerve, connected at one extremity to the nervous centre of the apparatus, and at the other distributed on the nervous surfaces of the laminæ of the battery.

In Torpedo there are two batteries which occupy the two spaces between the pectoral fins, the head, and gills. Each battery **consists of a** number of hexagonal, pentagonal, or tetragonal prisms, which **vary** in number from 400 to upwards of 1000, according to the age of the animal. The prisms extend perpendicularly between the dorsal and abdominal integument; and are separated from and connected to it by a thin but dense aponeurosis, which at the same time separates them all from, and connects them to one another, by passing inwards in single layers, so as to form a continuous series of prismatic aponeurotic compartments, in the interior of which the prisms are situated. Each prism consists of delicate, horizontal, superimposed laminæ, separated from one another by thin layers of fluid, so that the arrangement bears a general resemblance to a galvanic pile. It has hitherto been supposed that the laminæ are connected by their margins to the aponeurotic wall which surrounds the prism; but Pacini (*Sulla struttura intima dell' organo elettrico del Gimnoto, e di altri pesci elettrici*, 1852) has lately shown that the laminæ are attached by their angles only to the corners of their aponeurotic sheaths; and that an entire pile may be removed from its containing cavity, by cutting the four, five, or six series of attachments by which it is fixed. It is extremely important that the structure of the laminæ should be determined. Valentin ("Electricität der Thiere," in Wagner's *Handwörterbuch der Physiologie*) states, that each lamina consists of a thin prolongation of the aponeurotic wall of the pile, covered above and below by an epithelial layer, and affording a matrix for the ultimate divisions of the vessels and nerves, which, he is inclined to believe, are so arranged, that the terminal nervous plexuses are placed towards the upper, the capillaries towards the lower surface. Savi (Matteucci and Savi, *Traité des Phenomènes Electro-Physiologiques*, 1844) describes the elementary filaments of the nerves as forming a network by anastomosis in the lamina; but Rudolph Wagner (*Annales des Sciences Naturelles*, 1847) has shown that each elementary filament, enveloped in a very thick sheath, divides at once into twelve to twenty-five secondary filaments, which, passing towards the laminæ, splitting into two or three ternary filaments and losing their envelopes and dark contours, disappear in the soft, dotted, nucleated substance of the laminæ, without forming meshes. Pacini (*loc. cit.*) has lately made a most important addition to Wagner's description of the laminæ. The laminæ, or electrical diaphragms, as Pacini terms them, are attached, as has been already stated, by their angles only. The vessels and nerves enter at these points, but so as to be at first placed on the under surface of the diaphragm, and therefore in the fluid interposed between that surface and the upper surface of the diaphragm below. Passing inwards and ramifying in this fluid, they ultimately pass up to the under surface, and the nerves are distributed *on that surface only* of the diaphragm to which they belong. Now, as the dorsal surface in Torpedo is positive and the abdominal surface negative, it follows, as Pacini has indicated that the upper surface of each electrical diaphragm, consisting only of soft, dotted, nucleated vascular texture, is positive, while the under surface, on which the nerves only ramify, is negative.

Pacini was led to the observation of the position of the nerves in the electrical diaphragms of Torpedo, by the more complex structure which he had previously discovered in the corresponding parts of Gymnotus.

Gymnotus possesses four batteries, which extend nearly the whole length of its eel-like body, from behind the pectoral fins to the extremity of the tail; forcing the lateral muscles towards the dorsal, and the comparatively small abdominal viscera, with the anus, towards the cephalic region. The great or dorsal batteries are separated from one another above by the vertebral column, the great vessels, the displaced lateral muscles, and the air-bladder; below by a mesial aponeurotic septum, along which the nerves pass to the batteries and ventral fin. Laterally these dorsal batteries are intimately connected to the skin; and inferiorly are separated from the ventral, or small batteries, by a thin layer of muscle. The small batteries are, moreover, separated from the skin by the laterally-displaced muscles of the ventral fin; but are intimately connected to one another by a thin aponeurosis only. These small batteries are, therefore, peculiar, not only in their close approximation, but also in being enveloped in muscular substance.

The batteries in Gymnotus consist of a number of piles placed horizontally in a direction from head to tail. From this circumstance, as well as from their peculiar structure, they are aptly compared by Rudolphi to galvanic troughs. These troughs are in the form of flattened masses, separated from, but connected to one another by aponeurotic septa, which, diverging, extend outwards from the inner to the outer aspect of each battery. It is not easy to determine the exact number of the piles or troughs in a battery, as they vary in number in different parts of it, and are lost as they pass backwards and downwards. From the statements of Mr. Hunter (*An Account of the Gymnotus Electricus*; Phil. Trans. 1775), and Valentin (*loc. cit.*), and my own observations, the number of troughs in the great battery ranges from thirty to sixty; in the lesser from eight to fourteen. Hunter (*loc. cit.*), Rudolphi (*über die Electrischen Fische in Abhand. der Akad. zu Berlin*, 1822), Knox (*Edin. Jour. of Science*, 1824), Valentin (*loc. cit.*), and all observers previous to Pacini, state what may be easily verified, that the troughs in Gymnotus consist of numerous perpendicular laminæ, which extend transversely between the aponeurotic septa, with fluid interposed, as in the piles of Torpedo. Pacini's account (*loc. cit.*) of the structure and relations of the electrical laminæ or diaphragms of Gymnotus is much more precise; and elucidates in a remarkable manner a structure hitherto sufficiently obscure. The more important features of Pacini's account, as verified by myself, may be thus described. Each of the electric diaphragms in Gymnotus, instead of being, as in Torpedo, a single lamina with the nerves distributed on one of its surfaces, consists of two laminæ, with a thin layer of fluid interposed.

The posterior of these is a delicate, wide-meshed, fibrous layer, in which alone the nerves ramify; the anterior consists of a thicker layer of the peculiar vascular, dotted, nucleated texture which forms the laminæ in Torpedo. Both surfaces of the vasculo-cellular layer present an arrangement of prominent, close-set, undulating ridges, with thick, rounded, nucleated margins. The ridges are more fully developed on the anterior than on the posterior surface of the layer, and from the ridges of the latter a number of thread-like prolongations pass backwards through the interposed fluid to the fibro-nervous layer, so as to connect the two layers as one compound lamina. From the measurements and calculations of Pacini, the superficial extent of the anterior surface of the vasculo-nucleated layer is increased by this rigid structure from five to six times, the posterior about twice.

The electro-motor series, therefore, in Gymnotus, instead of simple laminæ, as in Torpedo, consist of compound laminæ separated by layers of fluid. There are thus two kinds of fluid in the electro-motor series of Gymnotus—firstly, that between the vasculo-cellular layers and the fibro-nervous, and which must be considered as an element of each compound electric diaphragm; and, secondly, that between any two electric diaphragms, which is the homologue of the fluid layer in Torpedo.

As the current in Gymnotus passes from before backwards, Pacini denominates the vasculo-cellular layer the positive, and the fibro-nervous layer the negative element, of the electro-motor series.

The batteries in Malapterurus are two in number, separated, but at the same time intimately connected to one another in the mesial plane, along the dorsal and ventral margins of the body, so as to form a continuous layer of a gelatinous consistence, closely adherent to the skin, and enclosing as in a sac the entire animal, except the head and fins. In the

Malapterurus of the Nile, of which species only dissections have hitherto been published (St. Hilaire, *Annales de Museum*, tom. i.; Rudolphi, *Abhand. Berl. Akad.* 1824; Valenciennes, *An. des Sci. Nat.* tom. xvi.), a subjacent areolar, laminated, fatty layer, has been described as a second and deeper electrical apparatus; and in the Malapterurus of Western Africa, with the examination of which I am at present engaged, this deeper layer exists in the form of longitudinal streaks of fat between the muscles and gelatinous layer. Pacini, however ("Sopra l'organo elettrico del siluro elettrico del Nilo, etc.," *negli Annali delle Sci. Nat. di Bologna*, 1846), has shown that this presumed deep electrical structure consists principally of fat (as it assuredly does in the species from Western Africa), and probably acts as an insulator to protect the fish from its own shocks; the electrical currents being presumed to pass from within outwards—that is, through any point on the surface of the body.

The determination of the intimate structure of the battery of Malapterurus is extremely difficult. Before Pacini, no precise description of it had been attempted. He represents the structure as consisting of octahedral cellules or alveoli, a form which in some measure explains the variable direction of the currents through the electro-motor mass. Professor Ecker, in a communication contained in Siebold and Kölliker's *Zeitschrift für Wissensch. Zoologie*, July 1854, states that Dr. Bilharz,* at present in Egypt, is engaged in the anatomy of the Nilotic species, and that he conceives he has determined the alveoli of the electro-motor layer to be lenticular in form, with their surfaces directed forwards and backwards. He would appear to have observed that they are arranged not in antero-posterior series, but alternately; so as to constitute

---

* The observations of Dr. Bilharz, the Professor of Anatomy in Cairo, have since been published *in extenso*, in a volume entitled, *Das Electrische organ des Zitterwelses*; Leipzig, 1857.—EDS.

decussating series, and to afford in certain sections the octahedral form attributed to them by Pacini. He also states that these lenticular alveoli consist of a fibrous membrane, covered by a very fine layer on which the nerves are disposed.

On each side of the tail of the skate (Raia), partly in contact with the skin, but chiefly enveloped in the so-called sacro-lumbalis muscle, is an elongated fusiform mass, which, although its electro-motor power has not yet been experimentally determined, nevertheless exhibits all the structural characteristics of an electrical battery. The mass consists of a number of longitudinally and somewhat spirally arranged series of discs; the series being separated from, and connected to, one another by thicker, the discs by thinner, layers of areolar texture. The discs are somewhat triangular, quadrangular, or pentangular in form, and are invariably arranged, so that their two large surfaces or faces are directed, the one backwards, the other forwards; and their three, four, or five smaller surfaces or margins enter into the formation of the surface of the series to which they belong. Of the two large surfaces, the anterior, or that towards the head of the animal, is smooth and slightly convex; the posterior slightly concave, and presents numerous alveolar depressions of various but graduated sizes, which penetrate two-thirds through the disc, and are separated from one another by corresponding straight or slightly-curved partitions, which diminish in size as they pass off from three or four primary ridges, which radiate from near the centre of the surface, and thus separate the alveoli into larger and smaller elliptical or angular groups. The discs consist of jelly-like dotted or granular nucleated substance; the granules being arranged in the form of spheroidal shells around clear spaces, in each of which a nucleus is situated. The ultimate ramifications of the vessels and nerves are situated not *in* but *on* the two large surfaces or faces of the discs; the former on the concave, alveolar, or posterior face; the latter on the convex, smooth, anterior face: and, like the vascular and nervous trunks and branches of the organ, lie in the midst of the areolar texture, which forms the greater and lesser laminæ of separation and connection of the constituent series and discs of the battery. The ultimate arterial twigs enter the areolar texture which lines the concave face of each disc; and pass into the alveoli as bundles of looped capillaries, which are continued into similarly arranged venous radicles. A number of ultimate nervous filaments spread from one of its margins through the areolar lamina, which clothes the convex face of each disc, preserving their double contours, until, becoming somewhat narrower, they divide into two or three secondary filaments, which, assuming an elongated fusiform aspect, and enclosing a nuclear mass, pass into corresponding secondary divisions of neighbouring filaments. The smooth convex surface of each disc is thus covered by an areolar lamina, which contains a network of ultimate branching and anastomosing nerve-filaments; the secondary or division filaments, which form the boundaries of the meshes of the network, having a peculiar festooned or looped fusiform aspect, with a mass resembling a nucleus in the centre of each.

This organ bears a resemblance to the batteries of Torpedo, and more particularly to those of Gymnotus, in the peculiar relations of the nerves, vessels, and nucleated texture; and if an electrical current exists in certain circumstances (probably when the animals are in season), it must pass in a contrary direction to that of the Gymnotus—that is, from tail to head.

These organs in the tail of the rays were discovered by Dr. Stark of Edinburgh; and their relative and general structure, as well as their probable function, described in an able paper read to the Royal Society of Edinburgh in 1844 (*Pro-*

ceedings of the Royal Soc. Edin. Dec. 1844). As Dr. Stark's description did not involve a sufficient account of the microscopic structure, which, in the absence of direct experimental evidence, could alone afford the basis of a legitimate hypothesis as to the function of the organ, I at the time undertook that inquiry, and stated the results in a paper read at a subsequent meeting of the Society.* In this paper the presumed electrical organ was described as consisting of antero-posterior, or linearly-arranged series of compressed chambers, lined by a nucleated gelatinous vascular substance; and suspended in the cavities of the chambers numerous sling-like anastomosing ultimate double contour nerve-tubes, with the centre of each loop occupied by a nucleus. There was also described a peculiar undulating ridge-structure (the alveoli of Robin), somewhat similar to the grooved and pitted marking on the dermal plates of certain fossil fishes; but the relations of this structure to the nucleated gelatinous texture were not determined; although its probable importance was indicated as a characteristic feature in an organ which could only be referred to electrical structures.

The entire structure of the presumed electrical apparatus in the rays, has, since Dr. Stark's discovery, been rediscovered, and most minutely and accurately described by Robin (*An. des Sci. Nat.* 1847); and from his descriptions, as verified by myself, the account in this lecture has been derived.

As the four nerves distributed to each battery of Torpedo are branches of the fifth and eighth cerebral pairs, the nervous centre of its electrical apparatus is situated in the medulla

---

* This paper was read before the Royal Society of Edinburgh, 6th January 1845; but its title only is recorded in the *Proceedings* of that day. In a manuscript found amongst his papers, he states that he was then engaged in observations on the structure of the electrical organs of two of the electrical fishes (torpedo and gymnotus), made during dissections for the University collection.—EDS.

oblongata, and consists of a large lobe on each side of its anterior part. Valentin ("Electricität der Thiere," in Wagner's *Handwörterb.*) states that these lobes consist of nucleated cellules so large as to be visible to the naked eye. The anterior or trigeminal electrical nerve is derived from the non-ganglionic portion of the third division of the fifth; the three posterior or vagal electrical nerves pass out along with the branchial divisions of the eighth nerve, but have no connection with the ganglionic masses developed on the branchial nerves. These electrical nerves belong, therefore, to the non-ganglionic series, with central relations similar to those of motor nerves.

The batteries of Gymnotus are supplied by about 224 pairs of nerves (J. Hunter, *Phil. Trans.* 1775; Rudolphi, *Abhand. der K. Akad. zu Berlin*, 1820) on each side. These are all derived from the inferior or motor roots of the spinal nerves; none being supplied by the lateral nerve, or combined branch of the fifth and eighth. The spinal cord exhibits no peculiar development, nor indication of the existence in it of a series of electrical nervous centres; but Valentin (Wagner's *Handwörterb. loc-cit.* 1842) has described a great lobe springing from each side of the brain between the peduncle of the cerebellum and the mesocephalon, extending upwards and forwards with its fellow of the opposite side, like an anterior or supplementary cerebellum. These lobes, according to Valentin, exhibit no trace of the large characteristic nucleated cells which exist in the electrical lobes of Torpedo. Whether the electrical lobes in Gymnotus be peculiar developments of the cerebellum, or of the grey matter at the cerebral extremities of the motor columns of the spinal cord, they present a highly interesting arrangement.

The presumed deep electrical layer of Malapterurus, which is merely a fatty mass, is supplied by branches of the spinal nerves; but the true electrical organs or batteries are supplied, the one on each side, by a longitudinal nerve, accompanied by an artery and vein, which pass along on their mesial aspects. This nerve was formerly considered to be a branch of the eighth pair; but Pacini (*sopra l'organo elettrico del Siluro elettrico del Nilo*, 1846) describes it as derived from the first spinal nerve. Ecker has more recently stated (Siebold and Kölliker's *Zeitschrift*, *July* 1854), that, according to Bilharz, "the electrical nerve on each side appears to be a new element intercalated between the third and fourth spinal nerves." From the same communication it appears that Bilharz has found the trunk of the electrical nerve of the Nilotic Malapterurus to consist not of a bundle of ultimate filaments, but of one such filament only, one-fourth of a line in diameter, surrounded by three fibrous sheaths, so as to present an entire thickness of one line. From this remarkable structure, Ecker has suggested to Bilharz further observations to determine whether the nervous centre of the electrical apparatus in this fish may not be a colossal unipolar nerve cell. From the peculiar structure of the trunk of the nerve, it is also evident that its branches and twigs of distribution must be subdivisions of the original single filament; in this respect resembling the subdivisions of the ultimate filaments in Torpedo, as observed by Wagner.

The presumed electrical organs in the tail of the skate are supplied by numerous nervous twigs, derived from the ventral or motor roots of the spinal nerves of the corresponding portion of the tail. These are distributed, as already stated, on the anterior faces of the discs, and do not exhibit at their spinal extremities any appreciable central development.

Physiologists admit, as a general fact, the disturbance of the electric equilibrium in the processes of the living organised body. In vegetables this development of electricity is remarkable. In animals the discovery of Galvani, and the researches of Matteucci, and more particularly of Du Bois

Reymond on the electro-motor phenomena of muscle and nerve, prove that in these structures currents take place, the result of nutritive process as well as of functional action; and the observations of Mr. Baxter (*Phil. Trans.* 1848-52, *Proceedings of Royal Soc.* 1855) have determined the existence of electrical currents manifested during secretion and respiration. There can be no doubt whatever, that in every living organism more or less numerous and powerful electric disturbances are produced by its organic processes; and that its general electric equilibrium is provided for by the resulting currents in the organism itself, and in the medium in which it lives. The problem which the physiologist has to solve, in attempting to explain the mode of action of the electrical apparatus in the fish, may be therefore thus briefly stated: What are the anatomical conditions, and the vital actions (meaning by vital all the actions of whatever kind, performed by the living structure), essential to the production of a sensible current of electricity, such as is produced by the apparatus in question?

Here it becomes necessary to review the more important successive opinions which have been taken of the electric property of the apparatus. Walsh (*Phil. Trans.* 1773) concluded that the electricity of the Torpedo resides in the electric organs; that their upper and under surfaces are capable, from a state of electric equilibrium, of being instantly thrown, *by a mere energy*, into a *plus* and *minus* state, like that of a charged phial; and that the current results from a conducting medium between their opposite surfaces being supplied, naturally, by the medium in which the animal lives, or artificially. The dependence of the electro-motor energy of the apparatus on the nervous centre has been more distinctly stated by Matteucci (*Biblioth. Univ.* xii.) and Dr. John Davy (*Phil. Trans.* 1834), the batteries being therefore viewed as analogous to Leyden jars, or an inductive apparatus. Rudolphi (*loc.*

cit.) considered the perpendicular prisms in Torpedo as galvanic piles, the horizontal series in Gymnotus as trough arrangements; but without entering into the details of the comparison. This view of their action does not explain the intermittent and voluntary character of the discharges. For, as Valentin (*loc. cit.*) has stated, the organs in the fish cannot be complete galvanic batteries, or they would be continually charged, and a discharge would follow every suitable closure of the circuit. Valentin (*loc. cit.*) proposes the following theory of the apparatus, based on Moser's (Dove and Moser's *Repertorium der Physik*, 1837) hypothesis of the action of the fluid of the cells of the battery on the substance of the nerves contained in it. He assumes the structure of the battery to be a series of closed spaces; the series enveloped in thicker, the spaces separated by thinner aponeurotic laminæ; each space being lined by a vascular epithelium, under which the nervous plexuses lie; and filled with fluid. He supposes that there results from the organic or nutritive reactions of the circulating blood, the epithelium, and the contained fluid of each space, a certain amount of electric force, not, however, sufficient to overcome the insulating obstacle opposed to it in the aponeurotic walls; all the spaces in the battery are, therefore, so far only insulated electrical spaces. As soon, however, as the will of the animal determines a flow of nervous force into the spaces, the organic reactions become so much exalted, that the resolved electric force overcomes the insulating power of the laminæ, and a current is produced— the current being confined to the series by their thicker aponeurotic walls. This theory, although it may account for a sudden increase of electricity in the organ, affords no explanation of its progressive character; the current is not accounted for.

The theory which most satisfactorily combines the anatomico-physiological as well as the electrical phenomena of the apparatus, is that lately propounded by Professor Pacini of Florence (*Sulla struttura intima dell organo elettrico del Gymnoto, e di altri pesci elettrici*, 1852). Having discovered the important anatomical fact, that the nerves are distributed on one surface only of the electrical elements of the battery; while the vessels and nucleated cellular texture occupy the other; he finds in these structural peculiarities the condition wanting in Valentin's theory—an explanation of the progression of the electricity—the current. Pacini refers the electrical batteries in the fish to two forms of structure, and two modes of action; of the first and simplest form the Torpedo affords the type, of the second and more complicated, the Gymnotus. The batteries of Malapterurus are probably referable to the Torpedinal type, those of Raia certainly to that of Gymnotus. In the Torpedinal type of battery, according to Pacini, the action is analogous to that which takes place in a thermo-electric pile, inasmuch as he conceives it to depend upon a dynamical difference, a certain different condition, in the two surfaces of each diaphragm of this *binary type* of pile. The nerve-surface and the vasculo-cellular surface of a Torpedinal diaphragm correspond to the bismuth and copper, or bismuth and antimony elements of a thermo-electric arrangement; the nervous influence in the former taking the place of the heat applied in the latter. There is here assumed, what on other grounds is highly probable, that the electrical and nervous forces are correlative; and here it must be admitted that in Torpedo, as pointed out by John Hunter (*Phil. Trans.* 1773), the bulk of the nerves in relation to the batteries is much greater than in Gymnotus, which exemplifies Pacini's second or *ternary type* of animal battery. When the Torpedo, therefore, wills a shock, or when, through the reflex action of its electrical nervous centre, a shock is induced, a sudden and copious nervous influx flowing over the under surfaces of its electric diaphragms, the upper surfaces are thrown into an opposite electrical condition, and a current is the consequence.

Pacini refers the structure of the battery in Gymnotus to a *ternary type;* consisting of a negative element—the fibrous layer on which the nerves ramify, together with the fluid which it bounds below; a positive element—the ridged vasculo-cellular layer; and a conducting element, the inter-diaphragmatic fluid. The vasculo-cellular layer predominating in this ternary type over the nervous, Pacini conceives the electricity to be evolved in the organic actions of the vasculo-cellular layer under the influence of the nerves. In other words, the will of the Gymnotus, or the reflex action of its electrical nervous centre, directs an influence along the nerves of its batteries over the fibro-nervous layer; which suddenly exciting the nutritive or other organic actions of the highly-developed vasculo-cellular layer, an electrical disturbance is produced; with an opposite electrical condition of the fibro-nervous and vasculo-cellular layers of the diaphragms, and consequently a current through the series. Pacini compares the wide-meshed fibrous layer, on the under surface of which the nerves ramify to the hollow cylinder of porous clay, which in a Bunsen's or Grove's galvanic arrangement separates the negative from the positive elements.

As to the manner in which the animal avails itself of the electrical currents which it has the power of exciting, without alluding to the numerous experiments which have been made on the Torpedo in air, I shall confine myself to the mode in which the Torpedo and Gymnotus use their currents as means of offence and defence in their proper aqueous medium. In the first place, it is evident that in water, the currents between the opposite surfaces of Torpedo, or between the ends of Gymnotus, instead of being confined to a transverse area of limited extent, as when they pass along a wire during a discharge in the air, must be diffused through a considerable extent of the water surrounding the fish. The entire current force of the batteries must, in fact, be subdivided into numerous subordinate axes of force arranged in lines which come round the margins of Torpedo from back to belly, and along the sides of Gymnotus from head to tail. It is evident, therefore, that another fish placed so that its antero-posterior axis is in the line of inductive action in the water, will be affected less powerfully by the circulating electric power than if it were placed across these lines. Mr. Faraday (*Phil. Trans.* 1839) found that although the Gymnotus can stun and kill fishes which are in various positions in relation to its own body, it can, moreover, by throwing itself so as to form a coil enclosing the fish, the latter representing a diameter across it, so concentrate its currents of one side as to strike it motionless as if by lightning. The Torpedo would also appear, from the observations of Dr. Davy, instinctively to elevate or arrange its margin so as to adjust the direction of its currents to the position of the object through which it wishes to pass them. "Thus," as Mr. Faraday observes, "the very conducting power which the water has; that which it gives to the moistened skin of the fish or animal to be struck; the extent of surface by which the fish and water conducting the charge to it are in contact; all conduce to favour and increase the shock upon the doomed animal" (*Phil. Trans.* 1839). Here, it is to be noted that one of the chief difficulties in explaining the operation of the electrical apparatus in the fish has been the necessity of admitting a certain amount of insulating property in certain of the textures composing and surrounding it; and in conceiving the apparatus acting at all in a medium which conducts so freely as water. The apparatus in fact owes its efficiency in such a medium to its peculiar combination of *quantity* and *intensity*. The battery of the fish, in relation to its final purpose, is a perfect instrument; yet, from another point of view, and in one sense, when compared with an artificial electrical apparatus, it is imperfect. It is necessarily most insufficiently insulated, and there is, therefore, an enormous loss of electricity; but the quantity produced is comparatively so enormous that enough remains to form an efficient circuit. It is, in fact, a remarkable example of the munificent power and perfect freedom of action, in combination with strict adhesion to law, which distinguish the work of the Creator in the formation and economy of organised beings; and it is only to be imitated in the most imperfect manner by human ingenuity.

The presumed correlation of the nervous and electrical forces in no way trenches on the psychical department of physiology, and has no tendency to exclude the psychical or proper vital element from the science of organisation. The physiology of man, at all events, can only be successfully studied and prosecuted by approaching it from two opposite poles. From the one, we approach its somatic department through anatomy, chemistry, and physics; by the kind of evidence and method of research common to all such sciences. From the other, guided by an evidence and method totally different in kind, we enter on its intellectual and moral departments through philosophy and revelation.*

---

* This lecture was illustrated by a selection from the very complete series of preparations of electrical organs in the Comparative Anatomy series in the Museum of the University.

XVI.—A BRIEF REVIEW OF THE PRESENT STATE OF ORGANIC ELECTRICITY.

The general Theory of Electricity has rapidly approached a consistent form through the labours of recent physicists and particularly by the researches of Mr. Faraday. The hypotheses of one or of two electric fluids, however modified, have been found tenable only so far as they involve the idea of force. In the phenomena of statical as in those of current electricity, there is constantly pressed upon the observer the necessity of admitting two forces, or two forms or directions of a force, inseparable from one another. And thus "the influence which is present in an electrical condition may best be conceived of as an axis of power having contrary forces, exactly equal in amount, in contrary directions."*

This peculiar form of force manifests itself in different kinds of inorganic matter, under circumstances such as friction, change of temperature, magnetic influence, and chemical action.

It is also manifested in organised beings, not only under circumstances in which they stand related to it as masses of mere matter; but more particularly during the actions performed by their component textures and organs.

Electrical science has been hitherto chiefly prosecuted in the region of inorganic nature; and although Volta opened

---

* Faraday, *Philosophical Transactions*; and *Experimental Researches in Electricity*.

up a boundless field of discovery, yet organic electricity still remains comparatively uncultivated.

In the investigation of electrical force as manifested in organic nature, the peculiar economy of the organised being must be taken into account. Each organised being, although dependent on certain external circumstances as the conditions of its existence, is, nevertheless, a system *per se*. Irrespective of those electrical conditions into which it may be thrown, through surrounding bodies, or through the medium in which it lives, it undoubtedly contains more or less numerous sources of electrical disturbance, in the numerous processes and arrangements productive of currents in the structures which collectively constitute its organisation. The organised being may be considered *electrically* as a system of electrical currents excited by electrical arrangements in the disposition of its fluids, textures, and organs.

So far as has yet been ascertained, these electrical currents, with the exception of those produced by the special batteries in the electrical fishes, are not employed in the economy of the being. They are merely necessary consequences of the organic processes carried on by the different structures; and effect, by their arrangement, the distribution of the resulting electricity, and the maintenance of the general electrical equilibrium of the organic sytem. The detection and investigation of these organic electrical phenomena are, however, important, not only for general electrical science, but also for the elucidation of the organic processes themselves. Residual phenomena, as such electrical disturbances must generally be considered in physiology, will, when investigated, indicate the probable nature of the actions from which they result.

Electrical Phenomena in Vegetables.

Various observers have proved the existence in plants of arrangements which affect the condenser and galvanometer.

The experiments of Pouillet[*] on electricity developed in, or in connection with, young plants in a state of growth, although valuable, present too many sources of fallacy to be available at present. Donné[†] was the first to point out the opposite electrical conditions of different parts of vegetables. He found the opposite extremities of certain fruits, and even the juices removed from those parts, to be in different electrical states; and thus opened up a new field of organic electricity, which promises, when more fully investigated, to lead to important results. The most precise information, however, regarding the effect of different parts of vegetables on the galvanometer are contained in two communications by M. Becquerel in the *Memoirs of the French Academy*,[‡] and in a notice by Professor Wartmann in the *Bibliothèque Universelle de Genève*.[§] The researches themselves are not yet sufficiently advanced to admit of a satisfactory analysis. Indeed, as M. Becquerel observes, the electrical effects are so complex that it is unsafe to draw any conclusion regarding the part which electricity takes in the organic functions. Hitherto, therefore, in his researches, he has considered electricity rather as an effect, serving to elucidate the study of physiology, than as a primary cause of organic phenomena. Much difficulty exists in determining whether certain currents, indicated by the instrument, are primary or derived; and also in ascertaining how far the observed currents are produced by

[*] "Sur l'Electricité des fluides élastiques, et sur une des causes de l'Electricité de l'Atmosphère."—*Ann. de Chim. et de Physique*, tom. xxxv. 1827.

[†] "Recherches sur quelques unes des Propriétés Chimiques des sécrétions et sur les courants électriques qui existent dans les Corps Organizés."—*Ann. de Chim. et de Physique*, tom. lvii. 1834.

[‡] "Recherches sur les causes qui degagent de l'électricité dans les végétaux, et sur les courants végétaux terrestres;" and "Memoire sur les effets électriques obtenus dans les tubercules, les racines, et les fruits, au moyen d'aiguilles de platine."—*Mem. de l'Acad. des Sciences*, tom. xxiii.

[§] "Note sur les Courants électriques qui existent dans les végétaux."—*Bibliothèque Universelle de Genève*, tom. xv 1850.

unavoidable injury of texture, and consequent mixing of fluids, by the insertion of the platina electrodes. The progress of animal electricity had, previously to the labours of Du Bois Reymond,* been impeded by similar circumstances; and until the electro-motor properties of the component parts of vegetables are in some way separately investigated, as those of muscle and nerve have been by the observer alluded to, no solid progress can be looked for in vegetable electricity.

The general arrangement of the parts of a plant, and the functions they perform, indicate the probable direction of the resulting electrical disturbances. The differences in the constitution of the ascending and descending portions of the axis, and of their different transverse segments, naturally indicate the existence of longitudinal currents; while the structural and functional differences between the central and superficial portions of the axis point to transverse or radiating lines of force. Accordingly, all the observations of Donné, Becquerel, and Wartmann, indicate currents, primary or derived, in the longitudinal and transverse direction, in roots, tubers, stems, leaves, flowers and fruits.

The Electrical Reactions of the Plant, Soil, and Atmosphere.—The soil is in a constant negative, while the air, when calm and free from clouds, is in a positive, electric condition.

According to the experiments of Pouillet,† plants in the later stages of germination, after they have protruded from the soil, exhibit, by the condenser, an excess of negative electricity. The explanation he gives is, according to Becquerel,‡ probably correct; that the action of the oxygen of the air on the starch of the seed, during its conversion, gives an excess of positive electricity to the air, and of negative electricity to the

---

* Poggendorff's *Annalen*, and *Untersuchungen über Thierische Electricität*, 1848.

† *Ann. de Chim. et de Physique*, loc. cit.

‡ *Mem. de l'Acad. des Sciences*, tom. xxiii. p. 60.

plant and soil. The electrical effects observed by M. Pouillet, in this first period of vegetation, correspond with the ordinary electrical conditions of the earth and atmosphere.

But according to M. Becquerel's own observations,* the electrical relations of the plant to the soil and air are reversed after germination is completed. If the electrodes of the galvanometer are inserted—the one into the stem or branch, or passed through a number of leaves laid together, but still adherent, the other into the soil—the former will exhibit an excess of negative, the latter of positive electricity, in proportion to the humidity of the soil and the succulence of the plant.

It may, therefore, be presumed that in the act of vegetation, after germination is accomplished, the ascending sap, which communicates by means of the root with the soil, conveys to it continuously the excess of positive electricity which it has acquired during its course upwards in its reactions more particularly with the descending sap; while the latter furnishes to the air, by exhalation, its excess of negative electricity.

Vegetation, therefore, produces electric effects contrary to those which render the air and soil respectively positive and negative.

Longitudinal Electrical Currents in the Dicotyledonous Plant.—Becquerel states† that if the electrodes of the galvanometer be inserted transversely into the parenchyma of the bark, the one a certain distance above the other, or if one be inserted between the bark and wood, and the other be passed through a number of leaves, superimposed and still adherent, the needle will indicate a current passing from below upwards‡

---

* *Mem. de l'Acad. des Sciences*, tom. xxiii. pp. 61, 62.

† *Ibid.*, tom. xxiii. pp. 55, 56.

‡ The statement of the *direction* of an electrical current is a conventional form of expression, which ought to convey merely an indication of *the relative positions of its positive and negative extremities*, and consequently of the two polar forces, both of which exist in the current. In the circuit formed by the

through the parenchyma, the upper electrode indicating positive, the lower negative electricity. M. Becquerel accounts for the relative electrical conditions of the green parenchyma from the leaves downwards by the removal of oxygen.

But the observations of M. Becquerel on the relative electrical conditions of the plant and soil indicate the existence of a descending current passing from the stem through the roots into the earth, which therefore becomes positive around the plant.

M. Wartmann, in the notice already quoted,* states that in the roots, the stem, the branches, the petioles, and peduncles, there exist a central descending current, and a peripheral ascending one, which he denominates axial currents ; and that the galvanometer indicates currents from every part of the plant, aërial or subterranean, to the soil, which is thus positive in relation to the plant.

From these observations of Becquerel and Wartmann, little doubt can be entertained that electrical currents exist in the dicotyledonous plant, in the course of the circulation of its sap, but in an opposite direction to it.

Currents passing from within outwards, and from without inwards in the horizontal section of the Dicotyledonous Plant.—According to Becquerel,† if one electrode be inserted into the pith, in a clean horizontal section of a young poplar, and the other into one of the woody layers, or into the bark, the needle is deflected 5°, 10°, 15°, or more, according to the delicacy of galvanometer, the current which traverses its wire, and which deflects the magnetic needle, is conventionally said to pass from the positive to the negative electrode ; while in the electro-motor portion of the circuit—*e.g.* a portion of vegetable structure—the current is said to pass in the opposite direction. But "there is never one current of force, or one fluid only." "In a current, whatever form the discharge may take, or whatever part of the circuit or current is referred to, as much positive force as is there exerted in one direction, so much negative force is there exerted in the other."

* *Bib. Univ. de Genève*, tom. xv. p. 302.
† *Loc. cit.* p. 44.

the instrument, the succulence of the tree, or the radial distance of the layer into which the second electrode has been inserted; a current from without inwards is indicated, the electrode in the pith being positive, that in the wood or bark negative.

If the one electrode be inserted close to the outside, and the other be removed from the pith, and be reinserted from place to place outwards, the current will diminish in intensity as the second electrode approaches the cambium. Beyond the cambium the current changes its direction and becomes stronger. The current which now deflects the needle passes along the wire from without inwards, indicating a positive electric condition of the outer part of the parenchyma, and a negative condition of the cambium.

On removing a piece of bark, and applying the electrodes, (which in this experiment should consist of platinum plates) to its opposite surfaces, the current becomes very intense. The piece of bark thus forms a voltaic couple, of which the exterior or parenchymatous side is positive, and the interior, covered by the cambium, negative.

It would appear then that, from the pith to the cambium, the woody layers are less and less positive in relation to the pith; whilst from the cambium to the cuticle, the parenchymatous layers are more positive, or at least comport themselves as such in the production of derived currents. This inversion of the electrical effects corresponds with the relative position of the cellular texture in the bark and wood. In the bark, it is on the exterior; in the wood, in the interior; in both it is positive.

In the notice by M. Wartmann, in the *Bibliothèque Universelle de Genève*,* that observer states that "in uniting by the galvanometer the layers of the stem where the liber and cambium touch one another (and where many botanists admit

* *Bib. Univ. de Genève*, tom. xv. p. 301.

a passage of descending juices), either with the most central parts (the pith or the perfect wood), or with the parts more exterior (the young bark), a lateral current will be found tending from these layers to the neighbouring organs."

It would appear, therefore, that currents pass from the contiguous surfaces of the bark and wood of the dicotyledonous plant outwards towards the cuticle, and inwards to the pith; or at least, arrangements exist in these directions which excite currents in the opposite directions through the galvanometer wire.

Currents in the Root and its Dependencies.—According to M. Wartmann,* in some roots the central structures and the cortical structures are, as in the stem, positive in relation to the layers by which they touch and are united.

Centrifugal transverse currents would appear to exist in certain roots, which resemble tubers in the quantity of their nutritious deposits. For Becquerel † has found the central part of the carrot, and of the red and white beetroot, negative in relation to the exterior.

In the potato, in the tubers of the *Helianthus tuberosus* and *Lathyrus tuberosus*, currents radiate from the centre to the cuticle; for the electrode at the centre is negative in relation to the other, the latter indicating a more positive condition the nearer it is placed to the cuticle. Becquerel, who has ascertained these facts, and refers them to the system of transverse currents in the bark, states at the same time that in the tubers of *Tropæolum tuberosum*, and *Ullucus tuberosus*, the currents are reversed, and correspond, therefore, with the transverse system in the wood and pith of the dicotyledonous stem.

* *Bib. Univ. de Genève,* tom. xv.
† Memoire sur les effets électriques obtenus dans les tubercules, les racines, "et les fruits, au moyen d'aiguilles de platine."—*Mem. de l'Acad. des Sciences,* tom. xxiii.

It remains to be determined how far the single transverse system of electrical currents in either direction, in certain roots, and in tubers, depends upon the disappearance of the central or peripheral elements of the axis.

On Currents in Leaves.—The relations and functions of the leaf indicate the probable direction of the electrical currents which may exist in it.

Becquerel's * observations lead to the conclusion that currents set from the cambium to the parenchyma of the leaf; while at the same time it is negative in relation to the pith and wood of the branch and stem. He states that the leaves comport themselves as the green part of the parenchyma of the bark—that is to say, the sap which circulates in their tissues is negative in relation to the wood, pith, and soil; and positive in relation to the cambium.

M. Wartmann † states that in most leaves the currents proceed from the limb of the leaf to its veins, and to the central parts of its petiole, and of the stem.

This centripetal current attributed to the leaf by Becquerel and Wartmann is evidently referable to the central or descending axial current of the plant; while the centrifugal current alluded to by the former belongs to the superficial transverse system, or that between the inner and outer aspects of the bark.

The Electrical Condition of the Flower.—From the energetic actions and rapid development of the flower, a considerable amount of electrical disturbance is to be expected in it. Various observers have ascertained the remarkable elevation of temperature which occurs during the development of this part of the plant; and the important chemico-vital actions which take place in it must certainly excite corresponding electrical phenomena.

* "Recherches sur les causes qui degagent de l'électricité," etc.—*Mem. de l'Acad. de Sciences,* tom. xxiii.

† *Bibliothèque Universelle de Genève,* tom. xv.

The only observations in regard to these which have been recorded are by Zantedeschi, quoted by Becquerel in his second memoir.* The Italian observer found that at the period of flowering in the tulip, jonquil, and anemone, a deflection of the needle to the extent of 3° or 4°, due to a descending current, occurs. He also found in an Azalea, an Amaryllis, a white lily, and in various species of Opuntia, a current passing from the stamen to the pistil; the one electrode being in contact with the pollen, the other inserted into the stigma.

Electrical condition of the Fruit.—The only recorded observations on this subject are by Donné,† in a memoir which may be said to have introduced for the first time the subject of vegetable, as well as certain important departments of animal electricity.

Donné found that when the platinum extremities of the galvanometer wire are plunged into certain fruits, the one at the stalk, the other at the opposite end, the parts exhibit different electrical conditions. In the apple and pear a current would appear to pass from the stalk towards the eye at the opposite end; whilst in the peach and apricot the current passes in the contrary direction. In the apple and pear the fruit is electro-positive at the distal end, electro-negative at the stalk; the contrary being the case in the peach and apricot.

Irrespective of the chemical causes to which these currents are ascribed by Donné and Becquerel, it might be well to determine how far their opposite directions may be referable to morphological differences in the two forms of fruit examined: whether in the monocarpal form, as in the peach, the current be not referable to the centripetal current of the leaf; and whether in the apple form (the fleshy mass of which is not a

* " Memoire sur les effects électriques," etc.—*Mem. de l'Acad. de Sciences*, tom. xxiii.
† *Ann. de Chim. et de Physique*, tom. lvii.

development of the carpellary leaf, but of the cortical layer of the receptacle, and of the end of the peduncle) it is not due to the same causes which produce the general superficial, or cortical axial current in the plant.

Are the Currents which affect the Galvanometer derived from Currents which actually exist in the Plant? or are they produced by the Insertion of the Electrodes?—M. Becquerel expresses himself very cautiously on this point; and blames certain physicists for entertaining inexact ideas regarding the currents obtained from organised bodies by the galvanometer platinum wires; and for assuming that such currents are necessarily derived from other currents which actually exist in the plant. But M. Becquerel adds,* somewhat inconsistently with his own admissions in other parts of his memoirs, that nothing at present authorises an induction of this kind. The effects, he states, appear to be due, at least in most cases, to the reaction of different liquids in contact with the electrodes; from which results such a disengagement of electricity, as that the liquid, which comports itself as an acid in relation to the other, sets free positive electricity.

At the same time, M. Becquerel admits that the two necessary conditions for the production of primary currents exist in the plant. The first is, that two liquids capable of acting chemically on one another should be arranged so as to do so gradually and continuously, or that there should be, as M. Becquerel expresses it, "le contact des deux liquides per transition insensible." The other is the intermedium of a conducting texture, or substance to complete the circuit. M. Becquerel, accordingly, both in his memoirs† and in his abridgments in the *Comptes Rendus*,‡ seems inclined to admit the two axial currents, and the horizontal system in the stem and branches of the dicotyledonous plant. Beyond this he

---

* *Mem. de l'Acad. des Sciences*, tom. xxiii.   † *Ibid.*
‡ *Comptes Rendus*, tom. xxxi. xxxii.

appears, at the date of the publication of his memoirs, to have drawn no more precise conclusion from the facts then observed; and states that the electrical effects which take place in vegetables are so numerous, that it has only been possible hitherto to observe a limited number of them.

M. Wartmann,[*] while he admits that the electro-chemical action, which results from the tearing of the textures during the insertion of the electrodes, produces at first a considerable deflection of the needle, states, at the same time, that when this action ceases, which it speedily does, there remains a more feeble current, which must be due to the normal electrical action of the parts. He states that vegetable currents probably form closed circuits; that the extremities of the root-fibres on the one hand, and the terminations of the leaves on the other, establish a continuity between the ascending peripheral and the descending central current; while the similarity in the electrical condition of the exterior of the bark and the interior of the wood probably depends on the medullary rays.

To what Actions and Arrangements in the Plant are its Electrical Disturbances and Currents due? From what has already been stated, it must appear that the knowledge hitherto obtained of the relations and circumstances of the electrical disturbances and currents in the plant is not yet sufficiently precise to afford a solution of this question. Before the publication of Du Bois Reymond's researches on the electrical actions of muscle and nerve, and of Pacini on the structure of the batteries in the Torpedo and Gymnotus, electrical excitement in the animal body had not been accurately connected with anatomical structure; and until a definite electrical current in the plant is distinctly referred to a demonstrable structural arrangement, a precise determination of the exciting causes of currents in the latter cannot be expected.

[*] *Bib. Univ. de Genève*, tom. xv.

We are not, indeed, acquainted with the actual chemical or physical causes of electrical excitement in any animal texture or organ; but we now know the direction and relations of the current in and to the anatomical structure in certain cases. This is a secure step in the proper direction, and one which has yet to be taken in vegetable electricity.

At present, therefore, it can only be stated generally that the disturbance of electric equilibrium in the textures and organs of the plant is due to the chemical action which plays so important a part in the organic processes—at its surface, as during transpiration, respiration proper, and the fixation of carbon—and in its interior, during the reaction of its ascending and descending sap, with the substances contained in the cells of its various structures. In the same manner, no precise statement can be made at present regarding the arrangements by means of which electrical currents are produced in the plant. The researches of Becquerel[*] have proved that a current is produced when two liquids of acid and alkaline reactions respectively, and separated from one another by a porous substance, are connected either by a fluid or solid conductor. It is quite evident that similar physical and chemical conditions for the production of currents exist in innumerable forms in the organisation of vegetables. It is, however, impossible in the present phase of the subject to define them with greater precision.

Animal Electricity.

The first discovery in animal electricity was the determination of the electrical character of the shock of the Torpedo by Walsh in 1772. The development of the subject has since been retarded, not only by its own intrinsic difficulty, but also by the greater attractions of those departments of general electricity which were opened up by

[*] "Recherches sur les circuits electro-chimique simple formé de liquides."
—*Comptes Rendus*, tom. xxiv.

the labours of Volta. Its history presents three distinct lines of research—that of the special electrical organs of the fish, commencing with the discovery of Walsh in 1772,* that of the electrical properties of muscle and nerve, starting from the fundamental experiment of Galvani in 1786-94,† and that of the electrical phenomena of membranes and glands, introduced by Donné in 1834.‡

The results which have ultimately been attained in these three directions will now be briefly examined; but in order to obtain a more comprehensive view they shall be taken up in the reverse order.

Electric Phenomena in connection with MEMBRANE *and* GLAND.—The experiments of Donné are now alluded to only because they were the first which proved electric disturbance in connection with secreting membrane and structure. He found that when the electrodes of the galvanometer were applied respectively to the mucous membrane of the mouth and to the skin, the needle deviated 15°, 20°, or 30°; the former being negative, the latter positive. In the same manner, when the instrument was applied between the mucous membrane of the stomach and the gall-bladder, or interior of the liver, the needle deviated 30°, 40°, or 50°.

Donné attributed these electric effects to the acid and alkaline properties of the secretions with which the electrodes were respectively in contact. Matteucci,§ again, while admitting the correctness of Donné's experimental results, attributed, as Drs. Wollaston‖ and Thomas Young¶ had previously

---

* "Of the Electric Property of the Torpedo."—*Phil. Trans.* 1773.

† *De Viribus Electricitatis in Motu Musculari Commentarius;* Bologna, 1791.

‡ *Ann. de Chim. et de Phys.* tom. lvii. 1834.

§ *Ibid.* tom. lvi.

‖ *Phil. Mag.* vol. xxxiii. "On the Agency of Electricity on Animal Secretions."

¶ Young. *Syllabus of Lectures on Medicine.*

done, the difference of the chemical composition of the secretions to the electric force itself. It is evident, therefore, that the ingenious conjectures of Wollaston and Young, and the experiments of Donné and Matteucci, merely indicated a promising field of discovery, and formed a prelude to researches which promised more precise results after the structures experimented upon had been more definitely selected.

The Electric Relations of Mucous Membrane.—Mr. H. F. Baxter has recorded the results of his experiments on this subject.* The principal object Mr. Baxter had in view was to determine the relative electric condition of the secretions of the mucous membrane, and of its vessels and blood; fulfilling, therefore, what has already been stated as an apparent condition of success in all such inquiries—viz. experimenting, as far as can be, on distinct textures or organs, and not on their aggregations.

The mucous membrane of the stomachs, and of the small and large intestines, of the rabbit, cat, and guinea-pig, were selected; and pointed and flattened platinum electrodes applied respectively to the surface of the mucous membrane, and inserted into the vessels. The following were the general results :—

1. The inside and outside of the gut were formed into a circuit without effect.

2. One electrode on the mucous membrane, the other inserted into an artery proceeding to the same spot, produced no effect.

3. One electrode on the mucous membrane, the other inserted into a vein proceeding from the same spot, indicated a positive condition of the vein or its contents, by a deviation of the needle to the extent of from 3° to 5°.

* *Phil. Trans.* 1848. "An experimental inquiry, undertaken with a view of ascertaining whether any, or what, signs of current electricity are manifested during the organic process of secretion, in living animals," etc.

4. One electrode on the mucous membrane, the other inserted into a vein emptied of its blood, produced no effect.

5. One electrode applied to the mucous membrane, the other inserted into a vein *not* proceeding from the same spot, produced no effect.

6. It was not necessary to insert the second electrode into the vein, for the needle was deflected if the second electrode was merely dipped into the blood flowing from the vein.

Having ascertained how far the different solid and fluid substances in contact with the electrodes might interfere with the result, and also in what manner the effects were influenced by the death of the animal, Mr. Baxter concluded from his experiments, that—

1. When the electrodes of a galvanometer are brought into communication—one with the mucous membrane of the alimentary canal, the other with the blood flowing from the same part—a deviation of the needle takes place, indicating that the secreted product and the blood are in opposite electric states.

2. The effect occurs during the life of the animal, and ceases after its death.

3. The effect may be considered as arising from the decomposition of the blood—*i.e.* from the changes which occur during the formation of the secreted product and venous blood.

4. These changes are effected by the organic actions of the part.

The Electric Relations of Gland.—In a second paper,[*] Mr. Baxter records the experiments which he had made to determine the electric relations of the secretions and blood of the liver, kidney, and mammary gland. The facts which his experiments tend to establish are as follow :—

---

[*] *Phil. Trans.* 1852. An experimental inquiry undertaken with a view of ascertaining whether any, or what, signs of current electricity are manifested during the organic process of secretion in living animals, etc.

1. During biliary secretion, the *bile* and *venous blood* flowing from the hepatic veins are in *opposite* electric states.

2. During urinary secretion, the *urine* and *venous blood* flowing from the renal vein are in *opposite* electric states.

3. During mammary secretion, the *milk* and the *venous blood* flowing from the mammary veins, are in *opposite* electric states.

In these experiments on glandular action, as in those described above on the alimentary mucous membrane, the venous blood was found to be positive, producing a deflection of the needle to the extent of 3°, 4°, 5°, 8°, 10°.

The Electric Relations of the Respiratory Mucous Membrane and the Pulmonic Blood.—Mr. Baxter, having ascertained that the venous blood flowing from a secreting membrane or gland, is in a positive electric condition, applied one electrode in contact with the mucous membrane of the lung, and the other in contact with the blood flowing from it—*i.e.* the arterial blood. He thus found the blood of the pulmonary veins, or of the left ventricle, invariably positive, producing a deflection of 2°, 3°, 4°, or 5°. At the same time, he ascertained that when the respiratory mucous membrane and the blood of the right ventricle are connected, a deflection of 2°, 3°, or 4°, occasionally occurred. All his experiments tended to the same conclusion— viz. that the blood of the pulmonary veins is positive; and that when a circuit is formed between the mucous membrane of the lung, and the blood in the left ventricle of the heart, a current is produced.

The Electric Properties of MUSCLE.—Galvani having discovered and investigated the contractions produced by electricity in the muscles of the frog,[*] afterwards observed similar contractions when two dissimilar metals, in contact with one another, are also brought into contact with the nerve and muscles respectively of the frog's leg.[†] At first he appears to

[*] *De Viribus Electricitatis*, etc.   [†] *Ibid.*

have conceived the contractions to be due to electricity evolved by the metals; but finally he concluded that it is produced by the animal textures themselves. The researches of Volta verified the original opinion of Galvani, that the metals, *when they are employed*, are the sources of the electricity which produce the muscular contractions;[*] but the discovery of the pile, with its consequences, threw into temporary oblivion the actual evidences of an electromotor property of the animal textures *independently of metals*, which the numerous experiments of Galvani and his supporters had afforded.[†] Even Humboldt's observations did not prevent the almost total neglect of the subject for a quarter of a century.[‡]

In 1827, Nobili,[||] having applied his improved galvanometer to the fundamental experiment of Galvani, discovered the electric current of the frog. He found that when the circuit of the nerve and muscles of the leg is closed by the instrument, a deviation of the needle to the extent of 10°, 20°, or 30°, occurs, due to a current which passes in the limb from the toes upwards, and which could be increased by inclosing in the circuit several frogs arranged as a battery. There could no longer be any doubt of the truth of Galvani's later opinion, that electricity is developed in connection with muscle and nerve.

The researches of Matteucci, carried on during a transitionary stage of the subject, and exhibiting occasional obscurity and contradiction, are, nevertheless, valuable, not only from having directed attention generally to electro-physiology, but particularly from having, in regard to muscle, indicated that its electric properties are due to its own texture, and not to the conjoined nerves. He had always, however, experimented

---

[*] *Nuova Memoria dell' Electricita Animale*, etc.

[†] *Dell' uso e dell' attività dell' arco conduttore nei contrazione de' muscoli*, 1793; and *Supplimento al Tratatto dell' uso*, etc. 1794.

[‡] *Versuche ueber die gereizte Muskel-und Nervenfaser*, u. s. w., 1797.

[||] *Ann. de Chim. et de Phys.* 1828

with masses, or aggregates of muscle, and had not attempted to ascertain the laws of electric action in the muscular fibre or bundle itself, or in a single isolated muscle.*

These laws have been investigated by Du Bois Reymond, who has ascertained that muscular structure presents two distinct electric conditions—firstly, during the intervals of contractions; and secondly, during contraction.

Electric Condition of a Muscle during the intervals of contraction.—Galvani conceived the outer surface of a muscle to be charged with negative, the inner with positive electricity. Matteucci had found that in order to produce contractions in the galvanoscopic frog, two parts of its nerve must be brought into contact with *two parts* respectively of the muscle of a living animal; and that the experiment uniformly succeeded if the nerve touched the bottom of a wound in the muscle and the margin of the wound at the same time. Du Bois Reymond has ascertained the actual relative electric condition of certain surfaces or aspects of the muscular fibre or muscle.† These aspects he denominates the *longitudinal* and *transverse sections*. These sections, again, may be either *natural or artificial*.

The *natural longitudinal section* is as much of the surface of a muscle as is formed by the exposed sides of its superficial fibres.

An *artificial longitudinal section* is any surface exposed by a section in the direction of the muscular fibres.

The surface or side of a fibre or fasciculus viewed as a cylinder or prism is its *longitudinal section*.

A *natural transverse section* is any part of a muscle formed by the extremities of its fibres, coated by tendon of attachment.

---

* *Bib. Univ. de Génève; Ann. de Chim. et de Phys.; Traité des Phénomènes Electro-physiologique.*

† "The Law of the Muscular Current," p. 498, vol. i. of *Untersuch. ueber Thier. Electricität.*

An *artificial transverse section* is a section made at right angles to the fibres.

The natural or artificial extremities of fibres are *transverse sections*.

By employing a very delicate galvanometer, and by certain refined precautions in the arrangement of his experiments, Du Bois Reymond found that the *longitudinal section, natural or artificial,* is invariably positive in relation to the *natural or artificial transverse section.* The following are the general laws of the *derived* muscular current.

1. If any point of the natural or artificial longitudinal section be put into connection, by means of the galvanometer, with any point of the natural or artificial transverse section, the needle will indicate a current in the wire from the longitudinal to the transverse section.

2. If one point of the natural or artificial transverse section of a muscle is brought into connection with another point of the same or of another similar transverse section, and if the points be unequally distant from the centre of the section considered as the base of a muscular cylinder, a current is indicated passing from the electrode furthest from the centre, and directed to that which is nearest to it.

3. If we now consider the mass of the muscle as a cylinder, and connect a point of the natural or artificial longitudinal section nearer the middle transverse section of the mass, with a point of the natural or artificial longitudinal section more distant from the middle, a current is indicated passing from the nearer to the more distant point.

4. If both connected points of one or of two natural or artificial transverse sections be equally distant from the centre of the surface, no current is indicated. So also in regard to longitudinal sections, points equally distant from the middle produced no current.

These laws are most satisfactorily illustrated in the muscles of rabbits and frogs, but they are essentially the same in man, in representatives of the four vertebrate classes, and in molluscs, crustaceans, and annelids.

The electromotor power, which is exhibited in the muscular current, does not depend upon the areolar texture, the tendons or vessels, etc., of the mass; or on the contact of dissimilar textures with the muscular fibre; for the power is exhibited when the smallest manageable portion, or even a single primary fasciculus, is employed. The power evidently resides in the ultimate fibre.

Du Bois Reymond has investigated the arrangement of the electromotor elements on which this power depends. After various experiments, he succeeded in constructing a model consisting of a solid copper cylinder, with its cylindrical surface coated with zinc, and suspended in or surrounded by an electrolytic liquid, which fulfilled by means of the galvanometer all the conditions of the current as derived from the natural sections of an entire muscle. He arranged another model, consisting of a number of similar but smaller cylinders, set in longitudinal series, so that the positive or zinc elements were directed laterally, and the copper or negative in the longitudinal direction. A combination of this kind, immersed in a fluid, exhibited by means of the galvanometer not only the currents of the natural section of an entire muscle, but also the currents of its artificial sections. Du Bois Reymond, therefore, concluded, that the conditions of the muscular current are fulfilled by assuming in the muscular mass the existence of electromotor centres, each of which may be conceived to be a molecule consisting of an equatorial positive zone and two polar negative zones, these molecules being arranged linearly, so that the polar zones are in the direction of the muscular fibre.

These investigations in no way anticipate the *cause of the electromotor property* of the muscular fibre; they bear only on the laws of its action. They leave very little doubt that the muscular substance during its life, and in the intervals of contraction, is in a state of electric tension; and that there are in it an infinite number of electromotor centres in connection with closed circuits, according to the laws already stated; and which must be infinitely stronger than those derived currents which are procured from a muscle, or a portion of it, by means of the galvanometer.

Du Bois Reymond having observed that the current derived from a longitudinal section and from a *natural transverse section* was generally weaker than that from an artificial transverse section, and that it was even occasionally not obtainable when the electric tension of the muscle was much diminished by cold, found, on further investigation, that it was necessary to admit the existence of a layer of peculiar electromotor elements at the ends of the muscular fibres in contact with the tendon. He denominates this the *parelectronomic* layer, as it produces a current opposed to the general muscular current, and must therefore present its positive elements towards the tendon. For the purpose of including this layer in his general theory, he modifies his conception of the electromotor molecules, and illustrates the entire action by a corresponding change in his model. Instead of the molecules being, as he had denominated them, *peripolar*—possessing an equatorial positive and two polar negative zones, he substitutes for each of such molecules a pair of *dipolar* molecules with their positive poles in contact, and their negative directed away from one another. If, now, the *parelectronomic* layer be conceived as formed of one set only of such dipolar molecules, they must necessarily have their positive poles next the tendinous surface.

This hypothesis not only satisfies the general law of the muscular current, but also affords a reason for the counteracting influence of the natural transverse section, and the facility with which it can be removed by any fluid which corrodes or acts upon the muscular fibre, or by the knife.*

The general Muscular Current.—Nobili discovered, by means of the galvanometer, that a current passed from the toes towards the head of the frog. If the animal be deprived of its skin, and bent backwards so that its feet dip into one vessel and its snout into another, the vessels being filled with a saturated solution of common salt, and connected by the electrodes, the needle will indicate a current in the galvanometer wire from the head to the feet. According to Du Bois Reymond, the general current may, by certain precautions, be detected even in the undissected frog, although the circuit is partially closed by the skin. This current is the resultant of the currents of all the individual muscles of the frog; for Du Bois Reymond found, firstly, that in some muscles the currents set from head to feet, in others in the opposite direction; secondly, that the electromotor power of a muscle is directly as its length and thickness; and, thirdly, that if two muscles are opposed to one another in a circuit, the thicker or the longer overcomes the other.

This general muscular current must therefore exist in every animal possessing muscular arrangements, at least in the four vertebrate classes. It does not, however, necessarily assume the same general direction in all.†

Electric condition of a Muscle during Contraction.—This condition has not yet been accurately determined. Matteucci observed, that when two prepared frog's limbs are so arranged that the nerve of the one lies across the muscles of the other, muscular contraction of the latter induces contraction of the

* The muscular current is investigated at great length, historically and experimentally, in the second and third chapters of section iii. of Du Bois Reymond's *Untersuchungen*.

† The fourth chapter of section iii., in the first part of vol. ii. of the *Untersuchungen*, treats "Of the influence of Contraction on the Muscular Current."

former. He concluded therefore, along with Becquerel, that during muscular contraction there is an evolution of electricity. But the galvanometer, even when a pile of contracting limbs is included in the circuit, gives no decided indication of a current. Matteucci, indeed, has latterly denied the evolution of electricity during muscular contraction, and is inclined to attribute the secondary contraction to another cause. Du Bois Reymond concludes from his investigations, that during contraction the ordinary muscular current is much diminished, if indeed it does not altogether disappear.

The contraction produced by a single act of excitement of a striped muscle is momentary. Any change, therefore, of its ordinary electric condition during such a contraction is too brief to be satisfactorily indicated by the needle. But if a muscle be included in the circuit of the galvanometer, and if, as soon as the deflected needle comes to rest under the influence of the ordinary muscular current, the muscle be put into a state of continuous contraction, or tetanus, by means of strychnine, or an interrupted electric current, the needle will pass backwards beyond zero, and oscillate unsteadily on the negative side till the muscular contractility is exhausted. That this negative deflection is not the result of any influence exerted by the current employed to tetanise the muscles, is shown by the fact that it occurs even when precautions are taken to prevent such an influence; and also by its occurrence when the tetanus is produced by strychnine, and other non-electric means.

If, again, an arrangement be made so as to enable the galvanometer circuit to be closed as soon only as the tetanus has commenced, the needle will be found, during the contraction, only to approach zero more or less, instead of passing to the negative side, indicating therefore a *diminution* of the ordinary muscular current.

That this diminution in the ordinary muscular current is

not due to an increased resistance to conduction in the muscle from its contracted condition is proved by placing the two corresponding muscles of the same animal, one before the other, in the same galvanometer circuit, but reversed so that their currents are opposed to one another, and then tetanising one of them, for when this is done the current of the other acquires the ascendant.

The negative deflection in the first form of the experiment is due, therefore, neither to invasion of the galvanometer circuit by the exciting current, nor to a change in the direction of the ordinary current, nor to increased resistance to conduction. It is the result of the counter-current produced at the platinum electrodes of the galvanometer during the passage of the ordinary muscular current; and this counter-current deflects the needle negatively as soon as the ordinary muscular current begins to lose its influence on it through the annihilating effect of the tetanus. The negative deflection is also in proportion to the intensity of the ordinary current, and is, moreover, increased by the negative effect of the parelectronomic layer, which, according to Du Bois Reymond, is not affected by the act of contraction.

The diminution or cessation of the ordinary muscular current has been employed by Du Bois Reymond to explain certain curious experiments which he has latterly made. The general muscular current of the frog sets, as has been stated, from the toes to the head of the animal. Now, if one of the legs of a frog be paralysed by cutting the sciatic plexus, the feet being then placed in the two conducting vessels for the electrodes of the galvanometer, and the animal tetanised with strychnine, it is evident that the ordinary general current will be diminished in the tetanised limb. Under these circumstances, the galvanometer indicates not only an increase of the upward current in the paralysed limb, but a downward current in the tetanised one. On the human subject a corresponding experiment may be made. The forefinger of each hand being dipped into the saline solutions along with the electrodes of the galvanometer, no deflection occurs. But if all the muscles of one arm be strongly and continuously contracted, a current is indicated as passing from the finger to the shoulder in the contracted arm, and in the opposite direction in the relaxed one. It is evident that this current is the result of the diminution of the ordinary general muscular current in the contracted arm, and the substitution for it of the closed circuit of the ordinary current of the opposite arm.*

The Electric Properties of Nerve.—The resemblance between many actions of the nervous system and certain electric phenomena has frequently impressed physiologists; but investigations of this subject have been so generally mixed up with that of the electricity of muscle, as to lead to no precise result. Matteucci had failed in obtaining any indication of electric currents in nerves; but, nevertheless, the singular parallelism between the two powers could not be overlooked; and Faraday has pointed out the importance of such considerations in his statements regarding electro-nervous action and reaction. More recently, Du Bois Reymond has admitted that electricity and the nervous force are at least equivalents. He was the first to derive electric currents from the nerves, and has procured many most remarkable results from his researches on the subject.

The Electric Condition of a Nerve in the Intervals of Functional Activity.—By employing a very delicate galvanometer, Du Bois Reymond has detected the electric current in nerve, and has determined its laws. They are similar to those of the muscular current, having the same relation to the longitudinal and transverse sections; except that as the nerve presents no natural transverse section, the relative conditions

---

* The general muscular current and the frog-current are treated of in the first chapter of section iii. of the *Untersuchungen*.

of the longitudinal and transverse sections cannot be detected before the nervous cord has been cut across. If a transverse section is in contact with one electrode, and the outer surface of the nerve with the other, the current passes through the galvanometer wire from the latter to the former. The current has the same relative direction whether the transverse section belong to the peripheral or central extremity of the nerve ; and, consequently, when a segment of nerve is doubled in the middle, the current passes from the loop to both sections. The currents derived from the natural longitudinal section—that is, the outer surface of the segment of a nerve—are similar to those derived from the outer aspect of a muscle ; and there is reason for believing that if the small size of the transverse section did not present an obstacle, it also would be found to be in the same condition of electric tension as a corresponding surface in a muscle.

It is a remarkable and important fact that no difference exists in the laws of the electric current in the two classes of cerebro-spinal nerves. The motor and sensory nerves, the dorsal and ventral roots of the spinal nerves, and the nerves of special sense, all present the same electric conditions. It is also remarkable that the spinal marrow and brain afford the same results as the nervous cords. The former has its natural and artificial longitudinal surfaces in a positive electric condition, and its transverse in a negative. In a brain the entire surface covered by the pia mater, whatever complication of form or direction it may assume, being morphologically a longitudinal surface, is electrically positive in relation to artificial sections of the organ.

Du Bois Reymond has discovered a very remarkable condition of a nerve produced by the passage of a continuous electric current through a portion of it. If a continuous current be passed along a portion of a separated segment of nerve, it alters the ordinary electromotor condition of the nerve in such a manner as to increase the force of the ordinary current at that extremity of the segment where they correspond in direction, and to diminish the ordinary current at the other extremity where they are opposed. That a new condition of electric tension is induced by the exciting currents along the entire segment is proved by the galvanometer, which indicates a current in the direction of the exciting current between points equally distant from the middle of the outer surface of the segment, where no galvanometric indications of the ordinary current can be derived.

From the resemblance which this peculiar condition of a nerve bears to the change which Faraday supposes to take place in a wire along which a current is induced by a neighbouring current, Du Bois Reymond adopts the term applied by the former to the induced change, and denominates the new condition of the nerve the *electrotonic* state.

In the electrotonic state the ordinary electromotor elements are evidently polarised, so as to have all their positive and negative poles turned in opposite directions. Du Bois Reymond conceives that the change may be explained by assuming that the ordinary electromotor elements consist each of two dipolar molecules, with their positive poles in contact, and that in the electrotonic condition one of the dipolar molecules of each electromotor element turns on itself from 90° to 100°.*

The Electric Condition of a Nerve during Functional Activity.—As Du Bois Reymond was the first to detect the ordinary electric current in nerves, so we owe to him the only information we possess regarding the electric condition of a nerve during functional activity. The question to be determined is the electric condition of a motor nerve while it is engaged in transmitting to a muscle the stimulus which

---

* The greater part of the first division of vol. ii. of the *Untersuchungen* is occupied with the subject of the nerve-current. The statement of the laws of the nerve-current will be found at pp. 262, 263.

induces contraction, and of a sensory nerve while it is conveying to the sensorium the impression produced at its peripheral extremity. In this investigation it was necessary to produce in the nerve that state of continuous activity which is required for overcoming the inertia of the needle. Such a condition may be procured by mechanical or chemical agents, or by the transmission of interrupted electric currents.

A segment of a nerve having been placed so that its longitudinal and one of its transverse sections are in connection with the electrodes of the galvanometer, if, after the needle has come to rest at the angle of deflection produced by the nerve-current, the other end of the nerve be burned or crushed, the needle will return towards zero a few degrees.

If the extremity of the nerve of a rheoscopic leg be connected with the galvanometer in a similar manner, and the leg itself be confined in one limb of a glass syphon, into which a boiling solution of salt is passed from the opposite limb, the needle will indicate a similar negative variation.

A frog having been fastened down, its sciatic nerve laid bare, cut across at the lower end, and turned up from the thigh, so as to have its longitudinal and transverse sections applied to the electrodes, the needle will exhibit the usual positive deflection. If the animal be now tetanised by strychnine, the needle will return towards zero, and continue to oscillate, approaching zero during each spasm, and receding from it in the intervals of muscular action—that is, while the nerves are not engaged in conveying their stimulus of muscular contraction.

From these experiments it appears, that when a motor or sensory nerve is in a state of functional activity, its ordinary electric condition is altered, as it no longer affords the same galvanometric indications, the current derived from it being diminished.

Electricity passed through a nerve excites that condition

which in a motor cord induces muscular contraction; and in a sensory, common or special, sensation. In order, therefore, to determine the nature of the change which occurs during the functional phase of a nerve, Du Bois Reymond had recourse to electric excitement.

It has already been stated that a nerve is thrown into what has been called the electrotonic condition as long as a continuous electric current passes through a portion of it. Now, as muscular contraction is induced at the closing and opening of the circuit, and at the movements of variation in the density of the exciting current, and as sensation also occurs most vividly under similar conditions, it was necessary to examine the electrotonic state, as produced by variable or intermitting currents. For, as a variable or alternating electrotonic state promised the greatest resemblance to a state of continuous functional activity, its investigation might be expected to throw some light on the change which takes place in the ordinary electric condition of a nerve when it is thrown into action.

Du Bois Reymond found that the galvanometer as distinctly indicated positive and negative variations in the currents which passed through it, when these currents were derived from the extremities of a segment of nerve which was in an intermitting, as when it was in a continuous, electrotonic state. When, however, the interruptions of the exciting primary current become very frequent, the negative variation of the derived currents becomes more marked, and even the positive variation, diminishes. It appeared probable; therefore, that by producing the electrotonic state of the nerve by rapidly alternating currents, the negative condition already indicated might be increased. It was consequently found that if, after the needle had come to rest in the deflection by the ordinary nerve-current from either end of the segment, a rapid series of alternating currents be transmitted through a portion of the cord from an induction-coil (in which each primary current induces an opposite in the other wire), the needle returns to zero.

These experiments appear to prove that when a nerve is completely excited or tetanised by electricity, its usual electro-motor power is diminished or in abeyance; and as a similar loss of electromotor power also accompanies intense functional excitement from ordinary agents, Du Bois Reymond conceives this negative electric condition to be in some manner related to the motor or sensory functional power of the nerve.*

To what is the Polarisation of the Nerve, when in a state of Functional Activity, due?—A nerve is thrown by a current of electricity into an electric condition apparently similar to that in which it is during excitation by its normal stimuli. Is its natural action due, therefore, to electricity? Is its natural electrotonic condition similar to its so-called artificial condition? Is it induced by an electric current? Du Bois Reymond's opinions on this subject are guardedly expressed.† He holds the so-called nervous principle and electricity to be similar or alike. A nerve in action is in an induced electrotonic state; and exhibits a consequent amount of negative variation of its ordinary electric current. The source of the inducing current is not stated; but its direction may be conceived as resulting, during its influence, from the direction and extent of the rotation which occurs in one or the other of the two dipolar molecules, of which the presumed ordinary peripolar electromotor elements consist, and on which the ordinary current of the nerve depends. The induced current

---

* Chap. vii. of the second division of vol. ii. of the *Untersuchungen*.

† See p. xv. of the preface of the *Untersuchungen*, in which Du Bois Reymond states that the electricity in muscle and nerve will probably ultimately prove to be not the mere consequence of their organic processes and actions, but the actual source of their activity.

will be more or less directly centrifugal or centripetal as long as the inducing current or power rotates the peripheral or the central dipolar molecule in each pair of double electromotor elements in the series, round an arc of from 90° to 180°.

The Electric Relations of Centrifugal and Centripetal Nerves are identical.—It would appear to be an important result of Du Bois Reymond's electro-physiological researches that motor and sensory nerves exhibit no difference in their electrical relations. The electrotonic condition can be induced in either direction. It may consequently be inferred that a motor nerve is capable of conveying its mere influence in either direction, but effectively only when it terminates in a muscle. On the other hand, a sensory nerve is capable of conveying its impression both ways, but with effect only when it reaches a sentient centre. In so far as the investigation has been carried by employing electricity as the exciting agent, Du Bois Reymond draws the following conclusion from his experiments: "that in both kinds of nervous fibres the innervation advances in both directions with equal facility."*

The Law of the Excitation of Nerves by the Electrical Current.—When a uniform current is transmitted through the nerve of the prepared limb of a frog, the leg contracts only at the closing and opening of the circuit. In order to keep up the contraction, or to produce a tetanic condition of the muscles, the current must be variable or intermittent. The action of a muscle is not, therefore, equivalent to the strength of the the electric current which may be transmitted along its nerve, but to the variations in it. The law is thus expressed by Du Bois Reymond :—" It is not the absolute value of the density of the current in a motor nerve which corresponds to the contraction of the muscle ; but the variation in this value

---

* *Untersuchungen*, vol. ii. p. 590.

from one moment to another, the excitation being greater the greater and quicker the variations in a given time."* This law is also illustrated by the so-called secondary contractions, which are produced by bringing the nerve of the prepared frog's limb into contact with a muscle during its contraction. If the nerve is laid upon a muscle which is in a tetanic condition, however produced, the muscles of the limb become tetanised also. This secondary tetanus is the result of that alternating negative variation which the ordinary muscular current undergoes during continued contraction.

The nerves of sensation, like those of motion, are more particularly affected at the closing and opening of the circuit, and by variations in the current; but they would also appear to be capable of excitement by a constant current.†

The organised being may be considered electrically as presenting a system of electrical currents, excited by arrangements in the system of its fluids, textures, and organs; the two systems representing each other. The electric disturbances and currents in the Microcosm are represented by similar but grander phenomena in the Macrocosm. These phenomena coincide in both cases with the disposition of component parts, and rank with other forms of material force alternately as causes and effects. But the organised being is, moreover, subordinated to those indwelling psychical powers and impulses by which it enjoys its prescribed freedom.

The Successive Opinions which have been entertained regarding the Action of the Electric Organ.—Walsh concluded that the electricity of the Torpedo is entirely due to the batteries; that their upper and under surfaces are capable, from a state of electric equilibrium, of being instantly thrown, *by a mere*

---

* *Untersuchungen*, vol. i. p. 258. † *Ibid.* p. 283.

‡ In the report, as originally printed, a description of the special electrical apparatus in certain fishes is then given; but, as it is substantially the same as that related in the preceding paper, it is not considered necessary to reproduce it.—EDS.

energy, into a plus and minus state, like that of a charged phial; and that the current results from a conducting medium between their opposite surfaces being supplied naturally or artificially. Galvani originally, Becquerel subsequently, and latterly Matteucci, conceived the batteries to be charged by electricity developed in the brain, or central organ of the apparatus. Rudolphi considered the perpendicular prisms in Torpedo as galvanic piles, the horizontal series in Gymnotus as trough arrangements; but without entering into the details of the comparison. This view of their action does not explain the intermittent and voluntary character of the electric discharges. For, as Valentin has stated, the organs in the fish cannot be complete galvanic batteries, or they would be continually charged, and a current would follow every suitable closure of the circuit. Valentin proposes the following theory of the apparatus. He assumes the structure of the battery to be a series of closed spaces; the series enveloped in thicker, the spaces separated by thinner aponeurotic laminæ; each space being lined by a vascular epithelium, under which the nervous plexuses lie, and filled with fluid. He supposes that there results from the organic or nutritive reactions of the circulating blood, the epithelium, and the contained fluid of each space, a certain amount of electric force, not, however, sufficient to overcome the insulating obstacle opposed to it in the aponeurotic walls; all the spaces in the battery are, therefore, so far only insulated electrical spaces. As soon, however, as the will of the animal determines a flow of nervous force into the spaces, the organic reactions become so much exalted that the resolved electric force overcomes the insulating power of the laminæ, and a current is produced; the current being confined to the series by their thicker aponeurotic walls.* This theory, although it may account for a sudden increase of electricity in the organ,

* "Electricität der Thiere" in Wagner's *Handwörterbuch*.

affords no explanation of its progressive character ; the current is not accounted for.

The theory which most satisfactorily combines the anatomico-physiological as well as the electrical phenomena of the apparatus, is that lately propounded by Professor Pacini of Florence.* Having discovered the important anatomical fact that the nerves are distributed on one surface only of the electrical elements of the battery, while the vessels and nucleated cellular texture occupy the other; he finds in these structural peculiarities the condition which is wanting in Valentin's theory to explain the progression of the electricity. Pacini refers the electrical batteries in the fish to two forms of structure, and two modes of action; of the first and simplest form, the Torpedo affords the type, of the second and more complicated, the Gymnotus. The batteries of Malapterurus are probably referable to the form in Torpedo, those of Raia certainly to that in Gymnotus. In the Torpedo, according to Pacini, the action is analogous to that which takes place in a thermo-electric pile, inasmuch as he conceives it to depend upon a peculiar dynamical difference in the condition of the two surfaces of each diaphragm of this binary type of pile. The nerve-surface and the vasculo-cellular surface of the electric diaphragm correspond to the bismuth and copper, or bismuth and antimony elements of a thermo-electric arrangement; the nervous influence in the former taking the place of the heat applied in the latter. There is here assumed, what on other grounds is highly probable, that the electrical and nervous forces are correlative; and here it must be admitted that in Torpedo, as pointed out by John Hunter,† the bulk of the nerves in relation to the batteries is much greater than in Gymnotus, which exemplifies Pacini's second or *ternary type* of animal battery. When the Torpedo,

---

* *Sulla struttura intima dell' organo elettrico del gymnoto, e di altri pesci elettrici*, 1852. † *Phil. Trans.* 1773.

therefore, wills a shock, or when, through the reflex action of its electrical nervous centre, a shock is induced, a sudden and copious nervous influx flows over the under surfaces of its electric diaphragms, the upper surfaces are thrown into an opposite electrical condition, and a current is the consequence.

Pacini refers the structure of the battery in Gymnotus to a ternary type. This type presents a negative element, which consists of the fibrous layer on which the nerves ramify, together with the fluid which it bounds below; a positive element formed by the ridged vasculo-cellular layer, and the conducting inter-diaphragmatic fluid. The vasculo-cellular layer predominating in this ternary type over the nervous, Pacini conceives the electricity to be evolved in the organic actions of the vasculo-cellular layer under the influence of the nerves. In other words, the will of the Gymnotus, or the reflex action of its electrical nervous centre, directs an influence along the nerves of its batteries over the fibro-nervous layer, which suddenly exciting the nutritive or other organic actions of the highly-developed vasculo-cellular layer, an electrical disturbance is produced, with an opposite electrical condition of the fibro-nervous and vasculo-cellular layers of the diaphragms, and consequently a current through the series. Pacini compares the wide-meshed fibrous layer, on the under surface of which the nerves ramify, to the hollow cylinder of porous clay, which in a Bunsen's or a Grove's galvanic arrangement separates the negative from the positive elements.

The Batteries of the Fish are Independent Electromotor Structures.—From the observations of Pacini, the terminations of the nerves appear to form important elements in the structure of the battery. On physiological grounds, however, it appears probable that the peculiar texture of the electric diaphragm is itself the seat of the electromotor power. As an ultimate muscular fibre contracts, although entirely separated from the nerve, it remains to be determined whether an appreciable electric discharge cannot be procured from an isolated element of the battery. If so, it may be presumed that the force which in the form of a contraction is elicited from a muscular fibre by the influence of a motor nerve is replaced by electric force when the same kind of nerve influences an ultimate element of the electric structure. The laws of the electromotor power of the electric organ cannot be determined by experiments on its entire mass, or on rudely-separated portions of it. The parts must be selected and removed on precise anatomical and physiological principles; and as Du Bois Reymond has stated his intention of investigating the electrical organs of the fish, his previous researches show that he will be guided in his proceedings by such considerations.

If the battery is separated from its nervous centre by section of the trunks of all the nerves which supply it, it will still afford discharges if the nerves are irritated; and the different portions of the organ, even the smallest, will do so likewise if the nerves which are distributed to them be similarly treated. Matteucci, who has latterly admitted that the nervous centre is not the source of the electricity in the fish, states that if even a minute fragment of the battery of the Torpedo is irritated by a spiculum of glass, it will yield a discharge.*

Peculiar Character of the Electricity evolved from the Batteries of the Fish.—The nature of the force evolved from the batteries of the fish is evinced by the shock and spark, by its influence on the galvanometer, its magnetising and heating powers, and its chemical action. The absolute quantity of electricity which the animal can put in circulation at each effort is enormous. For, as it can decompose water, and form magnets, it must greatly exceed the quantity which can be produced by any ordinary electrical machine. It is probable,

* *Traité des Phénomènes Electro-physiologiques,* etc.

therefore, that the animal has the power of continuing the evolution for a sensible time; so that its successive discharges rather resemble those of a voltaic arrangement intermitting in its action than those of a Leyden apparatus charged and discharged many times in succession. At the same time the power is one of low intensity, so that a dry skin wards it off, though a moist one conducts it.*

It is remarkable that the electric fishes, although affected like other animals by ordinary electric shocks, do not appear to feel the electric discharges which are produced by themselves, or by other individuals of the same species.

The Condition of the Water which surrounds the Fish at the moment of discharge of the Electric Organs.—At the moment of a discharge in water, the currents between the opposite surfaces of Torpedo, or between the ends of Gymnotus, instead of being confined to a transverse area of limited extent, as when they pass along a wire during a discharge in air, must be diffused through a considerable extent of the water surrounding the fish. The entire current force of the batteries must, in fact, be subdivided into numerous subordinate axes of force arranged in lines which come round the margins of Torpedo from back to belly, and along the sides of Gymnotus from head to tail. There is therefore at the moment of discharge an atmosphere of power around the fish which, in the language employed by Mr. Faraday in reference to the magnetic force, may be considered as disposed in sphondyloids determined by the lines, or rather shells, of force. "The magnet, with its surrounding sphondyloid of power, may be considered as analogous in its condition to a voltaic battery immersed in water or any other electrolyte, or to a Gymnotus or Torpedo at the moment when these creatures, at their own will, fill the surrounding fluid with lines of electric force." It is evident, therefore, that another fish, placed so that its antero-posterior axis is in the

---

* Faraday, *Researches in Electricity*, vol. i. p. 101.

direction of lines of inductive action in the water, will be affected less powerfully by the circulating electric power than if it were placed across these lines. Mr. Faraday* found that while the Gymnotus can stun and kill **fishes** which are in various positions in relation to its own **body, it can, moreover,** by throwing itself so as to form a coil enclosing **the fish, the** latter representing a diameter across it, so concentrate **its** currents of one side as to strike it motionless as if by lightning. The Torpedo would also appear, from the observations of Dr. Davy, instinctively to elevate or arrange its margin so as to adjust the **direction of its currents to the position of the** object **through which** it wishes to pass them. "Thus," as Mr. Faraday observes, "the very conducting power which the **water has,** that which it gives to the moistened skin of the fish or animal to be struck, the extent of surface by which the fish and water conducting the charge to it are in contact, all conduce to favour and increase the shock upon the doomed animal."

* *Phil. Trans.* 1839.

XVII.—ON THE CONFERVA WHICH VEGETATES ON THE SKIN OF THE GOLD-FISH.*

LADY BRISBANE having observed that a gold-fish which had lived for some time in a glass vase presented a very unusual appearance, as if a quantity of cotton were attached to its dorsal fin and tail, requested Mr. Bryson to explain the circumstance. That gentleman, having seen in the *Microscopic Journal* a notice of the occurrence of vegetables parasitic on living animals,† at once suspected that the cotton-like substance was a plant. Lady Brisbane kindly allowed him to remove the fish to Edinburgh for more accurate examination. Mr. Bryson sent it to me, with the information that the peculiar substance had made its appearance on the animal six weeks before.

The fish had been conveyed to town in a jug of water, but had died on the journey, so that I lost the opportunity of observing the parasite during the life of the animal. The water had begun to be tinged with blood and colouring matter from incipient putrefaction. The results of the examination were not, therefore, so satisfactory as I could have wished.

The parasite, when examined under water, presented to the naked eye a continuous mass consisting of minute filaments about three-quarters of an inch in length and extending all along the dorsal and posterior edge of the tail-fins. The

* Read before the Botanical Society of Edinburgh, January 13, 1842.
† See *Ann. and Mag. Nat. Hist.* vol. viii. p. 229, and p. 10.

filaments, although individually transparent, were so close to one another and so numerous that the mass appeared opaque. When the lateral portions of the mass were separated along the median line, so as to display the free edges of the fins, these edges were observed to be shrivelled, not, as appeared to me, by a process of ulceration, but by an irregular interstitial absorption. This absorption was more evident along the bounding edge of the parasitic mass, where it presented the appearance of a furrow, in which the parasite grew with more luxuriance than elsewhere.

What was the exact state of the surface to which the parasite adhered I am not prepared to say. I could detect no substance corresponding to the false membrane described by certain observers as constituting the soil on which vegetate those parasites which infest the air-cells of birds; neither could I satisfy myself that the substance which formed the infested surface was merely the mucous covering of the fish. I am inclined, however, to lean to the latter opinion, for two reasons—first, because the surface exhibited the pigment cells of the skin; and secondly, because I detected solitary individuals attached to the broad scales of the back.

Each plant consists of a jointed filament, in some individuals single, in others dividing dichotomously towards the attached extremity, but more frequently near the summit. The filament tapers gradually from the base to the summit. The former is very slightly dilated, rounded and closed at the extremity, which is destitute of appendages. The latter varies in different individuals under different circumstances, as will be afterwards described. The articulations are elongated, varying in length from ten to fifty times their breadth. Basal articulations were met with, having a breadth of the 800th of an inch; acute or barren terminal articulations were about the 2000th of an inch. The length of the articulations increased towards the summit, the basal being in general the shortest.

Each articulation was tubular, filled with a transparent fluid in which floated granules. Their walls appeared to be homogeneous; I could detect no double membrane, but at the spot where the neighbouring articulations were connected, the internal surface of each appeared to leave the external surface of the filament so as to form by conjunction the flat diaphragms. It would appear, then, that the walls of the cells are originally double, but have coalesced in the progress of growth. Towards the basal extremity of each articulation, generally close upon it, but sometimes a little removed, is a globular transparent vesicle. This vesicle varied in size, directly as the diameter of the articulation. I did not observe this vesicle in any instance exhibiting a nucleus or granular contents. I occasionally observed it floating free in the fluid of the articulation; but this might have been the effect of violence. The fluid of certain of the articulations contained granules about the 5000th or 6000th of an inch. Others again contained no granular matter. These granules did not exhibit molecular motion. I, on more than one occasion, observed a steady onward motion of the granules and transparent vesicle; but this appeared to depend on unequal pressure and level of the object-plates.

From certain spots on the external surface of the articulations—spots which appeared to be arranged in no appreciable order, there sprung bundles of very numerous, cylindrical, elongated, and transparent filaments. These were so numerous and so convoluted and twisted as to defy every attempt to disentangle them; in fact, they occasionally obscured altogether the stems or primary filaments of the plant. They arose from all the articulations except the basal and terminal, at least I never saw them springing from the latter, although I occasionally saw them arising from what I took to be the upper end of a basal articulation. They were quite cylindrical, as thick at their free as at their attached extremities, and about $\frac{1}{1000}$th of an inch in diameter. In structure they were homogeneous, apparently gelatinous, and covered with a fine membrane.

This parasite propagates by spores formed in its terminal articulations, which are developed into spore-cases for that purpose. Having observed terminal articulations in all stages of development, I may state the changes they undergo to be the following :—

1. A perfectly barren terminal articulation is elongated, spear-shaped, transparent, without granules.

2. A terminal articulation which is destined to become a spore-case does not elongate so much, and is from the first, or at least from an early period of its growth, full of granules, which give it a grey colour. It is also elongated, fusiform, and connected to the penultimate articulation by a narrow neck.

3. It becomes more distinctly fusiform, retaining its other characters.

4. The granules appear here and there to increase in size, or at least larger granules appear diffused through the mass. These larger granules or vesicles are more or less transparent. The articulation now becomes cylindrical, with rounded extremities and a constricted neck.

5. The articulation increasing in dimensions, but retaining the same shape, contains a packed mass of perfectly transparent globules, which are uncompressed and without appreciable internal structure.

6. The fertile articulation or spore-case bursts; that is, I have seen it with its contents hanging together from a rupture in its walls.

Proceeding to observe the changes which the spore itself undergoes, I detected lying here and there, among the attached extremities of the primary filaments, groups of spores corresponding in numbers and characters to those which I had seen escaping from the spore-cases.

The most careful examination revealed no nuclei or contents of any kind in these transparent vesicles, which in this their perfect state were about $\frac{1}{1000}$th of an inch in diameter.

The first step in the development was an opacity in the spore, due to the development of granules similar to those which have been so often mentioned.

2. The vessel elongates.

3. It appears double; that is, two-celled.

4. Both cells elongate and acquire additional cells at the extremity, which is known to be the terminal extremity by secondary filaments appearing on it.

A sufficient number of examples could not be met with to trace these changes with greater minuteness, so that certain circumstances which I was anxious to detect, and to which I shall allude immediately, escaped observation.

I may state that I met with one example of the incipient development of a dichotomous primary filament. It occurred at the point of attachment of a fertile articulation, and might therefore be considered, in some measure, as one mode in which the primary filament or axis of the individual is continued, when its elongation would otherwise have been interrupted by the development of the formal terminal articulation into a spore-case.

This incipient lateral filament appeared as a conical projection from the side of the upper extremity of the penultimate articulation. I could not make out the existence of a diaphragm at the base of the little cone; as however it, as well as the penultimate articulation, was full of granular matter, a diaphragm might have existed, although I did not observe it. A clear vesicle, such as I have formerly described, was situated at the terminal extremity of the penultimate articulation; but whether it belonged to the new articulation or to the old one, I could not determine.

I have been unable to determine, in a satisfactory manner

the exact nature of the clear vesicle which is found in each of the articulations. It may be the nucleus of the original cell of the articulation; but if it be so, it must be considered as a barren nucleus; having increased in size proportional to its cell, having lost the normal appearance of a nucleus, and having never performed the function of one. May it not, with greater propriety, be considered as some form of the endochrome, a result of development of the granules of the articulation? It exactly resembles the spores of the terminal articulations, which, as has been already stated, originate in the granular endochrome of this articulation.

The parasitic plant I have now described resembles in many respects those found by Hannover and Stilling on the newt and frog. As in these, the filaments swarmed with infusorial animalcules, *Monads, Bursariæ*, etc. Some of these doubtless lived among the filaments while the fish was still alive; others, again, as the *Bursariæ*, must have taken up their residence there after the commencement of putrefaction. Hannover, in Müller's *Archiv*, 1842, page 73, has described the development of the conferva of the frog and newt, and has mentioned the animal-like movements of the spores. Mr. Daniel Cooper (*Microscopic Journal*) has frequently observed a cotton-like conferva on the gills and fins of gold-fish. From a preserved specimen, an examination of which was afforded me by Professor Balfour, I am inclined to believe in the existence of more than one species of this genus of parasitic Algæ.

XVIII.—HISTORY OF A CASE IN WHICH A FLUID PERIODICALLY EJECTED FROM THE STOMACH CONTAINED VEGETABLE ORGANISMS (SARCINA VENTRICULI) OF AN UNDESCRIBED FORM.

Mr. ———, aged 19, consulted me about a stomach-complaint, under which he had been labouring for four months, and which had more or less resisted every attempt made for its removal. He informed me that he considered it to be waterbrash; that it attacked him on awakening in the morning with a feeling of distension of the stomach; that, without any effort of vomiting, a quantity of fluid, varying in volume from two-thirds to a whole wash-hand basinful, passed up from his stomach; that after this he was quite relieved, and experienced no further inconvenience till the evening of the same day, when, without decided distension, sounds as of a fluid boiling or bubbling, and proceeding from the region of his stomach, were perceptible to himself and to those around him; that he slept well enough, but was generally attacked in the usual manner next morning. Such was my patient's own account of his case.

On examining more particularly into the symptoms, I could ascertain nothing positive. His tongue and pulse were natural; he had no headache, nausea, or thirst; no tumour could be detected in the epigastrium, and no pain on pressure was complained of in the region of the stomach. The bowels were moved daily, and the stools were normal. His appetite was not affected, and the usual articles of diet appeared to agree with him. He was thin, but had a good complexion, and his flesh was firm. He stated that he had formerly been very fat, but that this had left him before the accession of his stomach-complaint. I was informed that one of his testicles had never descended beyond the groin.

Of the various remedies which had been tried for his relief, prussic acid appeared upon the whole to have exercised the greatest influence over the disease, preventing the attacks with considerable certainty for several days in succession.

Being unable to make up my mind as to the exact nature of the case, but conceiving it probable that there might be ulceration or some other organic lesion of the stomach, I ordered croton-oil, frictions of the epigastric region, and the internal remedies to be discontinued. I also requested that the ejected fluid might be preserved for my inspection.

Next day I found that he had had an attack in the morning as usual. No new symptoms presented themselves.

On examining the ejected fluid, I was struck with the truth of what had been stated to me, that it smelt like fermenting worts, with a faint acid odour. It appeared, after having stood for a few hours, moderately transparent and of a light brown colour. It had deposited in the bottom of the basin a quantity of a ropy matter, of a granular appearance; and on the surface was a mass of froth like the head of a pot of porter.

By a consideration of all the circumstances of the case, I was now induced to conceive it possible that this and other cases of similar stomach-complaints might depend on fermentation of the contents of the organ. Such a fermentation might, I presumed, be primary—that is, induced by the chemical constitution and relative conditions of the contents of the stomach; or it might be secondary—that is, induced by circumstances in the condition of the organ standing in the relations of primary causes of the whole complaint. But, whatever might be supposed to be the cause of the presumed fermentation, it appeared to me highly probable that, if it had really taken place, it would be indicated by the remains of ferment-vegetables in the ejected fluid.

In the meantime, till I had examined the fluid more minutely, I merely regulated my patient's diet. Animal food was recommended; vegetables and malt liquors were forbidden, and a little brandy was ordered in water for drink.

I now proceeded to examine the fluid ejected from the stomach, and in proceeding to do so, I expected, if I found any vegetable form at all, to see some of the globular or moniliform algæ, which it now appears pretty certain are concomitants of certain of the fermentations. What was my astonishment, then, to find, in the first drop I examined, not the vegetables I was led to expect, but numerous individuals of a form, with allies of which the zoologist is **familiar**! Drop after drop exhibited the same specific form, with a precision which convinced me that I had now to deal with an organism which, whether animal or vegetable, was closely allied to certain genera of BACCILLARIÆ, and much more closely to the genus GONIUM among the VOLVOCINÆ.

Before I proceed with the history of the case, or with the description of the organism which characterised it, it may be well to state that, in addition to a few fragments and shreds of undigested food, the ejected fluid presented the following microscopic elements:—

1st. Fecula-cells, globular, ovoidal, and kidney-shaped, with well-marked hila of attachment. Some of these cells were transparent and empty, others were full of starch-granules, and reacted powerfully with iodine. These cells were at first presumed, and were afterwards proved by comparison, to be nothing more than the remains of wheaten bread.

2*d*. Much larger, more irregular, flaccid, ruptured, or half-emptied cells, full of granular matter, which reacted with iodine, and were recognised as fecula-cells of the potato, as they appear after boiling.

3*d*. Minute shreds of muscular fibre, cellular tissue, and fat-cells, remains of the food.

4*th*, Globules or globular masses, from 500 to 100 of an inch in diameter, apparently oily, and presumed, although as to this no inquiries were instituted, to be some form of the chyme.

5*th*. Occasionally, but rarely, portions of bran, consisting of the perisperm of the wheat, recognisable by its internal surface presenting irregular-sized, ovoidal or hexagonal shallow foveæ, with included fecula-cells.

6*th*. The organisms themselves, which I at once recognised as belonging to the vegetable kingdom, and considered either as the cause of the symptoms in my patient's case, or at least as very remarkable and important concomitants.

I may state that these organisms could not have been swallowed in the water used for drink, as the water employed by the family for that purpose was regularly passed through a stone filter. I used every precaution also in ascertaining that they could not have been introduced along with any article of diet, and in satisfying myself that they were not portions of any animal or vegetable tissue.

I now recommended a return to the use of the prussic acid. I ascertained that it exercised a decided influence over the disease. After some time, however, I became satisfied that it acted more by enabling the stomach to retain its contents, than by any direct influence in preventing the formation of the fluid itself.

The case proceeded for about a fortnight without any change in the symptoms, the prussic acid being regularly taken at bed-time, with the effect of putting off the attacks occasionally for a day or two at a time.

I now determined to give creosote, from a belief that it would not only act, as the prussic acid had done, in preventing the ejection of the fluid, but that it would also put a stop to its formation. This I conceived it would do, whether the disease arose from a simple fermentation of the contents of the stomach, or from the development of the organisms as a primary cause.

A drop of creosote was ordered every night at bed-time. Supper was forbidden; a very light dinner of animal food was recommended, and breakfast indicated as the principal meal. Cessation of his somewhat sedentary habits, active country exercise on foot and horseback, and attention to the bowels were insisted upon.

A decided improvement now took place. The attacks, instead of recurring almost every morning, now took place only on the fifth or sixth morning, and latterly at intervals of eight or ten days. The fluid ejected also diminished in quantity, not exceeding six or eight ounces.

The attacks again increased slightly in frequency, and in quantity of fluid ejected, but this was at once controlled by a gradual increase of the dose to four drops at bed-time. It also appeared advisable to divide the dose, so as to take two drops in the forenoon and three or four about one hour and a-half after dinner, so as to stop the formation of the fluid. This effect my patient felt satisfied the creosote produced, as the bubbling or crackling sensation in the stomach usually ceased after taking his dose.

The bowels were now acted upon rather smartly, so as to promote the action downwards from the stomach.

At the present date I have it not in my power to state that the complaint is removed, although the attacks are much less frequent, and the quantity of fluid diminished. The creosote, however, has a most decided control over it, and will, I am inclined to believe, ultimately cure it. The disease, indeed, may depend on the patient's time of life, and on the peculiarity of his constitution, and may gradually disappear even without medicine, as a consequence of increased corporeal vigour.

The Structure, Mode of Reproduction, and Development of Sarcina ventriculi, the Parasite detected in the ejected Fluid.—The following description is drawn up from examination of the ejected fluid for a period of nearly two months.

In every instance the organisms presented themselves in the form of square or slightly oblong plates. The thickness of an individual was about one-eighth of the length of one of its sides. Under a moderate power the sides and angles appeared straight and well-defined; but under deeper glasses, the angles were rounded, and the sides sinuous; appearances which resulted from the uncompressed forms of the component cells in their particular directions. The flat surfaces were divided into four secondary squares by two rectilinear transparent spaces, which, passing from side to side, intersected one another in the centre like two cross garden-walks.

Each of the four secondary squares was again divided by similarly arranged, but more feebly developed spaces, into the four ternary squares.

The sixteen ternary squares thus constituted, when examined with deeper powers, were seen to consist each of four cells, which were not separated by transparent spaces, but simply by dissepiments formed by the conjunction of the walls of contiguous cells.

These sixty-four cells of which the organism consisted did not present in perfect individuals distinct nuclei; although in certain instances appearances presented themselves, having relation to the reproduction of the organism, and falling to be described in another part of the paper.

The individual organisms were transparent and slightly

yellow or brown. When carefully examined under favourable circumstances the cell-walls appeared rigid, and could be perceived passing from one flat surface to the other as dissepiments. These dissepiments, as well as the transparent spaces, were from compression of contiguity rectilinear, and all the angles right angles; but the bounding cells bulged somewhat irregularly on the edges of the organism, by reason of the freedom from pressure.

These circumstances gave the whole organism the appearance of a wool-pack, or of a soft bundle bound with cord, crossing it four times at right angles and at equal distances.

From these very striking peculiarities of form, I propose for it the generic term SARCINA.*

Perfect individual SARCINÆ, of the species now under consideration, vary from 800 to 1000 of an inch linear along each of their sides. They are, as has been stated, slightly brown or yellow under a high power—under moderate glasses they appear dark, and are defined with difficulty on account of the frequent reflections of the light by the dissepiments. Iodine does not react with them, as with starch, but tinges them deep brown or yellow. They shrivel but slightly in alcohol. In nitric acid, even after boiling for some time, the sixteen ternary squares retain their relative position, but diminished and shrivelled, appearing like minute crystalline granules arranged in a square. So persistent are those arrangements of granules in boiling nitric acid, that I at one time suspected the existence of silicious loricæ, or isolated raphides, but as I could not detect the same forms or arrangements in the ashes of the evaporated and calcined fluid, I do not now believe in their existence.

This species of SARCINA, therefore, consists of sixteen four-celled frustules, imbedded in a square tablet of a transparent

* SARCINULA would have been more appropriate, had not Lamarck already applied the term to a genus of polyps.

texture, as in the GONIUMS. The four-celled frustules correspond to the cells or globules; the tablet to the phycomater or gelatinous matrix of certain of the ULVACEÆ.

The generation of SARCINA is fissiparous, each individual dividing into four. This is proved by the following circumstances:—

1*st*. Specimens are frequently met with, which, instead of 16 ternary squares and 64 ultimate cells, exhibit 64 ternary squares and 256 ultimate cells. Such specimens are not, I conceive, to be considered as individuals, in as much as—1. Their four component squares are very loosely connected together. 2. One or two of the squares may be wanting, or two or more of these may remain attached by the angles—an arrangement never represented in the primary squares themselves.

2*d*. Large specimens are occasionally met with, which have most of the characters of composite individuals—that is, of individuals about to divide into four. Such specimens do not present 256, but only 64 ultimate cells, and these, exhibiting appearances not easily defined, but apparently consisting of four opaque spots, as if each cell were about to be divided into four parts, or were in the act of producing within itself four new cells.

Such appearances rendered it difficult to say whether certain specimens were simple individuals or composite—single adults, or adults about to divide each into four young ones.

I therefore conclude that a perfect individual SARCINA consists of 64 ultimate cells, but that as soon as each of these again divides into or produces four new cells, the individual becomes composite, and may forthwith divide into four young ones, each of these again to undergo the same quaternary division.

Such a mode of generation will account for what I frequently observed—two, three, or four SARCINÆ attached by their angles only, as in the baccillarian genera. It also explains why I could never detect more than four so united. It may account for the circumstance that the SARCINÆ were found grouped as it were in colonies, in certain portions of the ropy fluid, some drops containing numbers of them, others none at all.

Such is the structure, mode of reproduction and of development, of this species of SARCINA.

In tracing these out, it cannot but have been observed how beautiful is the symmetry of all the arrangements—how the parts of the individual are arranged in the square—how these parts increase in numbers in a geometrical progression—1, 4, 16, 64, 256,—and lastly, how the species propagates according to the same law, 4 in the first generation, 16 in the second, 64 in the third, 256 in the fourth, 1024 in the fifth, and so on with a rapidity peculiar to such a series of numbers.

Is SARCINA an animal or a vegetable? is it one of the infusorial Polygastrica, or a minute Alga? In order to give a satisfactory answer to this question, it becomes necessary to analyse the groups to which SARCINA is most closely allied.

Putting out of view for the present the FRAGILLARIÆ, DIATOMACLÆ, and other gonioid organisms, the animal or vegetable nature of which is yet a matter of doubt, I shall proceed to Müller's genus GONIUM, the genus of all others to which SARCINA has the greatest affinity.

The genus GONIUM consists of composite polygastric animalcules, each corpuscle of the whole animal having, according to Ehrenberg, the organisation of a monad, oral appendages, visceral sacs, etc. Ehrenberg does not enumerate eye-points among the characters of the family to which the GONIUMS belong (VOLVOCINÆ). Without coming to any decision as to whether the red points on certain species of GONIUM be really eye-points, or merely optical illusions,[*] I may state at once,

---

[*] It may be well to state, that the red dots do not appear in all the species,

that I am much inclined to believe that the genus GONIUM, as at present constituted, contains both animal and vegetable species—the former characterised by oral appendages, voluntary motions (eye-points?), the latter by their simple celluloglobular formation. GONIUM PECTORALE (*Pectoralina hebraica*, B. St. Vincent), GONIUM PUNCTATUM, contrary to the opinion of Bory St. Vincent and others, appear to be true composite animals.

But Ehrenberg has here, as in many other instances, decided for the animal nature of organisms in which even his experienced eye could not detect the characters of the family.

Such is the case with GONIUM HYALINUM, GONIUM GLAUCUM, and probably with GONIUM TRANQUILLUM.

These three species appear to consist merely of cells full of chlorophylle imbedded in the square plate which corresponds to the outer envelope of the NOSTOCHINÆ.

To such forms belongs SARCINA. It exhibits no mouths, no oral appendages, no visceral sacs, and its cells, instead of having the gelatinous appearance so familiar to the observer of the animal infusorials, are clear, transparent as if empty, and have that consistency of wall characteristic of vegetable structure.

Believing SARCINA to be a vegetable, I may state, in reference to its characters, that they are of a kind which distinguish it from all the gonioid plants at present known. It differs most essentially from PECTORALINA HEBRAICA of Bory St. Vincent, which, as we have already stated, appears to be a true animal. It makes the nearest approach to GONIUM HYALINUM, which with GONIUM GLAUCUM and GONIUM TRANQUILLUM, even Ehrenberg himself seems inclined to hand over to the botanists under the generic term GONIDIUM.

The generic characters of SARCINA are to be found in the

and it is interesting to observe, that those species in which they have not been detected are the very species in which oral appendages apparently do not exist.

predominance of the constituent cells over the outer coat or lorica, in each frustule being four-celled, and in the entire freedom of these from all coloured contents. Of the specific characters of a single species much cannot be said.

I define the genus thus :—

SARCINA. Plants coriaceous, transparent, consisting of sixteen or sixty-four four-celled square frustules, arranged parallel to one another in a square transparent matrix.

Species 1. SARCINA VENTRICULI, *mihi.* Pl. xi. Fig. 13. Frustules 16; colour light brown; transparent matrix very perceptible between the frustules, less so around the edges; size 800 to 1000 inch. Hab. the human stomach.

As soon as I had detected the SARCINA, I called upon my friend Dr. George Wilson for an analysis of the fluid. The following is his report :—

"The liquid sent me for examination was thick and viscid; by standing, it deposited a large quantity of ropy matter mixed with portions of undigested food, and when filtered through paper it had a pale brownish-yellow colour, and was quite transparent. It still contained much animal matter in solution, becoming opaque and flocculent when boiled, and giving a very copious precipitate with infusion of galls. It also precipitated nitrate of silver densely, and when evaporated to dryness, and exposed to a full red heat in a platina crucible, left an ash containing much chloride of sodium. It had a peculiar acid odour, which all who have observed compare to that of sour beer; it reddened litmus powerfully, and effervesced sharply with alkaline carbonates. These remarks, and all that follow, apply without exception to portions of liquid ejected at various intervals during a period of four weeks.

"To determine the nature of the acid which existed so abundantly in the ejected matter, a pint of the filtered liquid was distilled in a retort, till nine-tenths of the whole had passed over. The fluid in the receiver was colourless but opalescent, and a flocculent matter was diffused through it; it reddened litmus strongly, and gave, with nitrate of silver, a precipitate insoluble in nitric acid, and soluble in ammonia. The latter reaction seemed to point to the acid as the hydrochloric, but as the liquid had not the odour of that acid, and the presence of flocculent matter showed that substances not truly volatile, had been passing over with the vapour during distillation, I suspected that the precipitation of the silver salt had resulted from chloride of sodium transferred from the liquid in the retort by a similar process of mere mechanical convection. To decide this point, a portion of the distilled fluid was evaporated to dryness in a porcelain capsule, and strongly heated; distilled water poured upon the residue precipitated nitrate of silver, indicating the presence of some fixed metallic chloride.* To remove this, the liquid was filtered from the animal matter it held in suspension, and slowly distilled a second time in a capacious retort. The product of this distillation was colourless and transparent, and possessed a strong acid reaction, but gave not the slightest haze with nitrate of silver. It retained the vomit-smell, and along with it a faint acid odour, which was not perceptible to myself, but which others recognised, and pronounced to be that of vinegar.

* Berzelius has particularly pointed out the difficulty of distilling viscid animal fluids in retorts, without the transference of non-volatile matters, which appear to be projected upwards by the bursting of the bubbles of vapour produced during tumultuous ebullition.—*Traité de Chimie*, tome vii. p. 616, Ed. 1832.

Liebig has likewise called the attention of chemists to the remarkable power which vapours possess, of carrying along with them portions of bodies (such as nitre, boracic acid, chloride of sodium), which in their solid form resist dissipation by very high temperatures. When such bodies are dissolved in water, its vapour, even when far below the boiling point, determines their volatilisation along with itself.—*Organic Chemistry in its Application to Agriculture*, 1st Ed. p. 111.

"To ascertain the nature of the acid, six ounces of the twice-distilled liquid were neutralised with lime-water and evaporated to dryness. The lime-salt was then transferred to a tube-retort, and distilled with sulphuric acid slightly diluted. A colourless liquid collected in the receiver, which was at once recognised, by its odour, to contain acetic acid. This experiment was very carefully repeated with four portions of liquid distilled from different specimens of the ejected matter; the result was the same with all, an acid liquid was procured, which all who smelt it pronounced to be acetic acid.

"I was the more careful in repeating these trials, that Berzelius has shown that in the analysis of animal fluids, other volatile odorous acids may readily be mistaken for acetic acid. He particularly notices that lactic acid, accompanied by a chloride, may seem to be an acetate, when moistened with sulphuric acid ; the sharp smell of the evolved hydrochloric acid passing for the peculiar odour of the acetic. Even so expert a chemist as Leopold Gmelin has been deceived in this way.* But the liquid from the stomach, the lime-water, and the sulphuric acid, were all tested and found to contain no chloride, nor did the distilled liquid contain any ; moreover, the evidence of the acid being the acetic, did not depend on the perception for a moment of a faint and fleeting odour, when the salt was moistened with sulphuric acid ; a drachm of liquid was obtained by each distillation, so that the odour could be perceived and identified by many persons. In further trial of the acid, it was ascertained, that when digested in the cold on recently-precipitated oxide of lead, it formed a soluble salt, having a sugary taste, and possessing an alkaline reaction. The acquirement of the latter property, depending on the formation of a subsalt of lead, has been shown by Liebig to be distinctive of acetic acid.†

* Berzelius, *Op. et. loc. citat.*
† Graham's *Elements of Chemistry,* p. 785.

"The proportion of acetic acid in the twice-distilled fluid was ascertained in the usual way with the alkalimeter, by finding the quantity of carbonate of potass required to neutralise it. It was found by several trials, that, on an average, an ounce of the liquid neutralised 0·4 gr. of the carbonate; a quart (32 oz.) would therefore neutralise 12·8 gr. which correspond to 9 gr. of the hydrated (crystallisable) acetic acid $HO + C_4 H_3 O_3$.

"The liquid remaining in the retort after the first distillation was now examined and found still to be strongly acid. This property was traced in part to the presence of a small portion of free hydrochloric acid. The large amount of chloride of sodium which accompanied it made it difficult of detection; nor did I succeed in ascertaining its proportion. But I satisfied myself that it occurred only in small quantity by the following experiments:—Some ounces of the filtered liquid, along with a portion of red oxide of lead, were placed in a flask provided with a bent tube dipping into a wineglass, containing a very weak infusion of blue cabbage. The flask was then heated till the liquid boiled, and, by the quantity of vapour sent through the infusion, made the latter boil also. The cabbage was reddened, but not perceptibly weakened in tint; whereas, had free hydrochloric acid been present in any quantity, it must have been deprived of hydrogen by the metallic oxide and chlorine evolved. When the experiment was repeated, with the addition to the flask of a little sulphuric acid, the infusion was bleached in a few seconds. A similar experiment was made with the substitution of a solution of hydro-sulphuret of ammonia for the vegetable infusion, with a view to convert any evolved chlorine into muriate of ammonia. The hydro-sulphuret was then evaporated to dryness, and nitrate of silver added; a precipitate of sulphuret and chloride of silver fell, but when the latter was dissolved out by ammonia, its amount was found to be very small. Again, several ounces of the liquid from the stomach were boiled for some time with peroxide of manganese, and thereafter filtered. The filtered liquid was then tested for chloride of manganese, with caustic potash; a very slight precipitate of protoxide fell. As the quantity of hydrochloric acid discovered in this portion of the liquid was too small to explain its marked acidity, I made careful search for another acid, and soon detected the presence of one which was not volatile, but was destructible at high temperatures. Different processes were adopted for the isolation and purification of this acid, which was separated with much difficulty from the accompanying salts and animal matter. I state the results very briefly.

"The concentrated liquid from the retort, which now possessed a dark-brown colour and was very viscid, was evaporated on the water-bath till it ceased to lose weight. It formed a gummy mass, which remained moist after many hours' exposure to a heat of 212°, and retained unimpaired the power of reddening litmus strongly. The mass was boiled with successive portions of alcohol of sp. gr. 0·880, so long as the latter acquired an acid reaction; the greater part of the animal matter remained undissolved, but the alcohol was coloured dark-brown. On evaporating this solution on the water-bath, a viscid matter was left, strongly acid to litmus, and possessing a saline taste occasioned by the chloride of sodium dissolved along with it. The alcoholic extract was boiled with successive portions of sulphuric ether, recently rectified from carbonate of potass, and ascertained to be quite neutral. By this treatment the extract lost its acidity, which was transferred to the ether; but it required a large quantity of the latter to remove it entirely. The etherial solution was of a pale-yellow colour, and had dissolved very little of the salts or animal matter. When the ether was vaporised on the water-bath, there remained a thick yellow liquid, reddening litmus strongly. It was kept for an hour at the temperature of 212° without drying up; it could be dissolved in water and evaporated to its original consistence many times in succession, without dissipation of the acid; but when left in its most concentrated state, it absorbed moisture from the air, and became more liquid. When exposed in a capsule to a naked flame, it darkened in colour, the animal matter became charred, and the whole was destroyed.

"Leopold Gmelin and others have shown that when hydrochloric acid is accompanied by much animal matter, it may be entangled in it, so as to escape dissipation by heat. It will afterwards be shown that the acid was certainly not the hydrochloric; but to obviate any objection which might be founded on this fact, several portions of the liquid were treated in the following way:—Some ounces were concentrated by evaporation, and boiled on protoxide of lead, till the liquid had lost all acid reaction. By this treatment the hydrochloric acid should be converted into the insoluble chloride of lead. The liquid was filtered, decomposed by a current of sulphuretted hydrogen, boiled, and filtered a second time. It yielded a pale-yellow fluid markedly acid, which was subsequently treated with alcohol and ether by the method already described. The liquid, after the second filtration, still precipitated nitrate of silver, for it contained all the chloride of sodium originally present. Although this was no real objection to the distinction of the acid from the hydrochloric, I was anxious to satisfy myself that it could be procured quite free from chlorine. With this object in view, several ounces of the liquid were boiled with a portion of carefully prepared and crystallised sulphate of silver, till it ceased to give a precipitate with the nitrate of the same base. A current of sulphuretted hydrogen was then passed through the liquid, to precipitate the excess of sulphate necessarily added, after which it was boiled and filtered. It now contained free sulphuric acid, and sulphates instead of chlorides; it was digested on oxide of lead, until it lost all acid reaction, filtered from the sulphate of lead and excess of oxide, and submitted again to sulphuretted hydrogen, till a precipitate ceased to fall. After being boiled and filtered anew, it was evaporated on the water-bath, and digested with alcohol, which left the sulphates undissolved. The product of these operations, which contained no inorganic acid, reddened litmus strongly.

"Other processes were followed which need not be detailed; none of them yielded an acid quite free from animal matter, nor was it ever procured in large quantity; but it presented the same properties in whatever way obtained. I did not ascertain the solubility of the acid in ether, till the inquiry was nearly concluded, so that some of the experiments hereafter mentioned were made with the alcoholic solution, which was less pure.

"The following properties were ascertained by repeated trials to belong to this acid. It was soluble in ether, alcohol, and water, was quite destitute of odour, and neither volatile nor crystallisable. When the aqueous solution was digested on phosphate of lime prepared from bones burned to whiteness, and freed from carbonate of lime by boiling with acetic acid, and subsequent protracted washing with water, it dissolved a large portion of the salt; and it acted in the same way on the recently-precipitated phosphate. It formed a soluble salt with oxide of silver, which strikingly distinguishes it from hydrochloric acid. It formed soluble salts likewise with oxide of lead, with potass, soda, ammonia, baryta, and lime; the last soluble also in alcohol. It sustained a heat of 300° without decomposition, but when the temperature was much elevated it inflamed along with the animal matter accompanying it, and suffered destruction. It was always found, however, that the animal matter gave way before it, for after charring had occurred to some extent, water still dissolved an acid from the mass.

"On comparing these properties with the characters known to distinguish the organic acids of animal origin, they will be found to correspond closely with those of lactic acid, which accordingly I believe the acid I have been describing to be. Hydrated lactic acid ($HO + C_6H_5O_5$) is stated by Berzelius[*] and Liebig[†] to constitute a colourless syrupy liquid, inodorous, uncrystallisable, and not volatile, but decomposed at a temperature of 480°. It forms soluble salts with all the metallic oxides, and dissolves a large quantity of phosphate of lime. There is no single decisive test of its presence, nor does it present any other marked characteristics which could be sought for in the acid under examination. One method there certainly is by which the identity of this acid with the lactic could have been ascertained—an ultimate analysis namely, and discovery of its atomic weight; but it was impossible to put this plan in practice. Nevertheless, I think the conclusion will be admitted that the acid was the lactic.

"Three acids, then, were found in the liquid—hydrochloric, acetic, and lactic; the first was present in too small quantity to be considered a morbid product. So far as the organic acids are concerned, it is impossible to say whether their mere presence constitutes a morbid sign, for the statements on record concerning the normal acids of the stomach are very incomplete and unsatisfactory. Dr. Prout found in the stomachs of the lower animals no acid but the hydrochloric.[‡] Leuret and Lassaigne found only the lactic;[§] Schultz only the acetic;[||] Chevreul found only the lactic in the gastric juice of dog, and in the liquid brought up by an emetic from the stomach of a healthy man fasting.[¶] On the other hand, Gmelin found in the lower animals muriatic and acetic acids,

---

[*] *Traité de Chimie*, tome vii. pp. 612-620.
[†] Turner's *Chemistry*, p. 996. [‡] *Phil. Trans.* 1824, p. 45.
[§] *Recherches Physiologiques et Chimiques*, p. 115.
[||] Müller's *Physiology*, p. 564. [¶] Leuret et Lassaigne, *op. cit.* p. 117.

and in the horse butyric acid.* Dunglison, who analysed the gastric juice from the stomach of St. Martin the Canadian, whose case has been described by Dr. Beaumont, found muriatic and acetic acids.† Dumas, in his Lectures on Organic Chemistry, delivered last summer (1841), stated the normal acids to be the muriatic and lactic.‡

"To perplex the inquiry still further, Gmelin admitted no distinction between lactic and acetic acid, or, at furthest, conceived the former to be the latter modified by adhering animal matter. Now that we know these acids to be quite distinct in composition and properties, the observations of Gmelin, otherwise so high an authority, lose much of their value.

"In the preceding summary of conflicting opinions it will be observed, that whilst some chemists contend for lactic and others for acetic acid as the normal organic acid of the gastric juice, no one professes to have found both acids in the same liquid, as was the case with that which I have analysed. One of these acids, then, was abnormal, but which? It would be useless attempting to decide this question by an appeal to the relative worth of the authorities quoted ; it is not improbable that both acids are developed during healthy digestion. Lactic acid is so abundant, free or combined, in the milk, blood, urine, and other parts of the body, that its existence in the stomach is almost certain. As for acetic acid, it is a much rarer constituent of animal fluids, and there can be little doubt that lactic acid has often been mistaken for it.

"In the meanwhile however, till new researches are made on this subject, neither acid can be considered by its mere presence as a morbid sign. I may, however, remark, that lactic acid has already been found by Dr. Graves in the liquid

---

* *Recherches sur la Digestion*, vol. i. pp. 166-67 ; vol. ii. p. 317.

† Müller, *op.* and *loc. cit.*

‡ Manuscript notes kindly furnished by Mr. Norton.

vomited by a sufferer from dyspepsia;* and MM. Boutron and E. Fremy, in a paper on the lactic fermentation, observe, 'It is known that the liquids contained in the stomach can, in certain conditions, present a strongly acid reaction. Now, the analyses made on this subject demonstrate, in these liquids, the presence of lactic acid.'†

"One thing, however, is certain, and it is the main truth elicited by the analysis—viz. that the quantity of acetic acid found in this case was enormous. Although we have no account of the proportion discovered in the gastric juice or chyme, by those who maintain its presence there, it is certain that the quantity must be very small. Prout overlooked the presence of an organic acid altogether, and Gmelin, the great advocate of its existence, found only traces of it. But the quantity of liquid ejected at once by the patient often amounted to more than two quarts, which would contain eighteen grains of acetic acid; and the amount is rather understated, for some portions of the liquid were necessarily lost in the distillations, which, moreover, were never pushed to dryness.

"I am not aware of any case on record corresponding to this; but I forbear at present forming any opinion as to whether this remarkable development of acetic acid, and the occurrence of the curious organisms described by Mr. Goodsir, were mutually dependent or merely coincident.

"The liquid otherwise was not particularly examined as to its salts or animal matter."

Those who know the doubt which at present exists as to the acids which are found in the stomach in health and

---

* *Transactions of the Association of Fellows and Licentiates of the College of Physicians in Ireland,* 1804, vol. iv. Quoted in Tiedemann and Gmelin, vol. i. p. 167.

† *Annales de Chimie et de Physique,* 3me serie, tom. xii. 1841.

disease, will perceive the value of the foregoing analysis. Other questions arising out of the consideration of the case, as well as its future progress, will be taken up and recorded in future communications on healthy and morbid digestion —subjects with which Dr. Wilson and I are at present engaged.

XIX.—ON A DISEASED CONDITION OF THE INTESTINAL GLANDS.*

WITHOUT entering upon the question, as to whether the subject of the present paper constitutes a distinct species of disease, or be merely a form of the ordinary continued fever—a question which I am quite satisfied will never be answered so long as each pathologist confines the inquiry to the fever of his own district, without connecting with it the consideration of those forms of fever which occur in every separate district of a country or continent—I shall proceed at once to describe a lesion which I observed some time ago in a disease which I was led to consider as typhus or continued fever.

On opening the abdomen of individuals who had died of this fever, we could always recognise the diseased condition of the internal surface of the gut by the elongated bluish purple spots on its peritoneal surface, corresponding to the glands of Peyer on the internal surface; and this we could do, even in those cases in which, from other circumstances, the vascularity of the parts had disappeared after death.

On laying the gut open, the patches of Peyer's glands exhibited, according to the standing of the case, the various appearances which I shall now describe.

But before proceeding to detail the phases through which the patches pass, from the first appearance of the disease till the establishment of the typhous ulcer, or of perforation, I

* Read before the Med.-Chir. Soc., February 1842, and printed in the *London and Edinburgh Monthly Journal of Medical Science*, April 1842.

may remark, in regard to the condition of the mucous membrane in the neighbourhood of the patches, that it did not in every case exhibit unequivocal traces of inflammatory action. It might be highly congested, or it might be perfectly bloodless in cases of well-developed disease of these patches. I cannot say that I have often observed the mucous membrane pulpy or softened. The villi and follicles of Lieberkühn have always appeared to me to be healthy. The vascularity, when it did occur, was met with principally in the neighbourhood of the glandular patches, and resembled in all respects that described and figured by Dr. Bright in his report on the form of fever lesion now before us.

The commencement of the disease is first announced by the smaller patches becoming slightly elevated, so as to be hemispherical or conical, and by the more extended groups assuming a table-like appearance, with perpendicular edges, as if a flat plate had been placed on the mucous surface. The colour varies, according to the case, from bright carmine red to dark purple or black, continuous or in patches. In the more vascular specimens, the colour is a yellowish grey, contrasting with the dead white or greyish-white of the intestinal surface. More closely examined the surfaces of the patches exhibit, as usual, the follicles of Lieberkühn and villi, differing in no respect from those on a healthy surface, and arranged around the vesicles of the patch in the usual manner. An examination of this kind must be made under water, and when conducted in this manner the vesicles of the patch may be seen by floating aside the membranous border and circle of villi which surround each of them. The vesicles themselves may thus be seen to be much distended with a yellowish matter—a distension which is now perceived to be the immediate cause of the elevation of the patch.

In the second stage of the disease, the patches still continue to rise above the surrounding surface, and to exhibit the changes formerly described, in a more characteristic manner. As the elevation increases, a change begins to take place on the elevated surface. This change may be partial—that is to say, it may take place sooner on some parts of the patch than on others; but generally it extends over the whole surface, and is bounded by a line situated from a 10th to a 16th of an inch from the edge of the patch. The change itself consists in the surface beginning to alter in colour, becoming dirty-yellow or grey, and assuming a peculiar undulating or contorted surface, like a bit of leather seared with a hot iron. The villi have now in a great measure disappeared, but the orifices, or rather the circular folds or pits, in which are situated the vesicles, are still visible. At last the confines of the changed portion of the patch are rendered evident by a groove apparently produced by ulceration, which, appearing here and there on these confines, at last extends all round, and indicates some change about to take place in the whole arrangement of the parts.

In the third stage, the groove just described makes its way into the tissues; and as it does so, the healthy but elevated mucous membrane on its external edge gradually everts itself, as if by the upward pressure of the matter beneath it. While this is going on, the edges and surface of the altered portion become more rugged, and their former character somewhat obscured. The altered portion, which now assumes very much the appearance of a slough tinged with intestinal matters, becomes more and more detached from the surface to which it adheres. When the mass is gently raised under water, it may be observed that its attached surface sends processes down into the cellular membrane beneath; and if these processes be carefully drawn out, they will be found to correspond each with one of the original vesicles of the patch. When detached in this manner, they leave on the surface to which they adhered, dimples, or rather pits, which may be recognised as being the cellulo-vascular sheaths of the patch-vesicles.

Occasionally the free surface of the altered portion comes away first, in the form of flocculent laminæ, and the deep processes continue to be attached for some time in the cellulo-vascular capsules, like little nodules or pellets of a rounded or pyriform shape.

The altered portion, even immediately before detachment, may still present on its surface traces of its original structure. The orifices of the follicles in which the vesicles are situated are visible here and there on the surface, and the membrane retains sufficient consistence to bind the mass together.

Fourth stage.—When the sloughy mass has separated, the surface of what may now be called an ulcer appears flocculent; but, when examined under water with a couple of needles, a number of foveæ, the remains of the cellulo-vascular capsules, may be observed on it. In some of these, the little pellets of deposit may still remain attached, appearing like mustard-seeds scattered over the surface. The edges of these ulcers are thick and everted, and exhibit the natural structure of the mucous membrane. In some ulcers the eversion of the edges proceeds so far as to throw the mucous surface of the edge completely over, so as to apply it to the surrounding mucous membrane.

Fifth stage.—The ulcer may now heal, or proceed to perforation of the gut. In the former case, granulations, I presume, appear, and the reaction of these cellular elements carries on the contraction and cicatrisation so well displayed in some of the preparations on the table. In the present form of ulcer, as in others affecting the mucous coat of the bowels, it is some time before villi again make their appearance on the cicatrised surface; but these changes I have not watched or observed. When the ulceration proceeds towards perforation, it is generally one spot of the patch which is more particularly affected, the rest of the ulcer retaining its former granulating or flocculent appearance. At this stage of the process lymph begins to be deposited on the external surface of the gut; and if the patient survives the perforation eight or ten hours, the lymph rounds off the edges of the hole, and gives it that punched-out appearance so frequently observed. The omentum may adhere opposite the incipient perforation, and after contraction has concluded, it appears as if it had been forced from without into the hole, an appearance resulting from the contracting agency of the granulations.

Having now described the changes which the patches undergo in this form of disease, I have to point out the peculiar matter upon the presence of which these changes appear to depend. The grey matter which fills the vesicles or the spaces which they occupy, I find to consist of that universal element of every primitive tissue, healthy or diseased—nucleated cells. These cells are from 2000 to 4000 of an inch in diameter. They do not in general exhibit a nucleus in the sense in which that term is generally applied; that is, the individual cells do not present in their interior smaller cells holding certain relations to them. These cavities appear to contain a number of granules, four, five, or six, as far as could be reckoned. Whether these in the aggregate are to be considered as a nucleus proceeding towards the formation of a number of young cells, or whether the appearance is to be considered as analogous to that irregular form of nucleus and cell-contents characteristic of certain forms of tubercle, I do not know. This matter, of whatever nature it may be, appears first in the vesicles of the patches, and then spreads out on all sides, after the manner of other purely cellular structures, till the whole patch, before it is thrown off, appears to be principally formed of it; the surface of the mass, however, as has been stated, and certain parts of its interior, consisting of the somewhat altered mucous and submucous tissue.

The morbid changes which the glandulæ aggregatæ of the ileum undergo during continued fever, appear, from the observations I have just detailed, to be of the following nature—viz. the development of cells within the constituent vesicles of the patches to such an extent as at last to burst them, or cause their solution; the continued increase in the number of the cells, proceeding from as many centres as there are vesicles in the patch; the conglomeration of the whole into one mass above the submucous and under the mucous membrane; the distension of the latter, and the necessary ulceration and sloughing of the mass arising from this circumstance.

The whole mass, as detached from the gut, is not therefore to be considered as a slough; that portion only which consists of the upper halves of the vesicles and of the mucous membrane being dead; the greater part, consisting of the cellular mass, being merely detached from the submucous tissue, consists of those nucleated cells, which, at first confined within their generative vesicles, had at last vegetated so much as to break their natural bounds, and become one mass of cells, constantly increasing in numbers, except below, where the separate centres from which they originally proceeded are indicated by the processes and little pellets which are situated in the remains of the vesicle-capsules.

It will have been observed that I have not employed the term "*inflammation*" in the course of the description I have just given. Whether the changes I have described originate in inflammatory action or not, of this I am certain, that the ulceration and pseudo-sloughing is an immediate effect of the distension from the submucous vegetating mass, and would occur whether the latter were produced by inflammation or not.

In regard to the history of this department of the morbid anatomy of fever, I may state that Dr. Bright has given very beautiful representations of the sloughs and ulcers in his *Reports of Medical Cases*. Louis and Chomel have referred to the appearance of the matter which distends the glands, and compared the process to the tuberculous. Schönlein, in his *General Pathology*, has made a general allusion to the deposit, and to the changes which occur in the patches.* Gruby, in a work on the *Microscopic Character of Morbid Products*,† was the first, as far as I can learn, who figured and described the cells of which the deposit consists. Finally, Rokitansky‡ has generalised the subject, and considered the matter deposited as peculiar to typhus fever, and referable to the same category as cancer, tubercle, etc.

My own observations have been made without reference to any hypothesis as to the pathology of fever.

* Schönlein, *Allgemeine und specielle Pathologie und Therapie*, Zweiten Thiele, 1839, p. 23.
† *Observationes Microscopicæ auctore Dav. Gruby*, 1840, p. 44.
‡ Rokitansky, *Handbuch der Pathologischen Anatomie*, band iii. p. 265.

XX.—OBSERVATIONS ON THE STRUCTURE AND SOME OF THE PATHOLOGICAL CHANGES OF THE KIDNEY AND LIVER.*

RESEARCHES into the structure of the healthy human kidney, and into the changes which it undergoes in the granular degeneration described by Dr. Bright, have led me to the following conclusions:—

Without denying the existence of occasional blind extremities of the tubuli uriniferi, the result probably of arrested development, I may state that I have never seen the ducts terminating in this way. I have observed a structure which appears hitherto to have been overlooked by anatomists— namely, a fibro-cellular framework, which, pervading every part of the gland, and particularly its cortical portion, performs the same important part in the kidney which the capsule of Glisson does in the liver—forming a basis of support to the delicate structure of the gland, conducting the blood-vessels through the organ, and forming small chambers in the cortical portion, in each of which a single ultimate coil or loop of the uriniferous ducts is lodged. I believe that the urine is formed at first within the so-called epithelium-cells of the ducts; and that these burst, dissolve, and throw out their contents, and are succeeded by others which perform the same functions. The urine of man has not been detected by me within the cells which line the ducts, but I have submitted to the Royal Society of Edinburgh, within the last few

---

* Read before Medico-Chirurgical Society, Edinburgh, May 1842.

weeks, a Memoir,* in which it is proved that the urine, bile, milk, as well as the other more important secretions in the lower animals, are formed within the nucleated cells of the gland-ducts. I believe, therefore, that the urine of man is poured at first into the cavities of the nucleated cells of the human kidney. I do not pretend to decide whether the morbid changes in the kidneys, in the various stages of the granular disease of Bright, originate in inflammation or simply in congestion of the gland, but may remind the Society of those changes which, at a former meeting,† I announced as occurring in the vesicular glands of the intestine during fever—namely, the formation and progressive increase of nucleated cells (probably aberrant forms of the epithelium which lines the vesicles) within the vesicles of the patches, and may now state that granular degeneration of the kidney has a similar increase; that it consists essentially of the formation of nucleated cells within the uriniferous ducts; that these new cells were principally confined to the ultimate loops of the ducts, but that, in advanced stages of the disease, they may be formed even in the tubes of the pyramids of Ferrein; that when a single ultimate loop of the uriniferous ducts was gorged, or distended with the increasing mass of germinating cells, or when two or more neighbouring loops were in this condition, the little mass constituted one of the granulations characteristic of the milder forms of the disease; that when throughout the gland, or in certain portions of it, the germinating masses had so far distended the ducts and loops as to cause their disappearance, and to induce absorption of the walls of the little chambers of the fibro-cellular capsule, and consequently of the uriniferous ducts, the whole of the cortical portion of the gland, or that part of it more particularly affected, assumed the appearance presented in

* See the Memoir "On Secreting Structures," No. XXV. of this volume.
† See No. XIX. of this volume.

the more advanced stages of the disease. If the patient survive the stage last described, the kidney becomes partially or wholly atrophied—a change due to the contraction of fibrous tissue, produced either from the cells which constitute the disease or from cells resulting from effused fibrin. With the exception of the primary engorgement of the capillary system, and of the Malpighian corpuscles, and their subsequent diminution, I have not observed any very marked change in the vascular system of the kidney during granular degeneration of the organ.

In proceeding to describe certain parts of the healthy and morbid structure of the human liver, I may observe that very little remains to be done in reference to this gland, since the very admirable researches of Mr. Kiernan. In regard to two parts of the structure, however, we are yet quite in the dark—namely, the mode of termination of the hepatic ducts and the connection between them and the nucleated cells of this organ; but have been able, after considerable difficulty, to verify Mr. Kiernan's supposition that the hepatic ducts terminate by a network within the lobules of the liver, around the intra-lobular veins. But the most important feature in my observations is the detection of the real connection between these ultimate ducts and the nucleated cells, which are grouped in the form of acini on the sides of the duct. Each acinus may consist, first, of a single cell, the primary or germinal cell of the future acinus; or, secondly, of two or more cells enclosed in the primary cell, and produced from its nucleus. The enclosed cells may be named the secondary cells of the acinus; and in the cavities of these, between their nuclei and cell-walls, the bile and a few oil-like globules are contained, as has been already stated, in the memoir above alluded to. The primary cell, with its included group of cells, each full of bile, is appended to the side of the remote ducts, and consequently does not communicate with that duct—a diaphragm formed by a portion of the primary cell-wall stretching across the pedicle. When the bile in the group of included cells is fully elaborated, the diaphragm dissolves or gives way, the cells burst, and the bile flows along the ducts; the acinus disappearing, and making room for a neighbouring acinus, which has in the meantime been advancing in a similar manner. The whole parenchyma of the liver, then, is in a constant state of change—of development, maturity, and atrophy—this series of changes being directly proportioned to the profuseness of the secretion of bile. I find myself anticipated by Mr. Bowman in regard to one of the morbid conditions of the human liver—namely, the fatty liver; and have much pleasure in confirming that gentleman's observations (*Lancet*, Jan. 1842), as to the fat being deposited within the nucleated cells of the organ, and to be considered, in fact, as a redundancy of the oil-globules naturally existing in these cells. As in the kidney, so in the liver, contractile fibrous tissue may be developed, and produce partial or complete atrophy. Dr. Carswell had already indicated this as existing in cirrhosis. The matter, of which the rounded masses in cirrhosis consists, is not a new deposit, but merely the natural tissue of the liver, altered by the pressure exerted by their fibrous envelopes. These alterations consist in constriction, more or less powerful, of the vessels and ducts which pass out and in to the rounded mass, the necessary difficulty with which the circulation is carried on, and the bile advanced along the ducts; and, latterly, in a change in the constitution of the nucleated cells themselves, which, instead of being distended with bile containing oil-like globules, contain matter of a darker colour, and less oil. The cells may at last contain matter perfectly black, and then the rounded mass assumes the appearance of a melanotic tubercle, the black cells in some instances becoming pyriform and caudate. I am inclined to believe that the forms of cirrhosis and melanosis are due to the contractile tissue, as a product of inflammatory action more or less acute. The action of remedies, particularly of mercury, would appear to corroborate this opinion. From the observations made on the morbid anatomy of the human liver and kidney, I conclude that certain of the diseases of those organs are due to the development of new cells and new matter within the ducts and nucleated cells of the organs, in accordance with the normal laws of cellular development—this cellular vegetation at last destroying, more or less completely, the natural tissue of the organ.

APPENDIX TO PRECEDING PAPER.

[The following more detailed observations on the relation of the secreting cells to the bile-ducts, and of the distribution of the connective tissue in the liver, occur in a manuscript essay, we believe unpublished, entitled "A General View of the Healthy and Morbid Anatomy of the Liver." The observations on the relations of the cells and ducts are especially interesting in connection with the recent descriptions of Hering (Schultze's *Archiv*, 1867) and others on this subject, whilst the careful description of the distribution of the areolar texture, shows how thoroughly Professor Goodsir recognised the importance of this tissue in its relations to the pathology of the organ. There is no date attached to the essay, but from the appearance of the paper and ink it had evidently been written many years ago.—EDS.]

In the liver, as in every other gland, secretion is performed, not by the vessels, but by the particles which form its parenchyma. In glands generally these particles are packed in the form of a layer on the internal surface of the fine membrane (germinal or primary membrane) of the ducts, from their open mouths to their blind or anastomosing extremities. In the liver the arrangement is different, although in principle the same. Tracing the structure of the ducts from the transverse fissure up along the portal passages, where they accompany the vena portæ and hepatic artery on to the compressed spaces between the lobules, and where they form a network, they consist of a fine membrane, having vessels on its external, compressed particles (epithelia) on its internal surface. At the outer surface of the lobules, the fine membrane of these ducts does not seem to enter the lobules; only the portal vessels, and the secreting particles, the latter being grouped around the former, so as to leave passages continuous with the plexus of ducts on the external surface of the lobule, converging, and at the same time communicating, with one another from that surface to the centre of the lobule. If, then, we suppose the portal vessels, which pass in at the outer part of the lobule, the hepatic vein, which passes out at the base, and the intermediate capillary plexus to be removed, we shall have remaining in a lobule only a mass of flattened particles so arranged as to exhibit two sets of passages—one occupied by the vessels of the lobule, and communicating on the one hand with the portal, and on the other with the hepatic vessels. The other set of passages within the lobules are continuous with the hepatic ducts, and are the ducts of the lobule itself. The difference, then, between an extra and an intra-lobular duct is that the former possesses a fine membrane between its vessels and secreting particles; the latter presents no such membrane, the particles being so arranged as to be in the immediate neighbourhood of bloodvessels, and to leave free intercellular passages outwards for their secretion.

The lymphatics of the liver I am inclined to believe, for reasons which I cannot enter upon at present, to take their origin in the intercellular spaces of the lobule, to acquire distinct walls in the compressed portal spaces between the lobules. They then pass, some along the portal passages to the transverse fissure, others up between the lobules to the sub-peritoneal areolar texture of the diaphragmatic surface of the gland. The ducts of the liver may therefore be considered as communicating directly with the lymphatic system.

The areolar texture of the liver is of great pathological importance. There are two situations in which it can exist in this organ—the portal passages and those for the hepatic veins. In the latter situation it is extremely limited in amount and very dense, connecting firmly the bases of all the lobules to the sub-lobular veins, continuous, on the one hand, around the trunk of the hepatic vein with the areolar texture of the posterior region of the cavity of the abdomen; on the other, around the bases of the lobules with the areolar texture of the portal canals. Lymph and pus do not appear to be deposited in the areolar texture of the hepatic passages, for so firmly are the lobules attached to the veins, that when the texture of the organ is broken up by an abscess, the lobules adhere, in the form of masses of parenchyma, to the branches of the hepatic vein, the pus breaking up the texture in the direction of the portal passages and interlobular spaces.

The second and more important division of the areolar texture occupies the interlobular spaces, is continuous along these with the subserous areolar texture, and, passing along the portal passages, is continuous with the areolar texture of the gastro-hepatic omentum at the transverse fissure. In the interlobular portion of this division of the areolar texture the interlobular plexus of the portal veins and the hepatic ducts are situated. In its continuation under the peritoneum the branches of the hepatic artery for the serous membrane, as well as the superior lymphatics of the liver, lie. In the portal passages the areolar texture, or capsule of Glisson, contains the trunks and branches of the vena portæ, the hepatic artery, ducts, nerves, and inferior lymphatics, also the vaginal branches of the vein, artery, and duct. This division of the areolar texture is in certain respects the most important pathological element of the organ. It is the seat of the **more** important inflammations, of the effusions of pus and lymph, **of chronic** inflammation, and of the fibrous lymph, producing cirrhosis and atrophy, and probably of the heterologous formations, or cancers, which attack the organ.

ANATOMICAL AND PATHOLOGICAL OBSERVATIONS.*

"*Although it shew not the agent, yet it sheweth a rule and analogy in nature, to say that the solid parts of animals are endued with attractive powers, whereby, from contiguous fluids, they draw like to like; and that glands have peculiar powers attractive of peculiar juices.*"—BERKELEY.

"*Even herein consists the essential difference, the contradistinction, of an organ from a machine; that not only the characteristic shape is evolved from the invisible central power, but the material mass itself is acquired by assimilation. The germinal power of the plant transmutes the fixed air and the elementary base of water into grass or leaves; and on these the organific principle in the ox or the elephant exercises an alchemy still more stupendous. As the unseen agency weaves its magic eddies, the foliage becomes indifferently the bone and its marrow, the pulpy brain or the solid ivory.*"—COLERIDGE.

"The greater part of my share of these Anatomical and Pathological Observations will be already, to a certain extent, familiar to those who attended my lectures, in the theatre of the Royal College of Surgeons, in summer 1842, and winter 1842-3.

"The Memoir on the Secreting Structures is reprinted in a modified form from the *Transactions of the Royal Society of Edinburgh* for 1842, and that on the Intestinal Villi from the *Edinburgh Philosophical Journal* of the same year. Those on the Placenta and Lymphatic Glands were read in the Royal Society of Edinburgh in 1843, but were not sub-

---

* The thirteen succeeding Memoirs were published by Macphail, Edinburgh, 1845, in an octavo volume, entitled *Anatomical and Pathological Observations*, and were preceded by the accompanying preface.—(EDS.)

mitted for publication. Abstracts of some of the others have also appeared, from time to time, in the reports of various Societies.

"The observations on the healthy Structure and Economy of Bone are, with the exception of those on the contents of the corpuscles, an abstract of my lectures on this subject in the College of Surgeons in winter 1842-3. I have considered this explanation necessary, in consequence of the resemblance between certain parts of my description and those in the admirable chapter on the same subject in Todd and Bowman's *Physiological Anatomy*, drawn up from the observations of Mr. Tomes.

"My brother, Harry D. S. Goodsir, has added some of his own zoological, anatomical, and pathological observations, as confirmatory of the doctrines of Centres of Nutrition and of Secretion. (Nos. XXVI. XXXII. XXXIII.)

"To such as may be inclined to object to the theoretical views which run through and connect these anatomical details, I would only say, that we shall be quite satisfied, if, on finding the latter correct, they will allow us to retain the former for future use; feeling assured, that 'there is a certain analogy, constancy, and uniformity, in the phenomena or appearances of nature, which are a foundation for general rules;' and that 'these are a grammar for the understanding of nature, or that series of effects in the visible world, whereby we are enabled to foresee what will come to pass in the natural course of things.'"

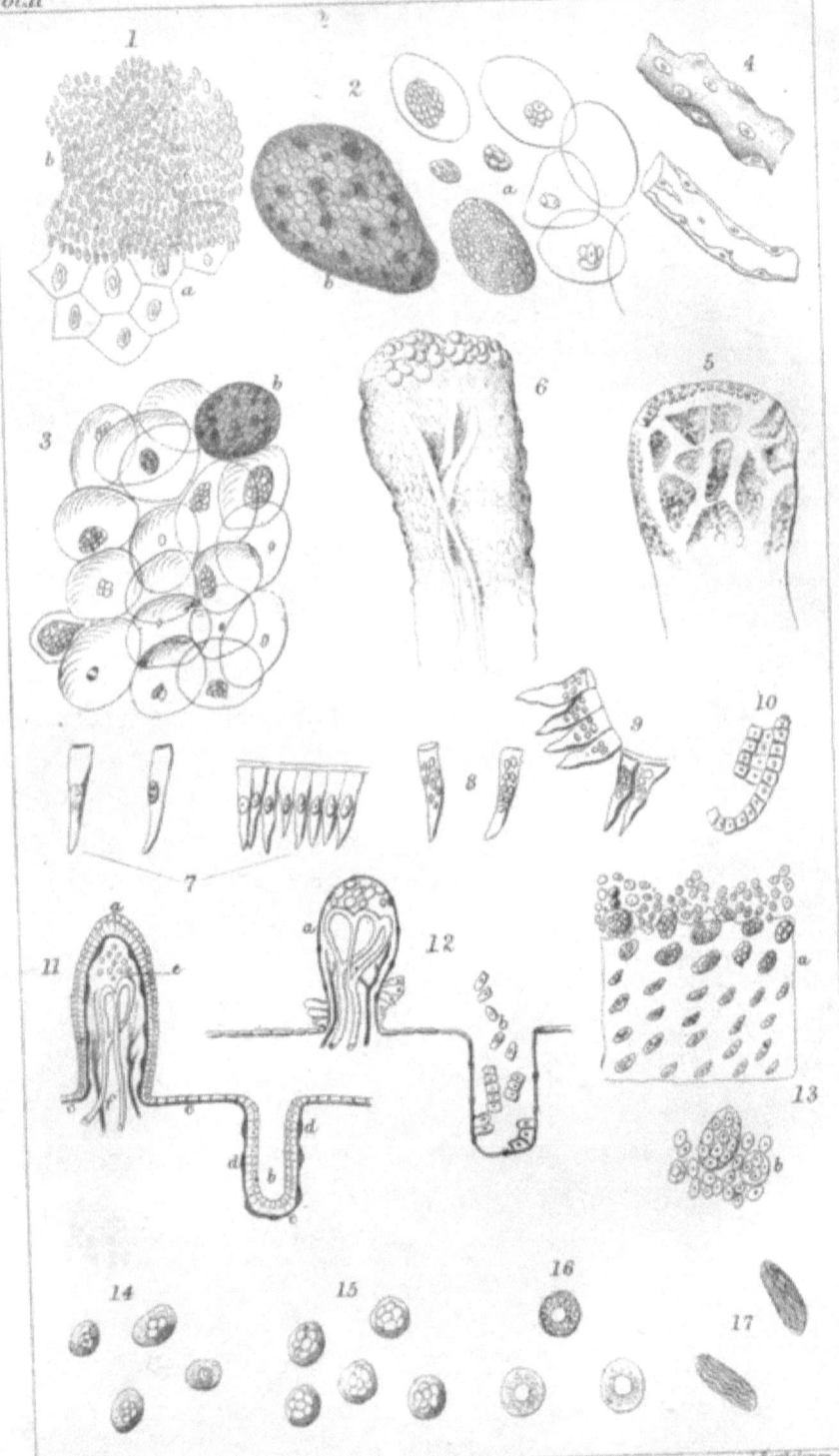

XXI.—CENTRES OF NUTRITION.—(Plate IV.)

By centres of nutrition I understand certain minute cellular parts existing in the textures and organs. With many of these centres anatomists have been for some time familiar,[*] but with a few exceptions have looked upon them as embryonic structures.[†] I am inclined to believe in the general existence of such centres, for a certain period at least, in all textures and organs, and to this I wish to direct attention at present.

The phenomena presented by these centres incline me to regard them as destined to draw from the capillary vessels, or from other sources, the materials of nutrition, and to distribute them by development to each organ or texture after its kind. In this way they are to be considered centres of germination; and I have elsewhere named them germinal spots—adopting the latter term from the Embryologists.[‡]

The centre of nutrition with which we are most familiar, is that from which the whole organism derives its origin—the germinal spot of the ovum. From this all the other centres are derived, either mediately or immediately; and in directions, numbers, and arrangements, which induce the configuration and structure of the being. As the entire organism

---

[*] The nuclei of the textures.

[†] Mr. Bowman, in his Paper on Muscle, *Philosophical Transactions*, 1840, Part I. page 485.—*Cyclopædia of Anatomy and Physiology*, art. "Muscle."— Dr. Martin Barry, in the *Philosophical Transactions*, and most explicitly in his Paper "On the Corpuscles of the Blood," 1841, Part I. page 269, paragraph 83.

[‡] *Trans. Roy. Soc. Ed.* 1842. "On the Secreting Structure, and the Laws of its Functions."

is formed at first, not by simultaneous formation of its parts, but by the successive development of these from one centre, so the various parts arise each from its own centre, this being the original source of all the centres with which the part is ultimately supplied.

From this it follows, not only that the entire organism, as has been stated by the authors of the cellular theory, consists of simple or developed cells, each having a peculiar independent vitality, but that there is, in addition, a division of the whole into departments, each containing a certain number of simple or developed cells, all of which hold certain relations to one central or capital cell, around which they are grouped. It would appear that from this central cell all the other cells of its department derive their origin. It is the mother of all those within its own territory. It has absorbed materials of nourishment for them while in a state of development, and has either passed them off after they have been fully formed, or have arrived at a stage of growth when they can be developed by their own powers.

Centres of nutrition are of two kinds—those which are peculiar to the textures, and those which belong to the organs. The nutritive centres of the textures are in general permanent. Those of the organs are in most instances peculiar to their embryonic stage, and either disappear ultimately or break up into the various centres of the textures of which the organs are composed.

A nutritive centre, anatomically considered, is merely a cell, the nucleus of which is the permanent source of successive broods of young cells, which from time to time fill the cavity of their parent, and carrying with them the cell-wall of the parent, pass off in certain directions, and under various forms, according to the texture or organ of which their parent forms a part.*

* For the first consistent account of the development of cells from a parent

There is one form in which **nutritive** centres are arranged, both in healthy and morbid parts, which is frequently alluded to in the following chapters, and which may be named a germinal membrane.* In a germinal membrane, the nutritive or germinal centres are arranged at **equal or variable distances**, and in certain directions, in the substance of a fine transparent membrane. A germinal membrane is occasionally found to break up into portions of equal size, each of which contains one of the germinal centres. From this it is perceived that a germinal membrane consists of cells, with their cavities flattened, so that their walls form the membrane by cohering at their edges, and their nuclei remain in its substance as the germinal centres.

Germinal membranes are only met with on the free centre, and more especially of the appearance of new centres within the original sphere, we are indebted to the researches of Dr. Martin Barry. Whatever may be said in opposition to Dr. Barry's views regarding the functions of the blood-globules, and the structure of muscular fibre, he is yet entitled, above all physiologists of the present day, to the merit of having kept steadily before him in his researches the principle of the central origin of all organic form.

* The membranous tubes of glands on which the epithelium is situated were described by Henle, Müller's *Archiv*, 1839. Mr. Bowman (*Phil. Trans.* 1842) "On the Structure and Use of the Malpighian Bodies of the Kidney," etc., has applied to the membrane of these tubes the very appropriate name of Basement Membrane. This membrane I consider to be a primary or germinal membrane. The term, basement membrane, is good as involving no hypothesis; it is therefore a most appropriate descriptive term. I have always considered the basement membrane, or elementary membrane of glands, as a form of the primary cells of glands, and the source of the secondary or secreting cells, and have therefore been in the habit of naming it primary, or germinal membrane. Mr. Bowman considers it to be simple, or homogeneous. This is true as far as it contains no bloodvessels, and as regards its external or attached layer; but as in its original condition it consists of cells, and when perfect contains nuclei at equal or variable distances, I do not consider it as simply molecular. These nuclei, or germinal spots, may be certain of the epithelial cells, which become mother-cells, between the two layers of the membrane; or cells belonging to the order of the nuclear fibres of Valentin and Henle.

surfaces of parts or organs. One surface of the membrane is therefore attached, and is applied upon a layer of areolar texture, intermixed with a more or less rich network of capillary vessels. The other surface is free, and it is on it only that **the developed or** secondary cells **of its germinal** spots are attached. These secondary cells are at first contained between the two layers of the membrane, these layers being the opposite walls of each of its component cells. When fully developed, the secondary cells carry forward the anterior layer, which is always the **thinnest,** leaving the **nuclei or germinal centres in the substance of the** posterior **layer in** close contact with the bloodvessels.

Of the forces which exist in connection with centres of nutrition, nothing very definite can yet be stated. When this branch of inquiry shall have been opened up, we shall expect to have a science of organic forces, bearing direct relations to anatomy, **the science** of organic forms.

XXII.—THE STRUCTURE AND FUNCTIONS OF THE INTESTINAL VILLI.—(PLATE IV.)

MR. CRUIKSHANK, in treating of the orifices of the Lacteals and Lymphatics,* states that he and Dr. William Hunter observed the openings by which the lacteals communicated with the cavity of the gut in portions of the intestine of a woman who died after eating a hearty supper. The two preparations of the intestine on which these anatomists made their observations, came into the possession of the College of Surgeons in Edinburgh, as part of the collection of the late Sir Charles Bell.

I removed one of the villi from Mr. Cruikshank's preparation, and had no difficulty in recognising what had been described and figured by the original owner of the preparation. With a low power the extremity of the villus appeared bulbous and opaque. With a higher power I observed that this opacity was due to the existence, at the extremity of the villus, of a number of vesicles of different sizes. The larger vesicles were pretty uniform in size, and about twenty in number. The smaller were of different sizes, and more numerous, and appeared gradually to pass into the granular texture of the attached extremity of the villus. No blood-vessels could be detected, but along the neck of the villus distinct traces of two or more opaque lacteals were visible. The vesicles and the lacteals, when viewed by transmitted light, were of a light brown colour; but when examined as opaque objects, they stood out of a dead white appearance,

* William Cruikshank, *The Anatomy of the Absorbing Vessels of the Human Body*, 2d ed. 1790, page 56.

contrasting strongly with the semi-transparency of the surrounding texture. Repeated examinations of these preparations satisfied me that Dr. William Hunter and Mr. Cruikshank were quite correct in describing and figuring radiating lacteals within the villi, but that they were led into error in describing those vessels as opening on the free surface of the gut, partly by imperfect instruments and methods of observation, partly by the general prejudice of the period in favour of absorbent orifices. I also satisfied myself of what appeared highly probable from the commencement of the observations, that the villi, when turgid with chyle, were destitute of their ordinary epithelial covering.* This circumstance I could not avoid connecting with the fact of the stomach throwing off its epithelia during the process of digestion. I determined, therefore, to investigate the process of absorption of chyle in fresh subjects, as the facts exhibited in Mr. Cruikshank's preparations indicated the probable existence of complicated processes going on in villi during digestion. The analogy of the vesicular bulbous extremity of the villus, to the spongiole of the vegetable, forced itself upon me, and the existence of milky chyle, within closed cells, led me to anticipate an explanation of some of the phenomena of digestion.

A dog was fed. Three hours afterwards he was killed. The lacteals were turgid, and the gut was found to be full of milky chyme, with an admixture of thin brownish fluid of a bilious appearance. The milky matter was situated principally towards the mucous membrane; the brown fluid occupied the cavity of the gut.

The white matter consisted of a transparent fluid, with a few oil-globules and numerous epithelia.

Some of the epithelia I recognised as those which cover the villi. They were pointed at their attached extremities,

* This opinion was subsequently abandoned by the author.—(Eds.)

flat at the other. Many of them were single, others were united in bundles, adhering principally by their flat or free extremities, as if a fine membrane passed over and connected the edges of their extreme surfaces. Occasionally these epithelia presented a distinct nucleus; but generally, and whether single or in bundles, they exhibited in their interior a group or mass of oil-like globules, which, when viewed as opaque objects, had a peculiar semi-opaque or opalescent appearance.* Others of the epithelia, contained in the chyme, were prismatic, single, or in columns. They were the lining epithelia of the follicles of Lieberkühn, and presented the usual nuclei.

The mucous membrane displayed the villi turgid, as if in a state of erection, and as I had anticipated, naked or destitute of epithelia, except at their bases, where a few still adhered. Each villus was covered by a very fine smooth membrane, which, from its free bulbous extremity, passed on to its sides, and became continuous with the germinal membrane of the follicles of Lieberkühn. These villi, when removed from the mucous membrane, and examined with a low power, were semi-transparent, except at their free or bulbous extremities, which appeared both by direct or transmitted light white and opaque. Under higher powers the summit of the villus, somewhat flattened, was observed to be crowded, immediately under the membrane before mentioned, with a number of perfectly spherical vesicles. These vesicles varied in size from 1000 to less than 2000 of an inch. The matter in their interior had an opalescent milky appearance. Towards the body of the villus, on the edges of the vesicular mass, minute granular or oily particles were situated in great numbers, and gradually passed into the granular texture of the substance of the villus.

* Is this appearance due to a partial absorption of chyle by these protective epithelia?

The trunks of two lacteals could be easily traced up the centre of the villus, and as they approached the vesicular mass they subdivided and looped. In no instance could one of these lacteals be traced to any of the spherical vesicles, nor could any direct communication between the structures be detected.* The bloodvessels and capillaries, with their columns of tawny blood disks, could be seen passing in radiating lines and in loops across the villus, immediately under the fine membrane already mentioned. This membrane, perceptible on the body and neck of the villus only by the smooth surface it presented, was most distinctly traced at the free extremity of the villus, as it passed from the surface of one vesicle on to that of another.† The vesicles, pushing the membrane forward, and grouped together in masses on its attached surface, gave the extremity of the villus the appearance of a mulberry. When viewed on a dark ground as an opaque object, the point directed to the light, a villus in this condition is remarkably beautiful, the play of the light on the surface of the highly-refractive semi-opaque and opalescent vesicles giving them the appearance of a group of pearls.

In villi turgid with chyle, which have been kept for some time in spirits, the contents of the vesicles are opaque, the albumen having become coagulated.

To understand the part which the vesicles of the villus play in digestion, it is necessary to be aware of certain of the functions of the cell, with which physiologists are yet unacquainted. Not only are these bodies the germs of all the tissues, as determined by the labours of Schleiden and Schwann, but are also the immediate agents of secretion. A

---

* See Gulliver's translation of Gerber's *General Anatomy*, pp. 272 and 273.

† Mr. Bowman, in the article "Mucous Membrane," *Cyclopædia of Anatomy*, does not admit this portion of the membrane. It certainly cannot be detached as a separate membrane.

primitive cell absorbs from the blood in the capillaries the matters necessary to enable it to form, in one set of instances, nerve, muscle, bone, if nutrition be its function; milk, bile, urine, in another set of instances, if secretion be the duty assigned to it. The only difference between the two functions being, that in the first, the cell dissolves and disappears among the textures, after having performed its part; in the other, it dissolves, disappears, and throws out its contents on a free surface. Now, it will be perceived, that before a cell can perform its functions as a nutritive cell, or as a secreting cell, it must have acted as an absorbing cell. This absorption, too, must necessarily be of a peculiar and specific nature. It is in virtue of it that the nutritive cell selects and absorbs from the liquor sanguinis those parts of the latter necessary for building up the peculiar texture of which the cell is the germ. It is in virtue of this peculiar force that the secreting cell not only selects and absorbs, but also in some instances elaborates, from the same common material, the particular secretion of which it is the immediate organ. And it is by the same force that the cell becomes the immediate agent of absorption in certain morbid processes.

"Absorption,"[*] says Professor Müller, "seems to depend on an attraction, the nature of which is at present unknown, but of which the very counterpart, as it were, takes place in secretion; the fluids altered by the secreting action being impelled towards the free surface only of the secreting membranes, and then pressed onwards by the successive portions of fluid secreted. In many organs, for instance in those invested with mucous membranes—absorption by the lymphatics and secretion by the secreting organs, are going on at the same time on the same surface." It appears, however, from what is stated in the present chapter, and in the *Trans. Roy.*

---

[*] Müller's *Physiology*, page 30—Baly's Translation.

Soc. Edin.,* that Professor Müller, and indeed all the physiologists hitherto, have been in error in supposing the forces of secretion and absorption as of different and opposite tendencies—the one attractive, the other repulsive. They are both attractive, absorption being but the first stage in the process of secretion. Secretion, in fact, differs from absorption, not physiologically, but morphologically.

What has been stated in the present paper explains also how, in the mucous membranes, "absorption by lymphatics and secretion by secreting organs are going on at the same time on the same surface." There is no physiological mystery in this. It depends on a morphological circumstance. The absorbing chyle-cells are on the attached surface of the germinal membrane—the secreting epithelia are on its free surface; the former are interstitial cells—the latter peripheral; the former cast their contents into the substance of the organism—the latter into the surrounding medium.

The primitive cell, then, is primarily an organ of specific absorption, and secondarily of nutrition, growth, and secretion.

As the chyme begins to pass along the small intestine, an increased quantity of blood circulates in the capillaries of the gut. In consequence of this increased flow of blood, or from some other cause with which I am not yet acquainted, the internal surface of the gut throws off its epithelium, which is intermixed with the chyme in the cavity of the gut. The cast-off epithelium is of two kinds—that which covers the villi, and which, from the duty it performs, may be named protective epithelium, and that which lines the follicles, and is endowed with secreting functions. The same action, then, which, in removing the protective epithelia from the villi, prepares the latter for their peculiar function of absorption, throws out the secreting epithelia from the follicles, and thus

---

* *Trans. Royal Society, Edin.* 1842, "On the Secreting Structure, and Laws of its Function." See also No. XXV. of this volume.

conduces towards the performance of the function of these follicles.

The villi, being now turgid with blood, erected, and naked, are covered or coated by the whitish-grey matter already described. This matter consists of chyme, of cast-off epithelia of the villi, and of the secreting epithelia of the follicles. The function of the villi now commences. The minute vesicles which are interspersed among the terminal loops of the lacteals of the villus, increase in size by drawing materials from the blood through the coats of the capillary vessels, which ramify at this spot in great abundance. While this increase in their capacity is in progress, the growing vesicles are continually exerting their absorbing function, and draw into their cavities that portion of the chyme in the gut necessary to supply materials for the chyle. When the vesicles respectively attain in succession their specific size, they burst or dissolve, their contents being cast into the texture of the villus, as in the case of any other species of interstitial cell.

The debris, and the contents of the dissolved chyle-cells, as well as the other matters which have already subserved the nutrition of the villus, pass into the looped network of lacteals, which, like other lymphatics, are continually employed in this peculiar function. As long as the cavity of the gut contains chyme, the vesicles of the terminal extremity of the villi continue to develope, to absorb chyle, and to burst, and their remains and contents to be removed along the lacteals.

When the gut contains no more chyme, the flow of blood to the mucous membrane diminishes, the development of new vesicles ceases, the lacteals empty themselves, and the villi become flaccid.

The function of the villi now ceases till they are again roused into action by another flow of chyme along the gut.

During the intervals of absorption, it becomes necessary

to protect the delicate villi from the matters contained in the bowel. They had thrown off their protective epithelium when required to perform their functions, just as the stomach had done to afford gastric juice, and the intestinal follicles to supply their peculiar secretions. In the intervals of digestion the epithelium is rapidly reproduced.

The germinal membrane, which, as I have stated, not only forms the outer membrane of the follicles, under the epithelia, but also the underlying membrane of the villi, contains in its substance germinal centres of an oval form, situated at pretty regular distances. From these the epithelium appears to be reproduced during the intervals of absorption, as stated in the first chapter.

During this process of development, the primary membrane appears to split into two laminæ, the epithelia passing out from its nuclei between these. This would account for the epithelia, particularly the prismatic and conical, adhering by their free extremities.

Such are the processes which would appear to take place in the villi of the intestinal tube during digestion and absorption. When considered in relation to the functions of digestion and absorption of chyle, these processes are highly interesting.

The labours of the chemist have now so far simplified the theory of digestion, as to deprive the stomach of the vitalising or organising powers so long ascribed to it.

Every step in this chemico-physiological inquiry leads to the conclusion, that the changes which the food undergoes while in the cavity of the gut are entirely of a chemical nature.

If we continue, then, to apply the term digestion to that series of processes by which the aliment is assimilated to the matter of which the body is composed, we must divide the series into two groups. The first group will include all those changes which take place within the digestive tube, but exterior to the organism. The second will include those which present themselves after the alimentary matter is taken up into the animal body, and becomes buried in its substance. The first group of processes are mechanical and chemical in their nature. They may be considered in a great measure as peculiar to the animal, although even vegetables throw out from their roots matter which, acting on some of the materials of the surrounding soil, prepares these for absorption.

The second group of processes is common to animals and vegetables. In these, for the first time, are alimentary substances taken into the tissues of the organism. In animals, as in plants, as I have already pointed out, these alimentary substances are drawn by a peculiar force into the interior of the cells, after escaping from which they pass on by the absorbent system. The chemist has not yet informed us of the change which the matter has undergone during its passage from the cavity of the gut, or from the soil, into the afferent lacteals and the sap-vessels; but if in vegetables, as in animals, this matter passes into the cavities of the cells of the spongiole before it passes on to the sap-vessels, then it is highly probable that the organising and vitalising part of the function of digestion commences in the cells of the spongiole and of the extremity of the villus.

The extremity of the fibril of the root of a plant elongates by the cells added to its tissue by the germinating spongiole. The spongiole is, therefore, an active organ of growth as well as of absorption. It is to the fibril of the root, what I have denominated in the animal tissues the nutritive centre. I conceive it to be probable, therefore, although as to this I have made no observations, that absorption by, and elongation of, the fibril of the root, vary inversely as one another. This supposition is founded on the assumption that the cells of the spongiole do not absorb by transmission, but by growth and solution.

In the villi of the intestines of animals, my own observations lead me to believe that absorption by growth and solution is the process which actually takes place.

The vesicular extremity, like the spongiole of the root-fibril, is the primitive nutritive centre of the villus. The villus originates in a cell. During the development of the villus, this spot or cell was employed only in procuring materials for the growth of the organ. In the perfect animal the formative function of the spot ceases; its action becomes periodical, active during digestion, at rest during the intervals of that process. The same function is performed, the same force is in action, and the same organ, the cell, is provided for absorption of alimentary matters in the embryo and in the adult, in the plant and in the animal. The spongioles of the root, the vesicles of the villus, the last layer of cells on the internal membrane of the included yelk, or the cells which cover the vasa lutea of the dependent yelk, and the cells which cover the tufts of the placenta, are the parts of the organism in which the alimentary matters first form a part of that organism, and undergo the first steps of the organising process.

XXIII.—ABSORPTION, ULCERATION, AND THE STRUCTURES ENGAGED IN THESE PROCESSES.

EVERY organic cell, the most simple as well as the most complicated, when a separate organism, or when a part of a more highly organised being, existing as a mere magazine of matter, or performing some of the more striking of the vital functions, invariably exhibits a phenomenon which is antecedent to all others—absorption from without of materials for its own growth.

The various kinds of cells in any organism differ from one another in this respect, that they have the power, each after its kind, of selecting and procuring from the circulating medium, or from other sources, the sort of matter necessary for their own growth : or they have the power of elaborating, or of conducing to the chemical change of the matter which is absorbed by them. In this respect, the component cells of animals and vegetables resemble the various species of beings of which they form parts : they have not only the power of selecting food, but the various species out of the same kind of food are formed of matter and of parts which are specifically different.

A most important circumstance in the history of cellular phenomena is the duration of existence of a cell. Like the various species of animals and vegetables, each species of cell has its own average term of existence, each after its kind. This average term is nevertheless contingent on the amount of action which each species may, by peculiar circumstances in the organism to which it belongs, be called on to perform. This variableness in the average age of each species of cell, is dependent on those circumstances which have been named "nervous agency," "peculiarity of constitution," "irritability of the parts," "morbid action," but may be studied independently of these agencies. The variableness in the term of existence of cells can no more be explained at present, than the variety in the duration of the lives of species of animals and vegetables: but the fact being known, its laws ascertained will afford a clue to the explanation of many organic phenomena and processes.

In the study of absorption, nutrition, and secretion, attention has been directed to the vessels, as the active agents in the performance of these processes. It is only a short time since we have been willing to admit that the new matter which is constantly replacing the old materials of the frame, is selected and laid down, not by the ultimate vessels, but by the non-vascular portions of the textures. It is only now that we are beginning to know that secretion differs from nutrition in its anatomical relations, and not in its intimate nature. We still, however, retain in full force the old belief in the active absorbent powers of the vessels, and in the agency of the capillary and lymphatic vessels in removing parts and modelling the forms.

It is not my intention to question entirely the active agency of the veins and lymphatics in absorption and ulceration, but merely to direct attention to the subject; and to point out, in some of the following chapters, a few organic processes in which these actions appear to be functions independent of the vessels, the latter to be passive agents, mere ducts for conveying away the products of action.

A rapidly-extending ulcerated surface appears as if the textures were scooped out by a sharp instrument. The textures are separated from the external medium by a thin film. This film is cellular in its constitution, and so far it is analogous to the epidermis or epithelium. It is a peculiarly endowed cellular layer, which takes up progressively the place of the subjacent textures—these being prepared for dissolution, either by the state of the system, the condition of the part, or by some influence induced by the contiguity of the new formation. Carrying out, therefore, the principles at present regarded as regulating the reciprocal functions of textures and vessels, the subjacent textures disappear in consequence of a disturbance of their own forces, consequent upon the appearance of new forces residing in the cellular layer. The disturbance and gradual annihilation of the natural forces residing in the subjacent textures, is indicated by the gradual disappearance of these. That new forces, not formerly existing in the part, are developed, appears from the formation of the cells of the cellular layer. As these appear in rapid succession, and disappear as rapidly, the subjacent textures also disappear, either by previous solution and subsequent absorption by the properties and powers of the former; or under the peculiar circumstances of inflammatory action by the more vigorous growth of the former, monopolising the resources of the part, the latter dissolving and disappearing by the usual channels of the returning circulation, more rapidly, but according to ordinary laws.

From this view of the process, it appears that, so far from consisting in a diminution of the formative powers of the part, such a progressive ulceration is actually an increase of it. The apparent diminution is a consequence of the extremely limited duration of existence of the cells of the absorbent layer, which die as rapidly as they are formed, disappearing after dissolution, partly as a discharge from the surface, but principally through the natural channels by which the debris of parts, which have already performed their allotted functions are taken up into the organism.

When a portion of dead or dying bone is about to be separated from the living, the process which occurs is essentially the same as that which has now been described. The Haversian canals, which immediately bound the dead or dying bone, are enlarged contemporaneously with the filling of their cavities with a cellular growth. As this proceeds, contiguous canals are thrown into one another. At last the dead or dying bone is connected to the living by the cellular mass alone. It is now loose, and has become so in consequence of the cellular layer which surrounds it presenting a free surface and throwing off pus.

In this process the veins and absorbents act on the osseous texture of the walls of the Haversian canals in no otherwise than in the natural state of the part. They are mediate, not immediate, instruments of absorption. It is the cells of the newly-formed cellular mass, contained in the Haversian canals, which are the immediate cause of the removal of the bone, either by taking it up as nourishment, and substituting themselves in its stead—the bone being prepared for this absorption in a manner analogous to that which occurs in the digestion of food previously to absorption of it by the cells of the gut;* or by the active formation of the cells of the new substance monopolising the resources of the part, and so inducing the disappearance of the osseous texture by the natural channels of the returning circulation.

The process by which a slough in the soft parts is separated from the living textures is similar to that which occurs in bone.

In this view of ulceration, there is substituted for the hypothetical active or aggressive power of absorption ascribed to the veins and the lymphatics, a power which is known

* "Hence, the digestive process, instead of being confined to the stomach and duodenum, is actually carried on without intermission, in all parts of a living animal body."—Prout's *Bridgewater Treatise*, page 534.

to exist in the organic cell during the progress of its growth; and the ultimate removal of the matter from the scene of action is ascribed, partly to the formation of discharge, partly to the yet unexplained, but at the same time undoubted, and in all probability **passive, agency of the returning** circulation.

XXIV.—THE PROCESS OF ULCERATION IN ARTICULAR CARTILAGES.—(Plate IV.)

The question as to the vascularity of cartilages cannot now excite much interest, when we know that all the textures are in themselves destitute of bloodvessels, which are accessory parts, carriers of nourishment, not active agents in its deposition. We do not consider cartilage as a texture into which no bloodvessels pass, but only as less vascular than some of the others. In a large mass of cartilage, as in those of the bulky mammals, or in the thick cartilages of the fœtal skeleton, canals containing bloodvessels are found here and there; but in the thin articular cartilages of the adult human subject few or no vessels can be detected.

It is evident, therefore, that in the process of ulceration in cartilage, it cannot be the usual bloodvessels of the part which are the active agents.[*] Still less likely is it that lymphatics, the existence of which has never been asserted in this texture, are the absorbing instruments.

If a thin section, at right angles, be made through the articular cartilage of a joint, at any part where it is covered by gelatinous membrane in scrofulous disease, or by false membrane in simple inflammatory condition of the joint, and if this section be examined, it will be found to present the following appearances.

---

[*] See Mr. Aston Key's Paper in the *London Med. Chir. Trans.* vol. xviii. Part I., "On the Ulcerative Process in Joints."

On one edge of the section is the cartilage unaltered, with its corpuscles natural in position and size. On the opposite edge, is the gelatinous, or false membrane, both consisting essentially of nucleated particles, intermixed, especially in the latter, with fibres and bloodvessels; and, in the former, with tubercular granular matter. In the immediate vicinity, and on both sides of the irregular edge of the section of cartilage, where it is connected to the membrane, certain remarkable appearances are seen. These consist, on the side of the cartilage, of a change in the shape and size of the cartilage-corpuscles. Instead of being of their usual form, they are larger, rounded, or oviform; and, instead of two or three nucleated cells in their interior, contain a mass of them. At the very edge of the ulcerated cartilage, the cellular contents of the enlarged cartilage-corpuscles communicate with the diseased membrane by openings more or less extended. Some of the ovoidal masses in the enlarged corpuscles may be seen half-released from their cavities by the removal of the cartilage; and others of them may be observed in the substance of the false membrane, close to the cartilage, where they have been left by the entire removal of the cartilage which originally surrounded them.

If a portion of the false membrane be gradually torn off the cartilage, the latter will appear rough and honey-combed. Into each depression on its surface a nipple-like projection of the false membrane penetrates. The cavities of the enlarged corpuscles of the cartilage open on the ulcerated surface by orifices of a size proportional to the extent of absorption of the walls of the corpuscle, and of the free surface of the cartilage.

The texture of the cartilage does not exhibit, during the progress of the ulceration, any trace of vascularity. The false membrane is vascular, and loops of capillary vessels dip into the substance of the nipple-like projections which fill the depressions on the ulcerated surface of the cartilage ;* but, with the exception of the enlargement of the corpuscules, and the peculiar development of their contents, no change has occurred in it. A layer of nucleated particles always exists between the loops of capillaries and the ulcerated surface.

The cartilage, where it is not covered by the false membrane, is unchanged in structure. The membrane generally adheres with some firmness to the ulcerating surface; in other instances it is loosely applied to it; but in all, the latter is accurately moulded to the former.

In scrofulous disease of the cancelled texture of the heads of bones, or in cases where the joint only is affected, but to the extent of total destruction of the cartilage over part or the whole of its extent, the latter is, during the progress of the ulceration, attacked from its attached surface. Nipple-shaped processes of vascular cellular texture pass from the bone into the attached surface of the cartilage, the latter undergoing the change already described. The processes from the two surfaces may thus meet half-way in the substance of the cartilage, or they may pass from the attached, and project through a sound portion of the surface of the cartilage, like little vascular nipples or granulations. The cartilage may thus be riddled, or it may be broken up into scales of varying size and thickness, or it may be undermined for a greater or less extent, or be thrown into the fluid of the cavity of the joint in small detached portions, or it may entirely disappear.

On the principles already laid down, if absorbents exist, as we have reason to believe they do in the false membrane, neither they nor the veins are to be considered as the active or immediate agents in the absorption of the cartilage. They certainly are not so in the absorption of the walls of the cor-

---

* The vascular loops described and figured by Mr. Liston are not vessels in the cartilage, but the vessels described in the text.—LISTON. *Lond. Med. Chir. Trans.*

puscules, and this, **as well as** the analogy of similar processes, gives weight **to the** opinion to which I have come, that they **are not the** immediate **instruments** in **the** absorption of the **free surface.** The cells **of new formation** appear to be **the** immediate **agents in** this **action.** They absorb into their substance **the** hyaline matter **of** the cartilage, the latter probably not being removed at once from the spot, but merely converted **into** soft cellular texture ; the process being one of **transformation rather than removal.**

XXV.—SECRETING STRUCTURES.—(Plates IV. V.)

MALPIGHI was the first to announce that all secreting glands are essentially composed of tubes, with blind extremities.* Müller, by his laborious researches, has brought this department of the anatomy of glands to its present comparatively perfect condition.† Purkinje announced his hypothesis of the secreting function of the nucleated epithelium of the gland-ducts, but made no statement to show that he had verified it by observation.‡ Schwann suggested that the epithelium of the mucous membranes might be the secreting organ of these surfaces.§ Henle described minutely the epithelium-cells which line the ducts of the principal glands and follicles, but did not prove that these are the secreting organs. The same anatomist has stated that the terminal extremities of certain gland-ducts are closed vesicles, within which the secretion is formed, and which contain nucleated cells. Henle has not, therefore, verified the hypothesis of Purkinje, although he is correct in stating that the terminal vesicles of certain gland-ducts are closed.‖ It will be shown, that the secretion is not formed, as Henle has asserted, in the closed vesicles, but in the nucleated cells themselves.

The discrepant observation of Boehm¶ and Krause** on the glands of Peyer, were in some measure reconciled by

---

* *Exercitationes de Structura Viscerum*, 1665.
† J. Müller, *De Gland. Struct. Penit.* 1830.   ‡ Isis, 1838.
§ *Froriep. Notiz.* 1838.   ‖ Müller's *Archiv*, 1838, 1839.
¶ *De Gland. Intestin. Struct. Penit.* 1835.   ** Müller's *Archiv*, 1837.

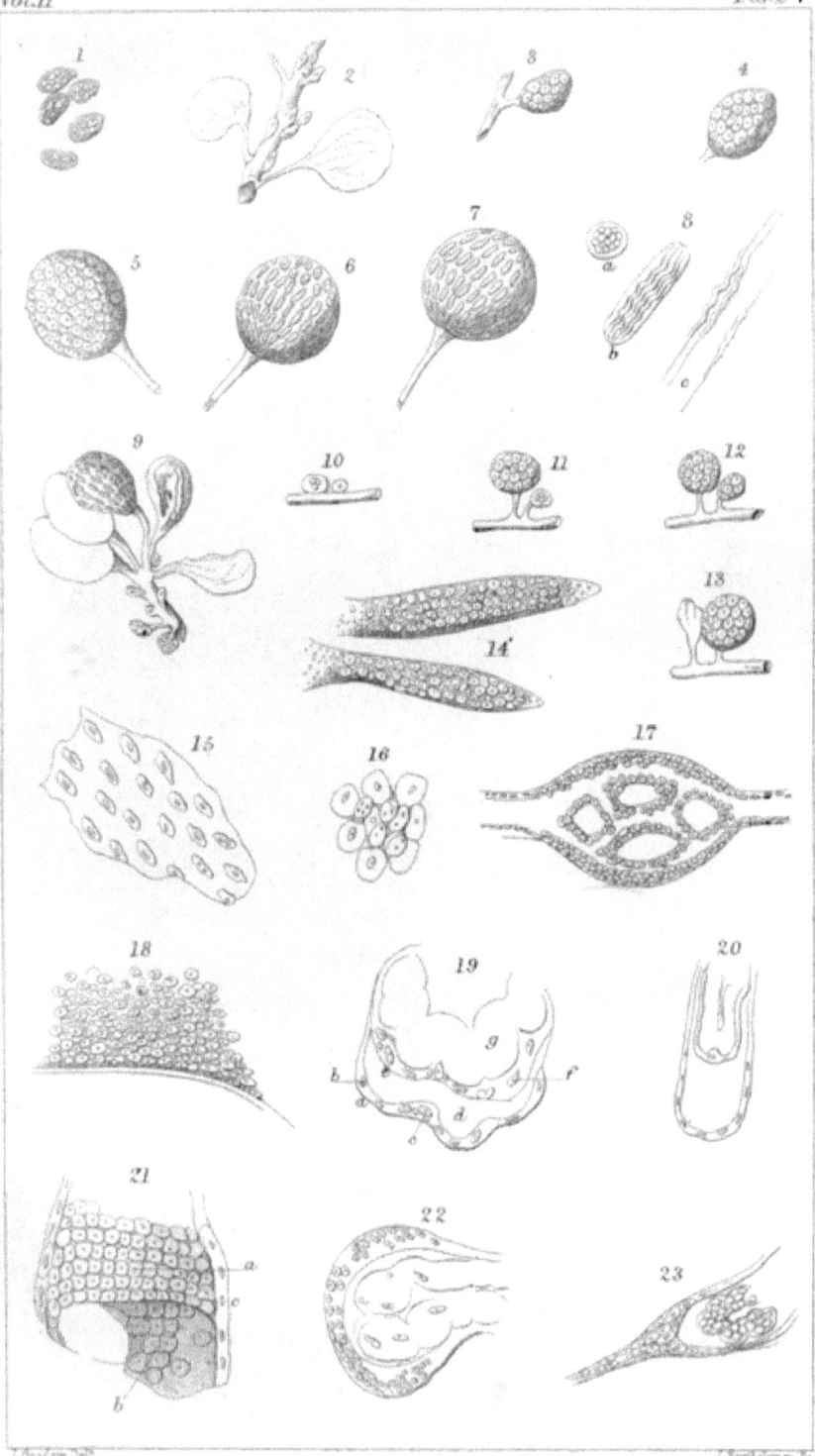

Henle, who referred them to the same class of structures as the closed vesicular extremities of the ducts of compound glands. Dr. Allen Thomson has observed, that the primitive condition of the gastric and intestinal gland is a closed vesicle.* Wasmann described the structure of the gastric glands in the pig; and his description will be fully explained by the following observations and views.† Hallman has given a detailed account of the testicle of the ray,‡ which closely resembles that of the *Squalus cornubicus*, as described in another part of this chapter. None of the recent observations on the development of the spermatozoa have proved that the vesicles, in which they are formed, are the epithelium-cells of the ducts of the testicle. I am indebted to Dr. Allen Thomson for directing my attention to a notice in Valentin's *Repertorium*, 1841, of a Dissertation by Erdl,§ in which he describes, in the kidney of that mollusc, cells, the nuclei of which pass out by the duct of the gland. It does not appear, however, that Erdl had discovered the uric acid within the cell.‖

If the membrane which lines the secreting portion of the internal surface of the ink-bag of *Loligo sagittata* (Lamark) be carefully freed from adhering secretion by washing, it will be found to consist almost entirely of nucleated cells, of a darkbrown or black colour. These cells are spherical or ovoidal. Their nuclei consist of cells, grouped together in a mass. Between these composite nuclei, and the walls of their containing cells, is a fluid of a dark-brown colour. This fluid resembles, in every respect, the secretion of the ink-bag itself. It

---

* *Proceedings of the British Association*, 1840.
† *De Digestione Nonnulla*, Diss. manq. Berol. 1839.
‡ Müller's *Archiv*, 1840.
§ *De Helicis Algiræ vasis sanguiferis*, 1840.
‖ Mr. Bowman has shown that the fat in the fatty liver is contained in the secreting cells.—*Observations on the Minute Structure of the Fatty Degeneration of the Liver*, January 1842.

renders each cell prominent and turgid, and is the cause of its dark colour.

The dilated terminal extremities of the ducts in the liver of *Helix aspersa* (Müller) contain a mass of cells. If one of these cells be isolated and examined, it presents a nucleus consisting of one or more cells. Between the nucleus and the wall of the containing cell is a fluid of an amber tint, and floating in this fluid are a few oil-globules. This fluid differs in no respect from the bile, as found in the ducts of the gland.

If a portion of the ramified glandular organ which opens into the fundus of the stomach of *Uraster rubens* (Agassiz) be examined, its internal surface is found to be lined with cells; between the nucleus of each of which and the wall of the cell itself a dark-brown fluid is situated. The organ secretes a fluid, supposed to be of the nature of bile.

The dark-brown ramified cæca of the same animal exhibit on their internal surfaces an arrangement of nucleated cells, the cavities of which contain a brown fluid. These cæca are also supposed to perform, or to assist in the performance of, the function of the liver.

The liver of *Modiola vulgaris* (Fleming) contains masses of spherical cells. Between the nucleus and the wall of each of these cells a light-brown fluid is situated, bearing a close resemblance to the bile in the gastro-hepatic pouches.

The nucleated cells which are arranged around the gastro-hepatic pouches of the *Pecten opercularis* are irregular in shape, and distended with a fluid resembling the bile.

The hepatic organ, which is situated in the loop of intestine of *Pirena prunum* (Fleming), consists of a mass of nucleated cells. These cells are collected in groups, in the interior of larger cells or vesicles. These nucleated cells are filled with a light-brown bilious fluid.

The hepatic organ, situated in the midst of the reproductive apparatus, and in the loop of the intestine of *Phallusia vulgaris* (Forbes and Goodsir), consists of a number of vesicles, and each vesicle contains a mass of nucleated cells. These cells contain a dark-brown bilious fluid.

The hepatic organ in the neighbourhood of the stomach, in each of the individuals of the compound mollusc, the *Alpidium ficus* (Linnæus), consists of nucleated cells, which contain in their cavities a reddish-brown fluid.

The liver of *Loligo sagittata* (Lamark) contains a number of nucleated cells, ovoidal and kidney-shaped. These cells are distended with a brown bilious fluid.

The nucleated cells in the liver of *Aplysia punctata* (Cuvier) are full of a dark-brown fluid.

The ultimate vesicular cæca of the liver of *Buccinum undatum* contain ovoidal vesicles of various sizes. These vesicles contain more or less numerous nucleated cells. The cells are full of a dark-brown fluid.

The hepatic cæca in the liver of *Patella vulgata*.—Each of these vesicles encloses a body, which consists of a number of nucleated cells, full of a dark fluid resembling the bile.

The simple biliary apparatus which surrounds the gastric portion of the intestinal tube of *Nereis* contains nucleated cells, full of a light-brown fluid.

The hepatic cæca of *Carcinus mænas* contains cells full of a fluid of an ochrey colour, along with numerous oil-globules.

The hepatic cæca of *Carabus catenulatus* (Fabricius) contain cells attached to their internal surfaces. Between the nuclei and the cell-walls a brown liquid containing numerous granules is situated.

The kidney of *Helix aspersa* (Müller) is principally composed of numerous transparent vesicles. In the centre of each vesicle is situated a cell full of a dead white granular mass. This gland secretes pure uric acid.

The ultimate elements of the human liver are nucleated

cells. Between the nucleus and the cell-wall is a light-brown fluid, with one or two oil-globules floating in it.

The vesicular cæca in the testicle of *Squalus cornubicus* contain nucleated cells, which ultimately exhibit in their interior bundles of spermatozoa.

The generative cæca of *Echiurus vulgaris* (Lamark) contain cells full of minute spermatozoa.

Aplysia punctata secretes from the edge and internal surface of its mantle a quantity of **purple fluid**. The secreting surface of the mantle consists of an arrangement of spherical nucleated cells. These cells are distended with a dark purple matter.

The edge and internal surface of the mantle of *Janthina fragilis* (Lamark), the animal which supplied the Tyrian dye, secretes a deep bluish purple fluid. The secreting surface consists of a layer of nucleated cells, distended with a dark purple matter.

If an ultimate acinus of the mammary gland of the bitch be examined during lactation, it is seen to contain a mass of nucleated cells. These cells are generally ovoidal, and rather transparent. Between the nucleus and the cell-wall of each a quantity of fluid is contained, and in this fluid float one, two, three, or more oil-like globules, exactly resembling those of the milk.

In addition to the series of examples already given, I might adduce many others to prove that secretion is a function of the nucleated cell. Some secretions, indeed, are so transparent and colourless, as to render ocular proof of their original formation within cells impossible; and we are not yet in possession of chemical tests sufficiently delicate for the detection of such minute quantities. The examples I have selected, however, show that the most important and most striking secretions are formed in this manner. The proof of the universality of the fact, in reference to the glandular structures which produce colourless secretions, can only rest at present on the identity of the anatomical changes which occur in their cellular elements. This part of the proof I shall enter upon in another part of this chapter.

The secretion within a primitive cell is always situated between the nucleus and the cell-wall, and would appear to be a product of the nucleus.*

The ultimate secreting structure, then, is the primitive cell, endowed with a peculiar organic agency, according to the secretion it is destined to produce. I shall henceforward name it the primary secreting cell. It consists, like other primitive cells, of three parts—the nucleus, the cell-wall, and the cavity. The nucleus is its generative organ, and may or may not, according to circumstances, become developed into young cells. The cavity is the receptacle in which the secretion is retained till the quantity has reached its proper limit, and till the period has arrived for its discharge.

Each primary secreting cell is endowed with its own peculiar property, according to the organ in which it is situated. In the liver it secretes bile—in the mamma, milk, etc.

The primary secreting cells of some glands have merely to separate from the nutritive medium a greater or less number of matters already existing in it. Other primary secreting cells are endowed with the more exalted property of elaborating from the nutritive medium matters which do not exist in it.

* In the original Memoir the cell-wall is stated to be the probable secreting structure. "Now, as we know that the nucleus is the reproductive organ of the cell—that it is from it, as from a germinal spot, that new cells are formed—I am inclined to believe that it has nothing to do with the formation of the secretion. I believe that the cell-wall itself is the structure, by the organic action of which each cell becomes distended with its peculiar secretion, at the expense of the ordinary nutritive medium which surrounds it."—*Trans. Roy. Soc. Edin.* 1842.

The discovery of the secreting agency of the **primitive** cell does not remove the principal mystery in which this function has always been involved. One cell secretes bile, another milk; yet the one cell does not differ more in structure from the other than the lining membrane of the duct of one gland from the lining membrane of the duct of another. The general fact, however, that the primitive cell is the ultimate secreting structure, is of great value in physiological science, inasmuch as it connects secretion with growth, as phenomena regulated by the same laws. The force, of whatever kind it may be, which enables one primary formative cell to produce nerve and another muscle, by an arrangement within itself of the common materials of nutrition, is identical with that force which enables one primary secreting cell to distend itself with bile, and another with milk.

Instead of growth being a species of imbibing force, and secretion on the contrary a repulsive—the one centripetal, the other centrifugal—they are both centripetal. Even in their later stages the two processes, growth and secretion, do not differ. The primary formative cell, after becoming distended with its peculiar nutritive matter, in some instances changes its form according to certain laws, and then, after a longer or shorter period, dissolves and disappears in the intercellular space in which it is situated, its materials passing into the circulating system if it be an internal, and being merely thrown off if it be an external cell. The primary secreting cell, again, after distension with its secretion, does not change its form so much as certain of the formative cells, but the subsequent stages are identical with those of the latter. It bursts or dissolves, and throws out its contents either into ducts or gland-cavities, both of which, as I shall afterwards show, are intercellular spaces, or from the free surface of the body.

The general fact of every secretion being formed within

cells, explains a difficulty which has hitherto puzzled physiologists—viz. why a secretion should only be poured out on the free surface of a gland-duct or secreting membrane.

"Why," says Professor Müller, "does not the mucus collect as readily between the coats of the intestine as exude from the inner surface? Why does not the bile permeate the walls of the biliary ducts, and escape on the surface of the liver, as readily as it forces its way outwards in the course of the ducts? Why does the semen collect on the inner surface only of the tubuli seminiferi, and not on their exterior, in their interstices? The elimination of the secreted fluid on one side only of the secreting membrane—viz. on the interior of the canals—is one of the greatest enigmas in physiology." Müller proceeds to explain this enigma by certain hypotheses; but the difficulty disappears, the mystery is removed, when we know that the secretion only exists in the interior of the ripe cells of the free surface of the ducts or membrane, and is poured out or eliminated simply by the bursting and solution of these superficial cells.

I have hitherto confined my observations to the structure and function of the ultimate secreting element, the primary secreting cell. I now proceed to state the laws which I have observed to regulate the original formation, the development, and the disappearance of the primary organ. This subject necessarily involves the description of the various minute arrangements of glands and other secreting structures.

If the testicle of *Squalus cornubicus* (Gmelin) be examined when the animal is in a state of sexual vigour, the following arrangements of structure present themselves :—

The gland consists of a number of lobes separated, and at the same time connected, by a web of filamentous texture, in which ramify the principal bloodvessels.

The lobes, when freed from this tunic, present on their surface a number of vesicles. When the gland is dissected under water, and one of the lobes is raised out of its capsule, an extremely delicate duct is observed to pass from it into the substance of the capsule, to join the ducts of the other lobes.

When a section is made through one of the lobes, it becomes evident that the vesicles are situated principally on its exterior.

If a small portion be macerated in water for a few hours, and dissected with a couple of needles, there are observed attached to the delicate ducts which ramify through the lobe vesicles in all stages of development. These stages are the following:—1*st*, A single nucleated cell attached to the side of the duct, and protruding, as it were, its outer membrane.

2*d*, A cell containing a few young cells grouped in a mass within it; the parent cell presenting itself more prominently on the side of the duct.

3*d*, A cell attached by a pedicle to the duct, the pedicle being tubular, and communicating with the duct; the cell itself being pyriform, but closed and full of nucleated cells.

4*th*, Cells larger than the last, assuming more of a globular form, still closed, full of nucleated cells, and situated more towards the surface of the lobe.

5*th*, The full-sized vesicles already described as situated at the surface of the lobe. These vesicles are spherical, perfectly closed; that part of the wall of each which is attached to the hollow pedicle forms a diaphragm across the passage, so that the vesicle has no communication with the ducts of the gland. The contents of the vesicles are in various stages of development. Those least advanced are full of simple nucleated cells; in others, the included cells contain young cells in their interior, so that they appear granular under low powers; in others, the included cells have begun at a certain part of the vesicle to elongate into cylinders, with slightly rounded extremities. In others the cylindrical elongation has taken place in all the included cells, with the exception of a few, which still retain the rounded form, at a spot opposite to that part of the vesicle in which the change commenced; and at the same time it may be observed, that the cylindrical cells have become arranged in a spiral direction within the parent vesicle. *Lastly*, Vesicles exist in which all the cells are cylindrical, and are arranged within its cavity in a spiral direction.

The changes which occur in the included nucleated cells of the vesicle are highly interesting. After the nucleus of each has become developed into a mass of cells, the parent cell becomes, as has been stated, cylindrical. The change in the shape of the cell is contemporaneous with the appearance of a spiral arrangement of the included mass of cells. This spiral arrangement is also contemporaneous with an elongation of each cell in the mass, in the direction of the axis of the parent cell. When the elongation has reached its maximum, the original mass of included cells has assumed the appearance of a bunch of spirals, like corkscrews arranged one with another, spiral to spiral. In particular lights the cylindrical cell presents alternate spots of light and shade, but by management of the illumination, the included spiral filaments become evident; the light and shade are seen to arise from the alternate convexities and concavities of the spiral filaments, combined in a spiral bundle.

In vesicles more advanced, the wall of the cylindrical cells has become attenuated.

In other vesicles the diaphragms across their necks have dissolved or burst, the bundles of spiral filaments float along the ducts of the gland, or separate into individual spiral filaments. These filaments are completely developed spermatozoa, pointed and filamentous at both extremities, thicker and spiral in the middle.

In the centre of the lobe, where the smaller ducts meet to form the principal duct, there is a mass of grey gelatinous matter through which the ducts pass. This gelatinous matter consists of a number of cells lying between the converging ducts, and from their peculiar appearance not presenting the usual nuclei. I am inclined to believe that they are either vesicles which have never become developed on account of the pressure of the surrounding parts, or that they are old vesicles in a state of atrophy after the expulsion of their contents.

Having now described the changes which are constantly taking place in the testicle of this shark when the organ is in a state of functional activity, I must defer till a future occasion an account of similar changes which occur in the parenchyma of an order of glands, of which the one already described may be considered as a type. I may state, however, that I have ascertained the following general facts in reference to glands of this order:—

1*st*, The glandular parenchyma is in a constant state of change, passing through stages of development, maturity, and atrophy.

2*d*, The state of change is contemporaneous with, and proportional to, the formation of the secretion, being rapid when the latter is profuse, and *vice versa*.

3*d*, There are not, as has hitherto been supposed, two vital processes going on at the same time in the gland, growth and secretion, but only one—viz. growth. The only difference between this kind of growth and that which occurs in other organs being, that a portion of the product is, from the anatomical condition of the part, thrown out of the system.

4*th*, The vital formative process which goes on in a gland is regulated by the anatomical laws of other primitive cellular parts.

5*th*, An acinus is at first a single nucleated cell. From the nucleus of this cell others are produced. From these, again, others rise in the same manner. The parent cell, however, does not dissolve away, but remains as a covering to the whole mass, and is appended to the extremity of the duct. Its cavity, therefore, as a consequence of its mode of development, has no communication with the duct.

The original parent cell now begins to dissolve away, or to burst into the duct at a period when its contents have attained their full maturity. This period varies in different glands, according to a law or laws peculiar to each of them.

6*th*, In the gland there are a number of points from which acini are developed, as from so many centres. These I name the germinal spots of the gland.

7*th*, The secretion of a gland is not the product of the parent cell of the acinus, but of its included mass of cells. The parent cell or vesicle may be denominated the primary cell; its included nucleated cells, after they have become primary secreting cells, may be named secondary cells of the acinus.

8*th*, There are three orders of secretions : (1.) A true secretion—that is, matter formed in the primary secreting cell-cavities; or, (2.) A mixture of a fluid formed in these cell-cavities with the developed or undeveloped nuclei of the cells themselves; and, (3.) It may be a number of secondary cells passing out entire.

In the liver of *Carcinus mænas*, and other Crustacea, it may be observed, that each of the follicles of which it consists presents the following structure :—The blind extremity of the follicle is slightly pointed, and contains in its interior a mass of perfectly transparent nucleated cells. From the blind extremity downwards, these cells appear in progressive states of development. At first they are mere primitive nucleated cells; further on they contain young cells; and beyond this they assume the characters of primary secreting cells, being distended with yellow bile, in which float oil-globules, the oil in some instances occupying the whole cell. Near the attached extremity of the follicle an irregular passage exists in the midst of the cells, and allows the contents of the cells which bound it to pass on to the branches of the hepatic duct.

This arrangement of the secreting apparatus may be taken as the type of an order of glands, which consist of follicles more or less elongated. Growth in glands of this kind is regulated by the following laws :—

1*st*, Each follicle is virtually permanent, but actually in a constant state of development and growth.

2*d*, This growth is contemporaneous with the function of the gland, that function being merely a part of the growth, and a consequence of the circumstances under which it occurs.

3*d*, Each follicle possesses a germinal spot situated at its blind extremity.

4*th*, The vital action of some follicles is continuous, the germinal spot in each never ceasing to develope nucleated cells, which take on the action of and become primary secreting cells, as they advance along the follicle. The action of other follicles is periodical.

5*th*, The wall, or germinal membrane of the follicle, is also in a state of progressive growth, acquiring additions to its length at its blind extremity, and becoming absorbed at its attached extremity. My brother, in a paper on the "Development and Metamorphoses of *Caligus*," read in the Wernerian Society, April 1842, has stated that the wall of the elongated and convoluted follicle, which constitutes the ovary in that genus, grows from its blind to its free extremity, at the same rate as the eggs advance in development and position. A progressive growth of this kind would account for the steady advance of its attached contents, and would also place the wall of the follicle in the same category with the primary vesicle, germinal membrane, or wall, of the acinus in the vesicular glands.

6*th*, The primary secreting cells of the follicle are not always isolated. They are sometimes arranged in groups, and when they are so each group is enclosed within its parent cell, the group of cells advancing in development according to its position in the follicle, but never exceeding a particular size in each follicle.

In my original memoir, I stated my opinion that there is an order of glands—namely, those with very much elongated ducts—which do not possess germinal spots in particular situations, but in which these spots are diffused more uniformly over the whole internal surface of the ducts. The human kidney is a gland of this order.*

We require renewed observations on the original development of glands in the embryo. From the information we possess, however, it appears that the process is identical in its nature with the growth of a gland during its state of functional activity.

The blastema, which announces the approaching formation of a gland in the embryo, in some instances precedes, and is in other instances contemporaneous with, the conical blind protrusion of the membrane upon the surface of which the future gland is to pour its secretion.

In certain instances it has been observed that the smaller branches of the duct are not formed by continued protrusion of the original blind sac, but are hollowed out independently in the substance of the blastema, and subsequently communicate with the ducts.

* "I am the more inclined to believe this, from what I have observed in certain secreting membranes. Thus the membranes which secrete the purple in *Aplysia* and *Janthina* are not covered with a continuous layer of purple secreting cells; but over the whole surface, and at regular distances, there are spots, consisting of transparent, colourless, nucleated cells, around which the neighbouring cells become coloured. Are these transparent cells the germinal spots of these secreting membranes? And may not the walls of the elongated tubes, and the surfaces of the laminæ within certain glands, have a similar arrangement of germinal spots?"—*Trans. Roy. Soc. Edin.* 1842.

It appears to be highly probable, therefore, that a gland is originally a mass of nucleated cells, the progeny of one or more parent cells; that the membrane in connection with the embryo gland may or may not, according to the case, send a portion of the membrane, in the form of a hollow cone, into the mass; but whether this happens or not, the extremities of the ducts are formed as closed vesicles, and then nucleated cells are formed within them, and are the parents of the epithelium cells of the perfect organ.

Dr. Allen Thomson has ascertained that the follicles of the stomach and large intestine are originally closed vesicles. This would appear to show that a nucleated cell is the original form of a follicle, and the source of the germinal spot which plays so important a part in its future actions.

The ducts of glands are, therefore, intercellular passages. This is an important consideration, inasmuch as it ranges them in the same category with the intercellular passages and secreting receptacles of vegetables.*

Since the publication of my paper on the secreting structures, in the Transactions of the Royal Society of Edinburgh in 1842, I have satisfied myself that I was in error in attributing to the cell-wall the important function of separating and preparing the secretion contained in the cell-cavity. The nucleus is the part which effects this. The secretion contained in the cavity of the cell appears to be the product of the solution of successive developments of the nucleus, which in some instances contains in its component vesicles the peculiar secretion, as in the bile-cells of certain Mollusca, and in others becomes developed into the secretion itself, as in seminal cells. In every instance, the nucleus is directed towards the source of nutritive matter, the cell-wall is opposed to the cavity into which the secretion is cast. This accords with that most important observation of Dr. Martin Barry, on the function of the nucleus in cellular development.

* Henle, in his *General Anatomy*, has made a similar statement.

I have also had an opportunity of verifying, and to an extent which I did not at the time fully anticipate, the remarkable vital properties of the third order of secretions, referred to in the memoir to which I have just alluded. The distinctive character of secretions of the third order is, that when thrown into the cavity of the gland, they consist of entire cells, instead of being the result of the partial or entire dissolution of the secreting cells. It is the most remarkable peculiarity of this order of secretions that, after the secreting cells have been separated from the gland, and cast into the duct or cavity, and therefore no longer a component part of the organism, they retain so much individuality of life, as to proceed in their development to a greater or less extent in their course along the canal or duct, before they arrive at their full extent of elimination.

The most remarkable instance of this peculiarity of secretions of this order, is that discovered by my brother, and recorded by him in a succeeding chapter.* He has observed that the seminal secretion of the decapodous crustaceans undergoes successive developments in its progress down the duct of the testis, but that it only becomes developed into spermatozoa after coitus, and in the spermatheca of the female. He has also ascertained that, apparently for the nourishment of the component cells of a secretion of this kind, a quantity of albuminous matter floats among them, by absorbing which they derive materials for development after separation from the walls of the gland.

This albuminous matter he compares to the substance which, according to Dr. Martin Barry's researches, results from the solution of certain cells of a brood, and affords nourishment to their survivors. It is one of other instances in which cells do not derive their nourishment from the blood, but from parts in their neighbourhood which have undergone

* See page 420.

solution; and it involves a principle which serves to explain many processes in health and disease, some of which have been referred to in other parts of this work.

I conclude, therefore, from the observations which I have made—1*st*, That all the true secretions are formed or selected by a vital action of the nucleated cell, and that they are first contained in the cavity of that cell; 2*d*, That growth and secretion are identical—the same vital process, under different circumstances.*

* In Mr. Bowman's elaborate Paper "On the Structure and Use of the Malpighian Bodies of the Kidney," read in the Royal Society of London, 17th February 1842, and in his Article "Mucous Membrane," in the *Cyclopædia of Anatomy*, written in December 1841, certain parts of the theory of secretion are well elucidated by a reference to human structure. In my own Memoir, read in the Royal Society of Edinburgh, 30th March 1842, I endeavoured, by an appeal to facts in comparative anatomy, to establish secretion as a function of the nucleated cell, and to show that glandular phenomena are only the changes which the cellular elements of these organs undergo. Mr. Bowman's own observation on the secretion of fat by the cells of the human liver in a state of disease was an important and positive result; and Professor John Reid, with whom I had frequent conversations on the subject of secretion, and to whom I had communicated my views on the subject a year before the publication of my Paper, was in the habit of supporting Purkinje and Schwann's hypothesis, by an appeal to the structure of *Molluscum contagiosum*, as described by Professor Henderson and Dr. Paterson in the *Edinburgh Medical and Surgical Journal*, 1841.

Vol. II   Plate VII

XXVI.—THE TESTIS AND ITS SECRETION IN THE DECAPODOUS CRUSTACEANS.—(Plates VII. VIII.)

THE organs of generation in the male crustacean consist of testes, vasa deferentia, and external or intromittent organs.

In no class of animals do these parts vary so much as in that now under consideration. In every family, and almost in every genus, they afford generic, and in some even specific, characters. This variableness of configuration and structure is not peculiar to the organs of reproduction, but exists also in the other systems—the vascular and respiratory, the nervous and locomotive. Such a variableness is to be looked for in a class, the forms in which pass from that of the annelids, through the articulata, to the mollusc. Throughout all this range of form the organs and functions vary in accordance with those in the group of animals to which the crustaceans presenting them are analogous.

In all the higher, or Brachyurous Crustaceans, the internal organs of generation are comparatively most highly developed. These organs exhibit the greatest complexity of form and structure among the *Triangulares*, but in the next order, the *Cyclometopa*, they are of great size. These crustaceans are accordingly the most prolific, and in greatest demand as articles of diet. The *Catometopa*, or rather the higher forms of that family, have these organs also very large; this family containing the land-crabs of tropical climates, which are used as food.

As we descend towards the *Anomoura*, the internal organs of generation are found to give way gradually to others, which have apparently a more important part to play in the economy; and in the lowest forms of the *Oxystoma* they are in a minimum state of development.

In this division (*Brachyura*) they occupy both sides of the shell, lying upon the liver, and sometimes entering the folds of that organ, and separated with difficulty from it. In others, as *Cancer* and *Carcinus*, when in an active state, they completely cover and conceal the liver.

In *Leptopodium* and *Hyas* the testis is a body of considerable size, lying upon the upper surface of the liver, and consisting of irregular masses, formed by the twistings of its constituent duct. It is covered by a delicate membrane, which is much stronger on the body of the testis than elsewhere, and is analogous to the tunica albuginea in the higher animals. The gland, extending forward, gradually enlarges, and when it has arrived in a line with the stomach, curves slightly inwards to the mesial plane, and terminates in a large tube on each side, which is its duct much dilated. This large tube, making a number of convolutions, proceeds inwards and downwards until it meets and forms a junction with that of the opposite side. The anastomosis is incomplete in this division of the class. After running in contact for some distance, the two ducts again separate, and each becoming much smaller, terminates by opening at the base of the external organs.

In the *Anomoura*, instead of being situated in the thorax, as in the *Brachyura*, the testes are contained in the abdominal segment of the body, lying on and above the liver. They are very small in all the animals of this section, the tubuli seminiferi being large, and after making a few convolutions ending in the vas deferens, which opens on the base of the fifth pair of legs, without the intervention of an intromittent organ. The elongated acini are confined to the lower part, and are contained within the external tunic of the gland.

Vol. II Plate VIII

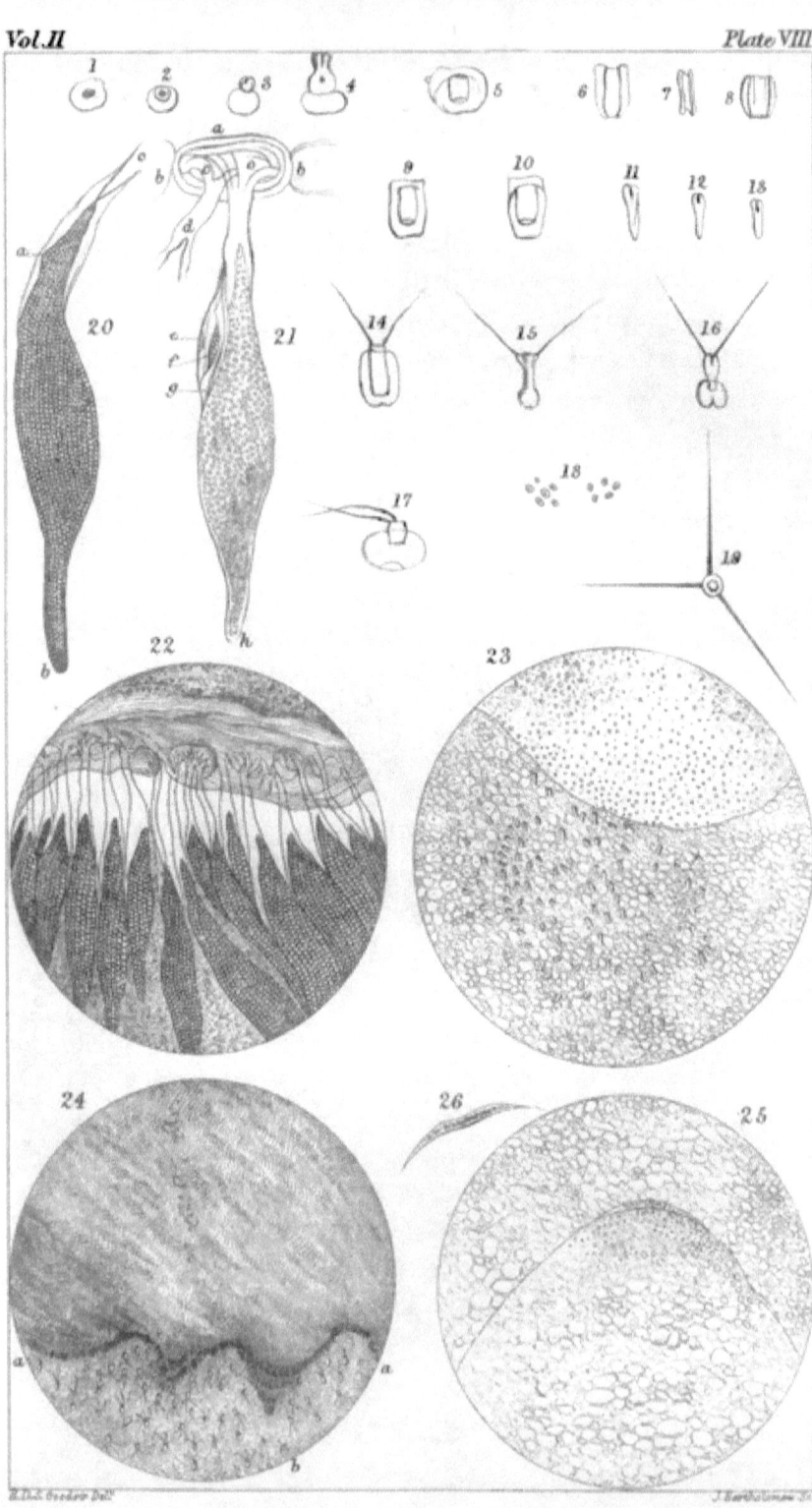

In the *Macroura* the testes commence on each side of the stomach, and extend down to the middle parts of the abdomen. In almost all the species of the section, these organs are narrow ribbon-shaped organs, connected with one another immediately behind the stomach by a narrow commissure; the vasa deferentia come off behind this commissure, and are more distinct than in any other of the sections. In *Galathea* these organs are more complicated, the tube being more convoluted.

The ultimate structure of the testis consists of a germinal membrane, covered externally by the common tunic of the organ, or by processes from it. The germinal membrane, in the upper or first part of its course, developes from germinal spots in its substance formative cells of a spherical shape and of small size, which will be afterwards described. In the lower part of the tube, the formative cells assume a peculiar linear or spindle shape, attached by one of their extremities to the germinal membrane, and projecting either into the cavity of the gland-duct, as in *Pagurus*, or from its external surface as in *Galathea*, and therefore in this case covered by the common enveloping tunic of the gland, or by processes of it which correspond to the areolar vascular matrix of the glands in the higher animals.

When the animal is getting into season, numerous small cells are found, as just described, on the internal surface of the seminal tube, and more particularly from that portion of the gland which lies on the surface of the liver. As the animal becomes stronger, these cells increase in size from the formation of young in their interior. That these young or secondary cells are produced from the germinal spots on the germinal membrane of the seminal tube, from which the primary cell took its origin, appeared highly probable, among other circumstances from this, that after the latter had burst, its cell-wall was smooth and regular, not broken up or rough, as might have been expected, had the secondary cells been formed from it. After these primary cells have burst, the secondary cells contained in them pass down the seminal tube, to undergo the changes to be afterwards described.

The spindle-shaped cells in the lower part of the seminal tube are large primary cells, two or three generally arising from a disc or spot in the germinal membrane. They correspond in every respect, except in shape and size, to the spherical primary cells further up the tube, and like them form in their interior young or secondary cells. These secondary cells originate in a germinal spot or nucleus, situated about a third from the attached extremity of the cell. In such of the spindle-shaped cells as are quite full of secondary cells, this nucleus cannot be seen, so that it probably disappears after the primary cells have become fully developed—that is, have become full of young. In such of these elongated cells, again, as are not quite developed, with cavities not entirely occupied by their progeny, the nucleus may be occasionally seen in various stages of development, with a brood of young cells surrounding it, and enclosed in a membrane carried off by them from the nucleus (*Pagurus*).

These spindle-shaped primary cells of the lower part of the seminal duct differ from the spherical primary cells of the upper part of the same tube, principally in this, that whereas the latter contain only a limited number of secondary cells, formed probably by a single act of nuclear development, the former are filled by successive broods from the nucleus.

In *Hyas*, when these spindle-shaped cells project from the external surface of the seminal duct, instead of into its cavity, the secondary cells pass off by a narrow valvular orifice in its attached extremity, and are replaced by others from the nucleus. The cell in this case has become a secreting follicle, with an active germinal spot.

The passage downwards of the secondary cells, both of the

superior spherical, and the lower spindle-shaped primary cells, is retarded in the neighbourhood of the latter by long slips or bands, which run up the cavity of the duct and terminate by free edges; the direction of these bands being opposed to the flow of the seminal fluid downwards.

These peculiar spindle-shaped cells or acini, although present in all the orders, are most apparent in the *Anomoura* and cuirassed *Macroura*. In the *Triangulares* and succeeding families of *Brachyura*, also in lower families of *Macroura*, from the *Cryptobranchiate* genera and downwards, they are by no means so elongated, resembling rather widened and contracted portions of the seminal duct. The arrangement is similar in the lower orders—as in *Stomapoda*, *Amphipoda*, and *Isopoda*—the *Læmodipoda* being apparently exceptions to the rule. Neither is this structure found in *Branchiopoda*, *Entomostraca*, *Siphonostoma*, and *Xiphosura*, in which orders the structure of the testis would require for elucidation a separate inquiry.

The secondary cells, as has already been stated, continue to be developed in their progress along the seminal tube. At the spot where they are retarded by the folds at the necks of the spindle-shaped cells, they increase much in size, from the increased number and size of their contained cells. After this no great change takes place, with the exception of a thinning of the walls. In this state they pass along the narrow part of the duct, or vas deferens, and are thrown during coitus into the spermatheca of the female, there to undergo the essential change which is to fit them for fertilisation of the ova.

That this final change can only take place in the spermatheca of the female does not appear to be the case, for precocious secondary cells may occasionally be found bursting in the lower part of the seminal tube, and even as high up as the spindle-shaped cells. The greater number, indeed, with a few exceptions the whole of them, are introduced into the female before bursting.

After lying in the spermatheca for some time, the wall of the secondary cell becomes so thin that it bursts, and allows the young cells to escape. These tertiary cells contain, and are, the formative cells of the spermatozoa. In the higher crustacea, *Brachyura*, they each contain one or more spermatozoa, in the *Macroura* one only. The spermatozoal cells are nucleated when they first burst from the secondary cells, and shortly the head of the spermatozoa is found to correspond to the nucleus.

The seminal fluid in all the species of *Macroura* is very peculiar, the tertiary cells being in all cases armed with three long slender setæ.* They are oblong, and dilated at the armed extremity. They are developed singly within their parent cells; sometimes, however, two may be observed in one cell. These parent or secondary cells are oblong, and bulge slightly in the middle. After they have remained for some time in the spindle-shaped cæca (*Galathea*), the three setæ of the tertiary cell expand, and the cells begin their descent. In the progress downwards, the unarmed extremity acquires a small nucleated spot, and in many instances small spherical cells are thrown off from this, which are quaternary, and probably spermatozoal cells. In the cuirassed and digging *Macroura* these tertiary cells are all armed with three setæ, many times longer than the body of the cell. In the prawn these setæ are short and truncated.

Throughout the whole course of the lower part of the seminal tube there may be observed during the active state of the gland, and while the seminal cells are being produced, a large quantity of albuminous matter in small irregular masses floating among the cells in an aqueous fluid. I am induced to believe that the cells derive their nourishment from this matter.

In the upper part of the tube, where the cells are small

---

* Von Siebold in Müller's *Archiv*, 1836.

and comparatively few in number, this matter is in small quantity; but in the lower part of the tube, where the cells are more numerous, more developed, and in a more active condition, it exists in the greatest abundance. Still lower down in the vas deferens, where the cells are in a state of satiety, and are in fact absorbing principally their own external wall, preparatory to bursting, it again diminishes in quantity, and disappears.

This albuminous matter would appear to result from the debris of dissolved cells. It is more abundant in the *Brachyura* than in the other forms of Crustacea, in accordance with the greater abundance of seminal cells.*

H. D. S. G.

* An abstract of more extended observations on the subject of this chapter was published in the *Ed. Phil. Journal*, October 1843.

XXVII.—THE STRUCTURE OF THE SEROUS MEMBRANES.

A PORTION of the human pleura or peritoneum will be found to consist, from its free surface inwards, of a layer of nucleated scales, of a germinal membrane,* and of the sub-serous areolar texture intermixed with occasional elastic fibres. The bloodvessels of the serous membrane ramify in the areolar texture.

There is one stratum only of the nucleated scales in the superficial layer of the serous membrane. This layer conceals the germinal membrane, which can only be detected after the removal of the scales.

The germinal membrane does not in general show the lines of junction of its component flattened cells. These appear to be elongated in the form of ribbons—their nuclei, or the germinal spots of the membrane, being elongated, expanded at one extremity, pointed at the other, and somewhat bent upon themselves. The direction of these flattened cells and nuclei is the same in any one part of the membrane, this direction being in general parallel to the subjacent bloodvessels, in the neighbourhood of which they exist in greatest numbers. The germinal spots are bright and crystalline, and may, or may not, according to their condition, contain smaller cells in their interior. They are not to be confounded with

* I stated this fact in my Paper on the Intestinal Villi, in the *Ed. Phil. Journal*, July 1822. Dr. Todd and Mr. Bowman, in their *Physiology of Man*, have described the same membrane in the serous texture.

the fibres of the areolar texture, or with elastic filaments, or with the nuclei of the capillary vessels of the subserous texture, or with paler, ovoidal, somewhat indistinct cells, scattered throughout that texture, and which appear to be connected with the common areolar fibres.

These flattened ribbon-shaped scales, and bright crystalline nuclei, which form the germinal or basement membrane of the serous coat appear to be identical with the objects described by Valentin,* Pappenheim,† and Henle,‡ and named by the latter nucleated fibres.

In inflamed or aged serous membranes, I have found it impossible to detect this membrane, or even the superimposed scales. The germinal membrane in such instances appears to break up into areolar texture, and to assimilate itself to the bursæ mucosæ, or the ordinary enlarged areolæ of the areolar texture.

If these germinal centres be the sources of all the scales of the superficial layer, each centre being the source of the scales of its own compartment, then the matter necessary for the formation of these during their development must pass from the capillary vessels to each of the centres acted on by forces whose centres of action are the germinal spots; each of the scales, after being detached from its parent centre, deriving its nourishment by its own inherent powers.

I have been in the habit of considering the highly vascular fringes and processes of the synovial membranes as more active in the formation of epithelium, and therefore more closely allied to the secreting organs, than other portions of these membranes. If this be the case, Clopton Havers§ was not mistaken in his ideas regarding the functions of these

---

* Valentin, *Repertorium*, 1838.
† Pappenheim, *Zur Kentniss der Verdauung*, 1839.
‡ Henle, *Anatomie Allgemeine*.
§ Clopton Havers, *Osteologia Nova*, 1691.

vascular fringes. They are situated where they cannot interfere with the motions of the joint. They hang into those parts of the cavity best fitted for containing and acting as reservoirs of synovia; and their high vascularity, and the pulpy nature of their serous covering, tend to strengthen this opinion.

The phenomena attending inflammatory action of the membranes are highly interesting. The capillaries are all on one side of the membrane, and yet the serum and lymph are on the other. The capillary vessels in healthy action have no power in themselves of throwing out any of their contents. They do not secrete in virtue of any power inherent in themselves. Do they acquire this power during inflammation? Or will any of the hypotheses of effusion account for the lymph and serum being on the free surface of the serous membranes, and so little, if any, in the subserous textures?

I do not see how we can, in the present state of the science, account for phenomena of this kind by referring them to actions of the extreme vessels. We must look for an explanation, I am inclined to believe, in a disturbance of the forces which naturally exist in the extravascular portions of the inflamed part.*

* "The primary change," in inflammation, " is in the *vital affinities*, common to the solids and fluids, and acting chiefly in that part of the system where the solids and fluids are most intimately mixed, and are continually interchanging particles."—*Alison's Outlines of Physiology and Pathology*, page 437.

XXVIII.—STRUCTURE OF THE LYMPHATIC GLANDS.—(Plate V.)

It is now generally admitted, that the afferent communicate in the interior of the lymphatic glands with the efferent vessels. These glands, indeed, consist of a dense network of lymphatics, in the meshes of which the arteries, veins, and nerves ramify. Much difference of opinion still exists, however, as to the nature of the communication between the afferent and efferent vessels, and no definite idea is entertained regarding the parenchyma of these organs.

We know that an efferent lymphatic, before it enters a gland, consists of an external tunic of filamentous texture, a middle tunic of fibrous texture, and an internal layer of epithelium.

Immediately after the branches, into which the afferent vessel divides, have penetrated the capsule of the gland, they lose their external tunic. For a short distance, indeed, until they have begun to anastomose with one another, a very thin external tunic, accompanied by a little fat, is still observable. This fat is continuous with the layer of adipose texture which generally exists immediately under the capsule of the gland, and through which the lymphatics must pass to and from the organ.

The branches of the extra-glandular lymphatics, then, which pass to and from the glands, possess a very thin internal tunic; but the network of intra-glandular lymphatics which enter into the structure of the gland itself, presents no external coat. The external tunic of the extra-glandular lymphatics—the afferent and efferent vessels—appears to leave them almost entirely at their entrance and exit from the organ, and by passing on to the surface of the gland forms its capsule.

This capsule is moderately strong, somewhat smooth on its free, more filamentous on its attached surface, sending inwards from the latter the processes already described, which not only support the larger branches of the vessels before they anastomose, but also bind together and strengthen the substance of the organ. The larger trunks of the arteries and veins, as they pass through the capsule, and plunge into the substance of the gland, carry along with them also a certain quantity of filamentous texture, which is derived from the internal surface of the capsule, and is continuous with the processes which surround the larger lymphatic branches.

The middle or fibrous tunic of the extra-glandular lymphatics, also begins to disappear after these vessels have penetrated the capsule of the gland. It is still sufficiently apparent on the lymphatics near the surface of the organ, but is met with sparingly towards the centre. Different glands, however, differ in this respect; the human intra-glandular lymphatics appearing to me to retain more of their fibrous tunic than those in the more granular and developed mesenteric glands of the dog and seal.

It is, however, to the changes which the internal tunic of the intra-glandular lymphatics undergoes, that I shall now more particularly direct attention, as these have hitherto escaped observation, and as upon them depend those appearances and peculiarities which are yet unexplained.

I shall first describe the internal tunic, and afterwards its arrangement.

If this tunic be traced from the afferent lymphatics, in which it presents the usual structure, into the branches immediately after they have penetrated the capsule of the gland, it is found to become thicker and more opaque. In the short dilated anastomosing branches which form the intra-glandular network this tunic has become so thick and opaque, that the vessels will no longer transmit the light, and appear as if they were stuffed full of a granular matter. When these thickened and dilated vessels are cut, torn, or broken, so as to display their structure, it may be observed that two parts enter into their composition—an extremely fine external membrane, and a thick granular substance, which lines the membrane.

The external membrane is extremely thin and transparent. In its substance there are arranged, at regular distances, ovoidal bodies, so placed that their long diameters are all in the same direction. The distance of these bodies from one another is somewhat greater than their long diameters. They are imbedded in the substance, and form a part of the membrane. They are hollow, and contain one or more rounded vesicles grouped together in their interior. I have seen portions of this membrane, after it has been acted upon by acetic acid, present an appearance of being broken up into flat semi-transparent scales, united by their edges—each scale consisting of one of the nucleated ovoidal bodies, and a portion of the surrounding membrane.

The thick granular substance which is attached to the internal surface of the membrane just described, is composed entirely of nucleated particles, closely packed together, and cohering to one another. The thickness of this layer of granular substance is so considerable as to render the vessel, of which it is a part, almost opaque, encroaching on its cavity, and leaving a comparatively narrow canal for the passage of the lymph and chyle. This canal appears to be somewhat irregular, in consequence of the greater exuberance of the granular substance in some spots, and its deficiency in others. This circumstance also accounts for the greater transparency of the vessels at certain parts of their extent. The canal is not lined by a membrane, but appears to me to be irregularly pierced through the granular substance, the projections and hollows of which, as well as the superficial layer of its nucleated particles, being freely bathed by the lymph and chyle.

The nucleated particles are on an average about the 5000th of an inch in diameter. They are spherical, and contain a nucleus, which consists of one or more particles. Their walls are very distinct, especially after being treated with acetic acid, which reduces their size somewhat, without dissolving or breaking them up.

The layer of particles which has now been described is thickest in the lymphatics towards the centre of the gland. If it be examined in either direction towards the afferent or efferent branches, it will be found to become thinner, and, at last, to be continuous with the layer of flat epithelium-scales of the extra-glandular lymphatics.

The anatomical relations of the membrane, and its layer of nucleated particles, are identical with those which characterise the primary cells or membrane, and the secondary or secreting cells of certain glands. The oval vesicles in the substance of the membrane are germinal spots or centres of nutrition, and the membrane is a germinal membrane. I am inclined to believe the spots on the membrane to be the sources from which the germs of the nucleated particles of the thick layer are derived. These spots are doubtless in a state of constant activity in all lymphatic glands, but must be called into much more vigorous action periodically in the mesenteric glands, during the passage of the chyle. If this be the case, these spots must exert a force by which matter is abstracted from the blood which circulates in the neighbouring capillaries, for the purpose of developing a steady succession of nucleated particles.

The arrangement in the substance of the lymphatic glands

of this highly-developed portion of the lymphatic system of vessels, or, in other words, the mode in which the afferent communicate with the efferent lymphatics, I have found to coincide with the account usually given of it. The terminal branches of the afferent form a more or less dense network with the radicals of the efferent lymphatics. The question which has been so often agitated, as to whether cavities exist, intermediate between the two sets of lymphatics, is not one of much importance. Some lymphatic glands, as has frequently been stated, exhibit, after injection with mercury, nothing but a mass of lymphatic vessels; others, again, a mass of apparently intermediate cells; and Cruikshank correctly remarks, that occasionally, when the mercury first passes through a gland, cells only may appear, but after the injection has been pushed a little further, vessels full of mercury may suddenly present themselves.*

These various appearances may be explained by the following facts :—In some lymphatic glands the meshes are elongated, in which case no force short of what is sufficient to burst the vessels can obliterate the vascular appearance. The intra-glandular lymphatics, like those in other parts, are liable to be over-distended with injections, or by their own contents, so that short vessels or rounded meshes, more especially after great distension, assume the appearance of globular cavities.

There is another apparently cellular appearance, which is not met with in the human lymphatic glands, but in some of the lower mammals, which is produced by another cause—the partial or entire obliteration of some of the meshes, so as to produce cavities more or less extended, with bars or threads passing from wall to wall, the lymphatics opening into them. This is the conversion of a network of lymphatics into cavities

* Cruikshank, *The Anatomy of the Absorbing Vessels of the Human Body*, page 82.

and connecting threads, by a process of absorption similar to that which I have to describe as occurring in the placental decidua.*

The external surfaces of the intra-glandular lymphatics are closely applied to one another. They are strengthened here and there by fibrous bundles, the remains of the middle tunic. These fibres are most distinct towards the surface of the glands, and at the angles formed by the junction of one lymphatic with another; and when viewed in thin sections seem to form arches inclosing circular or oval spaces, like the fibrous matrix of the human kidney.

The description usually given of the arrangement of the bloodvessels in the lymphatic glands is sufficiently correct. The ultimate capillaries, as I have observed, do not ramify in the substance of the germinal membrane of the intra-glandular lymphatics, but are merely in contact with its external surface. In this respect they resemble the ultimate ducts of the true secreting glands.

The capillary network which surrounds the intra-glandular lymphatics is as fine as that which supplies the ultimate secreting ducts, and for the same purpose in both, to afford matter for the continued formation of secreting epithelium on the internal surface of the germinal membrane.

The structure I have described affords, in my opinion, satisfactory evidence—

1. That the lymphatic glands are merely networks of lymphatic vessels, deprived of all their tunics but the internal, the epithelium of which is highly developed for the performance of particular functions.

2. That these peculiar lymphatics are supplied with a fine capillary network, to supply matter for the continual renovation of the epithelium.

* See page 457.

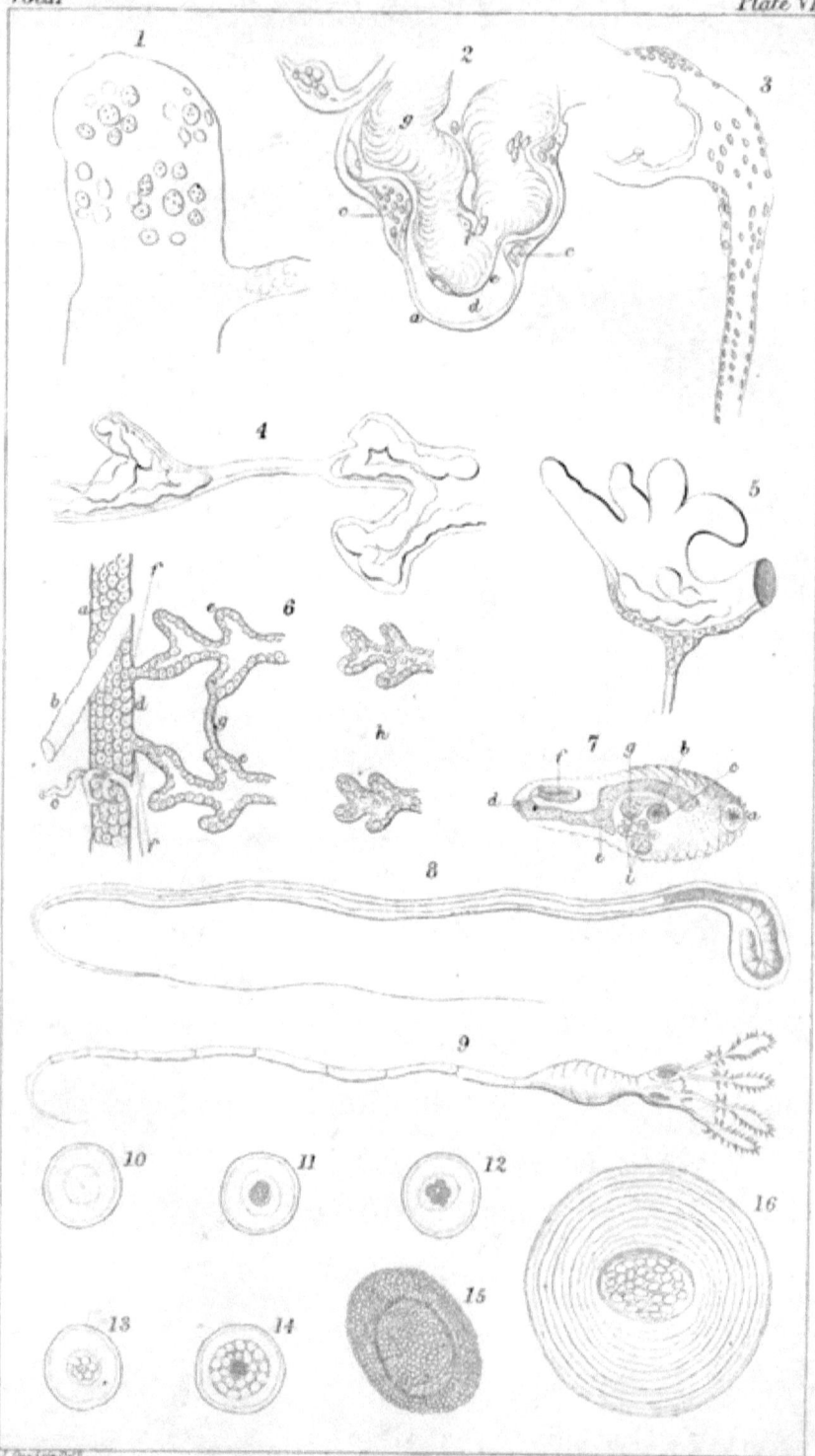

XXIX.—THE STRUCTURE OF THE HUMAN PLACENTA.—(Plates V. VI.)

I.—OF THE STRUCTURE OF THE TUFTS AND VILLI OF THE PLACENTA.

1.—*Of the Configuration of the Tufts.*

A PLACENTAL tuft resembles a tree. It consists of a trunk, of primary branches, and of secondary branches or terminal villi, which are attached as solitary villi to the sides of the primary branches, and to the extremities of the latter, in which case they generally present a digitated arrangement. The villus, when solitary, is cylindrical, or slightly flattened, or somewhat club-shaped; when digitated, each division may be much flattened, or is then generally heart-shaped. The digitated villi are only solitary villi grouped together at the extremity of a primary branch.

2.—*Of the External Membrane of the Tufts.*

The trunk, the primary branches, and the terminal villi of the tuft are covered by a very fine transparent membrane, apparently devoid of any structure. This membrane may be described as bounding the whole tuft, passing from the trunk to the branches, and from these to the villi, the free extremities of which it closely covers. Its free surface is smooth and glistening—its attached surface is somewhat rough.*

* Professor Reid, "On the Anatomical Relations of the Bloodvessels of the Mother to those of the Fœtus in the Human Species."—*Ed. Med. Surg. Journal*, 1841, page 7.

3.—*Of the External Cells of the Villi.*

Immediately under the membrane just described is a layer of cells.* They are flattened spheroids, slightly quadrilateral in outline, from the manner in which they are packed together. When a tuft is viewed in profile, under compression, its edges exhibit the appearance of a double line, which leads the observer to suppose that its bounding membrane is double, with the cells just described situated between the two laminæ. In the space between the two lines, the nuclei of the cells may be seen in the form of dark oval spots, and the septa formed by the walls of contiguous cells are also visible.

At variable distances the space between the two lines widens out into a triangular form, the base towards the external membrane, the apex towards the centre of the villus. This wider space is produced by a larger group of cells, which appear to be passing off from a spot in the centre of the mass. The groups of cells I am now describing are germinal spots. They are the centres from which new cells are constantly passing off, to supply the loss of those which have disappeared in the performance of their important function.

As in the case of the intestinal epithelium, I am inclined to believe that a fine membrane lines the internal aspect of the layer of cells. I have not been able to isolate it; but the very sharp outline in a profile view of a villus confirms me in my belief of the existence of such a membrane.

4.—*Of the Internal Membrane of the Villus.*

When a villus, under gentle compression, is viewed by transmitted light, there is perceived under the structures already described, and immediately bounding the blood-

---

* Mr. Dalrymple, "On the Structure of the Placenta."—*Med. Chir. Trans.* London, vol. xxv. pages 23, 24.

vessels, and other parts to be afterwards examined, a membrane finer and more transparent than the external membrane, but strong and firm in its texture. This membrane is most distinctly seen when it passes from one loop or coil of the bloodvessel of the villus on to another. It separates very easily from the internal surface of the layer of external cells. I am not disposed to believe that it is attached to this layer, but am of opinion that the spaces which frequently exist between them, even in villi which have undergone no violence, are due to the presence of a fluid matter, the nature of which will be afterwards considered. Be this as it may, pressure very easily separates this membrane from the external cells—the latter invariably remaining attached to the external membrane, the former continuing in every instance closely rolled round the internal structures of the villus, and following them in all their changes of position.

5.—*Of the Bloodvessels of the Tufts.*

Within the internal membrane, and imbedded in structures to be afterwards described, are situated the bloodvessels of the tuft. These vessels are branches of the umbilical arteries and veins.

In the trunk of the tuft, the artery gradually diminishes and the vein increases in size. In some of the primary branches the same relation holds. In others of the primary branches, and in all the villi, the vessel retains the same mean diameter throughout. This species of bloodvessel, although it cannot be considered as either artery or vein, cannot nevertheless be denominated, in precise anatomical language, a capillary. It differs from artery and vein in retaining throughout the same mean diameter; and from the capillary, properly so called, in its greater calibre, containing four or six blood-discs abreast. It is also peculiar in exhibiting sudden constrictions and dilatations, like an intestine.

These changes in form are most remarkable at the spots where the vessel makes sudden turns, coils, or convolutions. Like a capillary, however, this vessel may divide and again become single, and may send off a division to a vessel of the same kind. All such divisions and anastomosing vessels, however, preserve the same mean diameter, and are in this respect distinguishable from arterial and venous branches.

As regards the general arrangement of the vessels, it may be observed that—

1. One vessel may enter a villus, and, returning on itself, leave it again.

2. Two vessels may enter a villus, may anastomose, and leave it in one or two divisions.

3. One or more may enter, may each separate into two or more divisions, which may reunite and leave the villus as they entered.

Many other modifications occur, but the general rule is, that one vessel enters and leaves the villus without dividing.

As regards the particular arrangements of the vessels within the villus, we recognise those leading varieties :—

1. The simple loop, a vessel turning closely on itself.

2. The open loop, a vessel turning on itself, but leaving a space within the loop.

3. The wavy loop, resembling the first, except that the vessel is wavy instead of being direct.

4. The wavy open loops.

5. The contorted loop, the contortion being generally at the extremity or sling of the loop; the limbs of the loop being straight or wavy as the case may be.

6. The various modifications which arise from combinations of the five foregoing forms, in single, double, triple, or quadruple or anastomosing loops. The most common forms are the simple and contorted loop. The simple loop and the wavy loop are found in cylindrical villi. The open loop and

the wavy open loop, occur in the flattened and heart-shaped villi. The contorted and other varieties of loops exist in the club-shaped and tuberose villi.*

Lastly, It must be stated as a fact first recorded and represented by Professor Weber, confirmed by the observations of Mr. John Dalrymple, and to the accuracy of which I can testify, that the same peculiar vessel, or umbilical capillary, may enter and retire from two or more villi before it becomes continuous with a vein.

6.—*Of the internal Cells of the Villus.*

Within the internal membrane, and on the external surface of the umbilical capillaries, are cells which I have named the internal cells of the tuft. When the vessels are engorged, these cells are seen with difficulty. When the vessels are moderately distended, and the internal membrane separated from the external cells by moderate pressure, the cells now under consideration come into view. They are best seen in the spaces left between the internal membrane and the retiring angles formed by the coils and loops of the vessels, and in the vacant spaces formed by these loops. These cells are egg-shaped, highly transparent, and are defined by the instrument with difficulty; but their nuclei are easily perceived. They appear to be filled with a transparent highly refractive matter. This system of cells fills the whole space which

---

* Mr. Dalrymple, in his paper on the Placenta, in the *Med. Chir. Trans.*, has described with great accuracy the manner in which the fœtal vessels ramify and coil in the tufts of the placenta. I am indebted to Mr. Dalrymple for specimens of his injections of the placenta; and to Dr. John Reid, for a portion of a placenta injected by Professor Weber of Leipsic, and have satisfied myself of the accuracy of the descriptions given by these anatomists. My own observations have been made on the unprepared placenta. The drawings of the fœtal vessels in Dr. Reid's paper are plans, as the only point he was anxious to establish was, that the villi terminated in blunt extremities unconnected by cellular or other textures, the fœtal vessels returning upon themselves.—REID, in *Edinburgh Medical and Surgical Journal.*

intervenes between the internal membrane of the villus and the vessels, and gives to this part of the organ a mottled appearance.

II.—OF THE VILLI OF THE CHORION.

Without entering at present into the question as to the manner in which the villi of the chorion take their origin, I may state, that as soon as they are distinctly formed, they present a structure which has to a certain extent been represented and described by Raspail,* Seiler,† and others.

The substance of the tufts consists of nucleated cells. These cells are of different sizes. The smaller are situated, some in the interior, others in the spaces between the latter. The cavities of the larger cells are full of a granular fluid. The surface of the tufts is bounded by a fine but very distinct membrane, which, when minutely examined, is seen to consist of flattened cells united by their edges.

The free extremity of each villus of the tuft is bulbous. The cells which constitute this swelling are arranged round a central spot. They are transparent and refractive, apparently from not containing the same granular matter as the cells of the rest of the villus and tuft. However short a villus may be, it invariably presents a bulbous extremity, with the peculiar cellular arrangement already described. Here and there, on the sides of the stems of the tufts, swellings of a similar structure may be seen. Each of these swellings is the commencement of a new villus or stem, which, as it elongates, carries forward on its extremity the swelling from which it arose.

These groups of cells in the bulbous extremities of the villi of the chorion, and in the swellings on the sides of their

---

* Raspail. *Chemie Organique.*

† Seiler. *Gebärmutter und das Ei des Menschen in den ersten Schwangerschaftsmonaten.*

stems, are the germinal spots of the villi. They are the active agents in the formation of these parts. The villus elongates by the addition of cells to its extremity, the cells passing off from the germinal spot, and the spot receding on the extremity of the villus, as the latter elongates by the additions which it receives from it.

The bulbous extremities of the villi of the chorion, are not only the formative agents of these parts, but are also all along, but principally after the villi have become well developed, their functional agents also. They are to the ovum what the spongioles are to the plant—they supply it with nourishment from the soil in which it is planted.

Up to a certain period of gestation, the chorion and its villi contain no bloodvessels. Bloodvessels first appear in these parts when the allantois reaches and applies itself to a certain portion of the internal surface of the chorion. The umbilical vessels then communicate with the substance of the villi, and become continuous with loops in their interior. Those villi in which the bloodvessels do not undergo any further development, as the ovum increases in size, become more widely separated, and lose their importance in the economy. The villi, again, in which vessels form, in connection with the umbilical vessels, increase in number, and undergo certain changes in the arrangement of their constituent elements, so as to become the internal structures of the tufts of the placenta, as described in the first part of this Memoir. The villi of the chorion always retain their cellular structure. As the bloodvessels increase in size the cells diminish in number; but are always found surrounding the terminal loop of vessels in the situation of the germinal spot. The fine membrane, which was formerly described as bounding the villus of the chorion, always remains at the free extremities of the villi of the placenta; but on the stems and branches of the latter it coalesces with the contained cells.

The conversion into fibrous texture of the membrane and cells of the stems and branches of the tuft of the chorion, forms the tough white fibrous trunk and branches of the tufts of the fœtal portion of the placenta; in each of which runs a branch of the umbilical arteries and vein; and the fine membrane of the villi of the chorion, with its contained cells and terminal bloodloops, still persistent at the extremities of the villi, are the internal membrane, the internal cells, and the bloodloops described in the first part of this Memoir.

III.—OF THE MATERNAL PORTION OF THE PLACENTA.

The mucous membrane of the uterus presents on its free surface the orifices of numerous cylindrical follicles arranged parallel to one another, and at right angles to the surface. In the spaces between these follicles the bloodvessels form a dense capillary net-work.

From the observations of Professors Weber and Sharpey,[*] it has now been ascertained, that when impregnation has taken place, the mucous membrane of the uterus swells, and becomes lax, that its follicles increase in size, and secrete a granular matter, and that the capillaries increase in a proportional degree. "In a uterus," says Dr. Sharpey, "supposed to have been recently impregnated, and in which the vessels had been minutely injected with vermilion, the lining membrane, or commencing decidua, appeared everywhere pervaded by a net-work of bloodvessels, in the midst of which the tubular glands were seen, their white epithelium strongly contrasting with the surrounding redness." It must have been from a uterus in this condition that Von Baer took the sketch of the structure of the commencing decidua, which has been copied by Wagner in his *Icones Physiologicæ*. Von Baer and Wagner, however, have mistaken the enlarged follicles for

[*] Müller's *Physiology*, page 1574.

papillæ, and have represented the capillary loops in a manner much too formal. I have examined a uterus which was in a state described by Dr. Sharpey. There was a well-formed corpus luteum in one of the ovaries; the decidua had appeared on its internal surface, and presented in the most distinct and beautiful manner the orifices of the follicles, and the vascularity of the interfollicular spaces. The follicles, bounded by their germinal membrane, were turgid with their epithelial contents. The interfollicular spaces in which the capillaries formed a net-work with polygonal or rounded meshes, was occupied by a texture which consisted entirely of nucleated particles. This is the tissue represented by Von Baer and Wagner, described by them as surrounding what they supposed to be uterine papillæ, and considered by them as decidua. The free surface of the uterine mucous membrane was covered by a membrane which appeared to me to be continuous with the germinal membrane of the follicles.

Dr. Sharpey has not described this interfollicular substance, as his attention appears to have been chiefly directed to the follicles. As, however, it is to this interfollicular substance, as much as to the enlargement of the follicles themselves, that the mucous membrane owes its increased thickness, it appears to me worthy of being recorded.

A uterus in the condition which has just been described, is said to be lined with the decidua, consisting, as has been stated, of an interfollicular cellular substance, and of an extended net-work of capillary bloodvessels.

About the time at which the ovum reaches the uterus, the developed mucous membrane or decidua begins to secrete, the os uteri becomes plugged up by this secretion, where it assumes the form of elongated epithelial cells; the cavity of the uterus becomes filled with a fluid secretion, the "hydroperione" of Breschet, and in the immediate neighbourhood of the ovum, the secretion consists of cells of a spherical form.

The cells which are separated in the neighbourhood of the ovum I consider as a secretion of the third order. They have passed off from the uterine glands entire, and possess a power peculiar to the third order of secretions, the power of undergoing further development after being detached from the germinal spots or membrane of the secreting organ.

From what has now been stated, it appears that the decidua consists of two distinct elements; the mucous membrane of the uterus thickened by a peculiar development, and of a non-vascular cellular substance, the product of the uterine follicles. The former constitutes at a later period the greater part of the decidua vera, the latter, the decidua reflexa. This view of the constitution of the decidua, clears up the doubts which were entertained regarding the arrangement of these membranes at the os uteri, and entrances of the Fallopian tubes. It is evident that these orifices will be open or closed, just as the cellular secretion is more or less plentiful, or in a state of more or less vigorous development. It also removes the difficulty of explaining how the decidua covers the ovum, a difficulty which cannot be reconciled with the views of Dr. Sharpey, who is obliged to suppose the deposition of lymph, which is only the old view of the constitution of the decidua.

When the ovum enters the cavity of the uterus, the cellular decidua surrounds it, and becomes what has been named the decidua reflexa, by a continuation of the same action by which it had been increasing in quantity before the arrival of the ovum. The cellular decidua grows around the ovum by the formation of new cells, the product of those in whose vicinity the ovum happens to be situated.

At this stage of its growth, the ovum with its external membrane, the chorion, covered by tufts, the structure and functions of which have been described in the second part of this Memoir, is imbedded in a substance which consists entirely of active nucleated cells. The absorbing cells of the tufts are constantly taking up either the matter resulting from the solution of the cells of the cellular decidua, or the fluid contained in these cells. The ovum is now deriving its nourishment, not from the supply which it took along with it when it left the ovary, but from a matter supplied by the uterus. I am, therefore, inclined to look upon the cellular decidua as representing, in the gestation of the mammal, the albumen of the egg of the oviparous animal. They are both supplied by a certain portion of the oviduct, and they are both brought into play after the nourishment supplied by the ovary is exhausted, or in the course of being exhausted. The difference between them consists in this, that in the mammal the albumen is applied to use as quickly as it is absorbed ; whereas, in the oviparous animal, after being absorbed, it is kept in reserve within the chorion till required. I have also been in the habit of considering the uterine cotyledons of the ruminant and other mammalia as a permanent decidua vera, and the milky secretion interposed between them and the fœtal cotyledons as decidua reflexa in its primitive and simplest form.

I have been thus particular in the explanation of what I believe to be the nutritive function performed respectively by the chorion and decidua, as upon it I shall have to found my views regarding the actions of nutrition in the fully developed placenta.

When the ovum has arrived at a certain stage of its growth, the absorption and circulation of nutritive matter by the agency of cells alone is no longer sufficient. At this period, the ovum has approached the thickened mucous membrane, or that portion usually described as decidua serotina. About the same time, the allantois bearing the umbilical vessels applies itself to the internal surface of that portion of the chorion opposed to the decidua serotina, and the villi of that portion become vascular, as formerly described. The vessels of the decidua enlarge, and assume the appearance of sinuses encroaching on the space formerly occupied by the cellular decidua, in the midst of which the villi of the chorion are imbedded. This increase in the calibre of the decidual capillaries goes on to such an extent, that finally the villi are completely bound up or covered by the membrane which constitutes the walls of the vessels, this membrane following the contour of all the villi, and even passing to a certain extent over the branches and stems of the tufts. Between this membrane, or wall of the enlarged decidual vessels, and the internal membrane of the villi, there still remains a layer of the cells of the decidua.

From this period, up to the full time, all that portion of decidua in connection with the group of enlarged capillaries and vascular tufts of the chorion, and which may now be called a placenta, is divided into two portions. The first portion of the decidua, in connection with the placenta, or forming a part of it, is situated between that organ and the wall of the uterus. This is the only portion of the placental decidua with which anatomists have been hitherto acquainted, and I shall name it the parietal portion. It has a gelatinous appearance, and consists of rounded or oval cells. Two sets of vessels pass into it from the uterus. The first set includes vessels of large size which pass through it for the purpose of supplying the placenta with maternal blood for the use of the fœtus. These may be named the maternal functional vessels of the placenta. The second set are capillary vessels, and pass into this portion of the decidua for the purpose of nourishing it. These are the nutritive vessels of the placenta.

The account given by Mr. Hunter of the manner in which the functional vessels of the placenta pass through this portion of the placental decidua is still doubted by many, notwithstanding the more recent of Mr. Owen's* dissections,

* Owen. *Palmer's Edition of John Hunter's Works*, vol. iv.

and the observations of Dr. Reid.* I have dissected the vessels of an unopened uterus at the full time in the manner adopted by Mr. Owen, by opening one of the large veins over the spot to which the placenta was attached. Introducing a probe as a guide, I slit open the vein with a pair of scissors, and repeated the same process with the probe and scissors whenever a branch entered the vein already opened. I gradually passed through the wall of the uterus. In my progress, I occasionally found that when the probe was pushed along an unopened vein, its point appeared at another opening; and as I approached the internal surface of the wall of the uterus, these anastomoses of the veins became more numerous, the spaces which they inclosed presenting the appearance of narrow flat bands. At last, in introducing the probe under the falciform edges of the venous orifices, it was found to have arrived at the placental tufts, which could be seen by raising the edges of the falciform edges. Having passed over the falciform edges, the venous membrane suddenly passed to each side to line the great cavity of the placenta. The flat bands which I have just described as the spaces inclosed by anastomosing venous sinuses, became smaller, and, on entering the cavity itself, the bands were seen to have assumed the appearance of threads, which passed in great numbers from the vascular edges of the venous openings, and from the walls of the cavity of the placenta on to the extremities and sides of the villi and tufts of the placenta. The whole mass of spongy substance, that is the whole mass of tufts, was in this manner perceived to be attached by innumerable threads of venous membrane to that surface of the parietal decidua of the placenta which was covered by the venous membrane. On proceeding deeper into the substance of the placenta, I perceived that, throughout its whole extent, villus was connected to villus, and tuft to tuft, by similar threads of

* Reid. *Edinburgh Medical and Surgical Journal*, loc. cit.

venous membrane. Sometimes the apex of one villus was connected to the apex of another. In other instances the threads connected the sides of the villi. On minute examination these threads were found to be tubular, and the membrane of which they were formed was seen to be continuous in one direction with the lining membrane of the vascular system of the mother, and in the other with the external membrane of the tufts of the placenta, and passing from one tuft, or set of tufts, on to another, so as to form the central containing membrane of the bag of the placenta. These threads, as well as their cavities, are somewhat funnel-shaped at each extremity. The funnel-shaped portions of the cavities of threads, and, in some instances, the whole length of the tube, were found to be full of cells, which were continuous in the one direction with the parietal decidua of the placenta, and in the other with the external cells of the placental villi.*

This observation led me at once to perceive the real signification of the external cells of the placental tufts. I saw that this great system of cells was a portion of the decidua, all but cut off from the principal mass by the enormous development of the decidual vascular network, but still connected with it by the minute files of cells which fill the cavities of the placental threads.

This system of cells, the external cells of the villus, with the external membrane, are portions of the decidua, and, unlike the other elements of the placental tufts, belong to the organism of the mother. These cells, with their membrane, I name the central division of the placental decidua, to distinguish it from the other portion formerly described, and which I have already called the parietal division of the placental decidua.

1. My observations have confirmed the statements of

* These are the reflections of the venous membrane of the mother, described by Dr. Reid.

Professors Weber and Sharpey as to the mode of formation of the decidua vera; but have led me to attach more importance to the interfollicular substance, and to the secreted or non-vascular portion of the decidua.

2. The placenta, as has long been admitted, consists of a fœtal and of a maternal portion intermixed. But the maternal portion, instead of consisting of a part of the vascular system of the mother only, includes the whole of the external cells of the villi.

3. The external membrane of the placental villi is a portion of the wall of the vascular system of the mother, continuous with the rest of that wall, through the medium of the placental threads and lining membrane of the placental cavity.

4. The system of the external cells of the placental villi belongs to the decidua, and is continuous with the parietal division through the medium of the cavities of the placental threads. This portion of decidua has been named the central division of the placental decidua, and the threads decidual bars.

5. The function of the external cells of the placental villi is to separate from the blood of the mother the matter destined for the blood of the fœtus. They are, therefore, secreting cells, and are the remains of the secreting mucous membrane of the uterus.

6. Immediately within the external cells of the placental villi there is a membrane which I have named the internal membrane of the villi. This membrane belongs to the system of the fœtus, and is the external or bounding membrane of the villi of the chorion.

7. Inclosed within the internal membrane of the placental villi is a system of cells, which belong to the system of the fœtus, and are the cells of the villi of the chorion. These are the internal cells of the placental villus.

8. The function of the internal cells of the placental villi is to absorb, through the internal membrane, the matter secreted by the agency of the external cells of the villi.

9. **The external cells of the placental villi perform, during** intra-uterine existence, a function for which is substituted in extra-uterine life the digestive action of the gastro-intestinal mucous membrane.

10. The internal cells of the placental villi perform, during intra-uterine existence, a function for which is substituted in **extra-uterine** life the action of the absorbing chyle-cells of the intestinal villi.

11. The placenta, therefore, not only performs, as has been always admitted, the function of a lung, but also the function of an intestinal tube.

XXX.—THE STRUCTURE AND ECONOMY OF BONE.

A TEXTURE may be considered either by itself, or in connection with the parts which usually accompany it. These subsidiary parts may be entirely removed without interfering with the anatomical constitution of the texture. It is essentially non-vascular, neither vessels nor nerves entering into its intimate structure. It possesses in itself those powers by which it is nourished, produces its kind, and performs the actions for which it is destined, the subsidiary or superadded parts supplying it with materials which it appropriates by its own inherent powers, or connecting it in sympathetic and harmonious action with other parts of the organism to which it belongs.

In none of the textures are these characters more distinctly seen than in the osseous. A well-macerated bone is one of the most easily made, and, at the same time, one of the most curious anatomical preparations. It is a perfect example of a texture completely isolated, the vessels, nerves, membranes, and fat, are all separated, and nothing is left but the non-vascular osseous substance.

The osseous texture of a fresh bone, considered in this way, consists of two parts, a hard and a soft. The hard part, composed of earthy salts, deposited in a cartilaginous matrix, has already been carefully examined by anatomists. The soft has not yet attracted attention, in consequence of the manner in which it is isolated, divided into small portions, and concealed in the cavities of the osseous corpuscles.

The hard part of the osseous texture, considered in a long bone, presents four surfaces, all communicating with one another, a periosteal or external, a medullary or internal, a Haversian or intermediary, and a corpuscular or canalicular. The periosteal surface communicates with the Haversian in three ways: by those Haversian canals which open in it; by the canal for the medullary artery gradually subdividing and diminishing till it breaks up into arterial Haversian canals; and by the more numerous canals for the veins, principally met with at the extremities of the bone. The medullary surface is to be considered as a portion of the Haversian, having been formed by the enlargement, and subsequent blending of neighbouring Haversian canals into medullary cavities and cancelli. The canalicular or corpuscular surface forms the walls of the innumerable corpuscles and canaliculi, and communicates by the latter with the Haversian, medullary, and less freely with the periosteal surface.

The compact osseous substance, in which the corpuscles and their canaliculi are situated, is not homogeneous in texture. It consists of cells filled with bony substance, ossified or calcified primordial cells.

The soft part of the true osseous texture is not continuous like the hard, but is divided, as has been stated, into as many portions as there are corpuscles in the bone. Each of these portions consists of a little mass of nucleated cells of great transparency. They do not appear to extend along the canaliculi, but to be confined to the cavity of the corpuscle.

These two parts, the hard and the soft combined, constitute the true osseous texture. They differ from one another only in this, that the cells of the one are ossified, those of the other retain their original delicacy and softness. The masses of soft cells in the corpuscles, I am inclined to consider as the nutritive centres, germinal centres, or germinal spots of the texture. These centres are the source of all the hardened cells, each of them being the centre of all those comprehended within the range of its own caniliculi. Each of these soft germinal masses is the centre of attraction for the proper nutriment of bone, and is the active agent in withdrawing this from the vessels, and appropriating it, partly for the nourishment of the hard cells, each of which has a centre of attraction within itself, but more probably for the formation of new calcigerous cells, as the old cells dissolve and their debris falls back into the returning circulation. The canaliculi are undoubtedly the principal channels for the passage of nutriment from the capillaries to the calcigerous cells and germinal centres. They are necessary in a hard texture, and like similar canals and fissures in certain hard cells in vegetables, only appear at a late stage in the development of bone. Each osseous corpuscle has its own system of canaliculi, these extending, for the purpose of communicating with others, to the confines of its own territory; that is, to the boundaries of the space which was at one time contained within the sphere of the primary cell of which it was the nucleus.

The accessory parts of the osseous texture are the vessels, nerves, membranes, and oil. For my present purpose it is only necessary for me to allude to the membranes, as one of them, the periosteum, has been held to play a most important part in the formation and economy of bone.

The periosteum is not so important an element in the constitution of a bone as has usually been supposed. In the adult bone, it is nothing more than the fibrous sheath of the organ, similar to the bounding or limiting membrane of other organs, and in which the vessels ramify sufficiently to anastomose with those of the comparatively few Haversian canals which open on the external surface. In the fœtus it is much more vascular, the external surface of the bone being at that period actively engaged in growth.

There exists in every true bone a membrane or layer of much greater importance, and infinitely more extended than the periosteum. Between the bloodvessels and the walls of the Haversian canals there is a layer of cellular substance. This cellular substance is the product, its cells being the descendants of the corpuscles of the cartilage or matrix in which the bone was originally formed. It forms a blastema, originally produced round each cartilage corpuscle by development into a linear series perpendicular to the ossifying surface: each of the secondary cartilage corpuscles remaining as centres, or the sources of new centres of nutrition of the future bone, their progeny forming the cellular mass which becomes enclosed in the capsules of compact primary bone. When these capsules have opened into one another to form the Haversian canals, a process similar to the mode of development of gland ducts and capillaries, the cellular mass surrounds the vessels in their course, and separates them from the walls of the canals.

That this cellular layer plays an important part in the economy of bone, appears probable from the prominent position it holds in its development, and from the intimate connection of the Haversian canals with all the morbid changes of bone. Its existence, great extent, and probable powers, cannot be overlooked in any question regarding the economy of bone in health or disease.

The cellular mass, just described, fills the cancelli, or enlarged Haversian chambers, of foetal bones, and, in this situation, has not been overlooked by former observers. In adult bones, it is in the medullary cavity, cancelli, and, to a certain extent, in the larger Haversian canals, replaced by fat cells.

On the surface of young and vigorous bones I have observed numerous cells, flattened, elongated, and more or less turgid, belonging doubtless to the system of Haversian cells.

XXXI.—THE MODE OF REPRODUCTION AFTER DEATH OF THE SHAFT OF A LONG BONE.

THE question at issue regarding the source of the new osseous substance in regeneration of the shaft of a long bone, is thus stated by Professor Syme.* "Whether the periosteum, or membrane that covers the surface of the bones, possesses the power of forming new osseous substance independently of any assistance from the bone itself?" and the Professor has detailed some very ingenious experiments, which satisfied him that this membrane does possess the power of producing new osseous texture.

The first experiment consisted in exposing the radius of a dog, and removing an inch and three quarters of it along with the periosteum; and in the other leg removing a corresponding portion without the periosteum. In six weeks the cut extremities of the radius, from which a portion had been taken, together with the periosteum, had only extended towards one another in a conical form, with a great deficiency of bone between them, and in its place merely a small band of tough ligamentous texture. In the other, where the periosteum had been allowed to remain, there was a compact mass of bone, not only occupying the space left by the portion removed, but rather exceeding it.

The objection to this experiment is, that it cannot be performed accurately. I have satisfied myself, that it is

* *Trans. Roy. Soc. Edin.* vol. xiv. page 158. "On the Power of the Periosteum to form New Bone."

impossible to separate the periosteum from a dog's radius without removing along with it minute longitudinal, filamentary, or ribbon-shaped portions of the surface of the bone; more particularly, as may be conceived, when performed in the manner which under the circumstances would be adopted, by slitting it up in front, and detaching it transversely before separating the portion of bone. It remains to be proved that it is not from these minute shreds of bone that the regenerated portion of the shaft has derived its origin.*

In the other part of the experiment, in which the periosteum as well as the bone was removed, it was not to be expected that complete regeneration should have taken place, inasmuch as the bounding or limiting membrane of the organ had been removed, and the surrounding textures were allowed to collapse and unite. Even under these unfavourable circumstances, the cut extremities of the bone had lengthened themselves out in a conical form.

The two subsequent experiments, by the insertion of tin plates, though highly ingenious, differ in no essential particular from the first, and are liable to the same objections. If a section had been made through the denuded shafts, new bone would have been found deposited in their interior, just as it had been at the cut extremities in the first experiments.

The careful examination of numerous bones, the shafts of which had died, and were in progress of replacement by a substitute in the form of a shell, has satisfied me that in no instance do we ever see a new shaft, without at the same time observing portions of the old shaft ulcerated to a greater or less extent—the ulcerated portions invariably corresponding in the early stages to the scales of new bone in the periosteum. Whenever the old shaft is entire, its periosteal surface presenting the natural appearance of a macerated bone, the part corresponding to this in the new shaft is formed of bone which

* Baly. Note in his Translation of Müller's *Physiology*, page 471.

is seen to be shooting, in the manner peculiar to this mode of regeneration, from a point corresponding to an ulcerated portion of the old shaft. So striking is this peculiarity, that it will at once recur to those who have had an opportunity of observing new shafts in an early stage of formation; as well as the remarkable contrast between the smooth hard portions of the dead or dying bone and the nodulated scales lying in the separated periosteum, alternating with the former, and concealing from direct view the rough or ulcerated portions of the dead shaft. In those instances in which the shaft has died, with the exception of a ring or small portion at each or one end, close to the epiphysis, the new bone shoots in stalactitic masses in the longitudinal direction, their course, direction, and magnitude, corresponding to the forms of the rings or portions of ulcerated bone in the old shaft. This is an unfavourable form of necrosis, in consequence of the difficulty encountered by the extremities of the new shell in meeting in the centre, and the length of time required for the process of regeneration. This form has also given rise to a mistaken view of the source of the new bone in necrosis, a belief that it is derived from the epiphysis. I have never seen an instance in which the epiphysis supplied the new shaft, and I have had occasion to point out that the specimens on which such opinions were founded are in fact exemplifications of the formation of the new, from a ring or portion of the old shaft close to the epiphysis. An epiphysis is a distinct part, and has no greater tendency to supply the losses of the principal mass of the bone to which it belongs than the femur, fibula, or astragalus, to supply the loss of a tibia.

Another remarkable peculiarity, arising from the circumstance of the new bone invariably shooting from spots corresponding to ulcerated portions of the dead shaft, is met with in instances where one side of a dead shaft is not ulcerated, and the other side, or a portion of it, has undergone that process. In such instances, the new bone proceeds from points corresponding to the ulcerations, and shoots in the form of arches across the smooth portion of the old bone, meeting from either side, and giving rise to new processes which ultimately enclose the whole. In instances of this sort regeneration is effected with difficulty, and there is a tendency in the old shaft to ulcerate out on the side on which it has supplied no osseous centres of regeneration.

The death of the entire shaft of a long bone must be a very rare occurrence. In a case of this kind, the shaft would be found lying loose in a cavity formed by the epiphysis at each end, and the separated periosteum on the sides. The bone itself, although its surface might be opened up by inflammation, would present no ulceration or actual deficiency of substance. In a case of this kind, I believe no regeneration whatever would take place. The epiphyses have no tendency to assist; and the periosteum has separated without a single portion of the shaft from which new bone might be produced.

In the majority of instances of what is incorrectly named death of the entire shaft, ulcerated portions or deficiencies of the surface will be met with; and in the periosteal sheath, scales of new bone corresponding to these will be perceived. I have observed the process by which these ulcerations are produced, and have already described it in the chapter on ulceration.

The first appreciable inflammatory changes in bone occur within the Haversian canals. These passages dilate or become opened up, as may be seen on the surface of an inflamed bone, or better in a section. The result of this enlargement of the canals is the conversion of the contiguous canals into one cavity, and the consequent removal or absorption of all the osseous texture of the part. This removal of the substance of the walls of the Haversian canals is not to be explained by pressure arising from effused lymph, understood either in a mechanical sense, which is inapplicable to actions of this kind, or in the Hunterian sense in which it is employed, as a mode of expression for an action, the details of which have not been recognised.

By the enlargement of neighbouring Haversian canals, and the consequent removal of all the osseous substance of a portion of bone, an ulceration is produced, or a piece of dead or dying bone is separated from the living organ. A stratum of what, in the language of surgical pathologists, is named granulations, divides the dead from the living, and ultimately casts the dead off, by assuming a free surface towards it, throwing pus into the inter-space.

When the entire shaft of a bone is attacked by violent inflammation, there is generally time, before death of the bone takes place, for the separation, by the process just described, of more or less numerous portions of its surface. When the entire periosteum has separated from the shaft, it carries with it those minute portions of the surface of the bone. Each of these is covered on its external surface by the periosteum, on its internal by a layer of granulations, the result of the organised matter which originally filled the inflamed Haversian canals; the gradual enlargement and subsequent blending of which ultimately allowed their contained vascular contents to combine with the layer of granulations just described; and to form the separating medium between the dead shaft and its minute living remnants. These minute separated portions, after having advanced somewhat in development, appear, when carelessly examined, particularly in dried specimens, to be situated in the substance of the periosteum, and have been adduced by the advocates of the agency of that membrane in forming new bone, as evidences of the truth of their opinions.

In proportion to the equal manner in which these living portions of the old shaft are arranged over the whole internal surface of the periosteum, will be the facility and consequent rapidity in the formation of the new shaft. The shape of the new bone will also depend very much upon the same circumstances; for, if the centres of formation of the new shaft are separated from one side only of the old bone, then an unshapely mass of new bone is thrown out on the same side, for the purpose of strengthening the part during the time necessary for shooting across the bridges of bone which are to supply that side of the new shaft, for the formation of which no osseous centres had been separated. Every possible modification, resulting from these principles, may be observed in looking over series of necrosed long bones.

A remarkable fact in connection with cloacæ is, that they are almost invariably opposite a smooth or unaltered portion of the surface of the dead shaft. They result from the pus thrown off from the granulating internal surface of the new shaft making its way to the exterior by those parts not yet closed, in consequence of having been opposite to portions of the old shaft, which had not afforded separated osseous centres. After the new shell has gained its full strength the cloacæ, like sinuses of the soft parts, are prevented from closing by the continued flow of the pus. The situation of cloacæ is determined by circumstances in the death of the old, and kept open by the continued flow of the secretions of the new shaft.

As, therefore, it has been found impossible to separate the periosteum in living animals without detaching shreds of bone along with it—as in necrosis of the shafts of long bones, portions of the old osseous texture may be detected in the periosteal sheath opposite ulcerations of the dead shaft—and as consistent with what is at present held regarding the powers of capillary vessels, and the origin of the textures, we are compelled to assent to the doctrine that periosteum does not possess an independent power of forming osseous substance.

The participation of the periosteum in the office of regeneration—an important principle in surgery—is not denied in this conclusion.

Vol. II   Plate IX

XXXII.—THE MODE OF REPRODUCTION OF LOST PARTS IN THE CRUSTACEA.—(Plate IX.)

That all the species of crustacea have the power of regenerating parts of their body which have been accidentally lost, is a fact which has been long known. The particular manner in which these new parts are developed, and also the organ from which the germ of the new part is derived, has never yet been sufficiently examined or properly explained.

If one or more of the last phalanges of the leg of a common crab be seriously injured, the animal instantly throws off the remaining parts of the limb close to the body. It has the power of doing so, apparently for two purposes; to save the excessive flow of blood which always takes place at the first wound, and to lay bare the organ which is to reproduce the future limb. As soon as the injured limb has been thrown off the bleeding stops, the reason of which will be explained hereafter; but if the animal is unable, from weakness or other causes, to effect this, the hæmorrhage proceeds to a fatal termination.

It is apparently in the organs of locomotion only that the power of reproduction resides. That it does not do so in all parts of the body—in the higher crustacea, at least—is proved by experiment, and is also apparent from the circumstance of many species being obtained with the body and other parts very much maimed, and which have to all appearance been so for a considerable period. Wounds of the body in general prove speedily fatal, if they penetrate deeply, but if otherwise, a cicatrix only is formed, which remains until the casting of the shell, when the new shell takes on all the characters and appearance of the old one, before it met with the injury. When the animal is weak and unhealthy, and in that state meets with any severe injury of a limb, it is unable to throw it off at the usual place, and consequently very soon dies from loss of blood; but when strong and vigorous, it is enabled to throw the injured limb off with little apparent pain or exertion. It is a well-known fact, that these animals can throw off their limbs when seized by them, and also from several other causes, to which it is unnecessary to allude at present.

When the crustacean does throw off a limb voluntarily, it will be found on examination that this is always effected at one spot only, near to the basal extremity of the first phalanx. This part of the phalanx is very much contracted for the length of half-an-inch, or a little more, in the common edible crab. The whole of this portion is filled with a fibrous, gelatinous, glandular-looking mass; the organ which supplies the germs for future limbs. On looking closely into the surface of this body, we find that it is divided into two unequal parts, by means of a transverse line. The basal or proximal part of this body is the smallest. On tracing this line towards the shell we find that it runs into it, as it were, and forms, instead of one line, two; by which means a very thin ring is formed, and this ring is also found to run completely round the limb, being marked externally by means of a thin band of small scattered hairs. By dissection this line can be traced into the substance of the organ of reproduction, and is found in this way to be the exact spot where the limb is generally thrown off. Through the long axis of this, and near to one edge, a small foramen exists for the transmission of the bloodvessels and nerve. The microscopic structure of this gland or organ is extremely beautiful. When a thin transverse section is made, and placed under the microscope, it is found to present the following appearances:—The foramen, for the transmission of the vessels and nerves, which was distinctly seen with the naked eye, is obscured on account of the pressure arising from the glass plates, but its situation can be still distinctly made out near to one edge of the section, and also within a thick fibrous-looking band, which, when traced, is found to surround a considerable extent of surface. The space contained within this band is also found upon examination to be much more transparent than that beyond it, and to contain numerous small cells, all of which have nuclei or nucleoli within them. These cells appear to be suspended in a thickish transparent liquid. The thick fibrous band, mentioned above, is composed of a great many fibres, all of which run almost parallel to one another. Beyond this band, and occupying the remaining space between it and the shell, lies a confused mass of large primitive cells or blastema. The shell membrane, covered by the shell, encircles this,—thus the whole structure of the leg at this part consists of, 1*st*, the foramen for the transmission of the vessels and nerves; the fibrous band, with the semi-liquid mass containing small cells; the blastema of larger nucleated cells; and, lastly, the shell membrane, covered by the shell.

In reference to the fibrous band here mentioned, farther observations have proved it to belong to a very peculiar system of vessels, which are very generally distributed throughout the body of the animal. They ramify very freely over the membrane lining the carapace, throughout the ovaries, liver, intestinal canal, and on the bloodvessels of the organs of locomotion. In the latter, they are arranged at regular intervals, and run parallel to one another. They run in this manner, until that part of the leg is reached about half an inch beyond the reproductive gland, when they terminate by means of blind extremities. I have not yet made out the exact relative anatomy of this very peculiar system of vessels, or in what manner those running in the longitudinal direction of the leg are connected with the circular one which surrounds the foramen at the point of fracture, but immediately after the animal has thrown off the injured limb, the raw surface becomes covered with these vessels. Before the separation, the vessels had been partially empty; but immediately on the separation taking place, they became so distended as to become visible to the naked eye. In all the observations made, it was generally found that these vessels presented a radiated appearance on the newly made surface, running from the circumference to the circular one surrounding the situation of the germ. The greater number also appeared to terminate at the circumference by means of blind extremities. A dark circular disc was seen at the extremity of many of these cul-de-sacs, which had all the appearance of a germinal spot. When these vessels were first seen, they were thought to be connected with the reproductive gland alone, but after further observations, this appeared to be incorrect; and, as already mentioned, their relations are so extensive and complicated as to require much more time for their elucidation than I have had since they came under my observation. It is evident, however, they perform some important function in the economy of the animal, but whether it is connected with the reproduction of lost parts or not, is a question to be decided by future observation.

Immediately on the limb being thrown off, a quantity of blood escapes, which is soon stopped by the retraction of the vessels. After this takes place, we see the small open foramen for the passage of the artery and nerve, which becomes closed almost immediately by means of a slight film which spreads over the whole of the exposed surface. When this surface is examined some hours after the loss, we find that the small cavity of the foramen is slightly filled up with a body resembling a nucleated cell. This cell is the germ of the future leg, and very shortly increases in size, so as gradually to push out the film alluded to above, which is now become a thick strong cicatrix. During the time that this is going on, the whole of the exposed surface had become tense and bulging, but this gradually decreases round the circumference as the central nucleus increases in size, which it does at first longitudinally, and then transversely. As it increases in size, the cicatrix, which still surrounds it as a sac, becomes thinner and thinner, until it bursts, when the limb, which has hitherto been bent upon itself, becomes stretched out, and has all the appearance of a perfect limb, except in size.

In the lower crustacea, and even in the lower Macroura, we find the power of regeneration more extended;—a limb broken off at any part of its phalanges will grow. The mode of reproduction in the lobster is peculiar, and differs from the higher crustacea. Instead of the young limb being folded upon itself, as we found it in the Brachyura, it is quite extended, although apparently enclosed in a sac.

As far as my observations have yet gone, it appears to me that the germinal cell is derived from one of those which are nearest the central opening on the raw surface. This cell, following the ordinary course of development, by the nucleus breaking up into nucleoli, which in time become parent cells, each of which again undergo the same process. This proceeds for several stages, all the less important cells dissolving and serving as nourishment to the central or more important ones, until the number of centres are reduced to five, the number of joints required, which, by a constant process of a similar nature, assume the form of the future leg. H. D. S. G.

XXXIII.—OF THE ANATOMY AND DEVELOPMENT OF THE CYSTIC ENTOZOA.*—(Plates VI. X. XI. XII.)

I.—OF THE ACEPHALOCYST.

The acephalocyst, or simple hydatid, consists of a vesicle composed of several membranes containing a quantity of fluid, in which the young hydatids float, and from which they apparently derive nourishment.

Although found in all parts of the body, these animals are nevertheless more strictly confined to the liver, which appears to be their natural habitat.

In examining an acephalocyst from without inwards, there is met with, first, the natural tissues of the infested being slightly condensed, the condensation being greatest near the hydatid, and becoming gradually less as the distance increases. The next part met with in the dissection inwards, is a strong fibrous membrane, of considerable thickness, with numerous bloodvessels. This forms a sac for the hydatid. During the earlier stages of growth, hardly a vestige of this can be seen; for being formed of the condensed tissues of the infested animal, it becomes perceptible only after the parasite has attained some size. It is highly vascular, and forms a cushion, to which the external surface of the hydatid is applied. In this way, a steady supply of the blood, or of debris of the textures of the infested animal, is close at hand, from which the hydatid may extract nourishment. This membrane is best seen in aged hydatids, or in those in which the process

* Read before the York Meeting of the British Association, 1844.

Vol. II   Plate X

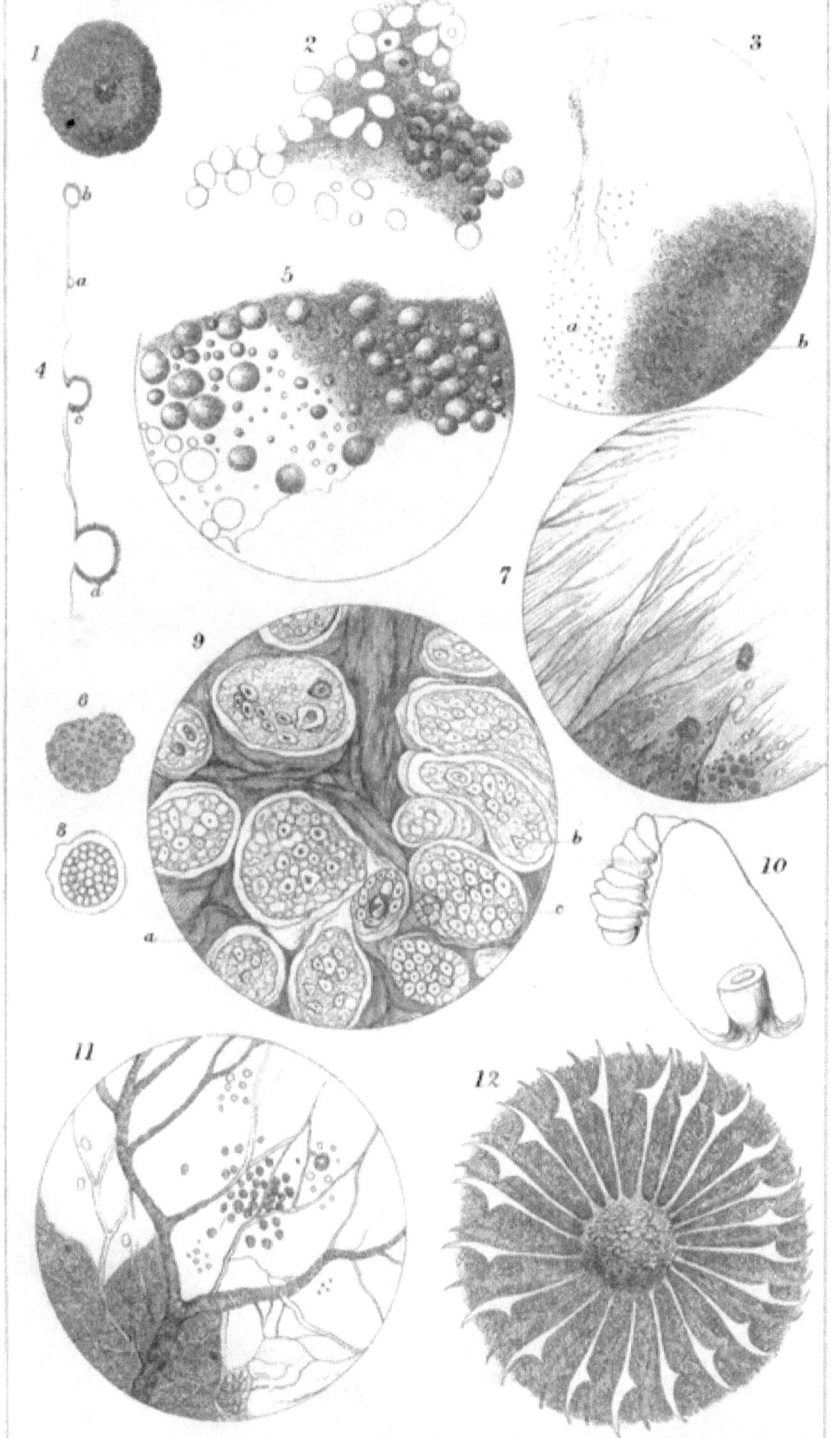

of obliteration has commenced, and in such can easily be demonstrated by dissection. In such aged individuals also it is found to be so intimately attached to the external membrane of the hydatid, as to appear to form one membrane with it; whereas in younger individuals a considerable space intervenes.

The external coat of the hydatid is gelatinous and slightly fibrous in appearance, and presents no structure.

The middle membrane appears to be of the nature of a germinal membrane, is much thinner, and more delicate than the external membrane. In this membrane numerous cells, in various stages of growth, take their rise, and project inwards into the cavity of the hydatid, carrying the next membrane along with them.

The internal membrane does not appear to be continuous over the whole internal surface; but observed only where it is reflected, as has been just stated, over the surface of the germinal cells. It may, therefore, be considered as that portion of the middle or germinal membrane which has been carried inwards by the rise of the germinal cells in the substance of the former membrane.

A small clear cell or vesicle, jutting from the internal surface of the second membrane, is the first vestige of the young hydatid. At first this vesicle is colourless, but as it increases slightly in size, it becomes opaque, and also carries the internal membrane inwards before it, which in time, as the young hydatid becomes more pedunculated before becoming free, almost covers it entirely. Vestiges of this membrane may be seen attached in shreds to the vesicle, even after it has attained a considerable size.

In all the hydatids which have already become independent animals, with their external coat still gelatinous, and are still enclosed within the cyst of the original acephalocyst, it may be observed that one side presents shreds of membrane attached to it; but that the other is quite free and almost transparent. This transparent part was that originally attached to the parent or germinal membrane; and the shreds are consequently the remains of the internal membrane of the parent. Shortly before the young hydatid separates from the germinal membrane of the parent, smaller cells are seen within it, which increase in size along with it. These are another generation of hydatids, and the fourth in the series I have been describing.

About this period in the process of development, there may be seen in some forms of hydatids of the tertiary growth, a dark irregular flat nucleated spot, which always occupies the same place, immediately opposite that of attachment. This spot is visible only before the separation. I am inclined to consider this spot as the first appearance of the pedicle, or what is generally termed a head in the class. This species I denominate *Acephalocystis armatus*. This appearance is merely the nucleus or central cell, from which all the others are produced; thus illustrating that the pedicles of Cænurus and Cysticercus are analogous to this nucleus, both being reproductive organs;—in the acephalocyst being a reproductive organ only, in Cænurus and Cysticercus being chiefly a reproductive organ with a slight adaptation for the purposes of prehension.

If the small cells which are seen in the tertiary hydatids are the young, they must be the first of those which are afterwards seen attached to the germinal membrane, for I have not met with secondary hydatids enclosing separated young individuals. It is only after the hydatid has obtained a nidus, or separate habitat of its own, that it begins to throw off its young from the germinal membrane, and those only which had been formed during the tertiary and secondary periods. Thus, if the original hydatid is buried deep in the textures of the infested being, or from other causes is prevented giving exit to its young (for it is by the dilatation caused by the young within it that the parent sac gives way), it soon becomes unable to extract proper nourishment from the infested being, the young within it become decomposed, and the whole animal degenerates either into a firm cicatrix, or, as is most general, into a fatty cretaceous matter. I have in many instances found this matter forming upon the external coats of young secondary hydatids, which were confined, as above stated, in old and degenerating parent sacs. In general this cretaceous matter originates in the internal and germinal membrane of the parent sac; these two membranes in old hydatids being always thick, gelatinous, and homogeneous, like pure gelatine. This thick gelatinous membrane presents no trace of the two membranes of which it originally consisted; it is generally about the eighth of an inch in thickness, and lies in the most dependent part of the cavity, quite loose and detached from the external coat. It presents no trace of young vesicles or hydatids, but has upon its internal surface a number of white, opaque, fatty looking spots of all sizes. Similar spots, but of much smaller size, are also to be seen in the substance of the membrane, and when examined by the microscope, present a peculiar cellular network. As these spots become larger, they, from being quite smooth, become rough and nodulated, each of the cells being apparently filled with the peculiar fatty substance. As this mass increases in size, it becomes more cretaceous, and sends out branches in all directions, so as in time to fill the whole cavity of the hydatid, which, as this process is going on, shrinks up very much, so that it meets the fatty matter, and enables the process of filling up to be more speedily completed. Shortly before the cavity is completely filled up, the fatty matter begins to lessen in quantity, being probably absorbed by the cretaceous matter gaining the preponderance. In this way more or less of the whole mass is absorbed, so that ultimately nothing is left but a small quantity of cretaceous matter which becomes very much condensed.

The middle membrane then appears to play the most important part in the economy of the hydatid; the external membrane acting only as an organ of defence.

Of this peculiar form of animal three species have been determined, the characters of which are derived from the structure and appearance of the germinal membrane. In *Acephalocystis simplex*, the lowest of these forms, the whole structure of the animal is much more homogeneous, transparent, and gelatinous, than that of the two higher forms; the cyst is not divided into separate parts, and the young are developed promiscuously throughout its internal surface.

In *Acephalocystis armatus*, the young are developed from a true germinal membrane, each of the young arising as a separate cell, and afterwards throwing off internally successive broods of young independently. It is also distinguished from the other species by the teeth which it possesses during the period of its attachment to the parent germinal membrane. These teeth are generally exactly opposite the spot of attachment, are quite straight, barbless, and form an irregular circlet, somewhat similar to that of Cænurus and Cysticercus. They are lost as soon as the animal leaves the germinal membrane and becomes free, and not the slightest vestige of them can be seen, even upon the shreds of membrane alluded to above, which at one period formed the internal membrane of the parent sac.

In the *Medical Gazette* for Nov. 22, 1844, p. 268, there is an abstract of a paper read before the Royal Medical and Chirurgical Society of London, by Erasmus Wilson, on the "Classification, etc., of *Echinococcus hominis*." There can be no doubt that the *Echinococcus* here described by Mr. Wilson, and the *Acephalocystis armatus*, are both one and the same species. The bodies described by Mr. Wilson as the echinococci, and which are attached to the internal surface of the membrane, are merely the young acephalocysts either of the secondary or tertiary stages of development. They will be, as already fully described in this paper, of the secondary generation, if found growing from the walls of the original containing sac, and tertiary if found growing from the walls of those sacs floating free in the fluid contained within the original sac. This animal is an acephalocyst, and not an echinococcus. Bremser, in the atlas of his work, *On the Intestinal Worms of Man*, calls it an echinococcus, but upon false grounds, for the proper definition of echinococcus, he says, at p. 294 of his work alluded to :*—"M. Rudolphi distingue les hydatides en vivantes et en non vivantes ; il regarde l'echinocoque provenant des intestins des bisulques (*Echinococcus veterinorum*) comme une hydatide vivante, par la raison que l'on trouve dans le liquide qu'elle contient les echinocoques, proprement dits, c'est-à-dire, des petits corps microscopiques, pourvus de quatre suçoirs et d'une couronne de crochets." The animal described by Mr. Wilson is also referred to in the same abstract by Dr. Budd, "who examined seven hydatid tumours which had been for many years in the Museum of King's College," when he found appearances exactly similar to those described by Mr. Wilson. It is more than probable that the animals here alluded to by Dr. Budd are similar to that I have called *Acephalocystis armatus*, which, if the case, from the want of suckers, cannot be an Echinococcus, being merely a transitory stage of the acephalocyst. For I have examined great numbers of these animals, preserved in the Museum of the Royal College of Surgeons in Edinburgh—a collection particularly rich in preparations of these animals—and in no instance have I been able to make

* *Traité Zoologique et Physiologique sur les Vers Intestinaux de l'Homme*, par M. Bremser. Traduit de l'Allemand par M. Grundler. Revu et augmenté de Notes par M. de Blainville.

out the slightest vestige of suckers. I had made out the existence of teeth, and was anxious to determine whether or not the animal was allied to the cephaloid hydatids.

The next form of Acephalocystis is one presenting a structure peculiar to itself, and which at once distinguishes it from the others. The external membrane is gelatinous and delicate; the germinal one is more fibrous, and is so slightly attached to the external one as to float in the contained fluid. When a small portion of this germinal membrane is placed under the microscope, its free or internal surface presents the following appearances:—1*st*, A fibrous texture forming the basis of the membrane; 2*d*, A series of large irregular ovoid vesicles, arranged in irregular rows. The fibrous texture surrounds the vesicles, and thus presents a peculiar appearance of ramification of a very regular form. Each of the vesicles contains one or more dark spots containing nucleoli—these spots are the young hydatids.*

II.—OF ASTOMA.—(PLATE XI.)

Astoma acephalocystis is an animal very nearly allied to Acephalocystis.† It was found attached to the peritoneum of an old subject, generally by means of a broad basis, but very often by a slender pedicle. The sac, composed of three membranes, of more or less delicacy, was very strong, and the membranes were easily separable from one another. They were all more or less composed of fibrous texture, and, as in the Acephalocystis, the external appeared to serve as a means of defence, while the two inner were devoted to nutrition and

* This species I have named *Acephalocystis Monroii*, after Dr. Monro, to whom I am indebted for the opportunity of examining the species, and from whom also I have received much valuable information regarding hydatids generally. A very beautiful figure of *A. Monroii* is given in Dr. Monro's work on *The Morbid Anatomy of the Stomach and Gullet*.

† *Edinburgh Medical and Surgical Journal*, No. clxi., p. 14.

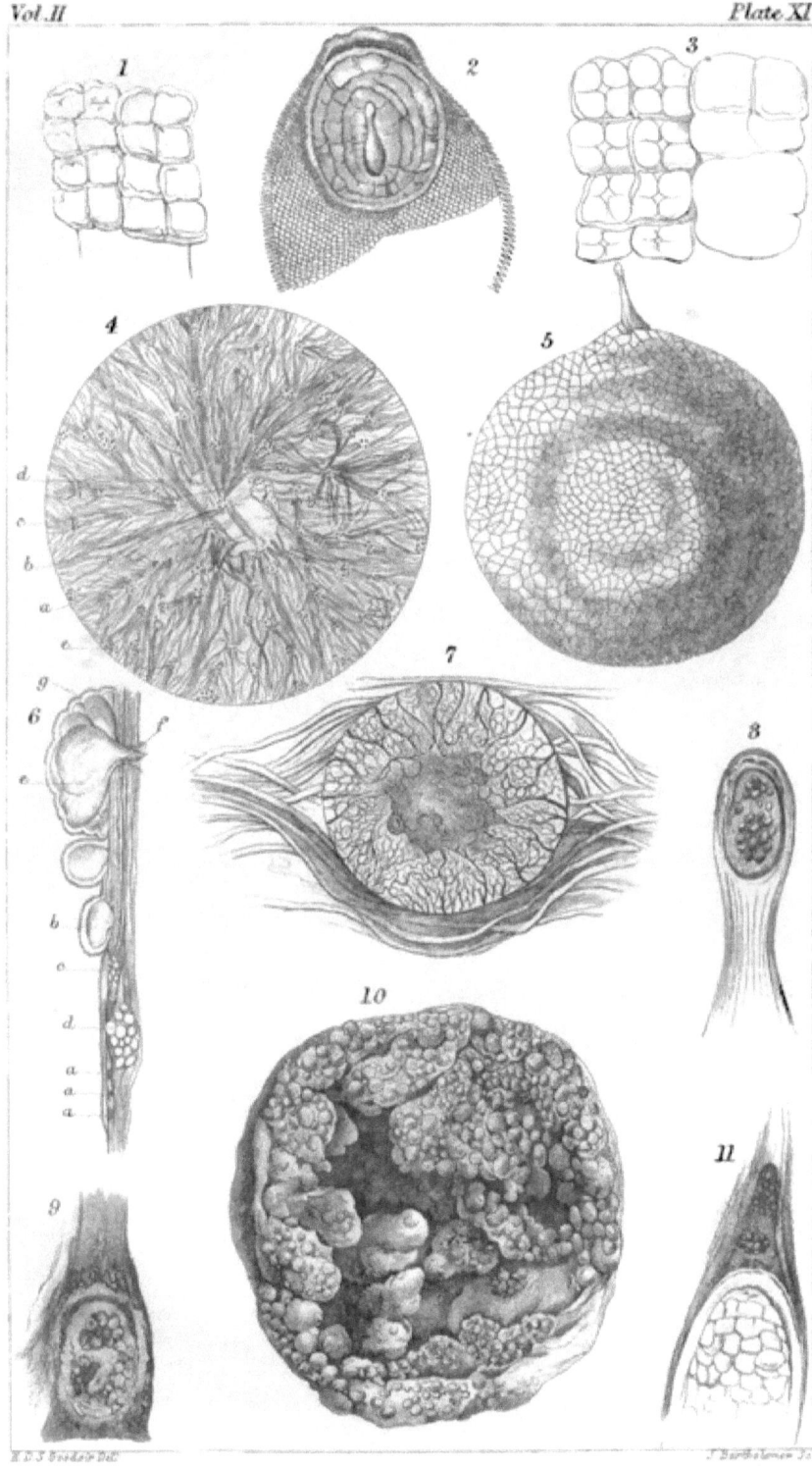

generation. The young cells, after acting for a time as the organs of nutrition, become free and independent animals after having thrown off young cells internally, which in their turn act as organs of nutrition to their parent until they are fit to become independent animals themselves. The particulars relative to the peculiar mode of development of ths aniimal will be adverted to more at length when we come to treat of that function in Diskostoma; in the meantime a few remarks on the external character of the animal may be useful.

It was of a greenish yellow colour when taken from its habitat, and varied in size from a millet seed to that of a middle-sized orange. The smaller specimens were all spherical, and very much corrugated; the larger were quite smooth and botryoidal—the first of which appearances arose apparently from the distension caused by the young; the second, from the young within it increasing irregularly in size. When a section was made of an adult specimen, the interior was found to consist of an immense number of young in various stages of advancement, and all of them apparently having their origin from the inclosing sac, either immediately or mediately. Along with these the interstices contained a great quantity of gelatinous matter, which appeared to be the assimilated food, analogous to the pabulum of the seminal cells already spoken of in another paper.

III.—OF DISKOSTOMA.*—(PLATE XI.)

Diskostoma acephalocystis is another animal belonging to the Cystic Entozoa, and very similar in many respects to the preceding genera; it is, however, more complicated in its structure than either.

Diskostoma was met with in great numbers in the peritoneal cavity of a middle-aged man. About six or eight

* *Transactions of the Royal Society*, Edinburgh, vol. xv., p. 564.

gallons were taken out of the abdomen after death, all of which had been apparently generated in the course of a few months.* Like Astoma they varied very much in size, but, with very few exceptions, were all regularly globular and of a bright straw colour, hanging, when undisturbed, from the surface of the abdominal cavity like the ova in the active ovarium of the common fowl. The sac consisted of two demonstrable membranes, the most external of which was rather complicated.

The basis of the membrane itself was fibro-gelatinous, and having a number of discs scattered at irregular intervals over its surface; these discs were connected with one another by means of numerous tubuli, which also ramified freely through the membrane. These were probably the organs of nutrition. The next membrane was much more delicate, and was that from which the gemmules arose. In some instances there was the appearance of a third membrane, but it was most difficult of detection. The greater mass of the body was composed of the gelatinous matter already alluded to as occurring in Astoma.

The function of generation in all these lower Acephalocysts is very interesting. In all of them the young cells or gemmules arise from the middle membrane of the sac. In Acephalocystis and Astoma the young cells act at first as organs of nutrition, and after a time become themselves independent animals. This is probably the case in Diskostoma also, but it could not be determined with certainty. The mode of development of the young in Astoma and Diskostoma is somewhat different from that already described as taking place in Acephalocystis. There appear to be two modes of generation, namely, one for the enlargement of the original group, and another for the formation of new groups in other parts of the peritoneum. The first of these modes proceeds in the Astoma,

* See *Edinburgh Medical and Surgical Journal* for October 1844, p. 1.

from the animal becoming so distended, in consequence of the increased size and number of the young within it, that it bursts when the young are exposed, and the parent sac, which is now useless, absorbed, the progeny in the meantime becoming attached to the peritoneum.* The external membranes in Diskostoma spread over the, as yet, uninfested portions of the peritoneum, and give origin to a number of cells from the attached surface, each of which, becoming parents, gradually increases in size, from the addition of new matter within the young cells. These young cells are the germs of the future animals. The other mode of development, or that intended for the formation of new groups, is similar in both animals. The young or secondary cells, bursting from their formative cell, by some means escape from the parent sac, and so gain a situation at some distance from the original group, where they become attached, in time throw off young cells, and thus become the origin of a new set.

Relative to the mode of reproduction in these animals, it is found that in Astoma, and the higher cystic entozoa, the numbers proceeding from one parent may be unlimited, whereas in Acephalocystis, generation ceases with the quaternary series of young, unless this series, or the gemmules of some of the preceding, escape from the original sac and are able to form a nidus in any portion of the liver, or other organ yet uninfested. For it appears necessary to the existence of the common hydatid that it be completely enveloped in the tissues of the infested being. To ensure this normal habitat, then, the animal must escape during the period of its gemmule existence from the parent; but, as most generally happens, if the parent hydatid be so deeply buried as not to allow free rupture of its coats within a certain period, decomposition ensues as already described, and so existence is

* See *Preparation in Museum of Royal College of Surgeons*, Edinburgh, No. 2244.

terminated;—if, on the contrary, the parent hydatid be so near a surface, or from other causes, as during its increase in size to rupture, then the young escape, and so form new and altogether independent animals. As the hydatid is by no means of unfrequent occurrence in the liver and other internal organs, this limitation of the increase appears to be a beneficent law of nature, for the purpose of preventing the fatal termination which the rapid increase of these animals would infallibly produce. In Diskostoma we have an instance of this rapidity of reproduction, which happily appears to be of rare occurrence.

It may be well to state here also the opinions to be deduced from the changes which take place in the germinal membrane of Acephalocystis, and the other acephalic entozoa. It has been already fully described in what manner the function of reproduction in these animals is stopped, namely, in consequence of the thickening of the germinal membrane. After having made out this fact, I was led to infer that many instances of the stoppage of cellular formations at certain periods of life might be traced to similar changes taking place in the germinal membrane of the formative organ, and, with the view of determining this point, examined the testes of several old men, after the fecundating power had in all probability passed away, when the germinal membrane in almost all cases had become thicker and quite different from what is generally seen in young males, a change which (as we have attempted to describe) had taken place in the germinal membrane of hydatids.*

* The stoppage here alluded to, in the function of reproduction of these animals, may be also greatly assisted, and the degenerating process made more active, in consequence of the thickening of the external membrane preventing the absorbing cells extracting from it a sufficient supply of nourishment.

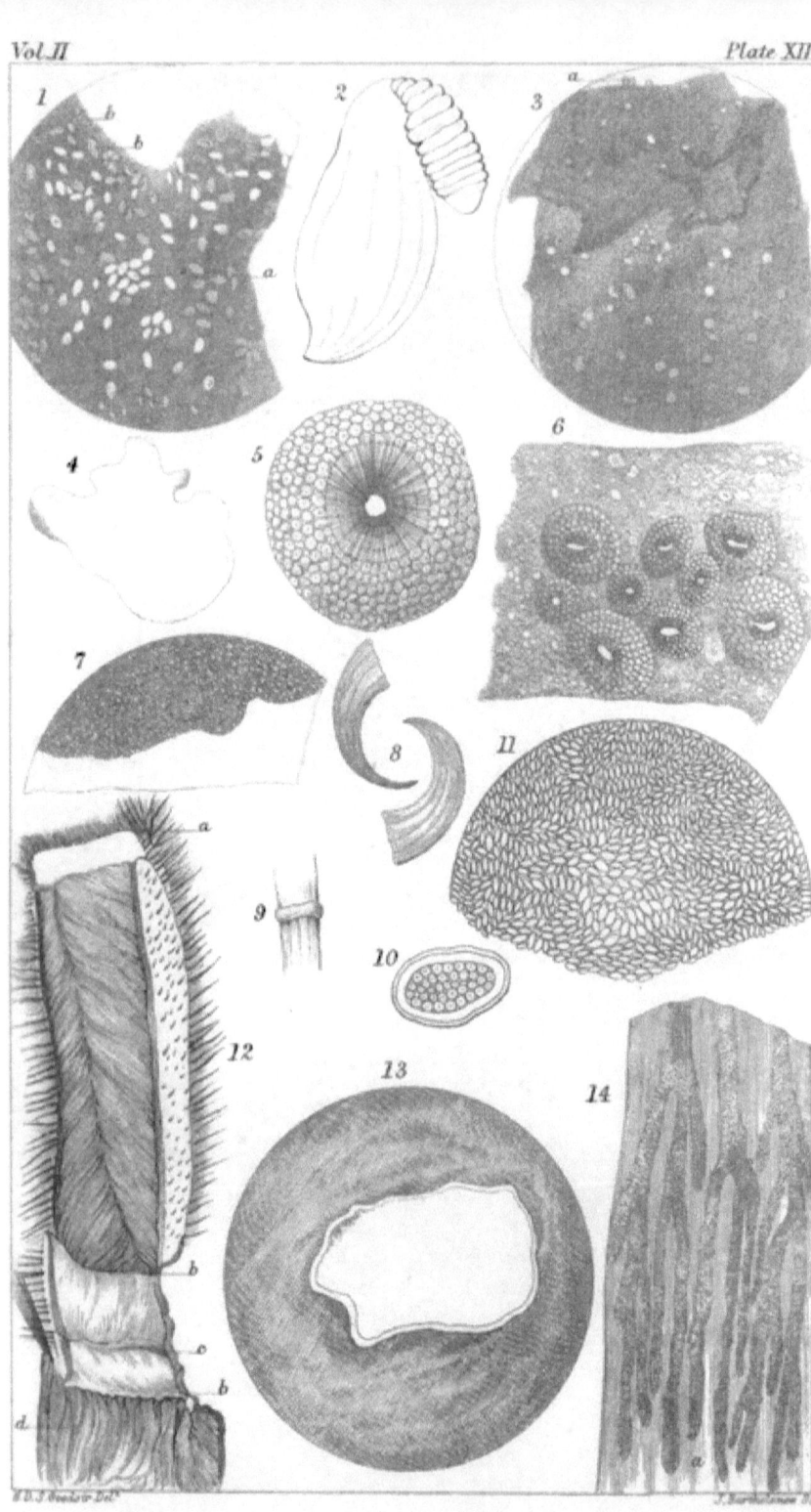

IV.—OF SPHAIRIDION.*—(Plate VI., Fig. 16.)

Sphairidion acephalocystis is an animal allied to Acephalocystis, chiefly from its acephalic character, but also from its reproductive organ being enclosed within the centre of its sac. This reproductive body or membrane is exactly similar to the pedicle of the Cysticercus, with the exception of its being entirely buried in the body of the animal, consequently also it is neither furnished with teeth nor suckers. There is no separate absorbent apparatus in the sac of the animal, and this part of its body appears to be composed of one membrane only, which is analogous to the external membrane of the sac of Acephalocystis. The cyst of this animal at first appears to be composed of three membranes, but a little examination proves the outermost to consist of peritoneum only, the two others being similar to the analogous membranes of the cyst of *Cysticercus rattus*, namely, an external for defence, and an internal for absorption of nourishment.

This animal was found attached to the intestines of the Balearic Crested Crane (*Balearica pavonia*, Vigors) beneath the peritoneum.

V.—OF CÆNURUS.†—(Plates VI., XII.)

The next animal we have to describe is Cænurus. It is in the species belonging to this genus that the first vestiges of extremities are perceived, to which form of structure we are led through Diskostoma—the discs described in the latter being without doubt analogous to the pedicles of the Cænurus.

Cænurus cerebralis, an animal frequently found in the brain of the sheep and other ruminants, has been long known

---

* Σφαιρίδιον, a globule.
† *Transactions of the Royal Society*, Edinburgh, vol. xv. p. 564.

to naturalists. This animal is composed of a double sac from the external surface of which proceed a number of small bodies, termed pedicles. These pedicles are contained between the two membranes of the sac, project at right angles from its surface, and are armed at the extremity with a double circle of teeth.

The sac of the Cænurus is composed of two membranes, the outermost of which acts as an organ of defence, the internal, containing a layer of absorbent cells, acts along with the larger cells contained in the pedicles as organs of nutrition. The natural size of a pedicle is about the one-eighth of an inch in length. It is divided into two parts, the basal and distal. The former contains the absorbing cells already spoken of, which, after a time, become themselves independent pedicles. The cells within the pedicle are arranged regularly in the form of concentric circles, each cell as it becomes a parent forming a centre. The latter, or distal portion of the pedicle, contains very few, if any, of these cells, but bears on its extremity a double series of bent barbed teeth, which enable the animal to attach itself firmly to the infested body. Four suckers are also placed at regular intervals round the sides of this portion of the pedicle.

When one of the smaller cells escape from the pedicles and obtains a situation between the layers of the parent sac, it shortly commences to take on a new action, the nucleus enlarges and presents a clear spot in the centre. As this spot increases in size, the nucleus becomes irregular on its edges, and shortly becomes nodulated, the nodules after a time are thrown off as separate cells, a central cell occupying the place of the clear central spot.*

This is the termination of the first stage of the develop-

---

* The great similarity which exists between the development of this animal and the mammiferous ovum, as described by Dr. Martin Barry, will be noticed by all observers.

ment of the ovum, after which the nucleus of the central cell undergoes a similar process, the cells proceeding from it pushing out nearer to the circumference those of the previous generation. Thus we have a great series of centres, round which all the other cells are arranged in circles. This I have termed the discoidal period of development.

After numerous circles have been thus formed, the cells nearest the circumference, and, of course, those first formed, become parents, and consequently centres; but a few of these gaining the advantage, dissolve the more peripheral cells and absorb them, thus becoming principal centres. As soon as this change in the development has taken place, the mode of growth, hitherto discoidal, becomes vertical, or at right angles to the sac, and so proceeds until the pedicle becomes perfect.

There is still another animal belonging to this series, and which requires to be noticed in this place. It is nondescript, and its characters resemble so much both those of Acephalocystis and Cænurus that I have not yet been able to decide with precision to which genus it belongs. It has certainly more of the characters of the Cænurus than Acephalocystis, although many also connect it most intimately with the latter. In the meantime, however, I have placed it along with Cænurus, and from its habitat called it C. hepaticus. In all its more important characters, it is very similar to the C. cerebralis.

VI.—OF CYSTICERCUS.—(PLATE XII.)

Cysticercus is distinguished from Cænurus by its sac having only one pedicle; it is also always contained in a cyst, which, in some cases, is formed from the compressed textures of the infested animal, while in others it consists of two membranes, viz., one similar to that mentioned, and another, *sui generis,* and belonging entirely to the parasite. The pedicle of the Cysticercus is exactly similar in its structure to that of the Cœnurus, with the exception of the cells, which are not arranged so regularly. The sac is also composed of two membranes, each having structures exactly similar to that of the Cœnurus.

I have divided the animals composing this genus of Entozoa into two classes, in consequence of the difference of structures met with in the cyst. Those species, in which the cyst is only composed of one membrane, derived from the compressed tissues of the infested being, have been placed near to the Acephalocysts; and those in which the cyst consists of two membranes already described, compose the other division.

The *Cysticercus cellulosus* is an example of the first of these divisions. In this animal the cyst is very vascular, *i.e.* more so than the surrounding textures, so that in this respect it is quite similar to the analogous structure in Acephalocystis. As an example of the animals belonging to this division of the genus, there is another species which appears to be nondescript. This Cysticercus was found in the Museum of the Royal College of Surgeons, but unfortunately the jar was not labelled, so that I am uncertain from what animal it was got. It is enclosed in a cyst formed by the omentum alone; these cysts are pedunculated, and although quite continuous with the healthy portion of the membrane, it is so puckered and constricted at the pedunculated portion as to be quite impermeable, so that the enclosed animal can obtain no nourishment from without, except through the portion of omentum forming the cyst. The cyst is very vascular, and generally contains a quantity of thin granular looking matter (probably the matter intended for the food of the enclosed animal). The double circlet of teeth in this species is remarkable for their great length. In many specimens which came under my notice numerous small globular bodies were observed, surrounded externally with hooked spines, and attached to the internal surface of the cyst, apparently by means of the spines. These bodies, although the intermediate stages between them and the young gemmules could not be seen, I considered to be young Cysticerci in an advanced stage of growth, and I was led to do so because they were often observed on the free surface of the omentum, attracting and puckering it together in folds, evidently the commencement of the process for the formation of a cyst, and in many instances they had completely enveloped themselves. It has not yet been decidedly made out in what manner the gemmules escape from the body of the Cysticercus, but from the observations I have made, it appears that they must first escape from the pedicle where they are formed into the sac, and then from the sac to the cyst. I am led to this supposition in consequence of having observed on several occasions the sac of the animal ruptured, and great numbers of the globular spined bodies attached to the inner surface of the cyst. How they escape from the cyst I have not been able to determine.

Those Cysticerci having the cyst composed of a double membrane, do not differ in any other particular from those of the preceding division of the genus. The best example of this peculiarity of structure exists in a species found in the liver of the rat, and which I have denominated *Cysticercus rattus*. The specific characters are given in the synopsis at the end of the paper.

In all the details, then, we find a great similarity between Cænurus and Cysticercus, with this exception, that the latter is simple, whereas the former, like all the other Acephalocysts, is a compound animal. Why the pedicles of Cænurus should all become attached to the same sac, is a fact, the cause of which it will be impossible to determine with any degree of certainty; probably, however, it arises from the difference of strength in the sacs of the two animals; the greater strength of that of Cænurus preventing the escape of the young gemmule from between its membranes. The mode of formation of the sac is also a point interesting to the physiologist, and one deserving consideration. In Acephalocystis and the other allied genera, the original gemmule, shortly after it has become an independent animal, begins to swell out and be distended from the accumulation of new matter within it. This new matter is drawn into it by means of the young internal cells which have just been formed, and which have a power, inherent in themselves, of attracting and assimilating nourishment from without. The cells referred to here are the young germs of future hydatids, and which afterwards, as already explained, become independent animals; but, at the same time, there is in many cases also another series of cells, whose only function is to act in this way, and throughout the term of their existence: these have been termed absorbent cells. Now, these cells drawing in the nourishment in this way cause the expansion of the original cell-wall, so that the enlargement of these bodies resembles a process of dilatation. This, then, appears to be the explanation of the peculiar forms assumed by the Cænurus and Cysticercus, as well as the different species of acephalocysts; that it is so can be proved from *Sphairidion acephalocystis,* an animal very nearly allied to Cænurus, and being a connecting link between the acephalic and cephalic hydatids; for in this animal we find that portion of its body analogous to the pedicle of Cysticercus, not exserted, as in the latter animal, but situated in the centre of the body, where it forms the attracting point for the nourishment absorbed, which accordingly dilates the external and containing sac.

What I wish to be inferred from this is, that the sacs of Acephalocystis, Cænurus, and Cysticercus, are analogous organs; and that the pedicles of these two latter animals are analogous to the reproductive nucleus, which may be observed during certain early stages of the development of Acephalocystis, as well as the reproductive and absorbing nucleus of Sphairidion.

Species of Cysticercus have been found in almost every part and cavity of the human body. In the brain, eye, lungs, liver, in the walls of the intestines, and in the muscles. In the present state of our knowledge, it is impossible to say how these animals gain such habitats as the eye, etc. This is a question, however, which has been the cause of much discussion.

VII.—OF THE HIGHER CYSTIC ENTOZOA.

Besides those already described, there are many other forms of entozoa of the higher orders, which are inhabitants of cysts similar to these of Cysticercus; we have examples of this occurring in the Nematoidea, Cestoidea, and Acanthacephala, etc. As examples of the worms alluded to, I may instance *Trichina spiralis, Gymnorhynchus horridus,* and a small filaria inhabiting the livers of some fish, but, as far as can be made out, not hitherto described by any author. As another example, too, of these peculiar forms, may be mentioned, a very interesting animal which will be afterwards described, namely, *Neuronaia Monroii.*

The cysts of all these worms have similar structures to those of Cysticercus, namely, an external membrane composed of compressed cellular texture, and an internal membrane containing absorbing cells, through which the contained animal obtains nourishment.

In the descriptions of the Acephalocysts already given, it will be remembered how the animal died in consequence of the thickening and hardening of the external membrane of the cyst, preventing the absorption of nourishment from or through it; so in like manner do these higher Cystic Entozoa—Trichina —die from a similar cause. In many cases where the subject is infested with Trichina, it is found on examination, that with few exceptions almost every specimen is converted into the hard cretaceous matter spoken of; many, at the same time, presenting all the intermediate stages of decay. Gymnorhynchus presents us with a very curious habit dependant upon this mode of structure, and which enables the animal to avoid the death from which all its co-geners suffer. This species, which I have fortunately had an opportunity of examining in its natural habitat, but which has been already described by my brother (*Edinburgh Philosophical Journal*, vol. 31), inhabits the liver of the sun-fish in great numbers, and from its peculiar structure is enabled to move slowly through the organ it infests. If the cyst of this worm is carefully examined, it will be found that the inner membrane, containing the absorbent cells, is covered anteriorly with a very thin layer only of the external membrane, so that it is enabled to absorb the nourishment from the external textures in great abundance, which thus enables the animal to move forward as well as obtain a supply of food; as we trace the cyst backwards, the external membrane will be found to become thicker and thicker, as also more impermeable, until we reach the tail of the animal, after which it becomes a mere cord. This cord can be traced for a great distance, becoming less and less perceptible, until it is lost altogether, and the course only marked by a simple line of a darker colour than the rest of the textures. It will be observed that the external membrane of this animal presents analogies similar to that of Acephalocystis; for instance, the cephalic portion of the membrane is so thin as to be hardly distinguishable, being thus analogous to the young hydatid.

In regard to the cyst of these worms, it has been long a question how far it is a part of the enclosed animal. Professor Owen[*] holds that it is merely condensed textures of the

---

[*] Owen, "Description of a Microscopic Entozoon infesting the Muscles of the Human Body."—*Transactions of the Zoological Society*, vol. i. p. 322.

infested being, and Dr. Knox* again, that it belongs essentially to the parasite. My brother, in the paper already alluded to, says, regarding the cyst—"May we not suppose them to be parts of the original ovum, within which the animal was formed, and within which it passes its term of existence." From observations made on the development of the Acephalocystic entozoa, it may be safely stated, I think, that the above statement is correct, for Acephalocystis must be considered as an enlarged ovum; but Sphairidion perhaps is the best example of this peculiar mode of formation, the "inserted pedicle" being analogous to the confined Trichina or Gymnorhynchus—for we must look upon the inserted pedicle as the active animal. In Cænurus, also, the pedicles are contained within the external membrane of the sac.

I shall finish these observations on the Cystic Entozoa, with the following account by my brother John, of *Neuronaia Monroii*.† (Plate VI., Fig. 7 ; Plate XI., Figs. 2, 7.)

"The observations of Pacini ‡ on the peculiar bodies which are appended to the digital nerves, induced me to direct my attention to the 'spheroidal bodies,' described by the second Monro, as existing on the surfaces of the brain and nerves of the gadidæ. I accordingly examined the 'spheroidal bodies' in the haddock, and found that they were entozoa, referrible to the family Distoma, and enclosed in cysts. I described these curious parasites at a meeting of the Anatomical and Pathological Society, and a short abstract was published in the *Monthly Journal of Medical Science*. Till lately, I had supposed that I was the first to observe the true nature

---

* Knox, *Edinburgh Medical and Surgical Journal*.

† Monro, *Observations on the Structure and functions of the Nervous System* p. 59.

‡ Pacini, *Nuovo Giornale dei Letterate*, March and April 1836, p. 109. J. Henle and Kölliker, *Ueber die Pacinischen Körperchen an den Nerven des Menschen und der Säugethiere*.

of these 'spheroidal bodies,' when Dr. Allen Thomson ascertained that Dr. Sharpey was in the habit of mentioning them in his courses of lectures in the University College. I accordingly wrote Dr. Sharpey on the subject, and I am indebted to that gentleman for the following interesting accounts of what has been already recorded regarding this entozoon :—

"When I was in Berlin some years ago, the late Professor Rudolphi remarked to me in conversation, that he thought it not unlikely the little bodies discovered by Dr. Monro 2d, on the nerves of the cod, haddock, and other allied fish, would turn out on examination to be entozoa; and he suggested that I should take an opportunity of inquiring into the point on my return to Scotland. Accordingly, in the autumn of 1836, I examined these bodies in the haddock or whiting, I really forget which, but I think it was the former, and found that each of them was a little cyst, containing a Distoma, which could be easily turned out from its enclosure alive. The specimens I examined were from the membranes of the brain.

"This observation was made in Edinburgh, and on going to London soon after, I mentioned the fact to Mr. Owen; and I have been accustomed to take notice of it in my lectures ever since, suggesting at the same time that it would be well to search for them, or for analogous parasites, in the nerves of other animals, as it was not likely that the gadus tribe of fishes should be the only example. Indeed, unless my memory deceives me, some one has met with something of the same kind in the nerves of the frog; and Valentin has seen the eggs of Distoma in the vertebral canal of a fœtal sheep. When I learned that the oval bodies, which all must have seen in the cellular tissue of the palm of the hand and fingers, were connected with the nerves, I at first imagined they might be entozoa (having been led to make just the converse of your conjecture), but Mr. Marshall, formerly of our museum, having examined these 'Pacinian' bodies two or three years ago (quite independently of any suggestion from me), I found nothing to confirm this conjecture on his showing me their structure. I have since seen Henle and Kölliker's memoir, which includes the substance of Pacini's observations.

"Rudolphi, as far as I know, never examined the structure of the spheroidal bodies of Monro; and the only notice of them which I have met with in his writings (to which he did not refer me) is in his *Historia Naturalis Entozoarum*, vol. ii. part ii. page 277, when, under the head of 'Dubious Entozoa,' he enumerates an object described and figured by Rathke, under the name of 'Hydatula Gadorum,' which that observer found in the *pia mater* of the *Gadus morrhua* and *G. virens*, often in great numbers, and which appeared to be a vesicle containing a worm. The nature of the parasite was doubtful, but supposed in some degree to resemble that of a Cysticercus, and hence the name applied to it by Rathke, but Rudolphi denies that it is a Cysticercus, though he does not know to what genus to refer it, he adds 'an Cucullanus?'"

This entozoon, as stated by Monro, is found in great numbers in the gelatinous substance which surrounds the brain, spinal cord, and semicircular canals, in the cod, haddock, and whiting. They are also very numerous in the larger branches of the nerves, and particularly on those of the pectoral and caudal fins. In the former situation they are suspended in the gelatinous fluid by fibres of areolar texture and by blood-vessels; in the latter they lie embedded in the substance of the nerve, the ultimate fibres of which are spread in bundles over the surface of the cysts.

The cysts are produced spheroids, somewhat flattened; their long axis measures about one-fourth of a line.

They consist of three tunics; an external, which appears

to be derived from the areolar texture of the infested animal, and of a middle or internal belonging to the parasite.

Upon the surface, and in the substance of the external tunic, the bloodvessels of the nerve can occasionally be seen, and recognised by their contents. One or two vessels may thus be observed coasting along the cyst, accompanied by single nerve-tubes, or by bundles of these, or by a mass which completely incloses and conceals the cyst. The second tunic is a fine transparent membrane, which lines the first, and has in its turn its internal surface covered by an epithelial layer, which is the third tunic of the cyst. The epithelia are flat, irregular in shape, and somewhat opaque. The third, or internal layer, formed by them, breaks up under the pressure of the glass plates, so as to present rents or fissures passing in various directions over it.

The cyst, in addition to the worm, contains a small quantity of fluid, in which oil-like globules of various sizes float.

The worm is a Distoma, oblong, dilated in front, tapering slightly towards its posterior extremity. The mouth, longitudinally oval, and rather pointed posteriorly, is surrounded by the usual suctorial disc. The acetabulum is situated at the junction of the anterior and middle third of the animal, and can be protruded from the surface of the body.

On the anterior edge of the acetabulum a minute pore is situated, and communicates with a sac, to be afterwards described.

At the posterior extremity of the animal another orifice is placed, which forms the outlet of the large chyle-sac, and apparently also of another sac, to be afterwards alluded to.

The integument of the two anterior thirds of the body is closely covered with short slightly-curved spines, directed backwards. These spines are largest round the suctorial mouth, and on the posterior part of the body are gradually replaced by minute tubercles or dots. Under this spiny or cuticular layer, the integument is muscular, the fibres being principally transverse, and so arranged that the animal appears to be made up of a series of rings, as may be observed along its edges, when examined by transmitted light.

From the anterior extremity to the acetabulum the integuments are so opaque, from the dense covering of spines, that the internal structure of the animal cannot be detected. It is probable, however, that the œsophagus terminates, as in the family Distoma generally, in two blind intestinal tubes. I have failed in detecting an arrangement of this kind; but I have observed about the middle of the animal, and along the sides of its posterior half, a sort of cellular structure, which may, probably, belong to the digestive system, as in *Distoma clavatum* described by Professor Owen.*

A large sac, evidently connected with the digestive system, opens externally by the minute orifice at the posterior part of the animal. This sac, in every individual, is full of a matter, which, by reflected light, is of a chalky whiteness, and described by Monro, and conjectured by him to be of a cretaceous nature. Examined by transmitted light, it is seen to consist of numerous spherical globules of variable size, and resembling the matter which fills the chyle-cells of the intestinal villi. The larger sac in which this matter is contained varies in shape, but it generally passes up from its outlet for about a third of the length of the body of the animal, then takes an acute bend to the other side, and passing forwards in a curved direction, ends in a dilated blind extremity between the acetabulum and the mouth. It is the "sigmoidal" or "serpentine body" of Monro. This sac is evidently the "cisterna chyli."

It does not communicate directly with the digestive

---

* Owen, "On the Anatomy of *Distoma clavatum*:" *Trans. Roy. Soc.* vol. i.

system, as in the apparently analogous receptacles in *Distoma claratum*, nor, as far as I could see, with the vascular system; but I have seen it discharge its contents by the posterior orifice, in the manner described by Nordman in *Diplostomum volvens*.*

From the movements of the walls of this receptacle, or from contractions of the animal itself, an active motion of the particles of its contents is occasionally observed. The movements occasionally resemble very much those produced by cilia. This sac is apparently a secreting organ, and is probably the only arrangement by which feculent matter is removed from the body of the animal. The food of an animal, living as this does in a cyst, is already digested by the walls of its cyst. Its food, therefore, yields no mechanical feculent matter, and its intestinal tube requires no anus. The only outlet which such an animal requires is for chemical feculent matter, which in all animals is the product of secretion, and principally of the lung, gill, or kidney. This sac, may, therefore, be considered as a respiratory organ or kidney.

There is another sac, very uniform in shape and size, situated at the posterior part of the body. This sac is elongated, extending from near the outlet of the "cisterna chyli," forward about a fourth of the length of the animal. Its posterior extremity is funnel-shaped, and appears to me, although I have failed in tracing it distinctly, to open externally along with the "cisterna chyli." It appears to possess circular fibres, which constrict it slightly at regular distances. The three anterior fourths of its wall are so thick that the cavity appears linear. This thick part of the wall exhibits an arrangement of fibres or particles perpendicular to its surface. The thick portion terminates by forming a curved projection into the thin posterior part of the organ, the whole arrangement resembling the projection of the

* Nordman, *Micrographische Beiträge*, p. 38, hft. 1.

human os uteri into the vagina. This organ, in its relations and structure, appears to be the analogue of the cavity described by Professor Owen, as opening into the posterior orifice of *Distoma clavatum*, and supposed by him to be a respiratory organ.

A pyriform sac, communicating with the exterior by the pore in front of the acetabulum, and two large, with occasionally two smaller globular masses, would appear to be the analogues of the reproductive organs. The pyriform sac always contains highly refractive oil-like globules, but larger than those in the chyle-receptacle. The two larger globular masses are very constant, and, as well as the two smaller, contain a mass of particles apparently nucleated. From the two larger, I have only been able to see faint traces of what appeared to be ducts passing in the direction of the smaller masses, and towards the neck of the pyriform sac. Whether these convoluted bodies be ovaries or convoluted oviducts, and the pyriform sac a uterus; or whether the former be the testes, and the latter the female organ, as in the arrangement described in the other Distomas; or whether they be reproductive organs at all, I have failed in satisfying myself, in consequence of the delicacy of their texture, and the comparatively dense integument of this part of the animal.

This Distoma possesses a vascular system forming a network throughout the body. The two principal trunks, as in the other genera, passing along the sides of the body and being most apparent at its posterior third.

I. ACEPHALOCYSTIS.

Completely buried in the textures of the infested animal young only consisting of three membranes; adult of four, the external one belonging originally to the infested being. Nourished by epithelial cells, which are contained in one of the membranes composing the sac. Generated by means of cells arising from a germinal membrane. Internal cavity filled with a watery fluid.

1.—*Acephalocystis simplex (Mihi).*

Parent sac quite transparent, with the membranes indivisible and the germinal cells very minute.

2.—*Acephalocystis monroii (Mihi).*

Parent sac transparent and gelatinous; germinal membrane intersected by membranous bands, which form flattened compartments, in which are large cells containing unequal numbers of young cells. Each of the young is marked with one or more dark spots.

3.—*Acephalocystis armatus (Mihi).*

Parent sac opaque, membranes distinct, germinal membrane composed of a soft granular matter, in which the germs are arranged irregularly; they are globular and armed with an irregular circlet of teeth at the part opposite that of attachment.

II. ASTOMA (MIHI).

Not buried, but attached by means of a pedicle, which becomes very slender as the animal increases in size. Young, globular and corrugated; adult, botryoidal and smooth; epithelial cells; with some appearance of tubuli in external coat. Young remain and increase in size within the membranes of the parent, till she bursts, when they become attached to the peritoneum.

4.—*Astoma acephalocystis (Mihi).*

Botryoidal, that part of the interior not occupied with the young filled with a yellowish gelatinous matter.

III. DISKOSTOMA (MIHI).

Peduncular. Whole group covered by a disk bearing tubular membrane.

5.—*Diskostoma acephalocystis (Mihi).*

Globular interior filled with gelatinous matter, of a transparent greenish ellow colour.

IV. SPHAIRIDION (MIHI.)

S. Animal enclosed within a cyst which is composed of two membranes. Sac single, containing the pedicle or reproductive body in its centre, and presenting a number of concentric coloured rings. *Hab.* Peritoneum of Crested Balearic Crane.

V. CÆNURUS RUDOLPHI.

Sac double, armed with numerous clusters of toothed pedicles. Epithelial cells in the sac. Germinal cells in the pedicles. Buried.

6.—*Cænurus hepaticus (Mihi).*

Sac botryoidal, opaque and thick; pedicles internal, small, suckers obsolete; teeth barbless, small, irregularly bent, and forming one irregular series. Gregarious. Infests the liver of man.

7.—*C. cerebralis (Rudolphi).*

Sac globular, transparent, thin, pedicles with four or five acetabula. Teeth thirteen, about three times as long as the breadth of the disc from which they arise. Infests the brain of sheep and other ruminants.

VI. CYSTICERCUS.

Animal enclosed within a cyst provided with a single pedicle.
1. Cyst formed from the infested animal.

8.—*C. neglectus (Mihi).*

Cyst formed from omentum of infested animal. Pedicle about three times the length of sac, head rounded, teeth twenty-one in number, very long, slender, and bent at the extremity, barbed on bent edge. *Hab.* unknown.

2. Cyst formed by parasite, as well as from textures of nfested being.

9.—*C. rattus (Mihi).*

Cyst small, globular, and transparent pedicle, not very long, teeth short, sickle-shaped, being curved throughout their whole length.

VII. ECHINOCOCCUS.

H. D. S. G.

XXXIV.—DESCRIPTION OF AN ERECTILE TUMOUR.*

This tumour occurred in the foot of an infant five months old, which was amputated by Mr. Syme. A fine injection of size and vermilion having been thrown into the arteries of the foot, the skin assumed a red tint, except where it was so attenuated as to display the peculiar bluish colour of the subjacent diseased mass.

It was then cut longitudinally into two portions. A gush of venous blood reduced its size very considerably. By means of a gentle stream of water, the rest of the contained blood was washed out, all pressure being avoided.

The two halves were then laid in a basin of spirit, and by means of a syringe that fluid was forced into the diseased mass, so as to distend the whole almost to its original size.

After having been hardened, fresh longitudinal sections were made, avoiding all pressure, and the structure was examined.

The venæ saphenæ, plantar, and posterior tibial veins were much enlarged, and had undergone a peculiar change, which consisted of increased bulk of the fibrous fasciculi of their coats, and of longitudinal and oblique foldings of the parietes, due partly to the fasciculation partly to actual involution.

About the centre of the foot the veins broke up into the general cellular arrangements which constituted the disease, the saphenæ forming a sort of central cavity on the dorsum, the plantar a much larger cavity or central areola in the sole of the foot.

The diseased mass itself consisted of areolæ, which de-

* Cormack's *Monthly Medical Journal*, 1845, p. 342.

creased in size from the central venous cavities to the surface of the skin, and to the deep limits of the disease, these limits being defined by the internal membrane of the venous system, which was continuous through all the areolæ.

The diseased mass had not displaced the surrounding textures, but had caused them to disappear before it, as in certain malignant growths and ulcerations—bone, ligament, muscle, and fat having equally failed in resisting its progress, the skin alone standing out against its advance, and along with the venous membrane forming the limit of its superficial position.

The areolæ of which the mass consisted were elongated from the central cavities towards the limits of the disease, being more elongated the nearer they were to the centres. The peculiar form of the areolæ was due to the radiated direction of the bars and imperfect laminæ which separated them, these being thicker, stronger, more elongated, and more separated from one another around the central cavities than near the circumference, where they were shorter, firmer, and much more numerous.

The bars and imperfect laminæ consisted of fibrous textures exactly resembling that of the tendinous ligaments, and aponeuroses with numerous germinal centres.

The bars and laminæ were all covered, and consequently they contained areolæ, lined by a fine membrane, consisting of tesselated epithelium, and continuous with the lining membrane of the venous system, at the central cavities or diseased terminations of the saphenæ and plantar veins.

In many of the bars and laminæ small arteries were situated, and one of these was traced nearly to the termination of the anterior tibial on the back of the foot. It was not ascertained how the arteries terminated, but it was presumed that they passed by small oblique orifices into the venous areolæ, as the curling arteries of the human placenta pass into the venous areolæ of the decidua.

XXXV.—DESCRIPTION OF A CONGENITAL TUMOUR OF THE TESTIS.*

This tumour was removed by Dr. James Duncan from a boy eight years old. When the tunica vaginalis was cut into, a considerable quantity of matter mixed with hairs was evacuated. The tumour possessed the following characters:—A mass of an irregular ovoidal form, about the size of the last joint of the forefinger, appeared to be the testis, so much altered in texture as to present no trace of its original structure.

It consisted almost entirely of fibrous texture, inclosing fat-cells in its areolæ, and, at variable distances throughout, small tubercular masses of a light yellow tough substance, of a granular aspect, resembling some forms of scrofulous deposit.

Near the reflection of the tunica vaginalis, on the surface of the testis, two club-shaped projections were attached, covered by a layer of a substance resembling the ordinary integument, with a quantity of fatty cuticular debris upon it. This portion of integument somewhat suddenly became continuous with the surface of the tunica vaginalis.

On the surface of the club-shaped projections, and at the angle of reflection of the tunica vaginalis, numerous long hairs were attached by bulbs. These hairs, of one-half to three-fourths of an inch in length, were conical, pointed, and of two kinds, some having their conical pulp-cavities prolonged in the form of canals, full of cells to their extremities; others were, with the exception of their conical pulp-cavities, solid.

The integumentary membrane in which the hairs were

* *Northern Journal of Medicine*, June 1845.

implanted, resembled in all respects the ordinary skin of the surface of the body.

A few hairs appeared to arise from the general surface of the tunica vaginalis.

In the substance of the club-shaped projections, but particularly in **the larger of** the two, where it adhered to the mass of the **testis**, there were irregular masses of soft cartilage, **presenting all** the ordinary characters of the corpuscles of that texture, and a few vascular canals.

In some places this cartilage had been converted into bone, in which were visible irregular Haversian canals and numerous corpuscles and canaliculi.

One portion of bone **resembling a sand-glass measured** half-an-inch in length.

XXXVI.—ON THE CURVATURES OF THE ARTICULAR SURFACES, AND ON THE GENERAL MECHANISM OF THE HUMAN HIP-JOINT.*

In consequence of the vague and unsatisfactory manner in which anatomists and physiologists have until lately examined the mechanism of the joints, it appears to have been assumed as self-evident that the cartilaginous surfaces of the head of the thigh-bone and of its socket must be spherical. If, however, the outlines of the transverse and antero-posterior curvatures of the head of the femur be attentively followed by the eye against the light, it will be at once observed that they are not arcs of circles. The transverse curves as seen from the front or back of the bone are two in number, one above, the other below the fossa for the ligamentum teres, and they increase in rapidity as they approach that fossa.

The transverse curves are also two in number, and may be observed by looking at the outline of the head of the bone from the inner side, holding it so that the ridge extending from it to the lesser trochanter may be perpendicular. If the line of the ridge be then traced upwards to the outline of the articular surface of the head of the bone, it will be found to intersect that outline at the point of osculation of the two curves of which it consists. This point is a cusp directed upwards, and the two curves increase in rapidity as they extend down to the front and back of the articular margin. On examining the articular surface, the eye will now be able

---

* This memoir ought to have immediately followed that on the Mechanism of the Knee-joint, but the manuscript from which we print was unfortunately overlooked until the greater part of this volume had gone to press.—Eds.

to trace this cusp to a ridge extending across from the neck of the bone to the fossa, dividing the surface into an anterior and posterior area. If the eye be carried along two series of lines diverging from the upper angles of the fossa, the one series outwards and forwards on the anterior area, and the other outwards and backwards on the posterior area, and with a convexity on each line towards the ridge corresponding to the curvature of that part of the surface on which it is traced, each series will be found to close with the anterior and posterior margins of the fossa for the ligamentum teres. It will also be observed why the transverse lines of curvature increase in rapidity from above downwards.

The cartilaginous surface of the acetabulum consists of three areas situated respectively on the pubic, iliac, and ischial portions of the cavity. They are more or less distinctly separated in the dry or recent bone by depressed lines. The marginal terminations of these lines are indicated at the brim of the cavity by the three notch-like hollows of the edge, that between the ischial and iliac at the middle of the posterior margin; that between the iliac and the pubic on the upper margin at the outer side of the ilio-pectineal eminence; that between the pubic and ischial by the fossa and notch of the lower part and margin of the cavity. These three notches, with the three intermediate wave-like projections, produce an undulating form of margin in the macerated bone. The three projections are respectively formed by the upper part of the iliac, the lower part of the ischial, and the anterior part of the pubic portion. The margin of the articular surface on the head of the femur is also undulating. It sweeps outwards opposite the front and back of the great trochanter, and slightly below opposite the lesser trochanter, and therefore recedes inwards opposite the upper margin of the great trochanter, also before and behind the ridge which connects the head to the small trochanter. In the erect position, that is when standing on both feet, the hip-joint being in full extension, the posterior area of the head of the femur is in close contact and congruent with the ischial area of the acetabulum, the undulation outwards of the posterior margin of the articular surface of the head of the femur occupying the broadest part of the ischial surface of the acetabulum; while the undulation inwards of its upper part occupies the notch in the margin of the acetabulum, between the ischial and iliac portions of the cavity.

In semi-flexion of the hip-joint, the anterior area of the head of the femur is congruent with the iliac area, this broadest or projecting portion occupying the undulation of the former, which extends outwards on the front of the neck of the bone; while the inward undulations on each side of it occupy respectively the acetabular notches between the ischial and iliac, and between the iliac and pubic portions of the cavity.

The anterior border of the femoral pit is the thread of this screwed area, and curves more rapidly as it approaches the posterior angle of the attachment of the lig-teres. The area itself is the rolling surface. It is a right-handed screw in the right hip, a left in the left. It therefore screws the head of the thigh bone out of the socket in flexion, but screws it against the iliac area, advancing its superior external angle or apex against the outer or projecting marginal portion of that area. During the action of this area the ilio-femoral ligament is slack; when completed the pubic and ischial portions of the capsule become tense and act as the tightening arrangements of the combination.

In complete flexion the lower portion of the posterior area of the head of the femur, which occupies the cotyloid fossa during semi-flexion, is applied and rests upon the pubic area; the posterior undulation outwards on the femur which occupies the ischial projection in full extension, now occupies the pubic projection, and the pubic notch is occupied by the posterior inferior inward undulation.

In complete extension, as in standing erect on both feet, the posterior area of the head of the femur is congruent with the ischial area of the acetabulum, and with the superior internal portion of the iliac area; being screwed backwards, upwards, inwards, and forwards, by the action of the extensor muscles of the hip, and by the tightening of the successive fasciculi of, and ultimate tension of, the entire ilio-femoral portion of the capsule. During extension, the thigh passes backwards and outwards, rotating outwards at the same time. It is, to use the current nomenclature, a combination of extension, abduction, and rotation outwards. These movements are the necessary accompaniments of the movements already described between the posterior femoral, and ischial articular areas. The movements of these two areas in extension are such that the male or femoral area advances by a combination of rolling and gliding along the female or ischial, apex towards apex, and base towards base, until the opposite convex and concave surfaces become congruent throughout, and the joint is screwed home in extension. If a portion of the inner wall of the acetabulum be removed, so as to display the respective movements of the areas under consideration, the most prominent portion of the femoral area will be observed to advance inwards and forwards, as it advances laterally along its action of rotation. The head of the femur is thus, during extension, screwed, and therefore forced into the acetabulum; from without inwards, and from behind forwards. The posterior border of the femoral pit constitutes the proper thread of this screwed area; its superior more rapidly curved portions at the posterior extremity of the attachment of the lig.-teres advancing during the movement forward and inward. The area itself constitutes the rolling surface. This area, with the ischial and deeper portion of the iliac, constitutes a right-handed screw combination in the right, a left-handed in the left hip.

The ligamentum teres.—When the posterior area is screwed home, the round ligament is quite slack and folded over on itself forwards; the posterior angle of its femoral attachment having revolved over and in front of its anterior, while the posterior area is screwing off, that is, performing the first half of flexion, by screwing and rolling backwards, downwards, and onwards, the ligamentum teres gradually tightens, so that when the shaft of the thigh bone has passed so far forwards and inwards as it is when the foot comes in contact with the ground in the step, when the trunk has inclined slightly forward to the same side over the head of the thigh bone, it becomes quite tight, flattened out, and lodged in the cartilaginous fossa below the femoral pit, and bounded on each side by the screwed anterior and posterior borders of that groove. The joint is now in mid flexion (or mid extension), that is, the posterior femoral area, and the corresponding cotyloid area are about to break contact, and the anterior femoral and corresponding area to come into action. When this takes place the ligamentum teres again gradually slackens, folding backwards with its anterior angle of femoral attachment revolving over the posterior. In extreme flexion when the lower part of the posterior area of the head of the femur passes across the non-cartilaginous fossa of the acetabulum and rests on the pubic area, a position which can only be assumed along with extreme abduction, the ligamentum teres folds still further backwards and inwards. As the hip joint is essentially a hinge joint, the ligamentum teres represents the internal lateral ligament, as the capsular is a modified external lateral ligament. The fossa for the femoral attachment of the ligamentum teres lies in the line of osculation of its two areas; and, therefore, like the internal lateral ligament of the hock-joint in the horse, becomes tense at mid action. The anterior and posterior bands of this ligament are reciprocally related to the anterior and posterior areas of the femoral head, and of the acetabulum, as the ilio-femoral and pubo-ischial femoral are.

On the Movements of the Hip-Joint.—The movements of the elbow and ankle-joints take place in an anterior and a posterior conical screw combination in each joint. These combinations are both dexiotrope or both scœotrope in each joint, according to the side to which the joint belongs. The axes of the fundamental cones lie more or less obliquely across the joint, one in front of the other—the apices of the cones pointing, the one outwards, the other inwards. The so-called movements of flexion and extension in these joints—that is, presumed movements in the same antero-posterior plane—are, in fact, movements of flexion and extension produced by combined gliding and rolling along one conical helicoid course in the anterior half, and along a second in a reverse direction in the posterior half of the articular path. As, however, the axes of rotation of both screw combinations are so nearly coincident with the axes of the presumed hinge movement, the actual variation from such a movement is not at first obvious. For the same reasons the movements are principally screwing or gliding, with a minimum of rolling; the gaping, therefore, is comparatively slight. It is evident that the path described by a point in either of the segments of the limb, between which the joint is placed, must be a double helix—that is, two conical helices, corresponding respectively to the anterior and posterior screw combinations of the joint oscultating with one another. It must also be evident from the double-threaded form of the screwed surfaces of these joints, and the peculiar configuration of their opposite articular surfaces, that they do not admit of the movements technically termed adduction, abduction, and rotation.

The anterior and posterior screw combinations of the knee-joint differ from those in the elbow and ankle in their axes being nearly perpendicular to the horizontal plane of the joint, that of the anterior being directed with its vertex upwards and slightly backwards and outwards; that of the posterior upwards and slightly forwards and inwards. The shallow transverse curvatures of the rolling areas of the male elements, and the wavy convex form of the corresponding curvatures of the female elements, would appear to render lateral and circumductory movements of the knee-joint possible. It will be found, however, that throughout the whole extent of its double helicoid movements, it only permits of eversion and inversion of the toes at the stage beyond semi-flexion; these movements, due to the action of the biceps and semi-membranous being again excluded when the joint is flexed home.

The hip-joint, from the ball and socket form assumed by its combined anterior and posterior screw combinations, is not only capable of pursuing its fundamental double helicoid path, but also of performing the so-called adduction, abduction, and circumduction movements in all parts of its course, but more particularly towards the close of flexion.

INDEX TO VOL. II.

ABSORPTION, nature of, 397; and ulceration, and the structures engaged in these processes, 403-407
Acephalocyst or simple hydatid, 476-482; *Acephalocystis armatus*, 478, 502; *A. simplex*, 480, 502; *A. monroii*, 482, 502
Acetic acid in fluid which contained *Sarcina ventriculi*, 370
Acids found in stomachs of animals, 368, 369
Acting facets of articular surfaces, their curvatures and movements, 246-264
Alpidium ficus, hepatic organ of, 415
Amaryllis, electric current at time of flowering, 315
Anatomical and pathological observations, 387-503
Anatomy, the study of, to be advanced by ascertaining the accurate shape, form, and proportion, geometrically, 209
Anemone, electric descending current at time of flowering, 315
Annulosa, eye how acted on, 280
Annulose type of organisation, on morphological relations of nervous system in, 78-87
Anomoura (Crustacea), organs of generation in, 430
"Antaxial couple," meaning of, 258
Aphotogenic rays, 278
Aplysia punctata, liver of, 415; secretion from mantle, 416, 425
Apple and pear, electrical current in fruit of, 315
Apteryx, nasal fossæ, arrangement of, 153
Arm in well-made man straight, 218
Arnold, paper in Salzburg Journal, 1831, referred to, 11, etc.; on formation of milk-tooth sacs, 51, 52
Articular cartilages, the process of ulceration in, 408-411; couple, what Professor Goodsir means by the term, 247; surfaces, memoir on the curvatures and movements of the acting facets of, 246-264; on the curvatures of the, 508-514
Artist, how he might draw better proportioned figures, 214-218
Astoma acephalocystis, 482, 502
"Axial" couple," meaning of, 258
Azalea, electric current at time of flowering, 315

BAER (Von) on morphological character of supra-œsophageal ganglion, 86, 87
Bacillary layer of the retina, 265; Gottsche and Hannover on, 268; its morphological relations, 271
Balearica pavonia, entozoon in, 487
Balæna mysticetus, tooth-germs in fœtus of, 54
Barry (Dr. Martin), paper on the corpuscles of the blood referred to, 389; development of cells from parent centre, 391
Basement membrane of Bowman, 391
Batteries in Gymnotus, 291, 292; in Malapterurus, 293, 294; of the fish independent electromotor structures, 341, 342
Battery in electrical fishes, 289, 299, 304, 305
Baxter on electrical currents during secretion and respiration, 300; on the electric relations of mucous membrane, 320, 322; of gland, 321
Beauty of proportion in human body, Hay on, 215
Becquerel on electricity in vegetables, referred to, 308, 318
Bell, Anatomy of Teeth referred to, 33, 35; note in Palmer's edition of Hunter's works quoted, 21
Berzelius on difficulty of distilling viscid animal fluids in retorts (note), 362
Bilharz (Dr.), on the electric organ in Nilotic Malapterurus,' 294
Biology, how its study has been promoted, 205, 206

Birds, centrum of pre-sphenoidal sclerotome in, 149-154; from size of organs of vision, have great development of principal frontal, 156
Birth, state of teeth at, 23
Blake, Structure and Formation of Teeth referred to, 21, 33
Blastema announcing formation of a gland in embryo, 425
Blastoderma, the first form after commencement of development, 73
Blennius viviparus, Rathke on cartilaginous streaks at the basis of head in embryo, 186
Blumenbach on the enclosure of bullets in ivory, 58
Bone: how dead or dying bone is separated from the living structure, 406, the structure and economy of, 461-464
"Bones of Bertin," 158, 163
Bowman, paper on muscle referred to, 389; fat deposited in liver, 382, 413; on basement membrane, 391; paper on the structure and use of the Malpighian bodies of the kidney referred to, 391, 428; on mucous membrane, 396, 428
Brachyura (Crustacea), organs of generation in, 430, 435
Brain in crustacea, its position, 80; in insects, annelids, and mollusca, 81
Bremser, Intestinal Worms of Man, quoted, 481
Bright, figures of ulceration of Peyer's patches, 378
Brisbane (Lady), sends gold-fish with parasitic conferva on it to Mr. Bryson, 345
Brücke and Hannover on the rods and cones of bacillary layer of retina reflecting light back, 269
Bryson (Alex.), on vegetable nature of growth on fin and tail of gold-fish, 345
Buccinum undatum, liver of, 415
Bulbs, tooth-pulp and its sac, 51
Burdach's Physiologie referred to, 20
Bursariæ on filaments of conferva of gold-fish, 350

Cænurus cerebralis, 487, 503; *C. hepaticus*, 489, 503
Camels, canine teeth in, 53
Camper on metallic bodies inclosed in ivory, 58
Canine and upper incisors, germs of, in embryo of cow and sheep, 53
Carabus catenulatus, hepatic cæca of, 415
Carcinus mœnas, hepatic cæca of, 415; liver of, 423

Carp, interorbital space in, 157
Carswell on cirrhosis of liver, 382
Cartilage, nature of, 408
Carus, view of the morphology of nervous system in annulosa, 79; division of skeleton, 102
Cassowary, olfactory chambers of, 153
Catacentric sclerotome, 110
Catametopa have large generative organs, 429
Cell (central), origin of others, 390
Cells, various kinds of, in animals and vegetables, 403
Cell-wall does not separate and prepare secretion, 426
Cement of elephant's tusk, exogenous growth of, 59
Centres of nutrition, 389-392
Centrifugal and centripetal nerves, their electric relations are identical, 337
Cetacea, substance in pulp-cavities of teeth, 62
Changes in pulps and sacs at various stages till the eruption of the wisdom-teeth, 26-43
Chemical action, cause of electricity in vegetables, 318
Chemistry, mechanics, and other physical sciences, how the knowledge of them was advanced, 206, 208
Child at birth, development of pulps and sacs of teeth in, 23; between four and five years old, sac and pulp of teeth in, 25, 26; six years old, 26
Chyle, absorption of, in fresh subjects, 394
Cirrhosis of liver, 382
Claudius on Corti's membrane, 283-286
Cochlea, on the lamina spiralis of, 282-288; Dr. Young's opinion that it was a "micrometer of sound," 287
Cod, interorbital space in, 156
Comb on a spear-head found in tusk of elephant, 64
Cones of retina, 265; seat of impression of light, 209; Goodsir's opinion that they are not nervous structures, 270
Confervæ, their mode of reproduction, 212; which vegetate on the skin of the gold-fish, 345-350
Contraction (muscular) electric condition during, 328
Cooper (Sir Astley) on structure of thymus, correction of one of his observations, 74; (Daniel), cotton-like conferva on gills and fins of gold-fish, 350
Corti, membrane of, in cochlea, 283
Cow, follicular stage of dentition in, 53

INDEX. 517

Crab, how it acts on the injuring of a limb, 471
Cranium of mammal, how it differs from that of the other vertebrata, 114
Crocodiles, observations made by Goodsir in dissection of, 98, 99; peculiar position of their nostrils, 118, 119
Cruikshank (William), Anatomy of the Absorbing Vessels of the Human Body, referred to, 393, 443
Crustacea, Geoffroy St. Hilaire's opinion of their relations, 79; brain in, its position, 80; development of seminal secretion in, 427; on the mode of reproduction of lost parts in, 471-475
Crystalline column, 278; of compound eye, 279
Cuvier, on the bone and ivory around bullets in tusks of elephant, 59; "os en forme de cuiller" in lizard, what, 151
Cyclometopa, the most prolific crustacea, 429
Cyclostomous fishes, nasal passage of, 173-175
Cyprinoid fish, post-stomal sclerotome, 176
Cystic entozoa, anatomy and development of, 476-503
Cysticercus cellulosus, 490; *C. rattus*, 491; *C. neglectus*, 503; species of, found in almost every part of human body, 493

DALRYMPLE on the structure of human placenta, referred to, 446-449
Davy (Dr.), on the torpedo, 344
Dexiotrope movements, 260
Diacentric sclerotome, 111
Diaphragms (electric) in torpedo, 290, 291; in gymnotus, 292, 293
Diatomaceæ, their mode of reproduction, 212
Dicotyledonous plants, electrical currents in, 310, 311
Digestion, functions of, 400, 401
Diplostomum volvens, Nordman, 500
Discs of mass on each side of tail of skate, their structure, 295
Diseased structure in one animal identical with normal structure in another, 62, 63
Diskostoma acephalocystis, 483-502
"Distal" margin in movements of joints, 248
Distoma clavatum, Owen, 499
Dodo, Dinornis, and other extinct birds, structure of bones of head, 152, 153
Donné, opposite electrical conditions of different parts of vegetables, 308; on electric phenomena of membrane and gland, 319-321

EAR, structure of parts of, 282-288
Echinococcus hominis, 480; *E. veterinorum*, 481
Echiurus vulgaris, cæca of, 416
Ecker, communication on Bilharz's anatomy of electric Nile fish, 294, 299
Edentulous mammals likely to have germs of teeth in fœtal state, 54
"Edinburgh Dissector," referred to, 35.
Electric organ, various opinions on its action, 338-341; fishes do not feel electric discharges produced by themselves or other individuals of the same species, 343
Electrical apparatus in torpedo, gymnotus, and other fishes, 289; disturbances in the processes of living organised bodies, as noticed by Galvani, Matteucci, and Du Bois Reymond, 299
Electricity (organic), a brief review of the present state of, 306-350; peculiar character of that evolved from the batteries of the fish, 342
Electrotonic state of nerve, 333-335
Elephant, successive dentitions conducted in a cavity of reserve, 41; on bullets and other bodies inclosed in the tusks of, 56-65.
Embryo of sixth week, dental arches in, 1; seventh week, 4; second month, 6; nine weeks old, 8; tenth week, 9; 11th or 12th week, 10; 13th week, 11; 14th week, 12; 15th week, 14; 16th week, 16; fifth month, 18; forms must be studied in morphological inquiries, 83
Enamel pulp of Hunter, 33; deposition of, 54
Endogenous growth of ivory, 59
Entomosome, a segmented animal, 84
Entozoa (cystic), Harry Goodsir on their anatomy and development, 476-503
Equiangular spiral, its characteristic property, 253
Eruptive stage of dentition, 44
Erdl, dissertation on *Helix algira*, 413
Ethmoidal sclerotome, 122-148; remarkable modification of, in the bird, 127-130; in the chelonian, 130; in the crocodiles, 131; in lacertians, 136; in ophidians, 137; in amphibians, 138; views hitherto taken of it, 139-143
Exogenous growth of cement of elephant's tusk, 59

INDEX.

External lamella of Blake, 33
Eye: on the mode in which light acts on the ultimate nervous structures of the eye, and on the relations between simple and compound eyes, 273-281

FACETS of patellar surface, peculiarity of, 234
Faraday on the power of gymnotus to strike fish motionless, 304; his researches on electricity, 306; on the atmosphere of power around fish at the time when electric organs are discharged, 343
Figures, Mr. D. R. Hay shows how they might be drawn in good proportion, 214-219
Filamentary layer of the retina, 267
Fin-rays of fishes, 105
Final causes, the study of, furthering the progress of biology, 206
Fishes, bony rays of, 104; composition of head, 113; from size of organs of vision have great development of principal frontal, 156
Flower, electrical condition of, 314
Follicular stage of dentition, 44; in ruminants, etc., 53-55
Food, changes of, in gut, of a chemical nature, 400
Formation and growth of ivory, 60
Fox, Natural History of the Human Teeth, referred to, 33
Frog, Galvani's observations on electrical contractions in the muscles of, 322; Nobili on electric current in nerve and muscles of, 323, 328, 330, 334; palatals in 161-163
Fruit, Donné's observations on electrical condition of, 315

GALATHEA, testis in, 431, 434
Galvani on animal electricity, 319, 322
Gelatinous body between pulp and sac of teeth, 20
Generation of *Sarcina*, 358; (organs of) in male crustacean, 429
Geoffroy St. Hilaire detects tooth-germs in fœtus of whale, 54
Geometrical formation of shells shown by Professor Moseley, 209-211; character of the configuration and movement of central articular facets, 247-264
Germinal membrane, 391-392, 400; spot of the ovum, centre of nutrition, 389
Germination of plant, electrical relations of plant to soil and air reversed after, 310

Germs of the teeth, 43; of canine and upper incisors in embryo of cow and sheep, 53
Giraffe, antlers of, 149
Gland, electric relations of, 321
Goethe on the elements of three distinct cranial segments, 197
"Go-lines" of ankle-joint, 237
Gold ball found at Amsterdam in elephant's tusk, 57
Gold-fish, on the conferva vegetating on the skin of, 345-350
Gonidium, a genus of Ehrenberg's, 360
Gonium, how its square form is produced, 211; characters of the genus, 359; *G. hyalinum, glaucum, pectorale, punctatum, tranquillum*, 360
Goodsir (Harry), paper on the development and metamorphoses of caligus, referred to, 424; the testis and its secretion in the decapodous crustaceans, 429-435; the mode of reproduction of lost parts in the crustacea, 471-475; on the anatomy and development of the cystic entozoa, 476-503
Granulations of surgical pathologists, in reproduction of bone, 469
Gray cellular layer of the retina, 266
Growth and secretion, centripetal, 418
Gruby, microscopic character of morbid products referred to, 378
Gymnorhynchus horridus in liver of sunfish, 494
Gymnotus, four batteries in, 291

Habenula sulcata, 283; *denticulata*, 284
Hæmal arch, Goodsir's remarks on Professor Owen's view of, 97-100
Hæmapod, Goodsir's term for a vertebrate animal, 85
Hæmome, hæmatome, terms of Goodsir's, 86
Hannover on conferva of frog and newt, 350
Havers (Clopton) on vascular fringes of synovial membranes, 437, 438
Haversian canals in bone, 406, 462; inflammatory changes, 468; glands or synovial pads, 227, 228, 235
Hay (D. R.) examined the geometric outline of the human body, 213-219
Head (vertebrate), morphological constitution of its skeleton, 88-197
Helianthus tuberosus, electrical currents in tubers of, 313
Helicoid curve of movement in knee-joint, 238, 241
Helix algira, cells in kidney of, 413;

INDEX. 519

H. aspersa, cells in liver, 414; kidney of, 415

Helmholtz on reflected light acting on the grey cellular layer of the retina, 269

Henle, System of Anatomy referred to, 231; on epithelium-cells of glands and follicles, 412

Hip-joint, general mechanism of, 513, 514

Human anatomy supplies keys for morphological solution of parts in presphenoidal sclerotome in birds, etc., 157

Human body, beauty of, arising from certain symmetrical and geometrical forms, 215-219

Hunter (John), account of the *Gymnotus electricus* referred to, 292; Natural History of Teeth referred to 20, etc.

Hyas, testis of, 430; spindle-shaped cells, 432

Hydatula gadorum, Rathke, 497

INCISIVES (central), how they pass through the gum, 37; (superior) teeth, tardy development of, 45

Inductive philosophy promoted the advance of physical science, 206

Infant eight or nine months old, state of teeth in, 24

Inflammation of membranes, 438

Infusorial animalcules on filaments of conferva of gold-fish, 350

Intermaxillary bones and incisors, 46, 47

Internal lamella of Blake, 33

Internuncial cord in electrical fishes, 289

Intestinal glands, on a diseased condition of the, 372-378

Intestinal villi, the structure and functions of, 393-402

Ivory of elephant's tusks, musket-bullets, etc., inclosed in, 56-65

JACOB's membrane of retina, 274

Janthina fragilis, mantle and its secretion, 416, 425

Joint-surfaces of mechanicians and of organic structures, differences of, 246

Jonquil, electric current at time of flowering, 315

KEY (Aston) on the ulcerative process in joints referred to, 408

Kidney and liver, structure and pathological changes in, 379-383; appendix to this paper, 383-386; granular degeneration of, 379-381

Kiernan, researches into the healthy and morbid structure of human liver, 381

Klockner, gold ball found in tusk of elephant, 57

Knee-joint, anatomy of human, 220-230; mechanism of, 231-245

Knees in female brought together, 218

Knox (Dr.) on tooth-substances, 62; on the troughs in gymnotus, 292; (F.) tooth-germs in fœtus of whale, 54

Kölliker on the rods and cones as the seat of the impression of light in the retina, 269

Læmodipoda, testis in, 433

Lamina spiralis of the cochlea, 282-288

Land-crabs of tropics, 429

Langer forms continued screws from upper articular surface of astragalus in horse, etc., 237

Lathyrus tuberosus, electrical currents in tubers of, 313

Law of the excitation of nerves by electrical current, 337, 338; of force, how made out by Sir Isaac Newton, 212; of production, what may prove to be, 213

Laws regulating the development of pulps and sacs, and period of appearance of each tooth-germ, 48-50

Lawrence on growth of orifices produced by balls in ivory, 58, 59

Leaves, Becquerel's observations of electrical currents in, 314

Leptopodia, testis of, 430

Leydig on structure of simple and compound eyes, 279

Liebig on power possessed by vapours of carrying along with them portions of bodies which in their solid form resist dissipation by very high temperatures, 362

Light, mode in which it acts on the retina, 273-281

Lily (white), electrical current at time of flowering, 315

Limbs, Goodsir on the morphological constitution of, 198-203; organ in crabs which supplies germs for, 472

Limitary layer of the retina, 267

Liver, observations on structure and pathology of, 381-386; the natural habitat of the acephalocyst, 476; (human) nucleated cells of, 415, 416

Logarithmic spiral in shells, 209-211; probably the law at work in the increase of organic bodies, 213

Loligo sagittata, secreting membrane of ink-bag, 413; liver of, 415

Louis and Chomel on matter distending intestinal glands, 378
Lymphatic glands, structure of, 439-444

Macroura (*Crustacea*), organs of generation in, 431, 433
Magnet formed by electricity of fish, 342
Malapterurus, electric batteries in, 293, 294, 302
Male and female figures, how they differ in harmonic ratio, D. R. Hay's views, 217, 218
Malpighi on secreting glands being formed of tubes with blind extremities, 412
Mammary gland of bitch, 416
Mathematical modes of investigation in the determination of organic forms, two lectures on the employment of, 205-219; principles on which shells are constructed, 209-211
Matteucci on the dependence of the electromotor energy of electric apparatus in fishes on the nervous centre, 300; electric properties in muscle due to its own texture and not to nerves, 323
Mechanism of knee-joint, Goodsir's memoir on, 231-245
Meckel's cartilage, 187-190
Membrane and gland, electric phenomena in connection with, 319-322
Mercury, effects of, on teeth, 38
Metasomatomic openings defined, 85
Meyer, on the peculiar curvature of the inner condyle of the femur, 220-224, 232; his Mechanics of the Human Skeleton referred to, 220, 232-234
Microcosm, electrical disturbances in, represented by similar but grander phenomena in macrocosm, 338
Milk incisives, growth of, 36
Milk-teeth, production of, 48, 50, 55
Modiola vulgaris, liver of, 414
Molars in man and elephant, their growth, 41; the anterior permanent molar the most remarkable tooth in man, 45
Mollusca, Moseley on the logarithmic curve in the shells of, 209-211; eye in, how acted on, 280
Monitor-lizards, "palatines" in, 160
Morphological constitution of the skeleton of the vertebrate head, 88-197
Moseley (Professor) on the geometrical formation of shells, 209-211
Mouth, position of, fundamental differences between morphological relations of annulose and vertebrate nervous systems, 80, 82

Movement (primary) or "along the thread," what it means, 248; (secondary) or "across the thread," 248
Mucous membrane, electric relations of, 320, 322
Müller on cyclostomous fishes, 174; on absorption, 397; on secreting glands, 412
Müllerian filaments of the retina, 269; not nervous structures, 270
Muscle, electric properties of, 322-331
Musket-bullets and other foreign bodies, how inclosed in tusks of the elephant, 56-65
Musical harmony in proportions of human frame, D. R. Hay's theory, 216-219
Myome, myotome, terms of Goodsir's, 86

Nautilus, the form of the shell in, 211
Nares, relative position of external and internal, 165
Nasal chamber in bird, 169; fossæ, their constitution, 165-173; passage of cyclostomous fishes, 173, 175
Nasmyth (A.) on resemblance of ossified pulp to diseased ivory, 62
"Negative" movement in joints, 249
Nereis, biliary apparatus of, 415
Nerves of batteries in electrical fishes, 289-291; in gymnotus, 298
Nerve-filament, the doctrine of Du Bois Reymond on, 276
Nerve, electric properties of, 331
Nervous centre in electrical fishes, 289; force and electricity equivalent, 331; system in the annulose and vertebrate types, morphological relations of, 78-87
Neurome, neurotome, terms of Goodsir's, 86
Neuronaia monroi, 493; John Goodsir's account of, 495-501
Neuropod, Goodsir's term for an annulose animal, 85
Newton from the geometric forms made out the law of the force, 212
Nobili on electric current in nerve and muscle of the frog, 323, 328
Noise, sound heard merely as noise in vestibule of ear, 287
Nostrils of chelonian more of the ornithic than mammalian conformation, 171; of crocodiles, peculiar position of, 118, 119
Nucleated cell, secretion a function of, 413-416, 428
Nutritive centres of textures permanent, 390; of organs embryonic, 390

INDEX. 521

Oken, views on cephalic limbs held by Carus, 198
Olfactory chambers in head of birds, 153 ; sense, its seat, 168
Operculum of the shell, its importance in regulating the form, 210, 211
Opuntia, current passing from stamen to pistil at time of flowering, 315
Organic electricity, present state of, 306-350
Organised and inorganised bodies, difference in the mode of studying, 207
Organs that have once acted an important part never altogether disappear so long as they do not interfere with other functions, 39
Osseous texture, 461
Ossific juice repairing injury in elephant's tusk, Blumenbach's opinion, 58
Ossification round balls in tusks of elephant, 60
Owen (Professor) on the relations of the endo and exo-skeleton, 79 ; structure of head of dodo, dinornis, apteryx, etc., 152-154 ; views on limbs, remarks of Goodsir on, 198 ; description of a microscopic entozoon infesting the muscles of the human body, referred to, 494 ; on the anatomy of *Distoma clavatum*, 499
Owl, bones of the head, 152

PACINI on electrical diaphragms, 290, 291, 292, 302, 303
Pagurus, generative organs of, 431, 432
Palatal arch and pterygoids in the bird, 158, 160 ; in reptiles and amphibians, 160
Palate-bone of bird, lacertian, and amphibian, 136
Parelectronomic layer of Du Bois Reymond, 327
Patella, movements and relations of, as observed by Goodsir, 223-227
Patella vulgata, liver of, 415
Peach and apricot, electrical current in, 315
Pecten opercularis, bile-like fluid in pouches, 414
Pectoralina hebraica, a composite animal, 360
Peptome, peptatome, terms of Goodsir's, 86
Periosteum as an element in formation and economy of bone, 463, 465, 470
Permanent teeth of independent origin, 51 ; developed from inner surface of cavities of reserve, 53

Peyer's glands, Boehm and Krause on, 413 ; patches, ulceration of, in continued fever, 372-378
Phallusia vulgaris, hepatic organ of, 415
Photæsthetic bodies of retina, 275, 278 ; surface, 278
Photogenic rays, 277
Pig, follicular stage of dentition in, 53 ; gastric glands in, Wasmann on, 413
Pirena prunum, hepatic organ of, 414
Pituitary body, Rathke on, 82
Placenta (human), Goodsir's memoir on the structure of, 445-460
Plant, soil, and atmosphere, electrical reactions of, 309
Polarisation of nerve, to what is it due? 336
"Positive" movement in joints, 249
Post-stomal cephalic sclerotomes, 175-197
Potato, electrical currents in tubers, 313
Pouillet's experiments on electrical development in young plants, 308 ; in old plants, 309
Prawn, seminal fluid, 434
Pre-sphenoidal sclerotome, 148-158 ; in birds, 149-154 ; in chelonians, 154 ; in crocodiles, 154 ; in lizards, 155 ; in ophidians and batrachia, 155 ; in fish, 156 ; hæmal arch in fishes, 163
Primary or fibrous sclerome, 93 ; secreting cell, 417
Primitive dental groove, 27-30
Principal frontal of birds, what, 149
Proboscidian mammals, simplification of sclerotome in, 111
Proboscis of elephant and tapir more than a mere elongation of external nose, 111
Progressive development, phases through which the tooth-pulp passes, 30
Proximal margin in movements of joints, 248
Pterygoid in fishes, 164
Pulmonic blood, electric relations of, 322
Pulps and sacs of human teeth, their origin and development, 1-52
Purkinje on secreting function of part of the gland-ducts, 412

QUADRATE-JUGAL bone of bird, Owen's analysis, 189

RABBIT, follicular stage of dentition in, 53
Raia, tail of, peculiar structure on the sides of, 295

2 M

Rathke on pituitary body, 82 ; on **branchial** clefts and quadrilateral bodies on each side of chorda dorsalis, 89
Ray, Hallman on the testicle of, 413 ; tail of, 295
Reflection of light from bottom of eye, 270
Reid (Dr. John) on placenta, observations of, 457, 458
Remak, observations on dorsal quadrilateral bodies, 89, 90
Reproduction of lost parts in the crustacea, Harry Goodsir on, 471-475
"Reserved" and "restricted," terms employed in distinguishing the articular elements in their respective conditions, 247, 261
Respiratory mucous membrane, electric relations of, 322
Retina, memoir on the, 265-272 ; how light acts on the, 273-281
Retzian tubes of ivory, 61
Retzius on microscopic structure of dental substances, 62
Reymond (Du Bois), on the law of the muscular current, 324 ; electric currents in nerves, 331-338
Rhinal sclerotome in mammals, 115 ; rudimentary in crocodiles, 117
Right angle, division of, enables artist to get a proper succession of lines in drawing, 214, 215
Robin on organs in the tail of the ray fishes, 297
Robison (Sir John), specimens of bullets in ivory presented by, 56
Rods of retina, 265 ; seat of impression of light, 269, 274 ; Goodsir's opinion not nervous structures, 270, 274
Root, electrical currents in, 313
Rokitansky, on matter peculiar to typhus fever, 378
Rudolphi on the troughs in gymnotus, 292 ; on the prisms in torpedo and gymnotus, 301
Ruminants, follicular stage of dentition in, 53-55
Ruysch figures bullets in ivory, 58

SACCULAR stage of dentition, 44
Sarcina ventriculi, history of a case in which a fluid periodically ejected from the stomach contained vegetable organisms of an undescribed form, 351-371 ; definition of genus and species, 361 ; how its form is produced, 211
Savi on the elementary filaments of the nerves in battery of electrical fishes, 290

Scæotrope movements, 260
Schönlein, "general pathology" referred to, 378
Schwann on the **secreting** organs of mucous membranes, 412
Sclerome of Goodsir, 85 ; in vertebrate embryo, its sources and modes of origin, 88, 93 ; sclerotome, 85
Screw-configuration of articular surfaces of elbow, ankle, and calcaneo-astragaloid joints, 237 ; movements in knee-joint, 243-245
Scrofulous disease of joint, 410
Secondary dental groove, 30-41 ; teeth, 55
Secreting structures, Goodsir's memoir on, 412-428
Secretion differs from absorption morphologically, 398
Secretions, three orders of, 423
Semilunar cartilages of human knee-joint, their movements and relations, as observed by Goodsir, 227-229
Seminal secretion of decapod crustacea, development of, 427
Serous membranes, structure of, 436-438
Serres, l'Anatomie et la Physiologie des Dents, referred to, 22
Shaft of a long bone, on the mode of reproduction after death, 465
Sharpey (Dr.), on impregnated uterus, 452 ; on the entozoa of nerves of haddock and whiting, 496, 497
Sheep, follicular stage of dentition in, 53 ; supra-renal, thymus, and thyroid bodies in the embryo of, 68 ; entozoon found in its brain, 487
Shells of molluscous animals examined geometrically by Professor Moseley, 209
Simple eye, its physiological superiority to compound eye, 281
Simplicity of natural law consists in the comprehensiveness of its general principles, 185
Skate, fusiform mass on each side of the tail in, exhibiting all the structural characteristics of an electrical battery, 295 ; nervous twigs, 299
Slough in soft parts separated from living textures, 406
Somatome of Goodsir, 84
Spear-head found in tusk of elephant, 64
Spheroidal bodies on brain are entozoa, 495
Sphairidion acephalocystis, 487, 492, 503
Sphenoidal turbinated bones, 158
Spongiole of root of plant, an active organ of growth and of absorption, 401

Squalus cornubicus, testicle of, 416, 419-422
Stages into which dentition is divided, 43
Stark (Dr.) on organs in the tail of the rays, 296, 297
Stomach: fluid ejected from the stomach of a patient which contained vegetable organisms, 351, 371
Strix flammea, optic foramina in, 152
Sun, his relations to the earth and other planetary bodies, 206
Supra-œsophagal ganglion, pre-stomal character of, 86
Supra-renal bodies, 66-77
Syme (Professor) on the power of the periosteum to form new bone, quoted, 465
Symmyotome, synhæmatome, synneuratome, terms of Goodsir's, 86
Synovial pads of the human knee-joint, their movements and relations, as observed by Goodsir, 227, 228
Synpeptatome, syssclerotome, syssomatome, terms of Goodsir's, 86

TEETH (human), origin and development of the pulps and sacs, 1-52
Terms in morphology must be precise, 84
Thigh-muscles action of certain, 222; and leg rotate in opposite directions at the close of extension and commencement of flexion, 234
Thomson (Dr. Allen) on primitive condition of gastric and intestinal gland, 413; follicles of stomach and large intestine originally closed vesicles, 426
Thymus, how formed, 66-77; Sir Astley Cooper on, 74
Thyroid, a portion of the membrana intermedia of Reichert, 66
Tooth-sacs (permanent), 35
Tooth-substance, deposition of, in embryo of sixteenth week, 18, 34
Torpedo, batteries in, 289; will of the fish, 302
Transition-teeth, 55
Triangulares (*Crustacea*), generative organs in, 429-433
Trichina spiralis, 493; Owen on its cyst, 494
Tropæolum tuberosum, electrical currents in tubers of, 313
Tufts of human placenta, 445-449
Tulip, electric descending current at time of flowering, 315
Tumour: description of an erectile tumour, 504, 505; of the testis, description of a congenital one, 506, 507
Turbinated shells, how their form is produced, 211
Turbines, the logarithmic spiral curve possessed by these shells ascertained by Professor Moseley, 209
Tusks of elephant, bullets and other bodies inclosed in, 56-65
Tusk-pulp of elephant, wounding of, 60
Twin-elements, what Professor Goodsir means by term, 247

ULCERATION, nature of, 404-407; in articular cartilages, 408-411; of Peyer's patches in continued fever, 372-378
Upper jaw dentition precedes that of lower jaw, 45
Uraster rubens, secreting organ in stomach, 414
Urine, where first formed, 379
Uterus, mucous membranes of, 452; dissection of vessels, 457

VALENTIN, Handbuch, referred to, 11, etc.; on the structure of the laminæ in batteries of electric fishes, 290, 298; on the action of, 301
Vascular border in gum, 38
Vegetables, electrical phenomena in, 307-318; organisms in fluid from stomach, 351-371
Vertebra (typical), applicability and convenience of Professor Owen's terms, 95
Vertebrate type, on morphological relations of nervous system in, 78-87
Vertebrata, eye in, how acted on, 280
Vestibules of ear, sound heard merely as noise, 287
Villi (intestinal), structure and functions of, 393-402
Vision, organ of, there are three fundamental forms of, 273
Vomer, its complete development in mammalia, 117
Vomerine sclerotome in mammals, 117; in crocodiles, 118; in the lizards, 119; in birds, 119, 120; in chelonian reptiles, 120, 121; in the osseous fishes, 121, 122

WAGNER (Rudolph) on structure of elementary filaments of nerves in batteries of electrical fishes, 290
Walrus, substance in pulp-cavities of tusk, 62
Walsh on the electricity of the torpedo,

300; determined the shock to be of the electric character in 1772, 318

Wartmann on electric currents in vegetables, 308, 314

Water decomposed by electricity of fish, 342; condition of water surrounding the fish at the moment of discharge of the electric organs, 343

Weber: the brothers Weber on the mechanism of the human knee-joint, 220, 231

White cellular layer of the retina, 266; Bowman on, 268

Will of the electric fish determines flow of nervous force into spaces of battery, 301

Wilson (Erasmus) on *Echinococcus hominis*, 480

Wilson (Dr. George), analysis of liquid in which the *Sarcina ventriculi* was found, 361-370

Wisdom-teeth, 40; **sometimes** decay at an early period, 45

Wolffian bodies, formation of, 67

Wollaston (Dr.) on the agency of electricity on animal secretions referred to, 319

Wounds in tusks of elephants, 63-65

YOUNG (Dr. Thomas) on cochlea being a "micrometer of sound," 287; on the electric force, 320

ZANTEDESCHI'S observations on electrical condition of different plants when flowering, 315

Printed by R. CLARK, *Edinburgh.*

www.ingramcontent.com/pod-product-compliance
Lightning Source LLC
Chambersburg PA
CBHW031936290426
44108CB00011B/579